3 Books in 1

Handbook for the New Paradigm
Volume I

Embracing the Rainbow
Volume II

Becoming
Volume III

Copyright 2018

BRIDGER HOUSE PUBLISHERS, INC.

PO BOX 599, Hayden ID 83835

1-800-729-4131   www.nohoax.com

ISBN: 978-1-893157-25-5

Typesetting & Design by The Right Type, www.therighttype.com
Cover Ocean Photo by Peter Melton

Published in the United States of America

A Personal Message for You

Table of Contents

Handbook for the New Paradigm
Volume I... 1

Embracing the Rainbow
Volume II 143

Becoming
Volume III 253

Epilogue 388

Suggested Reading........................... 390

Handbook for the New Paradigm
Volume I

I

This is a point in the evolution of the planet that brings to the forefront of each individual's thoughts the question of why me, why now and what is really going on in the reality that is right now in the time we are experiencing. What really is going on behind-the-scenes we are looking at through the five senses? Why is there this feeling that there is more to the story than just appearances. Who indeed has set this up and is pulling the strings. Is it really just a group of somebodies that is in charge? If this is the case, then is the God thing really a hoax after all? There are those who believe that to be the true essence of the scenario. Fortunately for the good of all, that is not the Truth.

The Truth is that there are multiple levels of activity behind what appears to be a play of incredible magnitude. Who then is writing the lines for the characters and what is the point of the script? Would it be a surprise to inform you that you are writing the lines and until you can figure out a point to the script, there is none? If that is the case, then which of the individuals on the planet

1

can figure one out? Well, indeed there is a focused group that has decided that they would like to put forth their point in the script. There is just one problem with this, they have decided to put forth a focus within the play that is not in harmony with the Creator of the stage and the theatre that this play is to be performed upon. In fact, the plan this group has in mind has a great surprise at the end for the audience and the actors on the stage. They intend to destroy the audience, the actors, the stage and the theatre.

Since the Creator of this theatre likes this particular theatre and thinks of it as a pet project, this idea doesn't appeal to Him at all. Since He is not in the business of standing in the way of the creative presentations that are produced within its confines, then He is hoping that the audience will decide to make changes of their own. There is a type of presentation that involves participation of the audience other than just sitting and observing. The theatre entrepreneur is wondering that if the play being presented becomes obnoxious enough to the audience, will they simply walk away and withdraw their attention? This would then allow the cast and its directors to destroy themselves, but then the theatre owner does not want his property destroyed along with them. He is hoping that the audience will come up with some other solution. Perhaps there could be audience participation that would perhaps introduce some new characters that would create lines of script of their own. If a new story line could be introduced with characters that could change the ending, then the performance could be a comedy or a mystery or a love story rather than a tragedy. Maybe, audience participation could indeed create a whole new genre of experience. Instead of depicting repetition of experiences already known, could the audience in the intensity of desire change the story line, come up with a creative scenario that would encompass possibilities not yet experienced? Why not? The greater the desire for change, the greater the opportunity for creative new boundary expanding story themes. Within the spontaneity of group focus, without the academic control of leadership with an intended purpose, conception outside of ordinary themes is not only possible, it is probable.

To what purpose is this discussion being instigated? It is time that you awaken to your responsibility to change the destination of the path you are now being pushed to take. It is far past the stage of leading you. It is at the stage of pushing you. It is at the stage where resistance cannot be successful therefore you are going to have to accomplish this by some other means. A way must be literally created that will bring about a solution. Nothing that you have done before will accomplish a change in this situation. Those who have brought you to this point know your current human nature so well that every possibility you can think of has been blocked. Every cell of resistance is well known by them and is allowed to exist because it has a purpose in their plan. These will be used as graphic examples of what they will not allow.

Now you must come into the understanding that there is a passage through this experience for mankind, but you must move into a creative stance, not a resistive posture. This is not what is expected of you based on your past modes of experience. I can assure you that your history has been analyzed and studied by minds and computer model to the point that you are known to an extent you cannot even imagine. Every reactive scenario has been dissected to the cellular level and restrictive actions planned for each of them. You are faced with the possibility of your extinction unless you can make a cosmic leap to a level of creative imagination that will completely nullify those plans. Have you not computers of your own? Can you not band into creative discussion groups and ask for entry into the mind of that which created you? "Where two or more of you are gathered together in my Name (within the focused desire for harmonious understanding), there am I also."

Cries and begging to be relieved of the situation by God, or Jesus, Buddha or Mohammed will not do it. You have allowed this evil to descend upon you and so it is you, individually and collectively, that must take it upon yourselves to conceive this solution. A new consciousness change must take place within you. Not all of humanity will choose to participate. There will be some that will hide their heads in blame and grovel in victimhood. So be it. Let them. You have no time to recruit among them, for what of creativity could they offer? This is a clarion call to the consciousness of those with the strength of character to stand up within their own conscious awareness and decide this situation shall not be allowed to continue to its planned completion. Even those who are in the midst of that abominable plan have no idea that the end is indeed to be annihilation. Unfortunately, it is not only planned to be annihilation of the people and the planet, but of realms beyond imagination.

How shall it be done? How can a change come about in the midst of such a lack of understanding of who and what you are? Now, while there is yet time, before the noose tightens, movement about the planet is yet possible. Groups shall come together to stretch their conscious awareness, to invoke the aid of the highest of sources of knowledge to assist them in conceiving a new way of experiencing manifested existence. This must not be copied from any other experience. It must be literally a conceptual leap, not in its entirety, but in invocation of the beginning framework of such an experience. This is not a process that can be spelled out. It is shadowy in the beginning as it is conceived as a possibility, and so it should be. Known boundaries of experience must be transcended. A super-human assignment? Indeed, but not at all impossible. Out of challenge born of desire and necessity comes the conception of that which is different.

Has mankind on this planet been presented with this opportunity before? Indeed, but each time he reverted to known strategies. Now it has been of his creation that this situation exists. It has been his task to make this leap and so he has now made it so that it must be undertaken or face the possibility he may cease to exist. All of this is his own doing. Mankind has no one else to blame, so it must be a 180 degree turn from past refusal to take on the whole project, to taking it on with resolve and dedication.

II

The focus of energy that holds this planet in orbit within this solar system does not require the power of force to do this, but uses an available process that does not require effort. The concept of power has within it the inherent understanding of effort as force. Since thought attracts, you have brought to you the experience of effort, force and power. There are other experiences available that do not use this concept. Rocketry projects are an example. Your resources are used to effort one rocket and its payload into the orbit of this planet and then beyond. Yet you are visited by beings of other planets that enter and leave your planet's gravitational field without this wasteful effort. Does this prove to you that there are other ways to accomplish movement without such wasteful and dangerous methods? The search for answers to this question intrigues the mind. There are many that know these possibilities exist, but are unable to envision the answers without the need of using great effort to resist what they envision ties them to the planet. It is not the gravitational field that ties them here. It is the consciousness. It is the interactivity of thought acting upon thought that eludes them. They know that their thoughts can influence the outcome of an experiment. However the concept that thought once projected can be released to interact within itself and that it can produce an outcome beyond a controlled (desired) outcome is not understood. The need to control, observe and to prove the process prevents them from reaching into new realms of understanding. What is lacking is the ability to trust that the process can only proceed within positive outcomes once it is released to act within and upon itself. Thought released to act upon itself will return in manifestation glorified and in a form more magnificent than the limited focused mind can imagine.

Now the challenge comes to those who desire to be the instruments of changing the negative plans for the destiny of this planet. Can you expand your consciousness to encompass the process that lies just beyond your "grasp"? It will be necessary for you to begin with the basic desire of participating within a new paradigm of experience. However, to leave the known and desire to venture into the unknown requires the courage to release what you feel is the advancement this "civilization" has made from its stone age beginnings into modern technological comfort for many on this planet. Do you know that the word civilization is synonymous with slavery? In order to accomplish this experience, it required giving up the freedom of personal choice in order that group organization might have precedence. Beyond the family, no organization is necessary. Personal responsibility is the keynote of freedom. Cooperation is a natural phenomenon as long as the need to control is absent. The need to control is a learned activity that becomes habitual through the experience of it.

How does one transcend this habitual activity when it is deeply ingrained at a planetary level? It has now reached a point that in and of himself, man cannot break this addiction. The adversaries know this well. They are sure that humanity cannot change it. How then will it occur as the primary starting point of the shift to a new paradigm of experience? It can be done by understanding that thought focused and released can indeed act within itself and upon itself. Though it sounds simplistic, and indeed in reality it is simplistic, it is a powerful tool. In order for this process to work, there are some criteria that must be present. Since it is a process of Divine Order, it must have at its intentional level the desire to co-ordinate within this perpetual process. The purpose of it must be conceived with the focus of the continued evolvement of those who will benefit from its inception through the outward movement of its spheres of influence. The intent of its purpose is the key to its success of coordination with and within the flow of Divine Order. If this is reduced to a mathematical formula, then its inclusion can not cause a change in any of the Divine formulas that allow the balance of the whole to exist in harmony. Thought thinking within itself would know if it was acceptable or not. That is the reason the opposition cannot take advantage of this process. Purity of intent to harmonize as the motive is a primary prerequisite. The outlining thought must be specific only in the intent of purpose. It must provide direction of purpose allowing the thought thinking process to proceed into Divine Order by releasing it in total trust knowing it is accomplished in what you call etheric levels and will then manifest into this recognizable reality using all the available triggers for appropriate interaction.

How can you know that this actually will accomplish the desired results and is not just another ploy of the opposition to keep you controlled? Have you heard of this on your media reports? Is anyone within the approved world of communication touting this as the thing for you to do? Indeed not! You are programmed to focus your energies into the salvaging of your sexy bodies and in your humanitarian thoughts for the suffering multitudes, as you have another bite of your steak dinner at the restaurant, or at least another convenient hamburger on your way home from your unproductive labors at the computer keyboard. The process through which you receive this information does use the wonders of your computer. It is a demonstration of thought interacting with itself with the addition of focus. It is the focus of your intent that will initiate the process that you desire. Then thought focused through purposeful intent will complete itself in magnificence through the energy of your faith and trust. Firmly holding to the knowing that the etheric form of it was completed in less than the blinking of your eye will allow it to manifest into 3rd dimensional reality. The computer-like processes of the Creation are indeed endowed with quickness. Then again the ball shall be returned to your court for more to be done within your dimension.

III

It is with careful and focused intent that the reality of this earthly experience is being engineered into a pattern of downward movement into the darker and heavier energies that are at the lower end of the scale in which the human body can exist. This makes the contact between the extension (spirit in body) and its Soul (focused source) more difficult. This is not the whole of the intent. This allows for the possibility of the separation of the two energies. Intricate manipulations of this extension energy must be accomplished in order for this to be a possibility. The "capture" of this Soul energy is for the purpose of causing a break in the chain of energies that extend from the matrix of the Soul. It is the belief of those doing this that it will cause a breaking down of the positive energies that comprise the basic building blocks of Creation. In other words, they perceive that causing a break in the return flow of this energy back to its source will cause a disruption in the larger combined pattern of the Galactic matrix. The conception of this group of separatists is that a chain reaction will happen allowing for chaos to such a degree that their focus can reorganize this chaos into their own matrix. This is quite an arrogant and ambitious undertaking. The plan includes many more quite fantastic steps to follow through to its completion. This is not a plan conceived on a moment's notice. It is one that has been put together over eons of time in your counting. However, since their plans are counter to the controlling parameters within which Creation has come into manifested experience, they are unable to take advantage of the processes that also act as failsafe guards available to the Creation for the purpose of preventing this planned procedure from causing such an event.

Your logical question is how has this rebellion been allowed to continue to this point? The freewill aspect is what has been exploited as the basis for their ability to manipulate humanity to be the vehicle of their power. Yours is the exact state of consciousness to serve their purpose. You are malleable enough to be influenced into desiring change when pressure is applied to the Soul/extension connection, and change is exactly what they want. At each critical juncture in the previous cycles, mankind has been influenced to change what was present rather than to desire an entirely new experience. Within the cycles of energy that maintain manifested Creation at the various dimensions, there are critical points which allow for changing the vibratory parameters of these dimensions. There is within this opportunity ways that they have worked out to create a downward spiral into heavier energy rather than the lifting of vibration as was intended. This can only happen when the mass consciousness of that vibratory level of planetary experience has its focus on experiences at the lowest level of that dimension. As we approach another of these opportunities, you can observe where the mass consciousness is with regard to what you call ethics and character by considering the role models that are currently popular. However, there is a risk for them in their process. There is a point at which their restrictive pressure of controlling the thought processes of the mass consciousness of the planet can backfire and cause exactly the opposite of what they have planned. This will cause them to miss the opportunity of the final dimensional vibratory change needed for completion of their plans.

They have been successful in their use of various techniques enabling them to greatly weaken the Soul/human extension connection. Because of technology and greater understanding of the nature of human experience, techniques have been developed that indicate success in the process of separating extension and Soul. There is considerable over confidence in the success of the techniques used on individuals as being applicable to large groups of a critical percentage of the mass consciousness. The results of these experimental successes have them quite intoxicated and already savoring the completion of their divergent goals. (However, it is possible to reverse those procedures and reunite the energies into wholeness again, though the complete healing of these beings that have been used as guinea pigs will require much help. The Grace of the Creator shall be showered upon those individuals to assure the Soul matrix is not distorted.)

The implications of this picture are many, but do not despair for in the knowledge of this, you can plainly see that you are not alone in the healing of this situation. It is just that freewill is at the essence of how you got yourselves into this situation and it will be the use of freewill that you will desire to finally do something drastic enough that will get you through it. You have used change to get you out before and it only altered the situation, it did not resolve it completely. In this case, the scenario is such that it is literally "do or die" to borrow your vernacular. Within the proper choice of focus lies your salvation. Smile, you are on the "winning side."

IV

As each of you come to understand this is the pivotal time in which to complete a spiritual journey involving multiple trips through the earthly experience, it will become obvious there is not a moment to be wasted in the final hours of this episode. If you are to accomplish this goal and end this chapter of the history of planetary experience, those who have chosen to mock the creator's plan must not write it. This is a time in which you cannot leave this change in the hands of others. It is too great a responsibility to be left to a few. You must make your contribution in order to be assured that it shall be accomplished and that you shall be included in the multitude that make this a reality.

To accomplish this, first you must open your eyes and see what is happening all around you. You must then come to the unpleasant understanding that you have allowed this to occur because overwhelming methodology of deception influenced you and you resisted becoming involved through taking any personal responsibility in changing it. Careful remembering of past intuitive feelings brings you to the truth. You are now and have been aware that something sinister is present. In all honesty you lacked the courage to look at what it might be because of the implications of what it could involve personally. Courage to do this has come through the change of your attitude. The magnitude of the implication of what the planners of this situation are capable of doing to your personal future and that of family and friends has allowed your desire to know to overwhelm your reluctance. This then leads to the necessity of considering its larger implication, the planet and its inhabitants as a whole. This process has brought you to the point of looking directly into the face of truth. Unfortunately, it is not some religious or esoteric concept that is the "truth that will set you free" but what it has been your desire to avoid at all cost. What you must understand is that this truth is about a situation that could end your earthly experience in extremely unpleasant circumstances, and places your eternal existence in jeopardy. The stakes are extremely high and the circumstances are dire indeed!

This is not a time to hide in your usual excuse of "what can one person do?" A large number of "one persons" can accomplish a great deal. Becoming "cannon fodder" is not the solution. It is required that you become a much more subtle influence. Learn one truth now. Subtle energy is powerful and the most powerful energy is subtle. Your bible says, "In the beginning was the word" but words are thoughts spoken out loud, an inaccurate translation. In the beginning was thought! That is the subtle energy that we are asking you to employ. Simply change the focus of your thought. Do not allow yourself to dwell upon the horrors of what is planned for you, but turn your thought to what it is that you would prefer to experience.

You are trained by their methodology to think only about the programmed thoughts of acquiring things, others opinions, self preservation among thieves and murderers, and escape from self directed thoughts through addiction to TV, movies and Soul jarring music. Last but not least, pursuit of sexual experience, be it in or out of monogamous relationships. There is also the mind-boggling profusion of religious entities to further lead you from the personal quest of understanding the connection to the source of your presence on this planet in the first place. I can assure you that Jesus, Buddha and Mohammed had nothing to do with it. It is not that these beings did not exist, nor that they were not here to attempt to give you guidance in getting through this dilemma, but the messages they brought were distorted long ago. Neither did they come here to "get you out" by your belief in their existence, past or present.

They came to teach you that you must get yourself through this by taking personal responsibility and creating through thought a new planetary experience. In this way only, will you be able to move through this painful experience.

You accept this responsibility by making a personal commitment between you and the creative energy that focused you through thought into this existence. You will know how to participate in creating what will replace this living nightmare with a new experience! How? You search for it through your desire to know and to participate in its creation. Then through seemingly miraculous coincidence, how to participate shall become known to you. The critical point of the process is in making the commitment within your own awareness that the most important thing is participating in the creation of an experience that is 180 degrees opposite what is now planned to be your final earthly sojourn.

The evidence of the necessity to do this surrounds you in irrefutable profusion. You need only to open your eyes, consider the changes in your personal freedoms that are happening in quick succession and listen to (hear) the researched evidence in both spoken and written presentations on your radios, internet and in books. Very soon those will no longer be available to you, leaving only word of mouth, so it is imperative that you respond to this information. You are encouraged to react only through your change of attitude and in your commitment to become a part of this subtly powerful movement. There will not be an Armageddon as suggested in their version of your bible. It shall be a replacement of their planned world through shifting the focus of the awareness of the beings on this planet toward that which is desired rather than that which is being forced upon them. It shall be individual inner change that shall conquer the outer forces that plan to control your very essence of self-awareness. Upon the acceptance of this clarion call lies the future of your survival and the experiences that wait for you within eternity.

V

Indeed, this is a glorious day. The rain falls and the air is clean. Rain is falling generously on the planet and Mother Earth begins the washing of herself in earnest. Is it being engineered? It would

appear so, but are their contemptuous machines all that powerful?
Do not be so sure. Remember that earth is a projection of thought
and thought is self-aware and interacts within itself to greater or
lesser degrees. Would earth think to a greater or a lesser degree?
That is a question to contemplate.

This is a moment in which to be aware of the changing of the
guard. It seems that the destiny of the planet has been wrestled
from the control of its inhabitants, as it would appear the control of
the Republic of the U.S.A. has been taken from its people. Movement within the conscious awareness of the inhabitants present has
begun. These levels of consciousness are subtle and they are powerful. Notice of this change in consciousness is not at a vibratory
level that will alert the negative forces. Its momentum builds within
the subtle powerful planes of energy forces that hold this planet in
focus. It is thought interacting within itself. It is acting in concert
as a changing perception of the mass consciousness that is similar
to a natural shedding process. Like the snake, there is an itchiness
that is being felt. This process allows for a time of vulnerability and
danger from enemies for it is an internal process. The snake indeed
goes within an available den because during this internal process it
becomes literally blind. All focus is within itself as the process goes
through its formation of a new outside experience for it has out-
grown its ability to continue as it is. Even the covering of the eyes is
changed so that it sees its world anew. Only the death of the snake
can prevent this cyclical occurrence, thus it takes great care during this process. This is an apt analogy for our consideration of the
progress of mankind through what appears to be a dilemma of great
proportion. Just as the fetus grows too large for the womb and must
give up its current experience and adventure out into a completely
new environment, there are guiding examples throughout nature to
suggest this process is a natural phase of manifested life experience.

The separation of man from nature through the herding of them
into metropolitan areas is not an accident. It has been used many
times to suppress individual power to control the experience of
life. Closely compacted form is more easily pushed to and fro in
the effort of moving individuals into experiences that are contrary
to their natural desires toward individual responsibility in choosing their life experience. This herding smothers the natural desires

and opens the psyche to influence by the confusion that is drawn within the totality of the being. There is a fundamental call within each for balance. The lack of ability to choose experiences freely causes a distortion of energy pattern that brings intuitional discomfort and searching to change that feeling. This need is then lead into unending streams of unfulfilling pursuits by those who would change the destiny of this planetary experience. However, there are ingrained patterns of experience that are reminiscent of the skin shedding process that cannot be distorted. The negative forces have their time schedule that must be met. The timing of this process of human "skin changing" is not one that they are privy to know no matter how they analyze and re-analyze the human experience from their perspective. Can you now realize that Thought thinking within itself has created fail-safe checks that prevent destruction if at all possible. Again we are faced with that one element that can put on hold even the fail- safe checks and balances. Freewill! Each has personal responsibility for the use of this great gift of the Creator. He has confidence that fragments of Himself may enjoy taking themselves to the edge of extinction for the fun of the adventure. But, just as in your action movies, (a depiction of this underlying adventurous focus) through perfect timing the hero moves through the scenario with hardly a scratch or at least nothing that can not be healed. Sometimes you miss the point of the movies.

You are now at the critical place in the script. It is time to write in the shift of momentum from the bad guys to the hero so that he can experience that unexpected twist of the story line that allows for his harrowing escape leaving the bad guys holding the bag. Let us hope that this is not a Superman or secret agent adventure in which again there is no end to the bad guy and another adventure between them is waiting in the wings. You have already experienced those scripts. Again you have missed the point of the movies. Do you feel that sense of satisfaction of evil vanquished when you leave that genre of movie? That is the point of it. To always leave you with the idea that evil remains no matter what you do. Were not your experiences in Korea, Vietnam and Desert Storm outward depictions of this same frustrating movie? All wars have this same result; it has just not been part of the plan until recently to flaunt it so plainly for you to see. Your ability to discern and react is being tested over and over. Why else would items of what is being "sanctioned" (withheld) from innocent people in Iraq be published in your newspapers. What do these items for personal use of individual innocent people have to do with the prevention of war preparations? These lists were published worldwide. How do you think the people, who uphold their degenerate president who is instigating this, are thought of by the rest of the world? A new movie genre is being released now. In these your people are being held accountable. These depict surges of justifiable retribution (terrorism) and are being planted in the minds of those of other countries. Their ideal of America as the Light of the world is being destroyed by your diplomacy of arrogance toward other countries' right of self-determination. These punishments are seen as appropriate by them for they are unable to resist on a larger scale to this injustice. The disturbances used as excuses to interfere within the borders of other countries are made to appear that there is necessity to intervene for the good of the citizens. These contrived situations are a hoax, created by subversive groups like the CIA. The resultant aftermath of your American intervention is hardly what you are told it is. Guilt because for being used as a tool will not serve to end this charade. Do not waste your time on it. Resolve to be a part of the solution in order that this error in perception maybe rectified.

The wake-up call is being sounded and the internal intuitional agitation to shed the skin of this deceptive controlled experience has begun in earnest. The time of choosing to move with the flow of Creation or to remain stuck within the hoax is upon all of humanity. Education, as it is known, is not an advantage. It is within each self-awareness that this process will take place. All are equal in opportunity in this process. Believe that! Purity of response outweighs educational degrees. Those who know the least of what is going on will hear first. You have been educated into the deception that provides the grease upon the wheels of their plans. You have been fooled into supporting them as they carried forth their plans that so far have been focused upon the uneducated and those unable to oppose the power you are giving the manifested evil ones through consent by believing their lies.

VI

In the reality that surrounds your awareness in 3rd dimensional experience, it is easier to allow the seduction of your 5 senses into believing this is all there is to the duration of your stay within your body. Indeed this has been further enhanced by the introduction of the visual aids of photos, movies, TV and computers. To this add telegraph, telephone, satellites plus music and sporting events all beginning in childhood at the earliest possible moment. Where is there, within this onslaught of mind boggling confusion of distractions, time or desire to contemplate within silence anything but a replay of these experiences? The conscious awareness tries to clear out the clutter of this overload so that contact can be made with an inner awareness and contemplation can begin of how and why you are within this experience. This is a process that goes on quite naturally, except when the conscious half of this combination is overloaded with stimuli. It should be immediately apparent to the reader that this is the case in modern North American/European parts of the world. Furthermore, it is spreading to the more affluent elements around the planet. Once exposed to this mind stifling process, it appears to be relaxing. It is not relaxing, it is mind suppressing! The creative, self-contemplating portions of the awareness are being shut down. The more the experience is repeated, the more of an addiction is acquired. Instead of enjoying mentally stimulating experiences, these are experienced as disquieting and downright irritating. Thus you see the joggers with their wired up ears listening rather than contemplating their own thoughts. Somehow, they must stay connected to their addiction to distraction. If not radios or tapes, then it is car phones to stay connected so one can pontificate with their "friends."

Can you, reading this, separate yourself from the distraction process to contemplate and absorb descriptions of the wondrous fantasy land existence you are experiencing? Where is what you call reality within a world that is mostly pretend? When you look in truth at the information you trade daily through your computer connections, how much of it is indeed concrete manifested reality? Is the money transferred from one account to another actually stacks of bills? Do that many stacks of denominations of money actually exist? Where are there bank safes to house trillions of dollars? Wake

up! You are dreaming! Ah, but if you wake up you will have to face
the solid reality that you have been used, and that is too frightening
to contemplate! How long do you think this dream bubble can go
on expanding before it breaks of its own thinness or just perhaps
there are ones that will enjoy pricking the bubble? Would it not
be best to wake up early and begin to dream a new ending to the
nightmare in disguise that you are now experiencing? Can you do
that? Of course you can. It is your dream. That you have been programmed to dream a particular scenario can only continue as long
as you allow it. There is something called lucid dreaming in which
you awaken to an awareness that you are dreaming, then you can
stop at that degree of consciousness, observe yourself dreaming and
change the scenario of the dream. If you are being chased, create a
safe hiding place, have the pursuer fall into a hole, or a train come
between you, and you escape.

You have been lulled into a dream state by the distraction of
your conscious awareness in order to separate you from your self-
aware state (which is the state in which you can observe your dream
process). You can correlate this into an awareness that will allow
you to reclaim the severed connection to both parts of your total
awareness. In truth, your intuitive awareness is beginning now to
become awake to the truth of this information. Do you know that
you have the power within yourself to encourage this feeling and
come out of the unnatural state of distraction into full awareness?
This waking process can allow you to avoid the fear and panic that
you think facing it might bring, and instead give you an ability to
discover yourself as a focus of energetic and creative expression.
It will not awaken the "brute caveman" reaction you might expect.
Instead a contemplative ability to focus upon solutions will come
forth that will replace what was formerly sensed as an undefeat-
able force and an unsolvable situation. This force was smothering
you in a deepening dream reality that you will discover does not
even exist. It may appear so to the five senses, but you perceive that
beyond those lies a potential that supersedes what you have known
before. It is the same potential that pulls entrepreneurs into successful businesses and explorers toward unknown places. It has an
enticing intuitional call that pulls them from the known, to desire an
experience that is unknown and holds such a vibration of potential

of success that it cannot be resisted. Many hear the call, but few choose to answer it. That does not mean that it does not exist. The success stories are proof enough of its existence.

It is hoped that this is information for you to contemplate apart from your normal mesmerizing existence. Is there something beyond this enticingly humdrum existence that could be even more rewarding? Indeed there is!

VII

"Around the World in 80 Days" was a marvelously funny satire on good and evil in competition. Don't we wish that the same scenario in one's own reality could be as carefree and funny with all the pratfalls and hair raising potentially dangerous scenes? You can rest assured that the observers of the play upon the stage of planet Earth are not laughing at the similar scenes as they pass through your manifested reality. Instead they watch through detached wisdom knowing that the ending will be a positive one, but with concern for how many awareness points shall move with the ascending transformation process and how many will be left behind to be shepherded through the process of another opportunity. It shall be a great relief to these when the Earth experience in this particular point of focus will have been completed. Just how it shall all come together has become of major interest, for indeed you have created your own grand and spectacular stage play. The story line is quite unique, something like "The Perils of Pauline of the Galaxy."

It is noted that the terms of Universe and Galaxy are tossed about with abandon and you find yourself puzzled in attempting to correlate these into a meaningful 3rd dimensional understanding. In truth this is not quite possible, but we shall make an attempt at doing so. Galaxy refers to the flow of manifested reality around a center of focus. Universe refers to the focused intent of coagulation of energy that in your terminology lies behind and supports this manifested reality. There are Universal Laws that allow for the creation and maintenance of this Galaxy. Since you are part of this Galaxy (you have named Milky Way), then if you are to experience in harmony within it, you must live within these laws. In this case, you are like children playing pin the tail on the donkey, for these laws have been withheld from you and you are left to discover them by trial and error. Right now, you are far into the error process. Is this how it has been ordained for you to learn them? INDEED NOT! The blindfold has been deliberately placed upon you and you have been fooled into thinking that you have no right to remove it. The blindfold is the game of deception in which you are enticed to look where the magician deliberately presents action for you to watch while he supports it with motions you do not perceive. Your attention is focused on what you think is the only action.

Fortunately not all the audience is fooled. They watch you and wonder why you do not see the process the magician uses. The fact is they wonder why you are now at a stage where you only perceive his spotlighted action and do not even see the magician. You are so mesmerized that indeed the supporting motions to the actions are no longer even hidden. They proceed all around him on the stage and still you see neither of them. How is this possible? By hypnotizing the conscious mind!

Luckily there is another part of the mind that is beyond this conscious thinking. Your psychologists call it your subconscious mind. They have painted it as holding your perception of Life hostage because it is full of dark, horrible experiences perpetrated on you by well meaning but abusive parents. As a result you fear it and block it from participating in your experience of Life. Why is the word Life capitalized? Because that is the purpose of your experience on this planet! You are alive, that is aware of experiencing this Life energy moving through you and played out on the screen of your observing ego mind. Ah, the ego, the devil of your existence, or so you have been led to believe. Anyone acting in a pushy manner is being egotistical. His ego has him by the necktie and is causing him to misbehave according to the imposed social norms. He is controlled by his evil sub-conscious acting out through his ego and he must be brought down a peg and that awful ego humbled into compliance. The successful businessman is successful because his inflated ego runs amuck over others and snatches success from the hands of the deserving underlings, etc., etc. Need I go on painting this picture of slight of mind?

What then is the true picture? If there is no ego, there will be no awareness of the manifested experience! The ego is your tape recorder. It is the observer of your thoughts, wants, needs and desires. It takes these thoughts in a type of robotic focused format, and this allows them to manifest into circumstances and situations that create your experience. It literally filters your thoughts, feelings and desires and causes them to coalesce into manifested experience. It is a process, not an entity. It is a process over which you have complete control, if you can take charge of thoughts, feelings and desires and actively direct them toward what you want to experience. These thoughts must be relatively depictive. For example, if you simply focus on change then expect chaos within your life for that will be the change you create until you decide upon some more precise idea of what you want in your experience. The process of how this works involves a Universal Law called Attraction. Once an idea is formed with the positive understanding that it is possible, then the ego holds this picture and completes the process through positive/negative polarity energy.

Through the action of the Law of Attraction and the malleable nature of the potential of an idea actually coming into your experience, it does. Since instant manifestation of ideas on this planet at the moment is very difficult, the ego incorporates the process within your supporting idea of time. If you are unable to remain focused on your desire of a certain experience, then often times you deny yourself that desired experience. There is a comment in your Bible regarding "praying amiss." Since that which you refer to as God is creative in nature, whenever you are focusing your desire in a sincere manner for an experience, then you are in "constant prayer" for you are within this creative, expansive expression that originates within the Source of your existence. But, what if you are asking for something that would cause problems for someone else? The law works! But, there is an effect for that which you have caused. As noted above you are using the Universal Law of Attraction and its process involves like energy attracting more like energy. If you cause a problem for someone else as a purposeful use of this Law, then what you create for someone else, you also will experience. It is like two sides of the same coin. One is presented to the other person and one is presented to you. If you are serious in attempting to understand this Law, then if you dare, look at the events that you have already experienced and you will see that this has been the case many times. When you have wished a blessing for someone else, you also experienced one, not in exactly the same way, but in something of meaning that came within your Life. Consider also difficulties. I believe there is a reference in the Bible that instructs you to "put a guard on your mouth for the words (including thoughts) that come forth do not return to you empty."

In utilizing this understanding, you must hold the desire steadily within your consciousness. If you error in desire by wishing to create a problem in the life of another you have time early in the process in which to reconsider and to withdraw the focus of that intent. Then it will not manifest for them to experience. Emotion, strong feelings, can increase the potential of manifestation and hurry the process, whether it is for your own "good" experience or for another one. The opposite is also true.

It is time for the entertainment portion of this purposefully written portion of the play and the distraction of your attention from your purpose for being within this experience on planet Earth to end. Now you must decide whether to take back your power, remove the blindfold of your own volition or wait until it's removed for you. The picture will be even more shocking if you wait, for you will be totally unprepared for the scene planned for you to view. There is little time remaining for you to make your decision. The glitzy world you are living within is an illusion. Behind its facade is another one that plays out a game of power that requires your total cooperation and the giving over of your creative power willingly by overwhelming your sense of possessing any personal power what ever. Example: "But, what can one person do?" Sound familiar. Answer: "More than you can possibly imagine, but first you must realize that you have the power!"

VIII

When the conditions of deterioration surround you, how can I comment that this is a glorious day? Indeed, it is, for those conditions are drawing to a close. The ending may contain many surprises. Your Armageddon will arrive, but it shall not be in a format that you have been told to expect. The forces of Light and darkness shall not parry and thrust in a format of war, but nonetheless the situation will have moments of what might be called confrontation but it will not be in a 3rd dimensional battle of armaments. This should be comforting for the power of even those 3rd dimensional devices can destroy the planet.

If indeed the Creator is a focus of Love, then methods of destruction would not be possible. These are only possible within the distorted use of negative polarity energy. Within the two foci of positive/negative energy lies the center point of harmony. This is the goal of all manifested energy, to exist within this harmonious point. However, it has one disadvantage in that the still point existence would allow for no movement at all, thus it can be maintained for only a relatively short period. As a result there is constant movement away from and returning to this ideal. Within the totality of the Galaxy, there is a balance between portions of it moving away and toward this still point. This is seen in the movement of planets and what you perceive as the Mazaroth or Zodiac as they move in cycles around the center point of the Galaxy. Within these revolving movements are many smaller cycles that you cannot observe. When a distortion occurs within one of the smaller cycles it is allowed up to a certain point. When it reaches a point at which this distortion begins to affect larger cycles, then attention is focused to correct this distortion. This attention is now on planet Earth. Destruction would indeed affect other cycles. One planet in your solar system was destroyed. Balance was maintained with great difficulty, but the loss of another planet would cause chaos that would be far reaching indeed. For this reason a great deal of attention now being paid to your situation.

If it were not for the limiting factor of the freewill of the inhabitants, balance could have been obtained long before this point. This emphasizes the importance of obtaining consent through deception of the inhabitants for the introduction of atomic destruction devices. Plans are afoot to create the very chaos that planetary destruction would bring. The stakes are very high indeed in this game of control. The plan behind this destruction is ambitious beyond your imagination. It involves the creation of a negative polarity universe/galaxy. To the perpetrators of this situation, you are not even small fry in the game. This is confrontational at the level of the Creator of this Universe/Galaxy. Have we made this up? Indeed we wish we could tell you that, but it is the usurping of your ability to make freewill decisions as to whether to cooperate or not that is the small key to the success of their plan. This will allow you to understand the multiple levels of control that have been used and why your complete control (which of course is impossible) has been used as the manipulation behind your deception. Indeed, there are many levels of control of the people on your planet. Those who think they are in control and planning this scenario are just as controlled as their plan for you. As this plays out, there are elements of this situation that are going to be more surprised than your general populous. However, perhaps that surprise will be at a higher level than even that plan includes.

What must be remembered in the greater perception of this is that all that exists and that does mean ALL, does so out of the potentiality that under lays manifested Creation. In following the layers of energy that coagulate into manifested realities in reverse order, the building blocks become finer and finer in vibrational quality until it reaches beyond what the Cabala calls Ain Soph or pure potentiality. In order to cause an entire Galaxy to change polarities it would be necessary to return to this point to cause such an event to happen. Needless to say, this is an extremely simplistic explanation, but should give you an understanding of the audacity of the idea and the relative chances for its success. However, the attempt to do this by working backwards through existing Creation to accomplish this goal holds within it the possibility of a pattern of resulting chaos of no small proportion.

Now to come upon the realization that your conscious consent had to be obtained in order to accomplish this should give you cause to take notice of your responsibility in all of this. Unless you wake up and change the path down which you are moving, there is great responsibility to be faced. Granted you have been lulled into a zombie like existence, but that has been your choice through lack of personal responsibility toward yourselves and your fellow man. At the end of this sojourn into Life experience, you stand and recount your experience in the light of full understanding and it is you who judge your own actions. No one judges you. You are then aware of what might have been had you lived your experience through extending the Love that created you rather than in pursuit of distractions that gave you no real satisfaction.

What now do you do at this pivotal point in your time? In the knowledge of this picture, which you are hardly able to acknowledge may even be a possibility, what can you do? First you must contemplate upon this understanding and come to face it within your own conscious thinking process. You must consider it as possibly being true. Then you must admit to your unknowing complicity in the treatment of your fellow human beings on this planet. You must move through your regrets for having been unaware through a process of denial, for the existence of these situations was plainly presented to you by the magician. This use of your consent was by real conspirators with very large agendas to put into place. You cannot linger in the destructive guilt process. You must resolve to come into your personal responsibility to cause this situation to change from its intended path. You are expected to stop being a victim and certainly not to become a martyr for there is no place to begin to resist this onslaught. You must vow and commit to become part of the solution. Then, despite the continued push of deceptive encroachment into your awareness, you must begin to discern what is truth. You must hold to your resolve to move through this to a new and greater understanding. When this becomes your greatest personal Truth, then you will find opportunities to become part of a different movement employing methods that will not constitute physical resistance, but will use an entirely new approach. There is no other way open for resistance on a physical level would be immediately snuffed out. Your constitution is no longer an effective shield and will be dissolved. But, that matters not. It is in assuming personal responsibility that when one accepts the challenge and does not fade in fear, others also shall come forth in like awareness and consciousness. Together this spreading group awareness shall provide the pivotal point that will bring an end to this situation. The resolve to be part of the solution from the depths of personal consciousness is the key that will open the lock, end the imprisonment of humanity and bring true freedom to the inhabitants of this planet. Many are called, but few choose to respond. Where do you stand at this pivotal point? You must ask yourself and you must answer yourself!

The question of "who?" is the focusing energy of the "messages" is a difficult question to answer tactfully and yet completely. "Isness" is the focus to be sought by each individual awareness. As each expands within the process of self-identification so does the ability to allow the flow of "Isness" to move through their experience. Each will attract into their awareness knowledge to live into wisdom. The vibratory rate of the planetary environment and of the members of humanity on earth is low enough that this ability is currently virtually inaccessible. To assist willing members of mankind to access the necessary information to provide a way to transcend this current aberrant state, various volunteer awareness points within higher vibrational frequencies have acted as booster stations to focus this information through those willing to participate on the earth plane. Knowing the custom of earth's inhabitants requiring the "personify to identify" mode, names from the exotic to the ridiculous have been given as sources of this information. The information included exercises in discernment, most participants failed the discernment tests. Much was filled with profound truth, but much of it was drained of energy by the continual parade of victims wanting their personal problems solved for them. The information became distorted as the foci were withdrawn and the volunteers winged it (faked it) on their own for their sincerity was lost in the notoriety and greed that resulted.

In view of this history, it was the mutual agreement between the parties involved in the dictation/translation/transcription process for these messages that the identities of the foci involved would remain unidentified and there would be no monetary rewards whatsoever involved. Further, there would be no personal information disseminated for any one individual's benefit. The totality of the foci involved is for the benefit of the planet and its inhabitants, period! The truth of the messages is to be discerned and used for the benefit of humanity first and then gleaned by the individual to apply personally as part of the wholeness to which it is focused without the necessity of personal names to identify truth. If that is not understood, then the messages need to be read again to transcend this need into commitment to the holographic intention of the information they contain.

It is hoped that the succinctness of this message is accepted in the tone of importance in which it is intended. The window of opportunity to accomplish the necessary monumental consciousness transition is small compared to the obstacles within the human belief systems that must be literally dissolved so that the whole may be transformed.

It is sincerely hoped that the truth contained will be a sword that cuts through the armor of deception and lays open the hearts and minds of the necessary quotient for success.

No. 1

It is time now for the people on earth to begin preparing for the planned changes in earnest. Many prophecies have been given to you, so many as to be confusing. This has made it possible for most to do nothing because how could they prepare for so many different possibilities? It is imperative to begin with the most basic steps. Consider what are the most basic needs of man in the particular climatic region that you live in? Where you are with winter coming on it would be food, warm shelter and water? If warmth would be critical, it should be addressed.

Let us take a hypothetical example of an earth change "disaster." Suppose there was an especially severe winter storm in your area. This would be a storm that involved high winds, extreme cold and quantities of blowing and drifting snow. The electrical power would of course be cut off. Even if as was available, it would be unavailable to you unless there was a gas powered fireplace. Without electricity, you could not cook on your electric stove. There would be no electric lights. The streets would be impassable and probably telephone lines would be out, so you could contact no one. What would be your plan? Have you even thought one possibility through to this extent? I suggest that you have at least basic emergency supplies available at home or perhaps in your auto as you are seldom anywhere without it being close by. A camp stove with fuel, some canned or dehydrated food, sleeping bag and most important of all — *water!* Be sure all is in working order, test them to be sure you know how to use them, see that all parts are there. Know what it is that you would do.

Watch your weather forecasts and be aware that any potential storm can be strengthened and steered. Instruments are in place and in use with the sophistication to do this. (HAARP) Inasmuch as we cannot interfere, we cannot protect you from this possibility. Of course this discussion has centered on only one of many possibilities. You may expect these to be happening around the planet as the equipment is tested in order to understand its capabilities before coming up with a planned sequence of scenarios to help them achieve their goals. Check your food supplies. Long keeping winter vegetables are a wise investment and do cook them to learn how, for most of you have fallen into the prepared food trap. Available lake or river water could be frozen and is seldom pure enough to drink. Water storage is wise and even that will not stay pure without special care. A camping purifier pump is available with extra filters. Consider adding a first aid kit, change of clothing, etc. I strongly suggest that you take stock, make a plan and actually put together a workable short term emergency kit and have it in place. Once that is completed then add long term necessities on a regular basis. Once this is accomplished, you can then turn your attention to the business at hand.

There was an old typing class exercise. "Now is the time for all good men to come to the aid of your country." It would seem to me that this is most appropriate now. But in coming to the aid of the country, one must put him/herself in a position of confidence so that in a crisis attention can be turned outward to those in need rather than scrambling to meet ones own personal needs.

In closing our first session, I would remind you that the days of greater chaos are drawing closer in an ascending quickness. Let us continue these sessions so that our clarity may increase and our messages may become truly a guiding light in the darkening of the days ahead. Sometimes it is necessary for darkness to descend before people can become aware of a light that has been shining all along. Thus shall the coming together of the true family of Light Bearers serve to vanquish the deeds of those with dark intentions. Always remember things work together to bring forth that which was planned long ago, for God's plans cannot be thwarted. The duration and complexity of events can be altered if there is a faltering of faith and action on the part of those that have been placed in stations of service. None are placed who do not have the ability to accomplish their missions. Some will falter and perhaps even fail. That, of course, is a possibility, but back-ups are in place and things will move forward in Divine Order. If you trust the knowledge that there is indeed an overall plan, a larger picture, and that it will succeed. Then your own courage and faith will be less likely to falter. TRUST THE PLAN AND PAY NO ATTENTION TO THE DAY TO DAY DETAILS. THIS KNOWINGNESS WILL BE YOUR ROCK ON WHICH TO LEAN. YOUR TOUCHSTONE OF FAITH.

No. 2

Let us begin on this new day in quest of a new day. The people of your planet sink further into the morass of depression and suppression. There is nothing but doom and gloom reported all around them and for lack of a vision of Light, all appears to be fading into darkness. The focus of attention to the devils of the dark doings does not resolve the issue. In order for Light to triumph over darkness there must be a vision of the Light that translates into a recognizable reality. Let us use the birth of the United States as an example. Though we cannot cover the details, we can look at the process, as it is known. There were those who came together to envision something that was different than what was currently being experienced by the planetary inhabitants. No one person brought forth the vision, it was a composite of the inspirations that were but pieces of the whole.

This process must be repeated again. There are those who believe that you should return to what you have had before. Let us say that even that would not resolve the issues at hand. The "founding fathers" did not have instant communication, the Internet, exotic surveillance methods, under and above the sea devices as well as horrendous weapons of destruction with which to deal. You have allowed these to be created and though you long to return to a simpler time, you will either tame these or they will destroy you. You must look past the need to merely survive the methods of trickery designed to annihilate you and dream what you would have instead of the chaos of darkness. It is as simple as that, for as long as you choose to merely withstand and only survive the onslaughts of the oppressors, you are sinking deeper into the morass. You will only rise to the top with a new vision. We cannot give you that vision. The book of Spiritual Laws provides some guidelines, however the vision must be simple to be powerful. It must be visual in its simplicity so that the people now surrounded in darkness can literally be struck with its beauty and feel called to its simplicity and clarity.

How do you do this? A small group cannot do it alone. A nucleus must come together and as they begin the process others of vision will be drawn to it, in fact literally sent. The time for beginning this project is not at a convenient time later, but now. There is no time to be wasted if you are to accomplish this. To tarry will only make it more difficult and bring more suffering to the already oppressed. The window will close in literally weeks if it is not begun. I know you are caught up in the process of illuminating the details of the chaos, but what has that done to stop it? Can you actually see anything happening to change the speed of the decline? Then you must change your perspective. Look in the opposite direction. Are you part of the problem by observing it or can you become part of the solution by looking for the building blocks of what you want instead?

Begin in your meditations to ask who would serve well in this project. This is not an esoteric process for people who are looking to give lip service and stand on the sidelines and observe. This is for visionary realists that may never actually observe the extent of the work they do now until the very end. These people will be able to look beyond the chaos and recognize the opportunity. I suppose you might say these are people with one foot in each world, who can look into both without losing their balance. Once you start looking for them you will find them coming into your experience in what may seem too unusual to be accidental. Meet in 3s, 7s and 12s. This is the most important step to be taken now. Know that all help possible will be given on request. Many ideas will float through, but those of value will take root and the dream will become real, but first it must be conceived before it can be born. You need not feel total responsibility for any phase, only for the initial promotion of the idea.

The hour is desperate and the plans of God hinge upon the people of service. The awareness of the need for change is well established in the consciousness of many, now the vision must be planted, that it may sprout and come to fruition. May your day be blessed with the Love that is yours, for you are Love in manifestation. It is your job and your privilege to focus it that God may stand forth in Freedom and Truth in the experience of his beloved children.

No. 3

It is our hope that the process being initiated will bring together a nucleus of such compatibility as to be a cohesive cell, which shall mimic the bodily process of cell division. Within such a process, the spread would be quite amazing. Remember a babe begins with the combining of just 2 cells and becomes a being of trillions in a matter of 9 months. By the Law of Attraction, a Universal Law, this is entirely possible. Of course the nature of the babe is determined by the birthing combination. It is the characteristics of these that shall have a profound effect upon the end product. Do not worry. Ones that should not be included won't be, but there are many that are appropriate. Just relax and allow the process to flow, which doesn't mean that this phase is yet complete. Indeed it is just beginning. Just setting minds to considering such a possibility will not bring commitment. You are most important in the birthing. It is receptive hearts that are willing to begin the processes that are important. The character, openness to act beyond the confines of the present moment, the ability to make and keep commitments, the love of fellow man beyond themselves, the desire to rise above the trees to see the forest that are the critical components for these parents. Through this process the awakening of man into again the "family of man" is possible. The ability of man to transcend the present self made dilemma into a new concept of experience will bring about a change not only individually, but to all and a ripple effect will be felt throughout the Universe/Cosmos. I know that this seems like a big assignment to begin from just 2, but each new child is also a miracle. Its beginning is hardly auspicious. Just a mass of dividing cells with no apparent organization into a miniature babe. But, at a miraculous moment, the appearance in miniature is there. Inspiration shall begin the change within the focused group consciousness.

The project assignment is that each new cell continues to divide. How exactly is this going to work? The first meets with two. Then each meets again with two others, then each again meets again with two others until there are 7. (3 plus 2 equals 5 plus 2 equals 7.) Then that group meets and the 4 additions split and create their own 7. Now the originals at that point can again begin a new cycle or drop out. The more times each individual repeats the process, the more the growth cycle accelerates. Can you see how the original organization can grow quickly without bringing great danger to the project or to individuals? At this point it is only the dream that is being promulgated. Then the babe takes shape at the critical point of greater group awareness, then the plan changes and the organs, so to speak begin to take shape for the different functions necessary for the creation of the dream. Since the focus is on the creation of a new experience, armaments are not a part of the picture and less danger is present. The focus is not resistance because forward movement into change is not factored into the detection process as presently set up by the oppressors.

I shall leave you to consider what you have been told this far.

No. 4

Fear in the heart, puts a damper on the appreciation of the wonderful gift of life. It also hardens the belief of separation and causes those wrapped up in it to become deadened and wooden in their ability to perceive changes going on around them. It is like a cloak being wrapped around the awareness. In this way the darkness wraps its insidious plans of subjugation and annihilation around your fellow earth beings.

Now begins in earnest the movement of the Light to bring an end to this situation. As with all things it begins with the process of thought and desire to bring an end to it. In this case, the subtle, modest beginning will go unnoticed. The opposing forces are plant-ing their seeds of perceived invincibility everywhere. If this were real, they would not need to do so at the level of a psychological campaign. Remember that humanity now numbers in the billions. That is an overwhelming number in itself. These are souls that are volunteering to be here for the benefit of this planet and these beings have incarnated here for the purpose of experiencing the next rising or at the least to assure its success. They shall not go unrewarded.

Remember that this is a play. It is difficult to get this under-standing across, but in a play, all you have to do is to change the lines to change the scope of the play. Well, you are a fragment of the whole of Creation and can begin changing the lines of the play. Is this an over simplification of this situation? It would appear so from your prospective, but indeed it is as simple as that. This project involves the formation of the group entity that can change the lines, or add a new character, however you want to visualize the process. Remember a visualization involves pictures. The words that you use in your contacts with those who might become the critical par-ents of this entity will respond to that which stirs their imagination and their emotions. Learn from your successful political elections, which appeal to emotion before logic. What works for this instru-ment of the opposition with the people can work for you also. The logical approach brings lots of rhetoric, but it is that which brings visualization and emotion that incites action. What is wanted here is action, not reaction. The resort to the use of arms against the plan for overwhelming mankind is doomed from the start. Yet the keeping of their guns by the citizen of this country, means that their freedom is not yet gone. When those are taken, then you will see a real overwhelming realization among your people of the gravity of what surrounds them. Thus the timing is again stressed. We do not mean to belabor this, but there are windows of opportunity that must be used for our advantage for these offer the greater chance of success with the least amount of suffering for the greatest number.

Insofar as grieving in regard to those that are suffering, let me assure you that the number of souls incarnating on this planet increases the difficulty of *their* plans. (Note that I avoid using cer-tain names, and you would be wise to do that also after all within your circle the exact identity of these forces can be assumed as known.) Their role is well known to them before they incarnate. They don't remember it now of course, but they come to assure the success of the process of our mission. Does that assure you of the importance of the earth in the total scheme of the grand picture? I would think so.

In the initial meetings of the small groups, no one visualization is likely to appeal to all, so one suggestion shall be given as guidance. "Ask and it shall be given." A composite will emerge that will provide the appeal when participation reaches a critical stage. This diversity will aid in the masking of the process. You are well connected, so do not be concerned about this aspect. Use the visualization of dominos standing on end and arranged is a pattern so that when one is made to fall, all follow in rapid progression. It has great application to our meaning and brings an identifying tie to their planned process.

No. 5

It is resistance to recognizing the situation and more resistance to being responsible for the changing of it, as well as the induced feeling of overwhelm that blocks the participation of the majority. The willingness to be responsible for personal conduct and to change the focus of perception is buried within the busy (frantic) schedules of daily existence. Individuals find solace in their excuses for not confronting the growing signs of coming oppression. Breaking down this line of resistance and drawing as many of these into the new planned pattern of Life remains the goal. Those of the dark plan have set their focus to overwhelm any human beings with plans to resist and have preconceived plans ready to move toward the crushing of resistance. However there are none for the coming of a new vision. This leaves that opening available to us, in fact, the ideal opening. Our plan is not to fix the old, but to create the new.

(There will always be the repetition of certain ingrained habitual thoughts, hopefully not to the point of nausea.) The skill of speaking, indeed even thinking, discretely on the subject of those with plans contrary to the will of Creation will aid in helping to bring that style of referring to them into usage. The more variety in this application of presenting the subject being discussed the better. It is easy for focused individuals to "get right to the point" but this will not serve in the long run.

It might be appropriate to point out that a linear progression within the scope of this project will not always be apparent. Divine Order is the "order of the day." And Divine Order does not follow man's ideas of sequence at all. You have set up certain unspoken, subconscious rules to give "sequential order" to your experience. The forces of God do not have to follow sequence to have organization. Therefore, it is important that once the process is initiated to a critical point, then you must trust in its completion of itself without the ego control so familiar to each of you. This is imperative, lest you monkey wrench your own dream.

Our co-operative effort and it is that, must begin, continue and end with focus on a completed goal. It is the composite of dreams of what a Utopian world would be like, one that each would truly like to experience that will bring this to pass. This is the opposite of the resistance that is expected. How much time do each of you spend in this "daydreaming" process? Survival daydreams are more the norm in the group that we are depending upon for this formative process. Granted such a thing, as easy earth compatible energy sources are a part of that dream, for luxuries of easy living are not appealing sacrifices for freedom from oppression. This is what is automatically supposed will be the cost of such change. Would a new paradigm of experience be without comforts? Different comforts probably, but I doubt anyone will feel any regrets for having given up the present situation. This again is the "resist or be shoved backwards" thought process that must be abandoned. That you want what will make your experience even better is a given, and it should be assumed. It must also be assumed there may be a short period necessary to endure in order for this change to happen, but it can be shorter than you might imagine. When this pivotal project is accomplished, our help is not only allowed, it is mandated. It is the beginning "think tank" discussions that will bring about the beginning of the change of expectation to an ever-expanding group. Think of a stone tossed into a pond. The ripples reach out to effect a greater and greater area. We call it a critical point, you refer to it as the "100th monkey theory." Think of the counter thought group as having to send the ripples in from the outside to the middle. Remember they are creating what is not in accordance with the laws of God. Their concentration is toward containment while your focus is toward rippling outward. Now, which one do you think works the best? When these ripples meet what happens? If you are using the same pond water, which one is likely to overwhelm the other, especially if the stone that is dropped is becoming larger and larger in what might be interpreted to be slow motion?

Remember there are vibrational effects that are and will be brought in to being that cannot be observed by you. Each time the thought pattern is focused toward the goal, the more it becomes intensified. As it intensifies, it becomes more magnetic and attraction begins to build. You are not likely to surprise any of the contacts. What you are most likely to hear is that it has been in their thoughts already, but they just hadn't made the effort to follow through with its implications. The process will become appealing and challenging when you begin to dream of ways to use the mechanisms put in place for the use of those of opposite intentions. Doesn't that sound intriguing? Rather than to destroy and resist, it might be possible to use some of what they have in place for your own intentions. You have focusing powers that are capable of many things when there is group participation and a few innovations of your own can be added. Remember the pipe that sends vibrations to the crops in the fields? Ever wonder what else it is capable of doing? You might be surprised. Even the sound embedded in Dan Carlson's music tapes for the growth of plants might be interesting in the presence of their focused vibrations. (Sonic Bloom). Just a thought or two about what you already have available.

No. 6

The light begins to change its focus as the window changes in what might be considered depth, as layers of intentional activity will be added. The focus becomes more intense in the area on which it is aimed. Now this can be an advantage as it can bring the focus to a greater clarity. That the cloak of darkness appears to you to be getting more intense can have its positive aspects. The closing of the noose is not as unobserved by the masses as you might think. Intuitive feelings are becoming aroused. The critical mass of awareness is being aroused and the other side is well aware of this.

Remember there is a weak link within their plan. They are going to demand that their army of militia turn on their own people, indeed their own friends and family. That is a key point on which there will be reactions that they cannot predict. This allows openings in their plan. They seem minor to you in your consideration, but these can be used to great advantage for sometimes a moment is all the focus of Light may need.

Ours will not be a plan of resistance. It will be the lifting up of a vision into manifestation through the minds of many. When the picture of what has been carefully planned for them is repulsive enough to their imaginations, don't you think that they will turn with enthusiasm to a vision that thrills them? Remember there will be those who will choose otherwise. There will be a division. There will be enough that have been either won over or will be lost in the desire of continuing to experience the menu which has been fed to them in the media barrage directed at them. This will be a point you will have to deal with, as will all that join in this plan for transcending the decayed into the new birthing opportunity. All will not choose to join, and here you must recognize the free choice of experience given to each. It is not so much hardening your heart toward them as an attitude of allowance. Remember there is no death. Only the end of an experience and eternity is incomprehensible. It is not for any of you to judge what the experiences of each individual means to the completion within each Soul. The Soul draws to itself a composite and makes of these experiences patterns that dazzle the imagination. The dance of duality, darkness and Light as you will, are part of the play.

You must not become disheartened at any time, for there will be those who will surprise you. It is for you to keep your eye on the vision and to watch it unfold into creation from your limited perspective. That too will be fascinating. How will you know? It will be difficult in the birthing phase, for in the beginning the process of a babe hardly looks like anything but a maze of dividing cells, with no apparent organization. At the critical point, all that miraculously changes into a form. Then the challenge of preventing an abortion will become a dual focus. However, that too shall be handled. Remember this, as you begin to help yourselves, more and more co-operation from various forms of manifested Light can assist in ways you, and even I, cannot imagine and may never be privy to know about. It is the focus on the vision that shall attract this assistance toward success.

We can continue to present this information to you, but there can also be discussion. Questions can be asked as long as they are pertinent to the process at this point. No divining allowed. Just focus on one stage at a time. As to what your continuing roles shall be as the plan unfolds will be revealed as each day arrives. There is no already existing vision except in a dim outline that is set up by the influence of the Universal Laws. At the time of filling in these outlines, those will be made known to the founding parents in very simplistic terms. KISS will be the "order of the day" for the entire project. How is that going to be possible within the contributions to the vision by many? Trust the process. The planet is experiencing on an entirely different level than it was when the founding fathers of the U.S. followed this same path. Note this time it is "founding parents," and that in itself is a raising of the level of experience. Both energies shall be present and it shall make for a doubled energy focus. Though women knew the last time and supported as allowed, theirs was not a contributory role except as an outside influence. Neither shall dominate, for the vision must move beyond such selfishness and bring about a synergistic wholeness.

At this point, you must not concern yourselves with the manifestation of their plan. You know of it, you are expecting it and so it must be ignored. Your focus must be on the moment and what is to be done. If that which you do now puts you in danger, perhaps you should begin laying plans for doing something different. Not yet in this moment, but soon. Perhaps this surface activity cycle is drawing to a close. It is only a suggestion to be considered, though you already have toyed with it. We leave it to your discretion. Corporate business will be allowed for activities that do not make big waves. Opportunities shall appear for your consideration.

Travel shall be safe for a time yet. If you miss a plane or a flight is canceled take it within your stride. There may be many reasons apparent in retrospect as to why you were not to be on a particular mode of transportation. When travel is no longer safe, you will know. The focus of your intent now is to work within the activities of the parenting process.

No. 7

There is much being done to bring into concrete experience the truth of the statement that the unseen world is more real than the one that is seen by the mass consciousness on the planet now. These concrete demonstrations of the nature of this unseen causal effect are not only stimulating awareness, but bringing forth the opportunity to use this knowledge to encourage the visioning of the process that together we are beginning to bring forth. (How is that for talking all the way around the subject?) It helps to bring it out of the realm of wishing into the realization that there is a way to counter their methods without adopting them. The work to be done is not at this 3rd dimensional level of resistance, but as I have emphasized before, at the causal level of creating what is another focus entirely. The reality of the possibility of this process has already been demonstrated in fields that indicate these processes can be adopted and focused in accordance with what is needed. The already proven success of these "theories" adds the inspiration needed to bring forth the birthing activity. It is recommended that the "messages" be held for those who would be encouraged to join the birthing process in the immediate future. These people will quickly see the correlation, and of course some are already in the awareness of some or all of its contents. A basic awareness of both sides of the forces present is needed and that information is available and it is necessary that it be known to those selected as the parents of this process. It is a human weakness to assume that what is known to one, is also known to all. Details are not necessary, but an overview would be most helpful with an available "catalog" of well documented information for those desiring a more comprehensive understanding in areas not familiar to them.

The processes mentioned in the "message" are of course known to those engaged in this broad research and these strive to be merely known, but not to create a situation that will bring public awareness. At that point their existence is a threat to the powers that assume invincibility. These would then be in a precarious situation as the noose tightens. Their importance cannot be stressed enough. This is the reality check needed to assure the success of the understanding that these higher vibrational realities need to be "pulled" into the experience of this planet. As the "message" reveals, the comfort zone under threat can bring violent reactions, not only in the circles of the opposition, but among the general public. The opposition at its highest levels knows that it is threatened by a possible collapse of their operation from the inside out. The mass consciousness is merely reacting in a "Pavlov's dog" fashion. Possibility thinking is not acceptable.

Herein lies the need for careful movements within the project until the critical mass is reached. This is why the approach to the plan must be by word of mouth to known individuals who then take the responsibility of approaching those who they know have the proper sympathetic awareness and desire to see the situation change. The ability to identify with the change to be made at levels behind the "5 senses" experience must be paramount in the beginning parenting process. It isn't the number of people involved at this stage, but the quality of the awareness that is important. The ability to possibility think, the openness to expansion of awareness and the ability to assimilate and postulate into new synthesis, the known and unknown, is of critical importance. In other words, choose carefully. With that step clearly in mind, the proliferation will take care of itself. The clarity of the first combinations will set the stage for the entire process.

No. 8

It is interesting that the power of thought has brought us to a meeting point of consciousness. This is a process of intent focused toward a mutual purpose. It is this bringing together of purposeful intent that is the magic of shared manifestation. It is evident in the perceived world that surrounds you in both its positive and negative forms. Now the plan is to raise that process to a higher level, to engage known processes to further your exploration of the process of manifestation. It is a matter of intention that brings forth the knowledge to be able to do this from a vantage point of awareness of the essential elements to ensure completion. This need not be done through blind faith in an unknown process. This would encourage an attrition rate that would ensure failure. It is a matter of making the data available to the conscious awareness and then allowing it to percolate. The inspiration for application will come forth into understanding. Manifestation is not a haphazard, lucky combination of synchronistic meetings. There are specific already existing procedures in place available to be used. It is a matter of bringing these purposefully into the awareness and then the creative imaginations will trigger the appropriate applications. "The luck of the draw" is simply too risky to be relied on in this project.

Here again the stress remains on the careful choices for the parenting operation. It is not desired to belabor this point, but it is awesomely important.

Ours is a most important combination of massaging your consciousness (plural) and stimulating your concerns without bringing forth panic. We are finding this to be a skill that is most rewarding. It is indeed bringing about the desired results. You are not the only ones to which this process is being applied. Just know that all that can be done from this level is being done. It is in the actual movement from the point of inertia that will allow this behind the scene help to aid in bringing forth the manifestation of the plan. Remember the birthing process begins with the dance of desires and culminates in an apparent miracle through processes that go on for the most part beneath the level of conscious awareness. These processes are not haphazard, but proceed within exacting synthesis of multiple complicated interactions. If there was an original plan for this common place happening, then don't you think that a plan for one as important as this one is also in place? If you do not need to be aware of the functions relating to the birth process of a child to complete itself, then do you need to know of all the processes that will happen in this project? The human birthing process would not happen if certain physical actions did not to take place to initiate its beginning.

What is being emphasized here is that you understand you will not shepherd the whole process to its conclusion. Neither do we want you to think you will be left out of the project once it is initiated. Indeed, you will be included in ways that are not in the most freewheeling of your imagination at this moment. In this case, we encourage you to trust the process and continue to be available, for you are all needed. You did not sign on for a short-term assignment.

Let us continue now by moving on to other subjects that are of course related. It is important to keep a balance in this stretch of your understanding of this commitment to the transcendence of the planet and its inhabitants. Know that this is hardly a single handed commitment, but the agreed upon commitment of countless numbers of beings who are not strangers to the process. In this case, the energy of this particular planet has reached a level of heaviness that is challenging to say the least. But after all, you must know that all of you thrive on challenge and this is no exception. However, this time it is not a game, for failure would have serious implications beyond the mere suffering of incarnated beings. This of course is known to you a your deepest levels, so it is not meant as a threat. In this case, we are allowed greater discretion to assist and we are stretching it to the utmost in order to initiate the beginning of this project. Much planning has gone into the methodology with contingencies covered for the art of improvisation is not limited to 3rd dimensional experience.

It is known that certain lack of sincerity exists in the realms of those who present themselves as leading the resistance to the planned changes. In this case, either these will find themselves involved in other activities or you will have a distinct knowingness regarding the appropriateness of their inclusion. The identity of some of these might come as a surprise, but again you are connected to a point now that you will know in the moment when it is necessary to be cautious. Most of what is included today in this contact is known to you, it is as yet not possible to reveal detail for two reasons. The proper sequences are not yet in place and this line of communication is not yet at a level for these to come through. All possible is being done to prepare this last phase so that there will be a coordination of these elements. Again, we ask your patience and that you trust the process, redundant as it may seems at times. As you say, just hang in there.

No. 9

The situation is this. Time is the primary element used to recognize placement within the 3rd dimension. However, the veil between dimensions is thinning. As the awareness grows of the availability of 4th and even 5th dimensional processes for usage in this 3rd dimensional realm, this veil will begin to thin even more. The new focus must include elements of the higher dimensions. How to do this! Thought moves between dimensions as long as the thought is within those dimensional parameters. 3rd dimensional parameters allow for interfering with the development of others. It allows for the forcing of one will upon another. Above that dimension, all are allowed freedom to develop without this interference. Personal responsibility is the keynote of existence. Contrary to the mass consciousness appearance of the lack of development of this level, it is there, simply smothered by the barrage of mind control techniques. However, those techniques are not as successful as it might appear. If it were, then the massive physical control that is being put in place would not be necessary. If it were, then there would be no problem of what to do in their view of over population. There would be masses of people following like lemmings into the sea. What is becoming a rising tide, is the ground swell of feeling of people longing for this personal freedom.

Through the moving of jobs from your country, people have found that they can create for themselves new opportunities, however nebulous they maybe within the "communications" dream of non-production. This success within planned failure has tweaked the creative urge within many thus the proliferation of home based businesses. It is this glimmering of personal success that has sparked a surge within even the most oppressed of the beings in your country, meaning the welfare recipients. This information has not stayed within the boundary of this country. It has always been alive in countries of great poverty. If it were not, more would have starved long ago.

This longing for freedom will be fanned into a blaze by the dream and its simplicity. It will be this new conception that will lift the spirits of those who will hear, and the lift will be literal. The inner prayer of the longing hearts shall be answered and their reaction to it will not be stopped. It can't be reached by third dimensional methods, for those who try to apply them will simply be left as helpless as was the dark plan for the people. Once the critical point of awareness is reached, support of the new paradigm will take the planet forward as a whole. The "ascension" of the new age dreamers is one of individual flights into the clouds, but this shall be a planetary change. Your bible mentions two standing in a field and only one is taken. The person who wholeheartedly believes in the dream shall accompany the dream.

The parents of this dream must have the understanding, that 3rd dimensional parameters must be transcended and thought must be focused into the higher expectations of a new dimension. Trust in the personal responsibility of its citizens will be the key to the foundations of that new perception. It is the password, so to speak, for entry into this experience. Honesty and forthrightness are practiced without question. Your 23rd psalm translation misrepresented this by the word "righteousness" which was given the meaning of judgmental attitude, in particular, the actions of others. Instead, it was meant that each was to be responsible to live rightly within the *personal* focus on their life attitudes and actions. This would result in finding that games of inappropriate action will not work if no one else will play by those rules. There can be no victims and no martyrs if no one will play that game. This may sound naive considering the chaos around you, but that is the difference. That is the leap that must be made, through the assumption that humanity has a critical mass that is ready to assume this shift in perception. The profit motive at the expense of all others has not lead to Utopia. Man in true prospective is a radiant being, meaning created to give outward the expression of the Creators Love, not to live as a usurper with only the intent of drawing all toward himself as depicted by the material experience. The experiment of this has left him hollow and unfulfilled. This shall be the opportunity to experience what will satisfy and fill his heart cup to running over.

How can you paint this vision with the color of emotion that shall magnetize all that hear it and catch them up into movement toward it? Intent shall be the alchemical ingredient, and the Creators Love of his children shall spread butter upon the path, to convert an old adage to a different focus. It can be done, it shall be done, on that you can place your life's focus and trust. The etheric winds of change are in motion and the momentum is building. Do you think there is anything that can stand against the Creator of the game in the first place? It cannot be so. Welcome to the winning side! Now isn't that a wonderful greeting?

This seems like a logical place on which to end this exchange of thought. Open your hearts and feel the love that is given to you for your trust and acceptance of our combined path in this marvelous adventure of adventures. How will we top this one? It is not for us to know, yet.

No. 10

The movie, "The Siege," contained heavy subliminal messaging. Just one point, remember that it used the constitution to resolve the difficulty. However, their intention is to use executive orders so that there is no constitution for where will there be a judge with authority to stand against the dark organization. The realization of that will quickly demoralize the people. That was another sleeping pill of greater magnitude than you realize. Asking for shielding and for discernment was quite effective and it will be most helpful to use it as the situation progresses. It is something that will need to be done by each and not something that can be done for a group by one person. Again we go back to the law of individual responsibility.

It will be interesting for you to know that the planetary consciousness is changing. Let us compare this to a breathing pattern. It is as though the planet is changing its steady intervals of inhale and exhale to an irregular pattern of a deeper inhale as compared to the exhale as a gathering of internal energies. That is an area of our discussions that has not been covered. The planet too shall participate in the plan to change the situation. Remember that all manifestation at all levels is the result of the projection of thought into the malleable ethers (your name for creative potential), and that thought is interactive within itself in the ability to maintain balance.

You can perceive that you are beginning to experience a focus of change in a co-operative energy vibration. This has the potential to synchronize the inhabitant consciousness to blend with that of the planet as a whole. Perhaps this will allow you to begin to understand why we belabor the point of the importance of the parenting cells being of the consciousness that will produce this blending vibratory ratio. There shall be a quickening of the latent emotional connections to the planetary consciousness, not to the suffering on her part because of mankind's infliction of selfishness and greed, but to the area of conscious desire for change to a new and different experience. Remember this is not the first civilization to experience here and you do not know the history of these previous scenarios. Just as you experience and learn, so also is this repeated in the evolution of the planet as a whole. Here you begin to see the damming up of energy that is occurring now. When a hole in this dam is released in a direction that the whole of this energy can blend into cohesively, then there can be a release that will flush away the infection and bring about a healing of marvelous proportion. Just as a journey begins with the first step, so also this begins with the tiny hole in the dam by the formation of the first cells of the birthing process.

It is not yet clear exactly what the planetary involvement will be as it depends upon the blend of energy that parents the part of the process that is contributed by humanity. It is the key that unlocks the whole of the project. We, of course, have observed various scenarios of possible energy combinations similar to your computer projections and find that each brings forth a vastly different combination of possible reactions. Each leads to a similar end conclusion, not only in different combinations of similar elements, actions and reactions, but in different elements, actions and reactions entirely. Therefore definite conclusions cannot be made even from this prospective. Isn't that interesting? We think so. Thus, once the selections are made and the first cells begin to act in the creation of the possible "dream" scenarios it still will not be possible to project much of clarity until it, the dream scenario, becomes clear in the minds of these groups as a whole.

Can we guide this process based on our test projections? We wish we could, but that would be unacceptable interference. In this case, the guidance will have to come from a higher Source than we are. There is little doubt that the Highest of High is most interested in what is happening here and that Source will be available for exactly the help needed. These miniature planetary think tanks will be allowed to play with possibilities, but the request for High Source help will no doubt have much powerful input into the completion of the process. I can assure you that this level knows mankind to its very core and will guide the process, but there must first be the movement beyond desire into active thought projection for the purpose of manifesting this new experience. After the creative dreaming of possibilities, then follows the purposeful focus process to place the skeletal outline in place. The great reward will be the painting in of the details with the experience of that which you will have created. The joy of this part of the process shall be wonderful indeed.

No. 11

The mantra of this project must be "In God We Trust!" You cannot trust manifested mass conscious beliefs. The seeds of death for your fellow human beings are beyond the planted seed stage and into sprouting and rapid growth. There is but one "salvation" from this trap. It is in the service to and total trust in the way through this situation. There is not a way out; there is only the way through. The subtle difference is not apparent, but is indeed of great importance. Out implies resistance, through implies movement through toward a greater goal lying beyond. Just as one does not get out of a mountain pass, but must move through it, so must you identify with the subtly different application. Mankind falls into the dream of a great leader being raised up in consciousness to "lead" them out of this or any other dilemma. It cannot be. It must be by the inspiration of visualizing a way of Life that fills the empty void of their consciousness that the political, scientific and religious dogma of the past and present has brought to each. The realization that only by their desire to participate, following a personal conscious decision, will lead them through this experience to what awaits beyond.

Man is an adventurous being, loving challenge. This desire for personal adventure has been diverted into the false desire for safety, the assurance of limited risk (insurance). Remember the navy posters that appealed to the young men by offering the adventure of sailing to unknown ports, only to end up with wooden guns guarding a metal fenced enclosure such as did Bill Cosby? Military combat is represented as an "adventurous" activity, but it is not on a personal responsibility level. Each activity is planned out not by the individual, but by the layers of officers. Yet military heroes are those that in the moment of need act on their own to accomplish a deed of great risk to themselves. For the public at large risk is left to such things as the risk of death on snowboards, skiing on possible avalanche areas, swimming in possible rip tide areas, climbing steep mountains, etc. These too shall soon be cut off, to further stifle the soul into greater limitation. The pent up feelings are then channeled into destructive outlets of wars, gangs, rape, pillage and other activities contrary to the purposes of manifested Life. This leads mankind from its original purpose of finding the connection and the path of return to the Creator.

You already know this, so of what point is this discussion? This is so that you might recognize the feelings that are prevalent, especially with the young people. What change is experienced when you remember that there is a plan to lead the human experience in the opposite direction, into the Promised Land of true personal adventure in dealing within the realms of personal self. This is what is being experienced in the greater manifested reality. It is but an enlarged mirror image of what is taking place within.

The identified 300 are but 300 focused tricks of these distorted egos given free rein through the manipulation of their minds. All effort has been made to assist individuals on the personal level to realize this. Now, the manifestation of the "evil" (misunderstanding and misuse) must be dealt with by the extreme method of bringing forth a movement to halt this process on the same level as has been achieved by the misused egos of the dark ones. This has occurred by the process of the ego empowering itself into areas contrary to its purpose. This process has reached proportions of imbalance, which endanger the integrity of the Galaxy/Universe. Extreme measures have been sanctioned by the Creator to bring this back into balance. Because of the Love of the Creator for his fragments, all possible means to return these into equilibrium is being made. Some shall indeed be denied manifested Life experience for what you would term long periods of time, as many opportunities to turn from their focus of separation have been given them. Others shall continue their lessons in other situations for they are but innocently duped during the experience they chose by incarnating here.

Those who have true intent and purpose shall move through the experience by their choices of participation within bringing forth this manifestation of the new creation scenario. This group-focused demonstration will carry a power of transformation that shall be thrilling indeed. It is a gift of the Creator. This shall be a blessing and a gift of Grace through a profound Love focus beyond all previous experience. Through this shall the raising of this planet occur, its transcendence shall ripple outward through all of creation allowing new levels of experience. The transcending participants will enjoy the rewards of participating within this completion. The mercy and grace available within the Loving focus of the Creator is included within the infinity of "His" Love. The finite mind is unable to fathom this, but there shall be an expansion of the ability to encompass this to a greater degree within this focus of human experience and expression within the changing of the dimensions. But even the dimensions shall change through this scenario so that all consciousness shall be thrilled by new experience and be further awakened.

Now, does the greeting "Welcome to the winning side" carry new meaning? Indeed! The intent of these messages is to deepen the resolve and to give all possible support to the tasks upon your plates. May your hearts be inspired to continue your devoted participation with the blessings of all beings of Light involved in this project. Your bible has a saying, "and she pondered this in her heart." An apt way of putting it. May you open your consciousness to experience the Love that surrounds, inspires and protects you on this day! Indeed!

No. 12

We find it interesting that the forces of evil are putting forth a dual effort. The ethnic and racial differences between individuals and groups are being stressed and agitated while at the same time you are being forced into a "one world government." This, of course, is not without planning. It is for the purpose of creating chaos and confusion within the psyche. In actuality, this serves our purposes also. It is a great deal easier to create change from chaos than it is to bring it about within a stable, static environment.

There are a great many planets that are highly developed within the adaptation and adoption of the Universal Laws. If this is such a wonderful state, then the question is why focus the opportunity of transcendence of such magnitude as is being hinged upon this process through a planet that is in the gross experience of this one. The answer is that it is the chaotic energy that offers the greatest potential for this particular process. That which you call God has not "created" your dilemma, but it is His Creation and certainly he can participate in the potential that it offers, much to your benefit we might add.

We are offering as many perspectives to this situation as possible, so that you might have as much understanding as possible. It is necessary that you rise above the stressful awareness that much suffering is being experienced by many of your fellow human beings that have incarnated upon this planet now. This is so that you can perceive from a level of perception that will allow you to have a "God's eye" view from which to conceive your plans. The conception of the "one world government" by the opposition also serves a purpose. Many of the incarnated beings have indeed put aside the nationalistic views they once had and are thinking in terms of global inclusiveness. The project plan will be one that will appeal to more than those of the USA. Of necessity it must be a plan of planetary scope. Necessarily, its beginning is focused here, but the total picture must be of global intent.

There will be a particular intensity of chaos that will be the pivotal time for change, either for them or for us. Thus the timing for the creation and birthing into the awareness of this plan or dream as we have previously called it is critical. In the nebulous unformed stage of the process, the word dream seems more appropriate in that a plan indicates something already in thought form. This is not yet the case and also keeps it in the mind-set of a more playful and creative format. It does not carry the heavy responsibility emphasis for the participating groups. It is intended to promote as much possibility thinking in the broadest possible ways. In the beginning phases, there must be no thoughts of boundaries. Remember that we are not to consider the actions or the reactions of the other side. We are going to be dreaming within little known possibilities; therefore all things are possible. The contingent plans of the other side can only work in their known reality. You are going to be setting up a reality that is far outside anything that they have even considered. It is this level of creativity that we are striving to encourage you to reach. This is creativity that will supersede and stretch beyond the current reality. Can you do this? Of course! Why do you think we tried out possible contingency plans? These are available for you in the etheric fields, not for the intention of you to choose one of them, but merely as beginning points for you to exercise your imaginations. Remember your imagination is the entry point to the "mind of God" which is infinite potentiality. The invocation of His Presence when "two or more are present," is true to the degree you limited ones have not yet perceived.

Any preconceived ideas individual members of these groups may have considered are to be used only as beginning points. No applicable possibility has as yet been conceived. This may challenge some egos in the early stages of participation, but this is a critical time in the education of egos. These observer parts of 3rd dimensional existence must be encouraged to enter into the imaging process and through this they will experience their true purpose. Even the ego will find joy within this process for in experiencing its true role it shall desire to experience more of this joy. Indeed, it is not an entity of separate identity, but is a very active aspect of the human experience that has received far too much emphasis within the complex union of Soul extension energies. Yet we must credit this distortion with the creation of this planetary opportunity, so from that perspective, this activity has contributed in its own unique way. God can turn anything into a purposeful synergy to benefit the whole. More faith on the part of mankind to the reality of this Truth would be of great assistance to them in this project.

The understanding of how individuals experiencing this incarnation fit into the cosmic scheme of things is a little like reading a corporate organization chart. However, this one would be amazingly complex for you to understand in totality for it does not follow the logical responsibility pattern of heavy at the top. Can you conceive of equality from top to bottom of something that has no top and no bottom? Stretches the logic of it, does it not? Does it make sense? Of course it does when linear sequence is not an essential parameter. How could a group accomplish anything without sequence being necessary? Quite well I assure you. How can things manifest without a beginning or an end? Amazingly, you think that it must begin as it appears in the formation of the baby. What appears to be the process in 3rd dimension begins in the etheric. The unseen part of the process is a complete being and already exists at the moment of conception. From completeness in one dimension, it manifests in your reality. A flower was not brought into manifestation from a plant cell, but was conceived in its wholeness not only in appearance, but also in process.

Will your group be responsible for the conception of the process of what needs to be accomplished to change this earthly dilemma? Why do you think so many "etheric" beings are present? We are here to help you with the unseen processes needed. Once the skeletal outline is in place, in a form that will bring the desired results, then you will not be able to imagine the activity that will take place, all focused toward a "splendid moment of creation." Are you being supported through this process? You had better believe it. But—it all hangs on the initiation by humanity of actively creating its own destiny through changing its perception of the ideal, in fact because of the chaos and confusion, in the creation of <u>an ideal</u>.

May the energy that awaits the initiation of the process in small part fill your experience. You are much appreciated and all possible support encompasses you this day. Be of good cheer as you go about your seemingly mundane tasks. Nothing in the lives of humans shall remain mundane for long.

No. 13

The energies as projected by those that would ensnare the inhabitants of earth in its plans to change the destiny of this planet moves in ever tightening circles as they attempt to incorporate the wheels within wheels that constitute a partial understanding of the cycles of creation. They are, oh so, careful to check each cog so that none are out of sequence. Linear thought is still the basis of their game for there is no spiraling toward evolutionary change. Evolution is the term given to change in your language. There is a lack of understanding what the process is. What are they evolving toward? The enslavement of the remaining population is the goal, but for what purpose? A stagnant Utopia? What makes them think that the Universe could or would support them in that process? To rebel against the process of creation is one possibility, but to maintain themselves outside of the focus of Creation would incorporate an ever-escalating process within its totality, and it is doomed to failure. To hijack a planet is one thing; to create an anti-universe is indeed grandiose, for there would be no other way. From where would that kind of energy come? Do they plan to hijack an entire universe? I doubt that which you call God is so impotent as to allow that.

Again I say "welcome to the winning side!" This may seem impossible to believe in view of the above comments. From one perspective that kind of arrogance is humorous. Of course it is not for those experiencing the day to day flexing of the muscles of their power and viewing it from the basis of 3rd dimensional experience. To bring a transition in the human consciousness, the largest view possible is necessary for those who would envision this change. Perhaps change is not the best term, for it implies merely readjusting that which already exists. This has been tried before in other opportunities to outwit the adversary. Obviously it didn't work or you would not be facing this situation. This time you must go a step farther in your refusal to play the game according to their rules. You must change your tactics completely so as to cause their plans to be as impotent as they have schemed to make you. You must transcend those plans. Much ado has been made for "ascending" and for "rapture." Well, this indeed shall be our version of that, accept "Jesus" will not do it for you. You must do more than claim to be a "Christian." It will not be necessary to get your hands dirty in the blood of your enemy. Neither shall you be required to turn the other cheek and look away as he does as he wills, for you shall have plans of your own that will employ God's methods that you have until now forgotten. The Armageddon of their vision shall never occur. There shall be an Armageddon, but it shall be played out on a different field and there shall be no conflict as has been envisioned for you.

Your desire for delivery and your will to thwart these puffed up antagonists to Creation shall be guided to fruition along paths of remembering. This shall bring forth the elements of the spiral of evolution that are missing from their carefully laid plans. Fear not, for you have on your side the energies that create solar systems, galaxies, universes and cosmos, indeed All That Is. Could you ask for more support? It is not that it has been lacking during the previous opportunities, but that the cleverness and focus of the antagonists have planned carefully to bring this action to a planned point of implementation at the moment of coinciding cycles. This they believe to be a point of vulnerability. Indeed, however, at those points of cycle endings, the Creator has planned opportunity for His holographic fragments to take advantage of the spiral acceleration that is potentially present. Attention is energetically focused toward that process which allows for those who will to take advantage of the opportunity.

This has been a very simplistic explanation of this unique situation. Indeed history will be written in the annals of this planet. The pot boils, the steam builds and the Universe holds its breath as the moment approaches. Could the process fail? No, but the degree of advantage taken within the opportunity shall affect all within this Universe. Remember that the Creator focus uses all within the flow of ever moving energy in Creation. Chaos is especially pregnant with opportunity for change. It is not to put pressure on you that this knowledge is being shared, but to add to your understanding of the opportunity that is being brought into the situation that appears so hopeless. You must have your eyes open and use your ability to observe and analyze the actions that are taking place about you. The avatars of the past have planted the seeds of understanding that lie dormant within human awareness. It is time to stimulate these seeds into sprouting and growth toward a maturation of 3rd dimensional experience. Those that can accept this stimulation will and those who cannot shall be given other opportunities. Shall any fragments be destroyed? All fragments of the Creator's awareness must be accounted for. Those aspects that have chosen to experience extreme imbalance are put into a space that is something like exile. It is not a burning hell as used to frighten you into submission, but in a space of separation to consider and to contemplate. Beyond knowing that this experience exists, it is unnecessary to know more for it is between those and their own inner Spirit.

Will those that brought this to bear and those that choose not to share the opportunity be judged? Judgement has been a word used to conjure up failure and guilt. Release that concept. It is another of the tools used to control you, for instead at the closure of this experience there is a releasing process. A review and a time for the Soul (source of each human focused into experience) to assimilate these experiences into the matrix of its totality. The experiencing focus cannot measure the impact of its life experience upon the matrix of the totality of that which focused it. It is that which focuses contemplating itself. It would be self-condemnation for judgment to take place. Self-condemnation does not exist in higher dimensions. There is a world of difference between self-condemnation and Self-contemplation. Condemnation and judgement are synonyms.

This message is given in Love. It is for enlightenment within the experience of communion with the flow of Creation. It is intended to bring you to the awareness of being within its flow. That is exactly where you are.

No. 14

A new day begins in the lives of those residing upon this planet! Does this sound beyond imagination? No indeed! The desire for what is entirely different creates a new vibratory opening. This indicates there have been others who have contemplated this possibility. The pieces of the puzzle have not been in their proper places before. In order for the chances of success to be at their greatest potential, certain sequential events and circumstances must be in pivotal positions. The mass consciousness of the planet has to reach a particular level of both the knowledge of the truth and a level of frustration within the feelings of resistance to recognizing the changes coming upon them. There is present within those with the advantage of media communication the awareness of the repressive process, but as yet they are in the denial stage. Even that is giving way to the suffocating feeling of the Inner Presence that is being psychically repressed.

You think of this as being a mind control game they are playing, but I tell you it is deeper than that. It is designed to imprison the Inner-Self, which then causes the brain to slow, and the mental sleep process appears as a symptom. If it were only a process of stupor at the mind level, then you could have all been drugged into sleep long ago. That is not the object of the process. What would that prove to the Creator? What is at stake is the proof of superiority through the capture and diversion of the Soul energy and the enslavement of those of particular energy matrix. At a certain point of the negative plan, those who have served them so faithfully will be among the first to be abandoned for they have already proved their corruptibil-ity. Their ideal slave has a different matrix entirely.

If the plan is to continue the game into larger foci of power, then of what use are sleeping slaves? How then do the planners of this escapade locate the ones of value to them? Would it be the ones that do not fall under the spell of their concerted efforts? Just whom do you think that identifies? Indeed, the stakes are high for each of you personally. Does this description fit? Why else have you been allowed to continue in the business of pointing fingers at who they are and what they are doing? These comments are not to instill fear into you, but to give you the greatest possible understanding of the situation that is now in front of you, indeed upon your plates. You have no place to go accept through this experience.

This is a short message, but it is one to be added to the previous knowledge. Let us considerate it the leavening of the bread to lift your intent to an even greater focus. Know that all this is given with the greatest of Love, for you are more valuable to the Light than to them. You are our key to the lock that now holds the totality of this planet in prison.

No. 15

There is within the organization of those with negative inten-tions for this planet and their contacts with the extra-terrestrials masterminding the entirety of this planned raping of Earth, a good deal of miscommunication. Each has their separate agenda. Each has plans of reaching their clandestine goals at the expense of the other. Herein lies a vulnerable point in their coordinated effort. It is like two pieces in a puzzle that almost, but not quite fit together Inasmuch as we look at situations in terms of holographic energy composites or matrix pictures, we are able to determine points of vulnerability. So, the point of this is that there is not a united effort within their reality of experience.

The second weakness in their methodology is that of feeding upon the negative energy that is created by the competition that is encouraged within their organization. When a weak link or defection is found or manufactured within the members of their groups, there is almost a feeding frenzy upon that departing energy. It is far more satisfying to them than the same event happening to one of the uninvolved human beings. There is more of their own energy to feed the void of separation that must be maintained in order to continue on their path. They do "eat up" the competition of sporting events. It is this point of clandestine divergence of purpose that is the major object of our attention. This opportunity is just that, our opportunity. Many scenarios to use this to our advantage have been considered. As yet no exact technique has been established, but several possibilities would accomplish the exact effect necessary. What we are saying here is that though your spearheading action is the key in the lock, there are forces at play here that are stacked up behind a dam that holds back energies that dwarf your ability to imagine them. Do not under estimate the importance of your role however, for it is the trigger that releases this energy build up. The forces of Creation are hardly impotent, however they must work within the Laws that create and maintain all of Creation, the magnitude of which only the Energies that allow the potential for creation can encompass. It is as if there is a holding of the breath until your freewill participation begins the shift in the flow of energies.

We on the one hand must encourage and guide you in your desire to fulfill your purpose and assist you to be ready to act so that you can participate in the flow of events that will manifest as this flood of energies is released into movement. Thus we are something like your sports coach, always with our game plan, but having to adjust and figure ways of compensating for the fluctuations in your synchronistic interactions, the movements and intentions of the adversary forces and the freewill aspects of manifested experience. Unfortunately we don't have any recognition for sainted patience in this level of experience. Neither do we have hair to pull out when you surprise us with your personal decisions. The degree of commitment to the changing of the destiny of the planet from how it is now moving, is our only organizational drawing power. The personal motive of the participating individuals is the primary element for inclusion in the beginning consideration of choice of contact. Then other elements of character must be considered. "Blabber mouths" must of course be excluded, but they are not likely to be "available." The last statement may seem a bit crude coming from our dimension of allowance, however it is necessary to make that point clear.

There are many levels of information yet to be considered. Until the primary contacts and discussions are begun, it would be impossible to go further with a cohesive formation of directions for you. There are no planned shots in the dark so to speak. Even your contributions to the totality of this change in your reality must fit within the confines of the Laws of this Universe and of Creation. The Law of Attraction is at the foundation of all other Laws. You shall see this in the coming together of the essential beginning groups and in the final assembly that shall be the cornerstone of this new evolution of experience. Within this pregnant combination of consciousness shall this conception and movement into the birthing process be possible. It is often quoted that there are no accidents, however the freewill ingredient within the evolutionary process certainly contains the seeds of both endless diversity and the leavening of the mix.

We come to the end of this portion of our continuing dialog as this process proceeds in an accelerating mode. Your days are blessed with synchronicity and healing. Love and Light are showered upon you in great amounts in appreciation of your commitment.

No. 16

The time, in your way of reckoning, is coming into a critical numbers of days. We prefer to see it as sequential events. But, since the knowledge of what these events might be is not available to you, time will have to be your way of being aware. We shall try to coordinate time/event correlation with regard to those events that are important for you to be aware of. At the moment, the contact between the parenting groups is the focus of the moment. As things progress, we shall give you such information as is appropriate. The methods of contact between the members must be in such a way that no clear pattern is apparent and the language used must be very vague. As we have mentioned before, certain words must not be used and certainly none consistently. Many of these people have their own pet names for those we often discuss. It would be well to avoid using these, but merely to allude to them or better yet not refer to them at all. This will help to prevent triggering the watch dog systems that monitor you on a regular basis. All systems of contact are monitored. You would do well to get accustomed to that understanding. The more recent that a method has come into use, the more easily it is monitored. Unfortunately wire and tomato soup cans just can't fill the bill, so it is with thought and caution that you must use your communication devices. The dilemma of face to face meetings is that if you meet in a public place you will be noticed and if you begin to meet in a clandestine way, you will be noticed. This begins to sound like one of your spy movies, but things are as they are. At this point of course, there is no problem, but as there begins to be meetings among those of you who are apt members of this project, two and two will begin to make sense to them. The "ball" must be passed onward and outward with little return contact regarding the project in a repetitious fashion. No one person or group of persons is to shepherd the project.

All future meetings for business or personal reasons must purposefully exclude any reference whatever to this project. Phone calls, etc., must not be for the purpose of comparing notes. At a certain time the appropriate group shall come together for one meeting in which the ideas for this future experience of mankind shall be blended together. A simple statement of purpose will arrive at identifying the new genre of experience as the focus of this project. This is the time that the choices of to whom the baton is passed must be carefully contemplated by each person and small group. Then each is to make their contact and the purpose explained in a face to face situation where it will be most difficult to be intercepted. Choosing within spur of the moment decisions of appropriate places is best. Your private offices are probably the worst. As I have pointed out before, you are considered entities with special talents and so are of special interest to them. Do not underestimate your stature in their eyes. We know of no other way to remind you of these parameters without setting the stage like a cloak and dagger movie, yet as this is but indeed as a play upon one small stage of Creation, perhaps that is not at all inappropriate. So—play your parts well. Just remember that your timing might not be as perfect as is Bruce Willis' in the movies.

This will come as perhaps a little late since the first of the meetings will have already happened, but that which is focused into this message has already been made known to each of the contacts through other levels of knowing within unconscious awareness. It shall be known to set this parameter. Other levels of your awareness are being instructed in this process as well as in this way.

We are pushing you, but once the process has begun, it shall move more quickly than you imagine for the pressure builds. The understanding of the hell that is planned for each and every human spirit shall cause the focus of a new paradigm to appeal to each contact at a spiritual level to a profound degree. A desire to participate and to help with the solution to the planetary dilemma will be like letting go of a long held breath within the spirit of each. An overwhelming gratefulness shall bring forth the action necessary, for it said, "God loves a grateful heart." This is true and much can be accomplished through this emotion. It causes an uplifting of the spirit. Certainly those of you who have been in service through the spreading of the Truth to your fellow human beings can use an uplifting. As the acceptance of the future planned for this planet has come into your understanding, the failure of the people to grasp this and their refusal to believe its existence, has caused you to face many a discouraging hour. But, you have each continued on with your spreading of the Truth. Isn't this a glorious change of focus?

The understanding that at long last there is a way, a plan to take shape and the forces of Creation are indeed here to give help. This shall be a pivotal point within each consciousness that will bring a change of attitude and will begin to draw in multitudes of awakening people. It is not that the message of the Truth of what is present and surrounding them will be different at this stage, but there will be a certain underlying attitude that will be the first trip of a trigger to each listening awareness. It will begin to be discussed and the message passes from one to another in a gathering momentum. No longer will it be limited to only those who listen to the talk shows and lectures. Those who have read and informed themselves shall be asked to inform and explain. Faithful tellers of the awful tale, you are the avatars of this time! But in the new paradigm victim/ martyrdom has no place. It is not in the plan to allow that pattern to continue.

This information is for your consideration. May your experience be filled with synchronicities and loving encounters.

No. 17

When the group consciousness came together to create the earth experience as a flow of Creation, the freewill element within the framework was given particular emphasis with the desire to allow the creative element to be given free rein. The hope was that this special emphasis would allow a blossoming of what you might term a utopian experience within the Universal Laws. It was not contemplated that the opposite would be created within the context of this focus. The joy of abundance was seen as a result of the proper placement of those laws at the center of the experience. Instead, the result was that the abundance of materiality became the focus and the concept of "the end justifies the means" became the framework of the distorted use of the Universal Laws.

If the distorted version of the Laws that indeed govern existence in this Universe of projected Thought is all that are known, then how do you create your way through this experience into a new paradigm which is in harmony with the totality of all that does exist in balance? This is the crux of the dilemma. If the earthly focus were created within a group focus, it would seem that a return to that beginning point would be the place to move toward. Picture as a beginning point, a small group of dots coming together into a single larger dot, then this dot expanding outward into a bubble with a focus point in the middle. All of this is within an expanding movement. Next see that bubble as starting to change shapes and become an elongated shape which continues to distort into various configurations until it is seems to be coming to a bursting point as more and more pressure is focused toward that point. Now, in your imagination, how would you return that configuration to a perfect circle? Think back to the way the circle was created in the first place and repeat the process. Isn't that what we have been recommending? You need not be all knowing upper dimensional beings to do this, for as you come together with the intention of creating this return to balance, you need but invoke the creative process to receive guidance. Believe us when we say that it is through your *concerted* intention that this distortion will be brought into balance.

It is the mass consciousness that controls the shape of the bubble. It exists within a flowing movement of the thoughts of all. As the negative pressure is purposefully pushing the mass consciousness to conform to its distorted thought forms, which are contrary to what supports the existence of the bubble, the mass consciousness begins to react. Certain available connections to the Source of each individual component of mass consciousness begin to enliven, to resonate as if being irritated by this pressure. The awareness of this reaction is causing more pressure to be applied through the methods that have brought the situation to the place that it is now. Think in terms of the bursting point on the bubble. If this bubble were to react, as would one of your balloons, this point would begin to thin and become more vulnerable. What if instead this point which consists of thought which thinks, would instead thicken and react in ways contrary to the apparent laws of the material world? Remember that thought thinking within itself couldn't accept thought that does not fit within the context of creation. Thought contrary to Creation is directional only by focus in what you might think of as requiring great effort. It cannot be released to complete the creation on its own. Thus this process requires that every contingency must be considered and contained within the plan or added to the plan which would then in turn affect the whole of the plan. Do you think this is possible when compared to the realm of thought that can think within itself and know every contingency in less than the blink of an eye? This all thinking thought has one incredible restriction called the "freewill" of the participants. However, when the freewill of the participants comes into resonance through intent and purpose, then indeed all "Creation" breaks loose, so to speak.

Is it as simple as that? What about all the Laws of Creation that have been broken by all those within the mass consciousness? Isn't each of them required to repent and give up all their erroneous thinking? Come now, isn't that what experiencing is all about? You have forgotten something. Each of you is thought manifested into 3rd dimensional energy! If thought can think within itself, then do you think that it can do that within each individual? It can, but it has the one restriction of "freewill." However, the desire to move through this experience and return this planet as a whole to its rightful place within the Creation is a "freewill" decision. When an internal boiling point is reached within each consciousness by the pressure being applied, don't you think that there shall be a call within each for help from their Creator? There is a point when those who are under the spell of religions that require an intermediary to their God will bypass that belief and undertake a call within themselves that shall awaken the understanding of their true connection. When that reaches a critical level, then that shall join in the new point of focus being formed at the center of the real circle (bubble) of existence which within Creation has always existed. It is a matter of identifying with the real bubble and not the one that is this play on the stage of the mass consciousness.

If that is the case, then why the big deal? Because the play is reality for the mass consciousness and in their freewill it is real and the continued existence of these Soul extensions is in danger of extreme damage with reaction that cannot be explained in 3rd dimensional terms. It is a matter of the realization by enough of these extensions that another reality is within their ability to identify and claim. Perhaps your greeting should be "Welcome to the winning side. Let us identify and claim!"

No. 18

The day begins anew as your planet turns on its axis and mankind sleeps on under the influence of the forces of darkness. Their plans seem to move in an inexplicable focus of disaster and only those few faithful ones appear to be awake and recording the movement of doom upon this lovely world of green and blue. The magic of the beauty becomes blurred and the very home upon which you depend is shutting down around you and still, if noticed, it is ignored. The final days descend into the abyss while your TV, sports and potions of sleep drug you figuratively and literally.

What now can you few do to stem the tide of blackness as it deepens more and more quickly? Shall we recount again all that you already know and groan and beat upon our breasts, as did the prophets of old and cry out for "God" to save us? Millions are already doing that to a Creator they think ignores their cries to answer their prayers. It is in the perception of victims that desire rescuing that they ask and cannot receive answers to such prayers. Indeed, only those prayers that ask for empowerment within the framework of Creation can be answered. Do you think that the stars stay up in your heavens by casual request of a god being? Indeed not! They are there within the design of balance and mathematical laws that underpin All That Is. Man continues in his mindless begging and blocks the very help he desires by being unwilling to participate except in ways that are contrary to the very Laws that support his unhappy existence. The story of these Laws surrounds them in what remains of nature, but in his misery he blinds himself. The scientific learned ones analyze the components but not the process of Life within the manifested structures of Life that surround them. The mental analysis of the mind deludes him into arrogant belief of his superiority over his surroundings rather than his brotherhood and kinship within it. How can those be helped that are becoming more and more blind to the very process within which they exist?

The victim cannot be rescued, but must pull himself up by his own boot straps and rescue himself by being responsible for his own rescue. Man is made in the essence of his Source. He is a tiny holograph of this Source. A holograph is a tiny fragment of the whole that has the potentiality of projecting the whole from which it came. Though the concept of the holograph has been encompassed in part, it has not been "analyzed" with application to the essence of Life that is within all self-aware beings. It is the refocusing of this fragment toward its source of existence that determines the degree of the totality of the Source that is brought forth into the known reality of each fragment's experience.

If you consider the degree of the focus that has brought forth the planet Earth from the fragment of its Source, you can begin to get the picture. Look at the magnificence of the human body that is the vehicle of your experience here. A vehicle capable of housing a self-awareness that can contemplate its Source if it but will, because that Source contemplates itself and in so doing fragments Itself so that it can further contemplate Itself through manifestation of experience. Within it is the freewill to do this. Since freewill is the vehicle for this contemplation, then it is manifest within each holographic fragment. This freewill allows for all experience within a further enhancement of this Self-contemplation process. This is the polarity that enables the recognition of that which serves the contemplation process and that which does not, so that the balance of these allows the completion of each exploration into the return of the fragment originally projected to its Source. To follow this process as presented, there is a spiral of understanding as this is contemplated by the mind reading this information. Each fragment returns itself to the Source that projected it. Thus you are lead to understand the framework of the process you are within, for each of you are a holographic fragment of the Source of all that is in the process of self-contemplation. Ah, panic, you will become as nothing if you follow the path of the return. Indeed not! With each returning phase toward the Source of your entry into experience, your own self-awareness grows and it becomes greater and greater until you have the absolute potential to being a total equal within the greater Totality of that Source contemplating Itself.

Does that boggle your finite minds? Indeed it should not. It should be the most comforting news that you have ever encompassed. Could there ever be a brighter picture of your future ever painted? What possible pleasures could ever compete with a future like that? Let me assure you that there are no fleeting pleasures of the body incarnate that can compare with those that await you as the fragmentary self-awareness begins to ascend the spiral of experience toward the ultimate goal. The problem is bridging the gulf of misunderstanding that has been set as a trap by ones that have become caught up in the distorted misuse of the aspect of freewill. These pitiful ones have become so caught up as to perceive themselves as powerful enough to reach not only total equality with the Totality of the Source of All, but that they can reach a place of Superiority. Even the distorted psychiatric paradigm of your time would consider this insanity if they could but encompass the scheme in its totality.

Within this distorted power grab, it is necessary to have a distorted replica of the process. A counter part to that which exists. Humanity is but one building block of this, for they cannot create from a negative potentiality. Try as they have, it will not work, so they are left with the process of converting what already exists from what you would term positive into its opposite, a negative counterpart. Now, this is not a recent event in your linear counting process. How much have they accomplished? So as not to overwhelm you completely, let us say that it has reached a critical stage. To allow it to continue would jeopardize more of manifested experience by the Source than is comfortable. Enough to bring a focus of the awareness of this "awesome totality" of Source to bear upon the problem. The potentiality of this Focus for bringing balance back into the totality of the process as explained above is awesome to contemplate, even within the limits of 3rd dimensional perception.

We have attempted to explain before that there is help available, that it is powerful and have even understated it. However, the key to the release of this awesome force lies within that which has created the situation in the first place. *FREEWILL!* If you were not of exceptional value beyond being the vehicle of change, other means of ending this could be employed. The fragment from which each and every individual fragment of that Focus is a portion must be accounted for in order for the balance of all to be maintained. You cannot be simply written off. That would create a flaw that would cause unacceptable repercussions. All fragments must return to the Source from which they were focused (projected) in order for that Source to remain in the balance of wholeness. That is not to say that those that have perpetrated this distorted experience to the extreme will not have some interesting educational experiences, for certainly they shall. Your perception of time does not allow you to contemplate such a process, so do not attempt to do so.

It is important that you gather into your awareness the wholeness of this situation so that you can begin to contemplate the understanding that even those of darkest behavior patterns are valuable to the Source that you call God. They are a part of the totality of all that the word Source implies. Simply telling you that they are a part of "All That Is" has not brought with it comprehension that encompasses the necessary understanding and so another approach to it has been attempted here. A back to basics lesson in your vernacular. Let us hope that this has now been accomplished. If not, perhaps the re-reading of this will bring it about. It is not that we wish a softening of your attitude toward what is being perpetrated which would further their negative cause, but that you understand why simply destroying the whole experiment is not an option, or why just messing up their plans is not enough. The Source, the Big Boss, wants it resolved and who are we to argue? We have this *key issue* to resolve. So, let us get on with it.

No. 19

Around the world there is a greater and greater feeling of unrest. The intuitive aspects of each being begin to awaken for the energy atmosphere of the planet is resonating with the focus of attention placed upon this single planet by the entire galaxy. Your fellow awake and aware co-inhabitants are certainly noticing what is going on here. This is different from the suffocating direct manipulative energies that are being diffused upon your conscious awareness. The galactic attention is coming through energies too subtle to be picked up by mechanistic methods in use by those of focused dark intent. The opposition must attain its ends by employing methods of suppression of the natural expansive movement of thought within manifested form. What is flowing into your mass consciousness from the galaxy that surrounds you is of a natural expansive quality. It is received within the awareness and then follows its expansive nature and arrives exponentially outward into conscious awareness as dreams and sleep patterns that are not restful. The governing factor with regard to the receiving of this galactic message is the degree to which the inner awareness of each individual being has been suppressed. How slow is the vibratory rate of the being? Can it still receive the stimulation of the higher and more rapid vibration of this galactic thought form? This is not a message of condolence that is being sent by sympathetic individuals. That is a trick of the lower dark energies, another of their suppression techniques. Rather, this is a focus of stimulation so that the receptors of Light which hold each in focus may be returned to greater use.

So you begin to see that there are two foci of energy in motion one of suppression and one of stimulation. We prefer not to use terminology of war here, but it can be noted that the "battle" for this planet is already underway. Not as depicted with carnage everywhere being created by both sides, but in the claiming and the retaining of Soul energies. The one side is planning for many, the other for all. Remember, if one tiny unit of energy is truly destroyed, then the totality of all is lost. The Source of All That Is is expansive in nature. The energy can change form through what appears to be the rise and fall, the birth and death of form, but the energy that is at the very basis of this phenomenon is *always* present.

A polarity always exists within the format of this ever-present energy, however it does not have to be present in the format of what you perceive as evil, dark forces. That opposite polarity is another subject. What you must understand is that what appears to be the opposite polarity in the experience of planet Earth is an aberration, a distorted use of this polarity in energy. It is the exception, not the norm.

The more clearly that you understand what is available to you within the context of this situation, the more easily you will be able to maintain the focus on your purpose within energies that are in motion around and through you. It is easier to succumb to the energies of suppression in some moments of your time than to maintain your focus upon the stimulating energies that are acting within you. The "battle" is not upon the surface of the planet as you have been told, but it is within the individual awareness and it is by definition also within the planetary awareness. It is either understood or misunderstood, that within the planetary awareness, the minds of humanity in combination is the conscious awareness of the planet itself. Therefore the transformation of the planet, earned by her through her repeated motherhood of evolving civilizations, hinges upon the transformation of her current resident civilization. You can begin to understand that the unity of this evolvement process brings forth the potential for misuse. This inner coagulation of energetic purpose is organized for the process of transcendence. The polar opposite conceived one world suppression rather than planetary expansive transformation into higher dimensional (vibratory) experience.

With the presence of so much heavy energy thought exchange between the planetary inhabitants, mind to mind exchange of conceptual understanding, has reached very low ebb. This has resulted in a proliferation of mechanized communication, each representing the abilities once in common use by you without a manifested device to make it possible. With the rapid advance of these technologies (devices) through the focus on heavy slow vibratory manifestation, what appears to be marvelous advancement is indeed quite the opposite. It represents a loss of ability to focus the formative, expansive use of the power of thought inherent within all Creation. Slight of mind is at work again diverting your attention from the potentiality of creating outward from within through the use of the outer mind activity of analysis and manipulation of your manifested reality. The natural flow would be toward the exploration of the inner awareness and manifesting outward into your realities the greater experiences to be found there. Where do you think the greater people serving ideas come? Instead these are being twisted into people suppressing uses right before your eyes while you fail to observe what is at work. All the while you are watching the show being staged, diverting your attention.

So, now the fun begins in earnest. You are making your final attempts to reach the inner awareness of as many as possible through the last available use of their technologies, but you are also beginning to join forces with the inner energy stimulation. You too are receiving this stimulation. Indeed you are like the repeater stations that your radio stations use. You are serving multiple purposes and you are perfectly aware of doing this within the inner awareness portions of your totality of experience. Trust the process and hold the pole, so to speak. All is far from lost. Welcome to the winning side! Focus and manifest!

No. 20

The glory of your nations fade before your eyes as one by one they are attacked from inside and out. Each is dependent upon the monetary handouts that require handing over mineral rights and other resources as ransom. The money is siphoned off into secret accounts that return to the usurpers as the leaders are deposed or assassinated. The cycles are repeated over and over. The people are abandoned by their governments and so must fend for themselves within situations of less and less available necessities and more and more regulations. Not a pretty picture to behold. So—what now?

Let us again consider possibilities that could bring change to this nightmarish situation. Could it be that the forces behind this situation could be creating causes to culminate this planned suppression of the people of this planet that might involve repercussions that are beyond their ability to control? Could there be small unknown glitches in those plans, which if exploited, could cause outcomes not planned? It is indeed not only possible, but probable. Let us consider Y2K as just one possibility. If indeed all of the technological wonders of the basics of power, water, communications, money, travel, etc., all depend upon computers to operate, then so also must the military and conspiratorial communication systems and other wonderful mechanisms of planned use. All of these were constructed by contract. It is well known that contractors deviate from specifications whenever and where ever it is possible to cut costs. It is entirely possible that at least some "off the shelf" computer chips have been used rather than the special designs that were specified. If those substitutions contain the same date problem as those purposefully in use for creating a chaotic breakdown of your world as you know it now, how will this effect their plans? Since there must be a synergistic exchange of information within computer systems there may well be repercussions within their own separately created system that will cause chaos within chaos. Portions of their plan may deploy, but in order to establish and then maintain complete control, which is their goal, all must proceed according to plan. What if enough of their plan moves into place for the people to realize the truth, but their own internal chaos allows for what we might call melt down from within? What if champions of mankind working within may have deliberately placed glitches within their systems? Interesting to contemplate.

Let us suppose that the above scenario is true. Now we have what might be called double chaos and exposure enough of the enslavement plan to bring humanity awake. This adds a 3rd layer of chaos. Out of all this chaos, how does the balance tip toward survival of humanity and the planet? There is one more element that must be interjected here. What of those extra-terrestrial beings that have been using the power structure they have coached into place? Would the above mentioned chaos serve their purposes? Could they have sabotaged the plans of their own henchmen in order to eliminate them from the game? Do they have in place a plan that overlays the ones that are in place? We might say that the plot thickens.

However, we could thicken it even more, since we are delving into possibilities. When one planet interferes with another to the detriment of the progress of that planet, we have the Universal Law of Attraction at work. Simply stated what you do unto another shall be done unto you. If you interfere with another planet, then you have given permission for other planetary forces to interact with you. Ah-ha! Does the thick plot begin to come into clarity? Let us hope that your heart just skipped a beat, and real hope has been born within your imagination.

We are still left with the dilemma of all that chaos. So, let us give a bit more clarity. Once a planet has been interfered with in a direct way, other than an advisory capacity, the inhabitants of that planet may *request* help in restoring balance and order. Herein lies the key. Help must be requested and prayer is considered requesting. However, it must be what is called affirmative prayer. Affirmative prayer is entering into the creative mode that is your pattern (made in the likeness and similitude of your Creator). Humanity must actually come forth in a group focus, in a harmonious creative mode within the upward spiral of the development of individual and planetary evolvement. Now, knowing human nature, there will be those who, when they have recovered from the shock, will immediately want to put back into place what is within their comfort zone. They will desire to take advantage of the situation to create another situation of power over the people, for indeed the cry will be for new "leaders." That would not be evolvement. The next level is based upon individual responsibility. Unless that is at the basis of the new paradigm the opportunity for the transcendence of this planet and its inhabitants will be lost.

The importance of an already perceived outline to be the "prayer of requesting help" needs to be in place to supersede any chances of returning to the old. The help you need to bring this into being will then be assured. This help will not be military in any way whatsoever. It will be the Love of the Creator manifested and shall be genuinely welcomed as it shall interact with the Inner Being that is the forgotten direct connection to the Creator. Love connecting and interacting with Love shall bring changes beyond your imagining abilities. It is also appropriate to note that on a planetary level, the planet itself shall have a like experience.

May this information offset your concerns about your futures! Welcome to the winning side! Focus and manifest, indeed!

No. 21

It is time to focus so that emphasis can be centered on the pivotal change necessary for the transition of the project from one phase to the next. This does not indicate that the first phase is already complete. That part, getting the information about the activities of the dark ones, is now in motion. From our point of view in watching energy composites, enough movement in the waking up phase is taking place to ensure its continuation. There are enough focused on getting the word out for it to continue within that momentum. Information is being discussed between people now, by those reading and hearing the information. As you know either by face to face discussion or through your computer Internet chat rooms, etc., the critical ripple effect is beginning. In order to keep the momentum, now that the wake up call is ringing, it is necessary to prepare the next step lest inertia caused by lack of understanding what to do next allows for the onslaught of mind numbing techniques to continue to hold the upper hand.

The next step is the choice of the individual to stand forth in determination to detach from emotion of overwhelm and to observe from a space that is beyond the reach of the control techniques. It seems like a small step, but is critical for it is the beginning of the separation from the herd, so to speak. It is a step that can be accomplished without the danger that physical resistance would present. It is something that can be done in safety without being detected by the apparently fearsome entities that are striving for control. It is also critical in the process of each individual becoming aware that there is a connection to awareness, a part of self that allows for this observation. It triggers the shift within the over stimulated ego function and begins the calming of the ego. This will begin to bring it back into its true intended purpose. This in itself is an empowering experience, for it begins the balance of expression intended in the manifested experience. This is a very critical point. By establishing the observation experience, a change in focus begins to happen in a smooth and easy way.

How is it best to begin to fulfill your assignment? By purposefully practicing the process within yourself you will begin to guide those who are in contact with you that are waking to the knowledge of what is happening all around them. There is a fear element very active in their consideration of this information and how it appears it might affect their lives. It is not easy to contemplate all the marvelous conveniences disappearing from their experience as well as wondering how they will continue to make a living. It spells total poverty to them and so it is easier to keep shoving it to the back of their conscious awareness and not consider it. However, it continues to pop up in to their thoughts like a bobber on a fishing line. It is appropriate then to suggest to them that they stand back from the problem and begin to consider what possibilities there are to use the situation to their advantage. Opportunities will present themselves through barter, trades and other methods yet to be created within the chaotic change period. Since it will be difficult to accumulate material wealth, this will free the creative aspect that is inherent in all fragments of the Creator. Creativeness is the keynote of experience at all levels, otherwise none of us would ever have been "thought" into existence. The key to all of this is asking for help from the focus of thought that brought forth this experience and holds us in it. If it were not for that focus the basic energy blocks (atoms, molecules and cells) would simply fly apart.

It seems difficult to correlate the probability of success for an entire planet. With only a few beginning a shift by simply changing their personal perspective and then encouraging a similar change in those in their sphere of influence, but that is how it is to be done. Just as a long journey begins with the first step, so also is change begun in individual experience. This is especially true when it follows the methodology that is the format for the operation of the Laws that govern manifested Creation. There must first exist something so that energy may be attracted to it. "In the beginning there was the 'thought,' and the 'thought' became flesh (manifest)."

Following the conceptual thought, there must be the desire for it to manifest. To think the thought only does not bring it forth. There must be an emotional desire to provide the fuel for the movement or change of energy from thought into expression. Through coagulation of "attracted" energies, manifestation begins. Form includes more than things; it includes situations, circumstances and stimulation of desire for additional thoughts that support the completion of the desired experience. It is within the Creative impetus once the process is begun to move toward completion when the purpose is in harmony with the Universal Laws. The focus desired must provide freedom within the spiral journey of return to the Source for all that it will affect. When this is the underlying purpose then the Harmonic of Attraction is set in motion with all its subtle power released.

It is well to review the basics when a shift in creative focus is to begin in purposeful action of great magnitude. Each and every change in the destiny of this planet is received with great anticipation to the highest (finest vibratory) level of awareness. Those changes that will lead to the establishment of balance and harmony receive input of supporting energy that strengthens and hastens the process. It would be well to acknowledge this with gratitude as part of your meditations. The attitude of gratitude creates a return flow and allows for greater exchange of this supporting attentive awareness.

Beginning a change within a flow as established as the planned hijacking of this planet, is the most difficult aspect of the project of returning this planet to the safety of harmony and balance. It has required considering responses to the recognition of distorted energies into action, and further to ferret out its source and its purpose. Then that understanding had to be put into written and spoken word and in finding ways to disseminate the information. All of this is to be accomplished within a flow of negative intention that not only is in motion, but also can be compared to a fast moving river. Yet you few are able to accomplish this seemingly impossible feat through intent fueled by desire to save your fellow beings and your planet from being exploited. Now, if we can continue the process with that same level of intent and desire to move many *through* the information about "them" to the next step, all shall continue toward the desired end result. Much of step one was accomplished without surface consciousness of where the knowledge and understanding of the situation engulfing humanity would lead. It was the need to inform and awaken so that "something" could be done. Thoughts of resistance through the original guidelines for continuing the government of the people fueled the process. Unfortunately government of the people by the people leads to tyranny in quick succession through many small steps.

Moving beyond into a new paradigm is the next step in the evolvement of the consciousness of humanity. Understanding the ideal of freedom through personal responsibility offers the true solution is a big jump in perceived reality and would seem more so to the beginning few in accepting this theory as being possible and begin to contemplate it. However, the impetus of the alternative of doing nothing during the collapse of the current experiment will supply pressure to consider new alternatives. Lack of personal responsibility within the ideal of elected governing entities will bring the realization of it as the key to success. The weakest link (muscle) must be strengthened by exercise. It must be given the opportunity of use in order to accomplish this strengthening. This must be the basis of the way out of the present situation to a new beginning.

Birthing this conception is next on the agenda. It will be like putting the second large rock into the flow of a fast river in order to divert it into another channel. But once the first rock is in place, then it is time to add the next one so that more water is diverted, however now there are more available to move that rock. There is a saying in your culture that in order to accomplish any difficult task; it is the willing horse that must be whipped. It is not easy for the compassionate driver, but he knows that it is what must be done. Indeed, we bless you willing ones in these critical hours of this salvage operation. As you also say, "hang in there." It is indeed worth the effort.

No. 22

The failure of the planned conflagration is to be expected, for there must be a foe in order for that to happen. If indeed there are no armaments to oppose them, what will the dark forces do? There have been such conflicts, but the end result was not something to be repeated. There were self-appointed ones who knew of no other way to oppose distorted energy forces, and this resulted in two wrongs, which did not equate to a right. It is imperative that it be understood that armed resistance is futile. Those of us charged with assisting in resolving this situation will not support it. Though it has been mentioned before, it seemed appropriate to make this point entirely clear.

There is an interesting method of resistance employed by workers within industry when they are working in a factory situation in which the owners/managers are oppressive. It is called "malicious compliance." It is extremely effective over a period of time. In this instance, the employees do only that which they are told to do. They execute their assigned functions, but *nothing* else. For example, if a machine is breaking down, they do nothing about it. If an item of production is out of place as it moves down the line and will become entangled in any way, they do nothing. It was not in their job description. They cooperate in exactly the way they are told. Nothing is done to create a situation; they just allow the process to follow its natural course. Total compliance, no resistance and the situation deteriorates into chaos by its own volition. An interesting course to contemplate.

Is this turning the other cheek? Not really! It is understanding the process of manifested creation outside of nature. That which comes into being through the focus of thought is maintained through continued focus. It continues as long as it serves its purpose and the focus of *positive* attention holds it in manifestation. When support for this is withdrawn, it returns to chaos. Management, as in the above example, rarely knows the exact functions and their focus is upon manipulating the workers, the customers and the balance sheet. There are too few holding the focus with positive intent for the manifestation to hold its form.

How then is nature different? Nature is Creation expressing in harmony with itself. Man did not create nature. Scientists are busy altering nature in your time. Ever bother to find out how long the hybrid distortions can be held in form? They cannot replicate themselves in perfection. The genes must be recombined, and often that does not happen according to past successes. It does happen when the intent is in harmony with Nature as in producing flowers of greater beauty and different colors. But the intent is to glorify, not exploit the process of nature. Most often, those who love the plant work *within the plant processes* to accomplish the successful changes.

The point of this discussion is to bring to your attention the importance of the intent of the group that desires to cooperate with Creation as they focus on the framework of the new paradigm. It is suggested that they consider nature as their ideal, this might give them a starting point. How indeed does nature fit into the whole of creation? How could humanity live in harmony with nature, rather than attempt to have dominion (power) over it? That does not mean that nature could not assist mankind in existing on this planet, but it should be a reciprocal relationship. The future would involve cooperating with nature within the Laws of the Universe.

But what are those laws? Where does humanity find those laws that have been hidden from them? In the small amount of time remaining, is there time to study nature and attempt to put together an accurate understanding that could be disseminated quickly enough? You must remember that what you need is available if you but ask. Already the Law of Attraction has been mentioned. But how many laws are there? Less than you might think. The number of applicable laws increases at each dimensional level, for the learning of these laws and their application allows for evolvement to the next level where there are more to learn and to apply within experience. Let us begin a review of these laws. It is a review because you have forgotten them in your sojourn to the 3rd dimensional experience.

The underlying Law of Creation is the Law of Attraction. Simply stated, like attracts like. It does this through the basic tool of Creation—*thought.* I believe your bible states "As a man thinketh, so is he." If you focus on the morass of evil once you are aware of it, you strengthen it. It is important to be aware of it, so that you may withdraw your support of it by using the second Law of Creation.

The Law of Deliberate Intent. Purposefully withdrawing your fear and fascination for the evil situation once you are aware of it, with the deliberate intent of doing so, is using this Law. You cannot do this by attempting to stop thinking about it. It is only possible to do this by substituting another thought on a completely different subject. In the case of the evil plan, it requires the total inclusion of those involved. It does not matter what the thoughts are as long as they support the plan. Complicity involves believing the intent of those involved is for the good of all. Perhaps now you can see the power of sympathy for the afflicted ones around your globe. This supports the victim consciousness that is required, for it is complicity in disguise. Do you not consider them victims of war or natural disaster or poverty? You must take a deep breath, accept your part in bringing support to their feelings of victimhood. They too have responsibility in the creation of those situations. Your sympathy will not solve their misery. Your deliberate choice to create a new paradigm of experience will do that. Withdrawing your focus of attention and bringing it toward creating a new experience will bring the change about far more quickly than repeatedly sending aid while considering them poor innocent victims. Does this sound hard hearted? From our point of view, it is hard hearted to be part of the creation of these horrendous situations in the first place. You must deliberately choose to implement your desire to create a whole new experience for them as well as yourselves. When you choose to place your intent beyond the play perceived by the 5 senses, and place it instead into the creation of a new experience, you are withdrawing your consent and support of the experience in which you no longer wish to participate. You are using the second Law of the Universe.

These are the two Laws that apply to this situation. There are yet two more and those shall be brought to bear within this information, as it is appropriate. It is important that we progress within the Laws, as they are applicable. It is important that you come to realize that the Laws of the Universe are immutable. They cannot be changed or distorted. They work without question as to whom is applying them. When you consider the plan of evil intent that surrounds you, you can see them at work. Like attracts like and intent of purpose brings situations into being. However, we have attempted to bring to your understanding that there are nuances within these Laws that allow for Creation to continue. There needs to be an understanding and awareness of the leavening ingredient of Freewill followed by its proper use. Through this we have infinite variety within Creation and expansive movement results.

It is our hope that you will contemplate the implications of this information and that it will enlighten your understanding as well as strengthen your resolve to serve with our winning team.

No. 23

When we last had occasion to deal directly with those behind this plot, it was within a conference type situation. At that time, they were informed that there was full awareness of what their plan was set to accomplish. They were told that it was a futile attempt, but it was their choice to continue on in their chosen path. Inasmuch as free-will is the loose cannon of the Universal plan for evolvement, there was nothing we could do. Now it has reached the point at which their plan is indeed a threat, not that it could ever fulfill their desired goal of a negative universe/galaxy. It can however create unimaginable chaos. Do not take this information lightly. It is indeed a serious situation. This is not the fault of the inhabitants of Earth, it is just that this was the planet with the consciousness and physical manifested body type to fit the most ideal criteria for their plan. This is not the first time they have tried to overwhelm your planet to use it and humans for this purpose. It was a long time ago in your sequential counting. They were far advanced then in their technological gadgetry, but did not understand humanity, which allowed them to be repulsed. Unfortunately humanity chose to use force to do so and in that way buried within their psyche the belief that force was the way to solve any encroachment upon their perceived freedom. In a way, it married you to them through this perception.

This time, they believe that the earlier error in understanding their foe will not be repeated, for they have studied you well. Every weakness is known and is being exploited for their purposes. However, their focus was upon inducing your cooperation rather than resisting them until it is too late for you to do so. They carefully laid plans to overwhelm you both sensually and physically. In particular, they have emphasized safety over adventurous risk except within military paradigms. So you have insurance for all risky portions of your regimented life. You have your addictive paycheck system to depend upon, along with Social Security. (Notice it is always capitalized right along with your references to God. Even omnipresent Satan Claus is capitalized.) Your heroes are all well paid sports or movie stars. How adventurous are these? Your movie star heroes are drugged and adulterous in open display along with your presidential movie star. Remember if you can be held at the lowest level of your dimension, you cannot take advantage of the dimensional leap at the shift of the cycles, but can instead be taken to an even lower level of vibration. At that point it is their intention to separate the soul energy from the body. They have no intention of putting it back into another body. It is the energy that they plan to use as power in the transformation of the chaos they intend to cause from positive to negative. They believe that the lower the vibration, the nearer it is to the still point, thus making it more malleable. All of these theories have been concluded by attempting to study Creation through the process of following its steps backward from manifestation to creative impetus.

Fortunately, there are many miscalculations in their plan. But not enough to avoid creating great chaos indeed if their plans progress much farther. Here again we are faced with the great stumbling block of freewill, the key ingredient in both bringing this situation into existence and causing it to self-destruct. This magical key is held by the consciousness of the beings on this planet. The consideration of the situation from the above point of view allows for it to seem to be a very bleak future indeed.

Enter the view from the other side, that of Creation. This view is adventurous, opportunistic and positive. It moves not upon long and exacting plans, but within a fluid and expansive mode. It moves within a creative stance that allows for enhancement of individual and collective experience rather than suppression and destruction. Remember the picture of the pond! The other side must control the ripples from the outside in, while WE may cause them great problems of containment by using just one small pebble, one idea continuing thought focused on creation. We have here two opposite modes of movement within the totality of Creation. Now, looking at the big picture, on which side would you place your bet?

It is not that our side does not have some problems to resolve, it is just that we have the innate natural expansive consciousness that harmonizes with the intended Life experience. Even though the conscious awareness appears to be mesmerized into sleep, how does one bring a hypnotized person back to consciousness? Is it not a snap of the fingers? But must that trigger be previously programmed? Not necessarily! Their planned trigger is the sudden mass realization of overwhelming control, an emotion they plan to feed upon with great enthusiasm. So, we have been busy triggering this realization in a slow and steady manner so as not to alert them to the damage that is being done to their planned trigger. Remember the 100th monkey theory? It is a slow and increasing dawning of understanding within the mass consciousness until a critical number reaches an awareness of a new concept and all know. Guess what! We are disarming their trigger. Are you aware of the awakening happening now? You were hoping for sudden realization while we were implementing the opposite. We are planning surprises of our own. It is indeed rewarding or fun as you put it, to be on the winning side and know it.

Now, is the time to begin preparing the step in the process of a new focus for the awakening awareness of your planetary inhabitants. A new paradigm of experience! How fast must it move into the fray? Don't sweat that for a minute. Just do your part and all will come into play right on time. Once the first crack in their plan is complete, things will pick up in momentum. Just remember that we are hardly impotent. It is just that we must play the game according to the rules that insure success. Not so for our opponents! Keep in mind that the Creator must retain all of his fragments; even those that are our perceived opponents. He cannot stop caring for any part of the whole of His being.

*Note that we use the masculine within this information when referring to the Creator. It is just that creating is an attribute of the masculine focus, while the womb or ability to contain the creation of the masculine function is considered the feminine attribute. Through this we have the depiction of the masculine Creator and the mother Earth. Indeed it is balanced in wholeness of experience. We would prefer that the women of Earth would come into this understanding and find their balance within it soon.

May these glimmers of understanding be blessings indeed, as you continue to fulfill your commitments within this wondrous event. Keep on keeping on!

No. 24

It is within the scope of the information to bring through the basic framework of the underlying movement of how we may assist you to spearhead the ripples of change that will spread outward through the mass consciousness. Remember that when the pebble is first cast, the first outward ripples would seem quite inconsequential, but in the moments that follow, they move outward in ever widening circles. This process works when the waters of the pond are still. The mass consciousness is indeed mesmerized into stillness through the methodology employed by the planners of this situation. That does not include ones involved in skirmishes of war, but when the totality of the billions of beings upon the planet is considered you must remember there are many who are not reached by the media communications and are unaware of any of this drama. Therefore the surface of the mass conscious awareness remains quite still. This is the reason that it is imperative that we accomplish our goals to interject our changes within the individual awareness of key individuals now. It is the slow and undetectable change of thought patterns within each individual that comes into contact with this knowledge, that is the underlying foundations of our building process. The talk radio programs as well as the supporting data available on the internet is making an impact with additional printed and visual material for those who are yet to understand and process the wake up information more completely.

This format is reaching countless individuals who have this within their conscious and sub-conscious levels of mind. Their degree of denial on the conscious level does not matter at this moment in the sequence of events. The information is there to be remembered when some item of news or event in their experience will trigger the remembering of it. The Internet reaches around the planet and the mushrooming of interest in available information is a measurement of the thirst for this knowledge and is a small indication of what is going on. Please note that had one of the talk show hosts indeed stopped his involvement, there was backup present and already in operation. Volunteers are given opportunity, but backups are standing by not only waiting, but already in position. Ours is not a slap-dash poorly planned operation. Just as the opposition has focused energy to lay their plans and to implement them; this was not unknown to us. In the observation of these, there were plans in readiness so that any possibility to end their endeavor at earlier stages was possible. Indeed, a chess game of great magnitude has been in progress for a very long time in your counting. Now we are down to the final moves.

The understanding of this basic framework of the plan involves seeing your part in the initiation of this phase as being within the first pebble. To bring change to a mass consciousness involving billions of individual points of awareness by a small group of focused group awareness is indeed a tiny pebble. It is the focused aspect that makes the difference, especially when that focus is in harmony with the underlying purpose of the Creator. As that focus encompasses a larger and larger group, the pebble becomes larger and larger. Just because it has reached the surface of the pond of mass consciousness of those inhabitants of the planet, it has not yet reached the level of the surface of the pond of awareness of the planet Herself.

The level of awareness of Earth consciousness is a whole new ball game, which has never been explored by the humanity in this sojourn you refer to as the current wave of planetary civilization. It was known and understood at what might be called "priestly" levels long ago, but the information was not disseminated. Just as there are what you call beings of awareness that have transcended 3rd dimensional experience and who are devoted to the task of assisting you in this process, so also are there foci of awareness that serve in that purpose at the planetary level. Those are fully aware of this situation and have not yet brought their influence to bear. What you perceive as influences involving Earth herself, are as yet just normal reactions to distorted patterns brought forth by the extreme misuse of your home base. If the action within the mass consciousness does not bring about the desired changes, then a pebble of different origin will ripple that conscious pond and indeed there shall be movement on that level which will not be kind to the inhabitants. Unfortunately that level of awareness is oblivious to individual humans and so all shall experience and survive, or not, those events by their own intuition as to placement and movements within the events as they occur. It is still possible to bring about the reversal of planned misuse of the inhabitants and the planet without that level of involvement.

As you can see by following the messages, there are multiple levels of involvement in this situation, and we have but barely scratched the surface. It is not planned to overwhelm you with information, but only to bring forth that which will serve your understanding that you are not abandoned, but are supported fully so that the opportunity to transcend through the cycles may be fully available. It is not necessary that all of humanity be given this information in order for them to participate at this moment in your timing. Most would not even consider it. It is for those that are open to it and find comfort in knowing that their efforts are acknowledged and supported. Most have moved on with their assignments without knowing why or how to accomplish them, but have taken advantage of opportunity and kept going because there was a knowingness that it was what they "had" to do. That is courage indeed, which does not go unrecognized in the final accounting of this endeavor.

Blessings to all that read and consider this information, for it is given in the focus of Love within that which is the Source of this opportunity through experience.

No. 25

Now that we are beginning to reach a level of understanding of the basic format that is the foundation for your cooperative focus within the larger view, it is possible to expand into more levels of information. These are not at the physical activity level, but in the more important area of using creative thought. Inasmuch as you are a focused fragment of the Creator's awareness, it is now time for you to begin to fulfill your purpose of expanding the use of the holographic concept that has been the vehicle of your trip into 3rd dimensional experience.

This is not a process intended to overwhelm or cause resistance within your awareness. These concepts are known to you at deeper levels, and will seem quite familiar provided you relax and follow the wording. These will begin to stir the inner remembrance process. It is within your understanding that a fragment of a whole can through the holographic process depict the whole. It is through the projection of light through the fragment that the illusion of the whole from which it came is reproduced so that the nature of the whole can be known. If this is the case, then you are a picture of the Whole from which you were projected. If this is true, then how can there be diversity in what is seen all around you? Shouldn't this be a world of exact replicas? If the Source of the replicated whole were limited to one focus of experience, then that would be true.

However, if the Whole of that Source is multi-dimensional and within its makeup holds the potentiality of multiple foci of purpose, then each projected fragment draws upon that unlimited field of possibilities. Thought provides the mobility that allows Creation to flow into manifestation. Thought has the potential of thinking within and upon itself. This is another way of describing Freewill. Thus these added levels of activity enable endless variety to be present.

Now if that is true, why then isn't every fragment *totally* different? You were created in the image and similitude of that which projected you into existence. Here the law of attraction of similar yet different is seen at work. If that was absent, then there could be no exchange of thought and Creation would be just an unending field of unrelated diversity. Enter what you call intelligence, which is nothing more than thought thinking within itself and observing itself observe itself, a spiraling activity. Focused thought thinks itself outward into manifestation. This is a slowing of the vibratory rate of the extended thought to the lowest level at which it can contain its purposeful intent. At that point the manifested thought can no longer perceive its Source. It is in a state of thinking awareness that can now perceive itself and its surrounding environment. In your vernacular, it can no longer clearly remember the nature of its Source, so it has forgotten. Since it is projected thought, it must maintain its connection in order to remain in manifestation. Through this connection, lies the potentiality of the fragment focusing its own thought processes purposefully back through this connective energy flow and then begin to "remember" what it is, which is again thought thinking within and upon itself.

Since the holographic projection is an extension process of outward movement of thought, the natural inclination is to continue the outward movement through the use, in this scenario, of its sensatory tools to think (observe). Indeed we could go on for volumes of books to cover the beginning story of this planet and its history of inhabitants, but that would take us afield from the purpose of this message. The point is to help you realize that thought thinking within and upon itself is commonly experienced by you because it is exactly what you are. Through choice you create diverse experiences. Through thinking and choosing, each experiences commonly shared situations differently. This is the natural flow of Creation within Itself.

This sounds idealistic when the current situation surrounding you is considered. When multiple human beings (extensions of thought from higher dimensional foci) experience interactions, combined thought patterns evolve. These thought patterns in movement are something like your breathing process. They expand to a certain point and then relax and contract by returning first to a restive state. Involved within this process you experience positive and negative polarities, or so you have named them. It is a slow spiraling process, just as your breathing process was intended to assist you in a slow spiraling process.

If these are the parameters of experience, then you can begin to perceive that the contraction-relaxation phase of your process in this moment of planetary experience is not in a normal state. It is very distorted indeed. Your intended freedom of thought choice process has been violated. It is layers of thought distortion experiencing contraction that has bypassed the restive point that normally allows for the return to the expansive mode. Hopefully you can now overlay this understanding upon the planetary experience. If so, you see that in order for the distorted plan to accomplish their moment of beginning, following use of planned chaos, which is to be their field of opportunity to cause a change of polarity, they must allow the restive point to be reached. There ideal is to attain this by overwhelming the greater part of the conscious awareness of this planet through a majority of its inhabitants. This is to be teamed with the ending, or shifting of a major Creative cycle in this Galaxy. There exists within their timing and their methodology their greatest weakness. For the contraction of awareness beyond the Universal norm, when placed in a momentary rest point, sets up the opportunity for a reactive expansion of major proportion. Carefully placed triggers within the same contracted awareness can ensure this expansion. Welcome to the winning side! Focus and manifest! Indeed!

No. 26

It is now appropriate through the shift of greater understanding within the key group of visionaries to begin the focus of the conception of the new paradigm of experience. As is the pattern, many will receive this cosmic stimulation, and the perfect few will respond when the opportunity to participate is presented. Keep in mind that this continuing process will move through phases of birthing within the awareness individually and collectively in a subtle calm transcending movement. Do not expect a massive jumping on the bandwagon type of reaction. It will move outward in a whisper of awareness. Again, think in terms of the patterns of nature. When you observe nature you see spirals in the slow process of growth as in the spiral of shell formation and within the functioning of breathing. Though, invisible to form, it is the process that begins at birth and carries each mammalian form through its sequential life. Consider the birthing process through the format of breathing, expansion and contraction causing movement toward the goal within a transcending spiral and carrying it to completion. You will see a traveling outward of conceptual information, and in breath of consideration, again a traveling outward and an in breath of shared discussion, moving toward the desired focus of new experience. The intent fueled by desire for new the experience will bring forth the process which is being built upon the foundation of foci provided by multiple levels of awareness with supporting intent for this situation to move into a new paradigm.

This is the appropriate moment to consider a self-defeating concept that needs to be corrected to insure success. Through long planted misinformation by the religions on your planet, you think of the focused assistance as coming to you from the outside. You look outward at the surrounding lights In your sky at night and presume it is coming from "out there." Indeed, it is possible to exchange energies at the level of manifestation, however the flow of Creation is from the inside out. It is an expansive process. Again we must remind you of the in and out flow of the breathing process. What your scientists observe as burn out and destruction through black holes, etc., is instead evidence of the breathing process incorporating the spiraling changes of shifts into higher vibratory dimensions.

As this happens, *appropriate* energy fields move through this process. If it was all energy, then what is observed would long ago have been "devoured" by one single black hole. (Here again you can begin to understand the magnitude of the plans of the negative focus in attempting to create through the process of pushing this Galaxy through a process opposite the creative flow into an opposing reality.) What is perceived by the scientists as the compaction of energy into a tiny ball of massive molecular weight, is of course, total nonsense. The energy is expanding within the conversion process by increasing its vibrational levels as it moves into a new paradigm of expression. Is this Galaxy, or a small portion of it going through the black hole process? There is no awareness of it. What if it was true? If it were to happen, it would hardly be a hellacious experience.

Let us return to the point. To say that our plan is in motion does not mean that conscious contacts with seemingly appropriate beings of shared purpose and dedication is near completion. It is this process of conception that is the focus of these lessons. That which is to be accomplished at more subtle levels depends upon this process proceeding within defined parameters. The outflow of this information to those of commitment is encouraged. It is most meaningful in the whole of it, but each can stand alone as is appropriate. Key words to trip the intercept triggers have been for the most part avoided and the references to beings and processes of "interest" are made as subtly as possible. It is time that the usage of those be virtually eliminated as our focus of intent is on information that educates and informs you of the true nature of yourselves and the energetic forms and functions of the Creation of which you are an integral part.

Let us make a point clear. This focus of information is not "God" speaking directly to you. That which you call by that name is a confused and misunderstood scramble of misinformation. What has happened is that what could be personified into the Creator of this Galaxy is not the focus of the whole of All That Is. To make this understandable, perhaps, let us return again to the breathing process as an example. The underlying All That Is is pure potentiality and even finer levels beyond that which are imperceptible because to perceive it is to limit it. At its conceptual level, breathing is expansion as you breath out, rest, in breath, rest and repetition. Potentiality is most available for "absorption" (big generalization) in the moments of rest. Throughout the entirety of the expression of Potentiality into experience are varying degrees of awareness that have begun their return trips by first realizing they are holographic tiny fragments of the focus of their Creator. This creative focus is in turn a tiny fragment of a finer more encompassing focus of the Potentiality that underlies a greater Creation that has at some point been birthed from that which lies beyond in an unknowable state. Will we return to that a state of unknowingness? Is that our goal at the farthermost reaches of eternity? Doubt it, for it appears that in order to move through the return trip, just exactly the opposite is necessary in order to progress. You must remember one of your greatest distortions in understanding Creation at this level is your concept of needing to measure experience as linear, in what you call time. It is also a great barrier for those of us who are too interested in experience to bother to measure it. We can conceive of no reason to do so, for we know Divine Order has no sequential parameters.

As we return to our discussion of your concept of "God" you can now see why we have substituted the term "Creation" and "Creator" instead of using "God" in the hope that we could begin to change your perception. The word "God" itself conjures up feelings that cause inner turmoil in many, since at a deeper level they know that the religious teachings through a long sequence of experience has brought them only confusion. It has given them a distorted representation of the Source of their origin. It is important that those who intend to bring forth the new paradigm have at least basic clarity of the nature of their identity and of the Source of their existence. What lies beyond this Galaxy is, at this moment, outside the necessity to understand. To know that it IS, is all that is necessary. Our focus lies within the Creation of our Creator. He (androgynous but in the masculine creative mode) can be called "God," but frankly a new name is recommended. You may address communication to Him, but it is only received when it harmonizes with the creative outflow of His expression. "In His Name" as an expression in your bible was meant to tell you to place your focus of prayer within that purposeful intention. You are to make a request that intends creation, within the harmony of His attitude of "all that is necessary to bring what you desire" is available for your use. You are a fragment of Him and through you, He (the "I am" awareness of your connection) is experiencing expansion of the total awareness that is "You/He." As you do this, it is a shared experience. As a fragment of Him, you create by attraction all your experiences. But, using the Law of Intention in harmonious cooperation within His expansive mode is how you create purposeful or new paradigms of experience.

It is hoped this information is a blessing through the expansion of your understanding of who and what you are! Yours is a glorious heritage, celebrate it!

No. 27

When your perception of time is adjusted to include the possibility of giving up the necessity of measuring experience in blocks, rather than allowing it to simply flow through your experience as unimportant, you will have surpassed a great impediment to your progress. Earlier in the existence of your planet, there was not a tilt in the axis and so the seasons as you know them did not exist. This confined plant and animal existence to the more moderate temperature zones, but the growth was more prolific and extended further into the colder areas than you might think because of adaptation. The effect of the tilt caused you to have the seasons as one more block of experience to measure as time.

A continuum of days and nights within an unchanging overall weather pattern brings a more relaxed focus on the necessity to measure time within survival experience. Before the distortion of the energy of competition, cooperation was one key to existence. When the lifestyles of what you refer to as indigenous tribes in the equatorial latitudes of your planet are considered, there is much less emphasis on measuring blocks of time and more cooperation within the survival groups. There is less competition between groups than is depicted in your movies, excluding areas like Africa because of planned outside influences. These are considerations to be included within your new paradigm. The greater the unbalance of the planetary inhabitants, the greater the imbalance of the planet as a whole. Within the changing of the galactic cycles lies the opportunity for re-balancing both the inhabitants and the planet. This does not mean that the planet would necessarily move 23 degrees back to perfect balance, but indeed some change could be made.

It is interesting to note that there is a move among what you refer to as "liberal political views" toward the elimination of competition within the educational experiences of your children and it is being met with stiff resistance. Of course there are ulterior motives for this would further calm the children into less and less creative modes of experience. Athletic competitions bring forth desires to excel and the concept transfers over into desire to excel in other areas. This has been a larger stumbling block for their plans than was anticipated. As an interesting side note, the greatest improvements in lifestyle, art and music happens during lengthy periods of peace when there is no competition within warring conflicts. The history of China has long periods of freedom from being overrun by other cultural groups and little intermarriage with outside groups. Unfortunately the over population counter-balanced and these improvements were not widely available to all the citizens. Nonetheless, the focus was turned inward toward contemplation and desire for greater experience of uplifting and more joyful existence. Much was accomplished during those periods.

The new paradigm must include within it the desire to lift the human experience above the pivotal thought and behavior patterns that force distortions to be repeated generation after generation. The desire to do this is apparent in the myriad of self-help books, tapes and well-trodden paths to the psychologist and psychiatrist offices. The approach is from the outside inward by considering the action and attempting to find the buried experience that has caused the reactive habits. Here again envisioning a new paradigm and focusing on experiencing this instead of fixing the old would empower the desired new realm of existence. However, even if accomplished, the ability to maintain a different level of experiencing within the surrounding environment would be difficult indeed. As more than one crab in a basket will not allow any to escape from the basket, so it is with human experience. The new paradigm must be a cooperative group focus of desire within a clearly stated purpose that can be held in focus for a period long enough to bring it into manifestation.

You can now understand what the focus group must accomplish is to create a clearly stated purpose that is appealing to all of humanity. Attached is the apologia of an essay written in 1899, long before instant communication. It chronicles what happened when it was published in a small inconsequential magazine. It was called "A Message to Garcia." If this one inspirational message could travel the globe then, think what effect one encompassing message of purpose could do within our goal! Though the focus of getting the information out about the existence of the evil planners and of their deeds as far as you have been able to discover them is indeed the necessary first step, it has not rallied a reactive response. It is just as well for as we have said before, victim/martyrdom which it might have engendered are not part of the true paradigm of experience within the Creative flow. What is needed is a pivot point that can be accomplished before the closing of the cycles. It need not be accomplished in a simultaneous moment. It is best as an event within each individual's conscious awareness. That process does not make it less of a pivot point. It would lay the groundwork for the greater pivotal changes in conscious awareness that *will* happen within sequential experience.

Again we remind you that freewill allows those who choose to remain in the pattern of present existence. *Do not be concerned with those*. The ingredient of freewill in the soup of experience teaches us another of the Universal Laws, that of Allowance. Personal responsibility is just that—PERSONAL. It means that one is concerned with the choosing of his/her own experience and is not responsible for the experience of others. All are allowed to participate within a group focus of cooperative experience or not. However choosing not to participate does have its consequences. Those who choose deliberately to withhold their participation in ending the present paradigm will be allowed to continue it elsewhere in a somewhat different format. They are *allowed* to choose their mode of experience in this situation. Allowance is the most difficult of the laws to be learned at the 3rd dimensional level because of the deeply ingrained need to control. Control is transcended through the practice of the Law of Allowance. At this point in this discussion, we encounter the situation of child abuse. Children are within the influence of their parent's belief systems. What the parents believe and focus upon draw experiences to the family group. Information of past family history is encoded within the combination of genes which accounts for events happening to some members of a family and not to others. It emphasizes the fact that parenting involves more than *dealing* with planned or unplanned children. It is the personal responsibility of each parent and both parents together to raise the children within an understanding of the wide scope of influences such an undertaking involves.

It is important at this point to discuss the capitalization of various words in this text. It is intended that this material be as free of *religious* connotations as possible. Current and past experiences with priestly manipulation and control causes immediate shut down or distortion of understanding information that contains these references because of the misinformation about the control of what you call god. We can assure you that the creator could care less if you honor him by capitalizing all references to him. He is much more interested in whether or not you harmonize within the outflow of his creative focus. There is a problem because the very words you choose to indicate awareness of this flow of energy engender reactive feelings. This cannot be helped, so it is best to at least do away with all the capitals. It is one trigger that is best left inactive.

It is our intent that this continuing discussion brings a deepening understanding with regard to the purpose that looms in your immediate future. It is hoped that it strengthens and supports your commitment to continue on with your progress along the path of completion of this segment of experience. However, don't plan on long R & R leaves at its ending.

A Message to Garcia
by Elbert Hubbard
(Fra Elbertus)

The Roycrofters
East ᐟ Avrora ᐟ Erie ᐟ Covray ᐟ NY

Apologia

This literary trifle, A *Message to Garcia,* was written one evening after supper, in a single hour. It was on the Twenty-second of February, Eighteen Hundred Ninety-nine, Washington's Birthday, and we were just going to press with the March *Philistine.* The thing leaped hot from my heart, written after a trying day, when I had been endeavoring train some rather delinquent villagers to abjure the comatose state and get radioactive.

The immediate suggestion, though, came from a little argument over the teacups, when my boy Bert suggested that Rowan was the real hero of the Cuban War. Rowan had gone alone and done the thing—carried the message to Garcia.

It came to me like a flash! Yes, the boy is right, the hero is the man who does his work—who carries the message to Garcia.

I got up from the table, and wrote A *Message to Garcia.* I thought so little of it that we ran it in the Magazine without a heading. The edition went out, and soon orders began to come for extra copies of the March *Philistine,* a dozen, fifty, a hundred; and when the American News Company ordered a thousand, I asked one of my helpers which article it was that had stirred up the cosmic dust. "It's the stuff about Garcia," he said.

The next day a telegram came from George H. Daniels, of the New York Central Railroad, thus: "Give price on one hundred thousand Rowan articles in pamphlet form — Empire State Express advertisement on back — also how soon can ship."

I replied giving price, and stated we could supply the pamphlets in two years. Our facilities were small and a hundred thousand booklets looked like an awful undertaking.

The result was that I gave Mr. Daniels permission to reprint the article in his own way. He issued it in booklet form in editions of half a million. Two or three of these half-million lots were sent out by Mr. Daniels, and in addition the article was reprinted in over two hundred magazines and newspapers. It has been translated into all written languages.

At the time Mr. Daniels was distributing the *Message to Garcia,* Prince Hilakoff, Director of the Russian Railways, was in this country. He was the guest of the New York Central, and made a tour of the country under the personal direction of Mr. Daniels. The prince saw the little book and was interested in it, more because Mr. Daniels was putting it out in such big numbers, probably, than otherwise.

In any event, when he got home he had the matter translated into Russian, and a copy of the booklet given to every railroad employee in Russia.

Other countries then took it up, and from Russia it passed into Germany, France, Spain, Turkey, Hindustan, and China. During the war between Russia and Japan, every Russian soldier who went to the front was given a copy of the *Message to Garcia.*

The Japanese, finding the booklets in possession of the Russian prisoners, concluded that it must be a good thing, and accordingly translated it into Japanese. And on an order of the Mikado, a copy was given to every man in the employ of the Japanese Government, soldier or civilian. Over forty million copies of *A Message to Garcia* have been printed. This is said to a larger circulation than any other literary venture of the author, in all history — thanks to a series of lucky accidents!

E.H.
East Aurora,
December 1, 1913

A Message to Garcia

In all this Cuban business there is one man that stands out on the horizon of my memory like Mars as perihelion.

When war broke out between Spain and the United States, it was very necessary to communicate quickly with the leader of the Insurgents. Garcia was somewhere in the mountain fastnesses of Cuba—no one knew where. No mail or telegraph message could reach him. The President must secure his cooperation, and quickly. What to do!

Someone said to the President, "There is a fellow by the name of Rowan who will find Garcia for you, if anybody can."

Rowan was sent for and given a letter to be delivered to Garcia. How the "fellow by the name of Rowan" took the letter, sealed it up in an oilskin pouch, strapped it over his heart, in four days landed by night off the coast of Cuba from an open boat, disappeared into the jungle, and in three weeks came out on the other side of the Island, having traversed a hostile country on foot, and delivered his letter to Garcia — are things I have no special desire now to tell in detail. The point that I wish to make is this: McKinley gave Rowan a letter to be delivered to Garcia; Rowan took the letter and did not ask, "Where is he at?"

By the Eternal there is a man whose form should be cast in deathless bronze and the statue placed in every college of the land. It is not book-learning young men need, nor instruction about this and that, but a stiffening of the vertebrae which will cause them to be loyal to a trust, to act promptly, concentrate their energies: do the thing — "Carry a message to Garcia."

General Garcia is dead now, but there are other Garcias. No man who has endeavored to carry out an enterprise where many hands were needed, but has been well-nigh appalled at times by the imbecility of the average man—the inability or unwillingness to concentrate on a thing and do it.

Slipshod assistance, foolish inattention, dowdy indifference, and half-hearted work seem the rule; and no man succeeds, unless by hook or crook or threat he forces or bribes other men to assist him; or mayhap, God in His goodness performs a miracle, and sends him an Angel of Light for an assistant.

You, reader, put this matter to a test: You are sitting now in your office — six clerks are within call. Summon any one and make this request: "Please look in the encyclopedia and make a brief memorandum for me concerning the life of Corregio," Will the clerk quietly say, "Yes, sir," and go do the task?

On your life he will not. He will look at you out of a fishey eye and ask one or more of the following questions: Who was he? Which encyclopedia? Was I hired for that? Don't you mean Bismark? What's the matter with Charlie doing it? Is he dead? Is there any hurry? Sha'n't I bring you the book and let you look it up yourself? What do you want to know for? And I will lay you ten to one that after you have answered the questions, and explained how to find the information, and why you want it, the clerk will go off and get one of the other clerks to help him try to find Garcia — and then come back and tell you there is not such man. Of course, I may lose my bet, but according to the Law of Average, I will not. Now, if you are wise, you will not bother to explain to your "assistant" that Corregio is indexed under the C's, not in the K's, but you will smile very sweetly and say, "Never mind," and go look it up yourself. And this incapacity for independent action, this oral stupidity, this infirmity of the will, this unwillingness to cheerfully catch hold and lift — these are the things that put pure Socialism so far into the future. If men will not act for themselves, what will they do when the benefit of their effort is for all?

A first mate with knotted club seems necessary; and the dread of getting "the bounce" Saturday night holds many a worker to his place. Advertise for a stenographer, and nine out of ten who apply can neither spell nor punctuate — and do not think it necessary to.

Can such a one write a letter to Garcia? "You see that bookkeeper," said the foreman to me in a large factory. "Yes; what about him?"

"Well, he's a fine accountant, but if I'd send him uptown on an errand, he might accomplish the errand, and on the other hand, might stop at four saloons on the way, and when he got to Main Street would forget what he had been sent for." Can such a man be entrusted to carry a message to Garcia?

We have recently been hearing much maudlin sympathy expressed for the "down-trodden denizens of the sweatshop" and the "homeless wanderer searching for honest employment," and with it all often go many hard words for the men in power.

Nothing is said about the employer who grows old before his time in a vain attempt to get frowsy ne'er-do-well to do intelligent work; and his long, patient striving after "help" that does nothing but loaf when his back is turned. In every store and factory there is a constant weeding-out process going on. The employer is constantly sending away "help" that have shown their incapacity to further the interests of the business, and others are being taken on. No matter how good times are, this sorting continues: only, if times are hard and work is scarce, the sorting is done finer — but out and forever out the incompetent and unworthy go. It is the survival of the fittest. Self-interest prompts every employer to keep the best those who can carry a message to Garcia.

I know one man of really brilliant parts who has not the ability to manage a business of his own, and yet who is absolutely worthless to anyone else, because he caries with him constantly the insane suspicion that his employer is oppressing, or intending to oppress him. He can not give orders, and he will not receive them. Should a message be given him to take to Garcia, his answer would probably be, "Take it yourself!" Tonight this man walks the streets looking for work, the wind whistling through his threadbare coat. No one who knows him dare employ him, for he is a regular firebrand of discontent. He is impervious to reason, and the only thing that can impress him is the toe of a thick-soled Number Nine boot.

Of course I know that one so morally deformed is no less to be pitied than a physical cripple; but in our pitying let us drop a tear, too, for the men who are striving to carry on a great enterprise, whose working hours are not limited by whistle, and whose hair is fast turning white through the struggle to hold in line dowdy indifference, slipshod imbecility, and the heartless ingratitude which, but for their enterprise, would be both hungry and homeless.

Have I put the matter too strongly? Possibly I have; but when all the world has gone a-slumming I wish to speak a word of sympathy for the man who succeeds — the man who, against great odds, has directed the efforts of others, and having succeeded, finds there's nothing in it: nothing but bare board and clothes. I have carried a dinner-pail and worked for day's wages, and have also been an employer of labor, and I know there is something to be said on both sides. There is no excellence, per se, in poverty: rags are no recommendation; and all employers are not rapacious and highlanded, any more than all poor men are virtuous. My heart goes out to the man who does his work when the "boss" is away, as well as when he is at home. And the man who, when given a letter for Garcia, quietly takes the missive, without asking any idiotic questions, and with no lurking intention of chucking it into the nearest sewer, or of doing aught else but deliver it, never gets "laid off," not has to go on a strike for higher wages. Civilization is one long, anxious search for just such individuals. Anything such a man asks shall be granted. He is wanted in every city, town and village — in every office, shop, store and factory. The world cries out for such: he is needed and needed badly — the man who can "Carry a Message to Garcia."

No. 28

As your need to experience in calculated time passes into relative unimportance, the momentum of your experiences of the new paradigm will flow smoothly into a release of the materialistic mode that holds you tightly within the power of the deviant perpetrators. It is the pursuit of the creation of your personal fiefdoms and in the competition to create one of greater opulence and grander physical pleasures that have you trapped. These are empty promises to fill the void of imbalance that you feel within. Subliminal messages are planted within all the advertisement to feed your materialistic addictions. The tangled and layered morass of information and lies is reminiscent of the fable of the lion and the mouse. The lion of humanity lies staked to the earth, held fast by the net of distraction of the conscious mind. In the story it took a tiny mouse to chew through the ropes to release the lion. In our version of the story, it is the radio talk show, the available Internet information and the publication of books and tapes that constitute the mouse. The information shared is based on personal experience and researches of archives of information available to any that care to take advantage of it. The integrity of the net is threatening to give way. Once released, the lion is then aware of the power of the tiny mouse so anything could happen. Unfortunately, there are more nets in place unless we take charge of the story line and change the scenario.

The point of these messages is to encourage and to inform, not educate in the format as it is practiced. There are no subliminal subversive intentions hidden within them. Each of you has programmed within the deep levels of your awareness the memory of the purpose you came into this lifetime to accomplish. We are simply keeping our agreement to remind you and to give guidance and direction to your actions. When the focus is on reacting to what is perceived as eminent danger, then momentum is lost. It is our agreed function to share the view that we are privileged to have from a dimension encompassing a greater vision of the situation. We view energy patterns in movement in a holographic display, and can model the various possibilities available. This is an advantage. It is the purpose of this information to share what is allowed within the universal laws governing freewill with as much clarity as possible. We find allegorical stories are remembered and applied to overall understanding most effectively. We are limited to those available through the experiences of the translator of this information. It is a dictation/translation/transcription process with the translation portion being the most critical component. It is important that this person continue to input information to enhance the available "database." Guidance is provided to appropriate materials.

It is within the allowable guidelines to bring to your attention deviations within those patterns that can be corrected because it is your freewill decision whether or not to do so. The problem of getting the information to you is massive indeed. Face to face discussions are not possible for many reasons but mostly because victim/martyrdom is not in our experience pattern and that would be the end result. Therefore we have this process as a more effective way. Though there is no 2-way exchange possible at this time and it is not necessary.

It is also possible for us to bring much information into the awareness of those committed to the project. Through the acceptance of this commission and a commitment to participate and see it though, the energy matrix of each change and this is observed. This opens a line of communication and also results in a change of activity within the inner dimensional (sleep) states. These changes are reflected in the outer dimensional activities during the day. Many changes in these lives will be noted, from the mundane to major shifts in attitudes and choices of activities. As mental and physical activities change, the intent and commitment becomes more focused and a spiral effect begins to occur within the levels of consciousness. You *are* being supported in this process!

It is with trepidation that we bring to your attention that the open communication lines are now under greater control and it is their intention to identify those yet unknown individuals who disseminate information that counters their plans. As yet it is in the identification process and has not moved beyond into retribution. This is because there are purposes for allowing you the privilege to do what you are doing that are not known to all levels of oppression. The word identification process is being further expanded. We suggest strongly that you edit your verbal and written conversations. Book wording can be read electronically, but titles especially are being processed. If suspicious, then scanning the forward/epilogue portions is taking place to be reviewed. Expect bookstore chains to be contacted and told to remove titles from the shelves and raids to take place at wholesale/distributor levels as the next step. Hopefully they will be discriminate and take only certain individual items, however that has not been the pattern. This will limit your freedom to print and distribute freely, so creativity must be used in the wording of titles, forwards and endorsement information. It suggests the possibility of setting up alternate locations and different names with books, etc., likely to pass through the first two tests. This might be considered as possible joint efforts if the hurdle of profit sharing can be worked *through*. If reprints are being considered, or new books or tapes, these considerations may be important. Creativity in promotional copy will be challenging. Intuitive inspiration is available on request. Smile! You are on the winning side!

No. 29

It is with *resolve* that you must *focus* the energy of intent into bringing forth this phase of the project. There is indeed a nuance of difference in these. One can intend to do something but never actually do it. Resolve is the spark that holds the intent in the forefront of the field of activity within your awareness. "This phase" refers to what might be called the second layer of activity toward initiation of the project. The phase of "getting the word out" does not cease because a new phase has begun. One simply adds the beginning of the next phase in a layering sense. Phase one was something like the foundation of a pyramid. Now we are beginning the second layer of the construction before the first layer is complete. Visualize how graphics complete a picture on the computer. It begins and does not always complete the picture in totally horizontal motion one line at a time and the picture is at some point complete. Next, consider this in a holographic focus for the planet. In your mind's eye, you can see where the information has gone and "paint" in areas where your information has been sent. If you see the planet as dark and the information painted in as lighted areas you can begin to "get the picture." You could see the sprinkles of light spread outward.

Even people who have heard and consciously rejected the information reflect a degree of light and it remains waiting to fully reflect. It is because you cannot know how many of these there are that you have difficulty in grasping the magnitude of accomplishment that this phase has reached and it continues to expand. The 100th monkey point is very close indeed. Portions of phase two are already in motion and momentum will expand it much more quickly than phase one. Because of the awareness brought forth by phase one, there are many that are waiting and wondering what it is that they can do, now that they are aware. We shall provide that answer and it will seem to them an easy thing to do, for they are being asked to do something that can be done privately and without drawing any notice. *And* it is the most powerful thing that needs to be done. It is a focused pivotal change of attitude from victim to empowerment.

The great resistance to phase one information was because each thought it would involve armed revolution to accomplish *change*. We know that a change is not our goal. A new paradigm of experience begins with totally different techniques and methods and there is no counter measure in place once it is begun. It can be countered only with reactive measures that would be deviations within the negative plan. This would bring forth, chaos within that focus. The negative plan is counter to the flow of creative energy within which it exists. It requires continuity and narrowly defined focus that links together. This is absolutely essential.

It is with joy that we share these segments of information so that you may begin to understand more than just the nature of the negative plans, but also to understand the weak links available within their plan are opportunities. We can continue to guide you as to how to "gnaw away" at those links as long *as we are asked!* Please remember to do this. To receive and follow through is of critical importance, but do remember to <u>ask.</u> Your appreciation is warmly received and your follow through is applauded with zeal at many levels. However, the key is always to use your freewill to *choose*.

There is a children's song used to teach the letters of your alphabet. The alphabet is the foundation of the written words in your languages. What we desire you to learn to use is what is the foundation of manifested self-awareness. Just as you must learn to apply the alphabet to written language and combinations of sound to speak the language, you must use the principles that form the foundation for directing the flow of thought into the coagulated energy that creates what is experienced as life. It is the utilization of the potentiality underlying all that is known at every level. This is accomplished through a process mentioned before and is reflected at the very basis of your ability to remain in your earthly form, breathing. In simple format it is drawn in through expansion of the lung, rest, contraction of the lung, rest and repeat. The lung is the vehicle of containment and motion. It in turn is contained within the totality of a greater conscious awareness vehicle, the body.

This is a pattern matrix that is repeated in endless variety. The stumbling block is to learn to appreciate this variety each time it is encountered and to remember that it is but a unique manifestation of the basic pattern matrix. This difficulty is especially true if there is distortion in the particular expressions encountered through experience. The more confrontational the experience, the more distortion is occurring, not in just one, but in both individuals. Distortion unfortunately ripples outward and encompasses groups of inter-acting individuals. When the interactive distortion becomes large enough, then in order to correct the distortion, a large number of those involved must return to the relearning *and application of* the basic fundamentals of manifested experience. Simply stated they must relearn and apply the universal laws. Guess where your plan-etary inhabitants are?

Fortunately you have at your disposal communications with a high potentiality of reaching vast numbers, at least at the moment. Mounting pressures of multiple layers of oppression are creating tension within those that can be reached and there are yet many ways of reaching them. 100 years ago this would not have been pos-sible, even though there were fewer to reach. These communication possibilities have been named "mass media" for good reason. There is no reason why these cannot be utilized for a reason contrary to what was originally intended. Perhaps there was even help in bring-ing them into such wide spread use. Could be! Guidance in many areas is available on request. Where are your requisitions?

The length of these daily messages depends on how much information can be received and assimilated and in the concise-ness of the message format. Clarity and conciseness are the goals, with enough repetition to assure the information is planted in fertile ground. If not, then another approach is used. For the greater part of human consciousness, the substitution of a new focus within their awareness is all that is necessary. For others of you, much more is involved. You have committed to physical action and the concep-tion and dissemination of this new focus. After all, someone has to plant the seeds of thought that comprise the foundation of this new paradigm before they can begin to grow, mature and re-seed them-selves. If you are reading this information, then you are chosen. Now the ball is in your court and you will choose to be chosen or not. It is your freewill decision.

Our blessings are given as you process the information and pro-vide it to others for their consideration. In your vernacular hang in there, the roller coaster ride is just beginning. You have not even gotten to the exciting parts. Just know you are strapped in and the ride will end. However, I doubt you will wish it had lasted longer. Not this time.

No. 30

The focus of these messages has been toward the dissemination of information that concerns the expansion of your understanding with regard to plans and appropriate attitudes and actions within group areas. There has been little information with regard to your personal experiences and application in that area. This was not to indicate that this area is of little importance. New age information, better called new thought which could be categorized even more accurately as "remembered thought," emphasizes the need to be balanced and chants "be in the now." In actuality, that is correct! As previous pointed out, all of the cycles within the cosmos/galaxy move toward and away from the center point of stillness or perfect balance. In order for the galaxy to be in balance, the cycles are moving within a balance of those moving away and those returning to each balance point. You could picture it as gyroscopes spinning and moving around a central gyroscope that remains in perfect balance and puts forth an energy pattern that holds all the smaller gyroscopes within its sphere of influence. Each gyroscope outside the central focus contains within it a myriad of smaller gyroscopes. In order for this entire system to continue in existence there must be an equality of energetic motion. If one gyroscope gets far enough out of balance to approach a point beyond its ability to return, then counter balancing must take place within the whole system with the focus of holding it within the range of safety. This is, of course, an over simplified picture, but gives you some understanding. It allows you to picture Earth at its tilt of 23 degrees approaching a point of losing its ability to return to balance.

If you consider that within the gyroscopic picture of Earth, there are 7+ billion tiny gyroscopes each spinning on their own axis, the balance of these influences the balance of the larger one. If most of these are out of balance, then of course the larger one cannot remain in balance. Grasping this picture leads you to the understanding that the 4th universal law is that of balance. One pattern of thought that holds powerful influence in the balance or imbalance of personal expression is that of past, present and future. Since all are necessary for various reasons of survival and progress, they are embedded within the ego observer mode. You remember the burn and so do not touch the stove again. You desire to build a larger house for your family so you envision the steps your future must contain in order to attract that experience, and so you migrate between the two. However, there is the moment of now that you experience that is not either past or future. That is your balance point. It is your place of rest. You return there during each sleep cycle. There was a time as the planet revolved in the cycle of light and darkness, all were active or resting in unison which brought greater balance to the whole. With the advent of artificial lighting, this balancing pattern is no longer present. Mankind now has constant activity first with the "industrial age." Now in the "technology age" even within the homes the hours of rest within a family are varied. A balancing technique is practiced in what you call the Far East and is called meditation. The new age group quickly adopted it. Techniques are often distorted and the conscious awareness is overwhelmed with media clutter and unable to find the still point of balance within the combination of conscious and subconscious. Entering that still point allows for connection with the Soul and balance to be reached for at least a short time.

Balance is reached through the understanding and practice of the three basic laws of the universe: attraction, deliberate creation and allowance. If you review the previous messages, you will find within the information suggestions for resolving this problematic situation of the population of Earth. In order to live the new paradigm of experience those participating will be required to focus within present time. Only the framework will be known and it must be fleshed out through "living it into existence" experience by experience. This will require living within present moment reality. Within this focused group experience balance will be attained. The past cannot be applied and the future will be unknown. That will leave only the present.

Let us consider the galactic cycle completion. Is it only a momentary instant that is available to accomplish a grand ascension or a ghastly dimensional crash? That depends. Again we return to your fixation of experiencing measured blocks of sequential events. Experience within what you call the present moment is a misnomer, an inapplicable designation. When you are focused *into* what you are thinking or doing with no awareness of any other activity, you "lose track of time." Each of you has experienced that. Only by looking at your time tracking device called a clock do you have any idea of what the time might be, other than the presence or absence of sunlight. If each of you were totally intrigued with what you were doing, that was your only required focus and there were no seasons to concern you, would you care what day it was? If that intriguing subject opened the door to another and another, would you care what day or what time it was? I doubt it. If you were in balance, would sleep be necessary? What about food? What about recreational pursuits? Aren't all of these necessities really just a search for balance?

This is not suggesting that you become breatharians. These are simply ideas to intrigue your imaginations. Your experiences are so far out of intended balance that it is difficult for you to imagine what balance during wakeful experience is like in 3rd dimensional format. It is far more pleasant than you know. No wonder you desire to leave this dimension thinking that respite is only to be found elsewhere. Without balance of the 3rd dimensional experience you could not exist in higher dimensions in your body format and current self-awareness. *First* you must come into balance. Because you are all interconnected, individuals have insurmountable problems maintaining balance even if it is achieved. It is necessary to bring a large number into balance to accomplish what is necessary in the bigger picture.

The bible warns you not to place "pearls of wisdom" before those who have no viable connection to their source of life. It is time to strike that idea from the books. It is time to do another 180-degree turn and to do it in practical, applicable terminology. The pattern has always been to hide it within religious and esoteric terminology so that only a few were privy to the information, lest it be lost through individual interpretations that might destroy it. Without written words, for few were literate, allegorical stories were the only method of disseminating even the basic understandings. These contained references to activities and other commonly known and understood references that were within that local cultural environment. Even these basic understandings became distorted when the stories were retold in cultural situations that had no reference points to those original understandings.

We find ourselves of necessity reintroducing the basics. A good place to begin a new beginning, don't you agree? Attraction, intention and allowance leading to balance through application within experience. A doctorate in those positively leads to ascension to higher dimensions. Welcome to the ascending team!

No. 31

We are entering the period of time that leads to the beginning of the shift of energies that will begin the days of tribulation. Unfortunately some of the predictions that have been made reflecting the plans of the dark side will manifest. Though they seem to indicate that the situation is irreversible, it certainly is not. This will be a time in which it will be critical that those of you who are privy to the behind the scenes maneuvers which you are part hold faithfully to the understanding and belief that they do indeed exist and are positively laying the foundation for the new paradigm. This new pattern of experience can be pictured as a shimmering castle coming forth amid a scene of frantic confused activity. It is at first very dimly seen. Though this is hardly the pattern of what the new paradigm will resemble, it instead draws on the Camelot myth as a recognizable fantasy containing within it desirable dream like ideals. It is a process of it rising through the mists of focused imagination amid what appears to be reality. This is the understanding that we desire to trigger. If you are not a Camelot buff, then choose some other picture.

The Phoenix perhaps, but choose for it to be transformed and to rise before the ashes stage. We would emphasize the recognition that the desirable already is manifesting before the undesirable has disintegrated. The focus of even a few with belief and knowingness that it does indeed exist and is coming forth is of critical importance. By choosing different pictures but the same focus then the process is held in place until the purpose is defined and becomes the ideal.

Defining the purpose will not be an easy process. Many versions will be proposed before ideal wording can encompass it. This is meant to encourage ones to begin, for the first step must be taken so that progress can be made toward the goal of bringing it forth. It is the brevity and the universal appeal of it within the diversity of 7+ billion beings that is the key. Though it seems impossible, we assure you it is possible. We remind you to ask for guidance and help at these sessions. Egos must be in their observer states for the credit of writing will go to no one individual. It is the desire that it comes forth in perfection that must be the motivation. It shall stand alone in its purpose of encompassing the foci present on earth into a focus of expression into greater experience. Again we remind you of the breathing process. It will be taken in by the conscious awareness, contemplated and expressed outward through desire for its manifestation into each personal reality and held dearly while it happens. We wish it were other than a lifeline for drowning beings, but that is the experience you have created.

It is through the approach to the universality of scope that the encompassing appeal shall be addressed. The focus on this aspect will begin to draw the feeling of oneness to the beings on the planet. A realization will begin to dawn that all are facing the same dilemmas as the itchy feeling that something ominous is present continues to intensify this feeling keys understandings that the causes of it are beyond local, regional or national scope. The oppression is being felt with greater and greater intensity. What about the indigenous peoples? As we have mentioned before, they already know. Their "shamans" already have the message and are aware that a new paradigm is being born. They are steps ahead of you and are already at work on its expression. Their people are aware and already in harmony with the process. Do not be concerned with them.

Survival is their way of life. You may find yourself wishing you had incarnated into a more indigenous way of life in the days ahead. (I did say may!) Inasmuch as all have incarnated from the same source, you are indeed connected and do communicate at subtle levels. The mass consciousness (awareness is malleable through coercion, but always certain levels of it remain connected to the source. It is through these connections that we can achieve subtle changes that will lay the groundwork for future shifts at the conscious levels. The oppressors must work with the levels of the mind while it might be said that we have available the levels of the "heart." The heart feels. A feeling can transform the beliefs held by the mind. When the feeling vibrates within the being at a certain level, it overrides the belief and the being simply tosses it out and follows the feeling to a new conclusion. The feeling of oppression is soon to override the insistence of the mind that all is well and that big brother government will work things out to the benefit of all. The magician is about to lose his facade of darkness and be seen in the full light of recognition and it may not be at the time of his choosing.

Inasmuch as you live within time as your controlling focus, we must deal with it. The sequence of linking interfacing actions and events now enters a phase of critical importance. It is important that each of you feel the inspiration, the divine urge, to push ahead with this project. The dominos are in place and it will take but a nudge for them to begin their sequential trip. The placement of the final few must be preempted in order that the dark plan is unable to be carried to its planned conclusion. If a critical few can be removed, then the planned sequence will go awry and glorious confusion will result, the perfect time for the new paradigm to rise amid that confusion. Its conception must, however, have been completed and the birthing process well underway at the subtle levels.

It is difficult for the information contained in these messages to stress the importance of various facets without becoming repetitive. We also are aware that some are reading these that have not had access to the prior information, thus we attempt to make them at least somewhat inclusive. The window of time available to complete the second phase that is focused toward the completion of the worded purpose is continually shrinking. Therefore, we feel it necessary to continue to prod and poke lest it close without its completion. Chaos would then indeed reign and the birthing of the new paradigm could become unimaginably difficult. The period of chaos could stretch on for a painfully long time in your counting. *It is not this information that is important, it is the conception and completion of the writing of the purpose!* We do not want this information on file in your Library of Congress. *We p*refer it to be exchanged on a personal, need to know level. It is purposefully written so as to exclude words that trip the communication scanners so that it may yet spread easily to the chosen ones. We wish to be very clear about this. Our translator spends much time in the thesaurus mode looking for synonyms so word patterns are varied within each document. What appears to be but a few paragraphs involves much dedicated attention to this facet of caution. The purpose of this information weighs heavily on this conscious awareness, however commitment carries the process forward day by day. We are finding that commitment matched in like manner by the readers of it and are grateful indeed.

It is your resolve to bring this new archetype of experience into being that holds the progress made in place so that the building of the pattern can continue on. Visualize the pattern of a snowflake only now beginning to crystallize from a drop of water. Just the very beginning of one corner of what will be a unique picture is happening. You are not only watching the creation of something uniquely beautiful, you are providing the focus that will cause it to happen. How could you avoid continuing to be an important part of this beautiful demonstration?

No. 32

When the time arrives for what could be termed the crash of all your systems of communications, utilities and supplies, there will be turmoil and confusion of massive proportions. It behooves you who are well aware of this possibility to survey your personal situations and to make contingency plans. It is amazing to us that this information is known but each assumes that it will happen around them but not to them. You are aware of the existence of various mechanisms that would provide at least minimum replacements for your utility needs; even coordinated systems are available. The project will not make the shift in consciousness before this break down of current lifestyle. There will be a period of chaos. How long that will last depends on the completion of phase two and three, the conception of the new paradigm and then the spread of it through the conscious awareness of your brethren. As you can deduce for yourselves, communications are relatively easy before the breakdown, and difficult at best after it. It is critical that you truly realize and begin preparing for this advancing menace with as much focus and dispatch as possible. We are long past the, "I can hardly wait for it, but I just don't have time prepare for it just yet," syndrome. It is necessary for you to look carefully at your priorities and to remember that you have made commitments that involve the survival and transcendence of as many of your willing brethren as possible. This does mean that they have to be occupying their bodies for this to be successful. This is indeed a heavy responsibility, but we again remind you that all possible help is available if you but ask and "move your feet."

It would appear that it is necessary to also remind you that the discussions of phase 2 must be conducted in places that are not likely to contain listening wires. It is suggested that you view the movie called "Enemy of the State" and listen carefully when the character Brill describes the capabilities of the electronics. He goes through the list at top speed and so you must be listening carefully. It was also given on TV when the filming process of the movie was reviewed. Brill, in the movie, reminds the hero that the capabilities he is listing were available many years previously, however the capability to apply them in a massive manner was not possible until recently, but the added sophistication's since exceed what is demonstrated in the movie. All of you are being observed and when you gather, you can be sure your discussions are of interest. We would prefer that this project continue unnoticed for as long as possible. If this sounds melodramatic, so be it. Ask for discernment and then view the movie and you will understand.

As our arrogant planners flaunt their methodology before your eyes assuming that sleeping minds have little discernment between programming and entertainment, there is no reason we cannot use this information to our advantage. When you ask for discernment within our purposes, the ability to interpret and to envision ways of applying the Laws given you will provide avenues avoiding their entrapment techniques. As all encompassing as they appear, they are inventions of opposite focus and thus contain the elements of self-destruction. Just as Divine purpose contains within it the impulse for self-expansion the opposite contains the tendencies of self-destruction. When the negative polarity is expanded, then its innate tendencies are magnified, just as the opposite is true within the positive polarity. It is within the path between the two that the spiral of evolution exists.

It is important to note here that the meaning of the word "evolution" has been purposely distorted by implanting the idea that evolution and adaptation are synonymous. Animal life and even human life at one level adapts. Evolution refers to the spiral of spiritual experience through (think holographically) its return trip to the source. Here you can see correlation of spiral to spirit and holographic to holy.

When the appropriate moments arrive, you will have the discernment to bring forward into your conscious awareness that prickly feeling that causes you to move to a more appropriate place and it will be available. Planning ahead does not work; it is necessary to be flexible and move in the moment. It is spontaneity that provides the atmosphere in which creation moves without restriction. Since creation is what you are about, then it is important to move within the framework of purpose as spontaneously as possible. Though this would seem that opposites are at counterpoints, indeed this is combining the polarities in a complimentary fashion allowing for the spiraling effect that is desired for movement in a balanced fashion. Polarities are not limited to extreme opposites as in black and white, on and off, good and bad, etc. Pink and gray are opposites, but of a different intensity. These intensities are available in abundance to apply and through this principle diversity within a focus are accomplished.

How does this apply to the project at hand? It is through the diverse contributions toward the goal of completing phase two that the appropriate composite will come forth. Each session will be a think tank of spiraling ideas toward the goal fueled by combining the individual minds into an empowered group focus. It is the addition of the group focus that is the increased power of the creative presence. Because the creator is not a personal presence at the 3rd dimensional level, he literally cannot be present, but the combination of focus provided by the shared common goal brings forth a greater power, particularly when numerical combinations are observed. The common language of creation is mathematical formulation. The practice of numerology touches upon how these formulations apply to individual lives. Spontaneity is allowing the conscious awareness to relax and for harmony with these foundations of existence to bring forth desired results within the framework of defined purpose. The purpose of these think tank sessions provides the framework to bring forth a greater purpose that in turn will be the framework for the new paradigm. It will be the framework to provide for individuals to continue the process within their own experience. This may seem simple enough, however it is in the understanding and follow through of the steps within the universal laws that is the trick. Allowance is the most difficult to incorporate. Rising above the need to control is the leavening of the loaf so to speak. Volumes could be written regarding this, but it would not change anything. It is in the doing that it is accomplished. It is the doing of this one facet that opens the door to the transcendence of this dimension. The ability to apply this principle is built upon the use of the previous two and through application of all three that the fourth is reached and bingo, you are there at the point of choice. To go or not to go! Graduation requires the release of attachments, than not now. Just as you have been misled regarding your ego, so have you been misled regarding your attachments? There is a difference between attachments and addictions. That is for you to discern and now is the time to release the addictions. You must ask yourself what it is that you think must remain in your experience and what it would be pleasant to have, but not absolutely necessary. You will be surprised if you take a few moments to make even a brief list of your technological wonders and contemplate what life will be like without them. You will then be prepared for your not so distant future. This is not to say that to plan to provide for the *basic* necessities is addiction rather than wisdom. Here again ask for discernment.

We remind you that it is our concern for all that motivates us to share as much guidance as possible, for this project is of critical importance. The creator is non-preferential in the desire to retain every fragment; we however value our ground team greatly. Friendship is a wondrous part of the shared experience of self-aware manifested fragments. You don't remember us, but we remember you!

No. 33

The days are now upon us for gathering the focus that will bring about the transformation of the mass consciousness. It will be an interesting process of inter-linking various consciously begun projects at different places on the planet. There are more than one ground crew with purposeful assignments. While it is natural to feel that what one person or one group is attempting is too little too late, this is not the case. All are now in place, or nearly enough so that the concerted beginning can be initiated. It is necessary that the resolve, intent and purpose be held securely within the scope of each of you, as the days ahead may seem discouraging. You must hold to your commitment with a calm and trust that does not waver. This experience is a manifested reality that must be dealt with inside that reality. The game must be continued on until completion. It can no longer be changed or delayed. Humanity is sinking into greater fear and confusion furthering the plans of the manipulators at a rapid pace. The spiritual levels of each are becoming more and more inaccessible and the reaction of the spirit expressing through the body to this process will continue to reflect through the reaction of the planet also. It is not a pretty picture from our prospective. It is not our intent to focus your attention into this picture but it is also necessary that you are aware of what you are working within. It is unfortunate that it has had to proceed this far into the levels of suffering before the consciousness becomes vulnerable and desperate enough to pause and reflect that enough is enough. Perhaps now enough can be reached with the desire to bring this situation to an end to be willing to accomplish it through a total change of ingrained habitual reactions.

The locking mechanism has been what has been called "the opium of religion." The religious doctrine of "ours is the only way, and all else is wrong" has literally created cells with in a dungeon of ignorance with every modern religious sect present and accounted for. This is not to say that some truth is not present within them, but there is not enough either within any one, or even a composite of the truth known within all of them, now to guide mankind in anything but unending circles of frustration. The innate desire is always within each to progress toward the goal of transcending this entrapment with in 3rd dimension and now religion offers no way to continue the journey. The aspiration of each soul extension as it incarnates to earth is to assist in bringing this situation back into balance. Each desires to *become* part of the pivotal pebble in the pond, but instead are caught in the entrapment of the heavy oppressive pattern of energies and become part of the chorus calling out for assistance. The assistance can not come from without; it must come from within through self-empowerment, not for the purpose of placing the self over and above others, but in the genuine desire to inspire others to follow suit. In this way, these individuals come into harmony with the creative flow and with the focused conscious desire of those who are dedicated to this purpose that have accomplished this transcendence before. Unfortunately the situation has reached such a sad state that dedicated ones of higher dimensions have now volunteered to incarnate and act on behalf of the inhabitants and set into motion a wave of self-empowerment on the planet. These volunteers are numerous and await the triggers planted within their awareness to remember their roles. The time has come for this to begin!

Now is the time for these self-appointed ones to lead mankind from being into *becoming* what was intended. Human being is a misnomer; each is a human becoming! Knowing this and referring to themselves in this way, each would be constantly focused upon the true purpose of incarnation. Then the internal cry that those on the planet and the planet herself in this moment of time would become "I am a human (god-man) *becoming!* Help me to do this!" Then response is possible. It changes the focus from "I am a victim, help me!" which implies help me to continue being a victim, to a focus of desire for self-empowerment. After centuries of calling for someone or some ritual or miracle to accomplish the impossible, man has been unable to figure out that it must come from within his own awareness and the empowering of himself so that it can be accomplished. Instead the self-empowerment urge was distorted into self-aggrandizement and the result is seen all around you. *The shift* of your own consciousness toward your desire for this end has brought forth your ability to attract these messages. As the wake up triggers are tripped, the ripples of the pebble shall become waves. Then the action shall begin and many levels of links shall form and wheels shall begin to turn. A beleaguered mass consciousness shall experience a shift as will the planet. This will not be the shift, but will be the beginning of the necessary upliftment that must precede that process.

Keep in mind the vibratory level of the mass consciousness. No inhabitant of planet earth could survive a shift to 4th dimension at this time. No amount of meditating and listening to channeled entities has accomplished this feat. It must be a shift in self-perception and focus of the purpose of this incarnation in great numbers to accomplish this, as the flow is downward in vibratory rate into disease and death. To halt this movement and change its direction will require a shift of major proportion. The normal vibratory rate of a human body has been determined to be between 62 and 68 MHz. The brain functions optimally between 72 and 90 MHz. When the body vibration lowers to 58 MHz it can "catch a cold"; at 57 MHz the flu; 55 MHz candida, 52 MHz Epstein Barr; 42 MHz cancer and at 25 MHz death begins. By considering the health problems of your friends and family, you can begin to get a true picture. Our interesting negative planners simply lower the MHz of someone they would like to eliminate through their recently devised methods. Within a short period of time, the body either develops a fatal disease or if lowered enough, death occurs and whatever disease already present is the excuse. Allopathic *medicine* (a misnomer), chemical prescriptions, lower the MHz of the body. Radiation from TV and computer screens lower the MHz, and consuming processed and canned foods, which have 0 MHz to support the body, continue the process. Starvation is the least subtle of the ways to lower the MHz and bring on the lowering of the mass consciousness before each die, in that way these make their contribution to this descending cycle. The human body has amazing adaptive abilities, but the onslaught of ways to bring down the vibratory level to tie you to this planet has reached a critical point. The good news is that the shift in focus of purpose by the critical mass within the encompassing planetary consciousness can go beyond removing a few critical dominos as placed by the interesting planners. It could reverse the way they fall thereby releasing the lowering process and allowing the MHz of the bodies to increase. Now that is an interesting supposition to consider!

The picture as it is at the moment is beyond discouraging; it is appalling. However, in playing out various scenarios in holographic possibilities it is not at all hopeless. The keys lie in the cards held by the "ground crew." How these are played will determine which of the scenarios are available to ensure success. Keep playing! The last game has just begun and the Creator never gambles. He only plays the sure bets. After all he made up the game and he never forgets the rules. You can rely on that! His turn to shuffle and deal is about to come up. Don't wait for it to happen elsewhere. Be here now!

No. 34

At the point in your timing when this project was initiated, there was a very small window in which to begin the process. Once the idea was grasped and acted upon, the next window encompassing moving into the process was much larger. This step allowed for the contact of various new individuals to be made aware and to continue the enlarging of the window. The addition of other minds grasping the basic idea and focusing their intention of participating has continued opening the window to allow for the continuing inclusion of additional participants. The expansiveness of this movement allows the process to come into harmony with the expression of divine order, which is expansive in its very nature. The momentum of the outward movement of this information forms the basis continuing this harmonious flow and insures the divine participation that is essential to success. It is important that you realize the key to success is in expansive outward movement. It is the combination of grasping the various aspects of this intended change of attitude and focusing it through the needed number of points of individual awareness. The importance of these aspects is the establishment of an outward flow and maintaining this flow. New contacts must be made by as many of the recently contacted individuals as possible to keep this expansive flow in motion. As memories are keyed to think of other appropriate people not yet contacted, then ones can continue to make additional contacts. This insures that those without commitment to carry the "Letter to Garcia" do not impede this essential outward expansion.

If these messages were to be sent out to new contacts that are considered to be ones sure to follow through and actually continue the flow, it would perhaps be appropriate to send the first few as an introductory packet. A cover note suggesting that if theirs is a real commitment, then on request more of the messages will be provided. This would allow a spread of the cost for reproduction and mailing so that it would not be burdensome to a few. Each committed one would in all probability make only a few *appropriate* contacts. This also allows for anonymity and protection. It is assumed that only those known and deemed appropriate would be contacted so that discussions could be carried on in the groups of 3s, 7s and 12s (this is to again remind you of the numerical power available within divine mathematical order.) It is entirely appropriate that attempts to formulate a possible statement of purpose should be made at small group levels. The more of these attempts that are made, the sooner the "perfect one" will stand forth. When that happens, that group will be totally aware that completion has been accomplished for that phase. What to do next will also be drawn into that group awareness attracted by the power of the fusion of all the input from the totality of the groups? (Here again you are reminded that thought thinks within and upon itself when it is in divine harmony.) How many participants are necessary for this parenting phase? That depends on three factors: whom, how quickly the phase is initiated and the productive discussions actually taking place. The ball is in your court. Responses in terms beyond intellectualizing the shift in perception are the keys. We can participate further when you return the ball to our court. In the meantime, we are limited, in this project, to this flow of information and encouragement.

The overall view from our prospective is somewhat encouraging. The plans of the interesting participants of opposite purpose continue right on schedule. It is important that the view of our focus is one of action and not reaction. It is in the ability of our group to have a balanced dual prospective that spreads with the awareness of our project. This will sustain the momentum. There must be an awareness of the awesome inevitability of the probable success of their "plan" and a balancing awareness that ours is the only shift available that offers the power to bring release from the intended horrendous future. If followed with dedication and resolve through application of the universal laws of attraction, focused intention to create a new paradigm of experience and allowance through lack of resistance, return to balance and harmony must be the end result. Only through this format can the help so ardently sought by suffering humanity be answered. All of the above discussion of bringing others into the awareness of the possibility of creating a new paradigm of experience for this planetary focus when simply stated is that the *return to personal responsibility* is the only avenue leading to success. As individuals assume responsibility, group responsibility through cooperation is the inevitable result. Those unable to move beyond the desire for personal material gain and the need to control the proceedings and the outcome will soon drop by the way side. If discernment is used in choosing appropriate contacts, those may be considered but not contacted.

If at first appropriate names do not come into your awareness, as you continue to desire to participate, names and coincidental contacts will "happen." The law of attraction works! Just hold the desire in your consciousness, especially at times of least attention to other activities. As you retire, when you awaken, at the end of meditation or intentional prayer times are appropriate. The more often it comes into your mind and you *feel* strongly about desiring to be part of this positive after exercise in participation with the creator within his modus operandi, the greater the contribution you will make. Commitment and resolve are the buoyant qualities that hold this desire on the surface of your consciousness so that opportunities for you to participate are attracted to you. Through this process you will indeed be a blessing and a focused beam of light in this darkened world. A spotlight spreads into a larger and larger circle at the end of the beam. A greater understanding through your choice to become a part of this project will allow you to spread this light of understanding in the midst of a darkening world. Your inner confidence and the peace of knowing that something powerfully new is already being created as the present reality is changing is a powerful positive pole. This attitude will attract to you those desiring change and ready to transcend the victim-state. You will be the pebble within your own pond of experience. Your service will continue to expand to other levels of experience. Don't plan on a dull and boring life from this point on.

Your participation in this project will bring with it personal rewards. Recognized sainthood is not one of them. Changes in consciousness will happen as you participate and as your body is able to accommodate them. Those of you who continue to dishonor the living temple of your spirit will miss out on some of these rewards. Caffeine, carbonation, a diet of prepared (over cooked) foods, etc., require you to reconsider your priorities. Many of you are without a mate that results in choosing to eat out. Consider your choices and opt for food cooked for shorter periods and include raw foods. If you eat at home, many supermarkets now carry some organic foods. Over eating causes the body to use its energy digesting rather than using it for more productive modes. Smaller amounts of nourishing foods allow the body to use its available energy in other activities and to possibly require shorter sleep periods.

Much is being asked of you, but knowing you incarnated herein this lifetime to participate in this project allows you to stop wondering "why me, why here and why now?" This in itself will bring you to change your priorities. As participation in it becomes your priority, those activities that are not important to it will shift out of your life. It is the way it works. Will this take over your life? We would hope not. It is where the action is and so your life will take *it* over. A different and energizing perspective! The taking on of *personal responsibility* and moving within the flow of creation for the purpose of expanding creation, bring rewards of a personal nature as well to the larger picture. It is a most enjoyable experience. As you participate you will remember how it feels to be in balance and harmony and this will assist you in knowing and making your necessary contributions to the wholeness of the project. To bless is to be blessed indeed!

No. 35

It is interesting from our perspective to see that you are busily building a reservoir of energy that is standing in stagnation. There is a growing number of people aware of the paradigm project, but few if any have sat down to play at composing what might be their personal idea of a statement of purpose. It is as though you must wait until you meet in some type of formal meeting to accomplish anything. Where is personal responsibility in this response? It would seem to me that bringing your personally defined idea along with you would bring: different level of intent to a meeting to define a purpose. It was hoped that this would be a natural outcome of the suggestion that you begin this process for your own salvation. Do not assume that your ground crew status will be enough. You are in 3rd dimensional experience and are governed by it the same as all other inhabitants of the earth planet. If personal responsibility is the keynote, then operate within it, especially with regard to the project if you hope to achieve its purpose.

We are finding it difficult from the perspective of our experience to comprehend just how difficult it is for you to experience
within the vibrational level of earth. The combination of planned
lowering techniques being applied to all aspects of earthly existence
is inevitably lowering the vibration in measurable calibrations. It
is the concerted effects of the multiple techniques that are accomplishing this. The critical mass of humans now within the control of
these combined techniques will soon be reached. It is important for
you to have the understanding that the critical mass point needed for
evil intent is different than it is for intent of upliftment. This cannot
be calculated in simple percentages, for the degree of evolvement of
each soul and its extensions must be considered in this calculation.
As the vibratory rate descends the critical mass point ascends while
the opposite is true from our point of view. Lowering the vibratory
rate is much more difficult than raising it. A simple realization can
cause a jump in vibratory rate. So why don't we just trigger a big
planetary realization and fix the whole thing? As the vibratory rate
lowers the brain synapses become more and more difficult. Also
the use of the sugar substitute such as equal is slowly destroying
the ability of the brain to function as it destroys the nerve endings.
It can and does cross the blood brain barrier. Further, low fat/high
sugar bearing carbohydrate diets are starving the brain cells. All
of this is part of the plan, remember they understand the functions
of the physical body well enough to be able to develop techniques
to weaken the connection of the being to its vibratory source in
hopes it can be broken at their moment of choosing. May we stress
that you think carefully about this information and that you read
your labels and take personal responsibility in the care of the bodily
functions necessary to participate in this project. Beyond that which
was mentioned in this message and the previous one, the remaining
critical factor is the pH level of your body and your blood.

If you are serious about wanting to return to higher dimensional
experience then you are required to master the 3rd dimension and
the completion of this project is recommended as your ticket. Personal responsibility is being responsible for your personal expression of this life experience, starting with your body temple. To do
that now you will need to think independently of what is being
touted in your media and by the medical community. Even most

alternative "professionals" are versed in less than holistic understanding and offer only partial assistance with their expensive products. Massage is a pleasant interlude but is not a replacement for the personal responsibility of regular gentle exercise.

Are we lecturing you? What is offered is in way of guidance. If you take it in any other way, then you are reacting through the distorted ego function. It depends on whether you can act rather than intellectualize. The ego has been distorted so that it loves to pontificate and to excuse so that personal responsibility can be avoided. It is so much easier to talk that to do when changing established patterns are involved. It can be overcome by ignoring it and placing the focus beyond the chaos of change and instead to visualize the end result. Picture bypass the intellectualizing process. In order to come up with a statement of purpose, the parenting groups must spend personal time visualizing (dreaming) what each can conceive through imagination (going within the mind of God) and then attempting to put it into concise wording. The process can begin with words, then mental movies, then words again, etc. This would bring into practice purposeful meditation, a wonderful tool of higher dimensions. I believe it has been referred to as *"becoming* that which you desire." Those known as shamans and oracles use this technique and walk in two "worlds." There are nuances of the universal laws that serve the intended purpose of experiencing your way back to the source of all. It is an adventure offering challenge and joy far beyond 3rd dimensional physical challenges. These leave the empty feelings that ones feel can only be filled with more challenging experiences that bring the same frustrating results of emptiness. The paths of learning are blocked and mankind on earth is left chasing its nonexistent tail and is being lead in a downward spiral.

Continuing in our focus of accepting personal responsibility, it is important to consider another aspect. The ideal of personal responsibility is perceived as being heavy on the responsibility aspect. It would serve humanity better if the accent were on the personal aspect. Again personal has been distorted to assume the meaning of selfishness which is translated from the deliberate focus of denying that one can create independence and must take what is needed from someone else. The bankers on your planet illustrate this law of the proposed negative system and carry out this concept to the extreme. This group is not only visualizing their planned result, but are living it now. This increases the available energy required for their plan to move forward. Your bible has a statement within it that reads something like "The rain falls on the just and the unjust. How do you feel about that?" The rain refers to the universal laws working within the focus of either polarity. You are programmed to think that the negative pole is always "bad." Within the context of the whole this is not true. There is no electricity (energy moving) without both poles. It is distorted use beyond the norms of balance that are at issue in this instance. Personal has the true meaning of the harmonious, expression of the fragment of creator energy expressing radiantly by continuing the flow of expansive energy into what ever dimension it is within. The word was devised within the focus of referral to the fragments as the family of god, perSONal. Again the masculine reference because it is within the perception of expansiveness being a masculine aspect. In other words, personal responsibility reflects the willingness to be a flow of expansive energy within the realm of your pattern of experience. With the cycle of energy surrounding you moving in an opposite directional flow, you must swim upstream so to speak to accomplish what you intend.

Hopefully these messages will provide a convenient rock on which you can stand above this flow in order to get your equilibrium, gain strength through resolve and then start to gather the rocks necessary build a dam to divert the flow in a new direction. Yours is a holy project reflecting the wholistic nature of how "it all" works. Within your sequential focus it must come together piece by piece, but it may not, in true reality, work that way. This is why it is so important that you trust the process especially when you think things are not working as they should be. Just do your part and all will come into place! Trust!

No. 36

Let us continue with these messages for a few more sessions. These pertain to the parenting phase of project new paradigm. The ball then is in your court for action. Either you pick up the ball and move into actually doing the conception of the "babe" or not.

Certainly we have been making every effort to encourage your participation. If it is necessary for the pebble to be dropped at the next level, you are going to have an interesting ride on space ship earth. This is a further wake up call. The snooze bar is reaching the end of its program. If you are reading this information, you are a part of the ground crew and need only realize it is time to drop your disguise and begin your mission. The flight crew cannot land until the field is ready and the invitation is issued. As suggested before, begin formulating and dreaming scenarios within your own personal awareness. This triggers the resonance of the law of attraction. "In the beginning there was the thought and the thought became flesh."

It is a matter of bringing the information shared previously into a cohesive understanding that allows you to operate within the appropriate process. Since the paradigm can only be brought forth within a holographic format that resonates in harmony with the wholeness of creation, it would seem logical that you must understand the basic parameters required ensuring success. Since this involves feeding this information to you in bits that can be pondered and assimilated, it ends up spread over many pages. You are then left to combine the bits into a composite that formulates a sensible basis for moving into the creative process with confidence.

It will be necessary for you to assume the study mode and reread these lessons in order to bring forth your own understanding and to formulate your personal foundation. There are nuances of the laws that will blossom into your awareness through the study-assimilation process. It would be convenient for you if we would simply provide you with an outline, but that would not allow the flowering process to be reached as an end result. It is nice to receive a bouquet and simply enjoy the beauty and the fragrance, but the growth process would be skipped. It is necessary that you "grow" your understanding. The Handbook of the New Paradigm is a precious treasure given to you so that you may step into your radiant stance of service and fulfill your chosen destiny in the history of planet earth. Through this suggested process the burden of responsibility will transcend into the pure joy of bringing "en-*light*-enment" to a world of darkness.

Within the holographic process is the element of maintaining the focus to enable manifestation to complete its intended cycle.

The focus of thought is maintained for long periods of time (again staying within your reckoning mode) by setting the vibratory oscillations within a range that emanates sound. This is duplicated in crude form by your music. In purity it can be grasped as being of a crystalline bell like quality. Tibetan bells give you an inkling of the reverberations that continue for long periods of time, beyond what the human ear can hear. Within a holographic context, a continuous vibration is set forth in an over unity mode carrying forth the expansive paradigm. Each holographic creation is unique, reminiscent of your snowflakes. There is present within each galaxy a continuous melody of bell like sounds which is perceived in part by some and referred to as "the music of the spheres" which is a perfect description.

Earth is at the moment quite out of tune. Contemplate the resonance of the crystalline music of the spheres and then think of punk rock. That might be thought of as the resonant sound of the planned new galaxy. Would you want to live there all the time? Perfect resonance is attained through balance. This is the reason that rock music is so destructive to the balance of the young people. It is designed to be unbalanced and discordant in its basic construction. It reflects outward the inner imbalance of its composers and it enhances chaotic tendencies with in the psyche of those spending long and frequent time listening to it. The bridge for this phase from romantic sexually stimulating music was the Beatles. Their early music contained melodies with a lessor amount of distortion as is demonstrated by the orchestral versions. It did however open the door for the more destructive distortions that inevitably followed. Again all part of the plan to slow and hold down the human vibration.

In order for you to conceptualize a higher dimensional experience, it is necessary that you have some understanding of the experience of it from the creational perspective. Holographic interaction is basic to this understanding. Current methodology to produce this phenomenon involves a beam of light focused through a transparency that produces a floating dimensional replica. In an existing holograph (you) conceive a thought of a desire to be reproduced in like holographic mode. This thought thinking (you) focuses by enlarging this thought with details that further define the holographic desire and increases the energy of the beam like thought with emotions of what the experience of enjoying this new holograph will be like therefore empowering it to come into form.

You call the holographic concept 3D or third dimensional. How then is the 4th dimension different? 3D encompasses the conception of height, width and depth, but involves no motion within the holograph of its own volition. (3D movies involve dimensional glasses. Virtual reality is also a manipulation.) The next step into 4th dimensional experience superimposes the living or vibratory dimension of action within the purview of the holograph itself. A true holograph is projected through thought, not by a mechanism. Since thought has the power to act upon itself with further thought, it is self-aware. The higher the degree of self-awareness implies a higher vibratory rate or dimension of experience. The seeds of one dimension are planted within the lessor one.

This brings you to the understanding that you are already aware of being self-aware. However, this seed must be nurtured and cultivated in order to flower into transcending to a point of outgrowing its present placement through increasing its vibratory rate until it lifts itself into a dimensional shift allowing for greater opportunity to grow even more self-aware. What you are attempting to do is to cause this process to manifest on a planetary scale because earth's vibratory environment is so distorted that individuals can no longer accomplish it. Just as Moses had to cross the Red Sea at the exact moment of a planetary shift, this is timed at the exact moment of a galactic shift. How will you know? That is our job.

As usual, you are being reminded that unless you create a plug and pull it, some other backup plan will be employed that will bypass the opportunity for humanity to cleanup their own act and use it as a stepping stone for advancement. We continue to stress the power that you hold in the palm of your hands. It is such a gift to be in the position of assisting this planet and its inhabitants into a shift of such major proportion and it carries with it an opportunity for literally jumping up the vibratory scale. We can only bring the opportunity to your attention and act in an advisory capacity. You must be the ones to do it. It is not the first time you have participated in similar roles. This is the mission you have literally trained yourself to take part in, so don't drop the ball now. There is *nothing* more important in your current realm of experience.

No. 37

Progress is being made within the hearts and minds of those who are reading these messages. By progress we mean there is a shift within the consciousness that is reflected within the holographic activity that is you. In other words, the thought that each of you are, is thinking and acting within itself. Your psychologist/psychiatrists would say there is a shift in the data stored within your subconscious. The prayer given previously, *"I am a human becoming, help me to become!"* is powerful enough that simply reading it and considering it in a positive attitude begins the shift. The victim attitude is deeply ingrained within humanity as a whole. It shuts down the light of each child as soon as it is absorbed from the parental attitude. With the realization that victimhood is a falsehood and an ideal to be released, the holographic pattern immediately begins to brighten. Use it as a mantra, especially when encountering situations that have in the past triggered what has been referred to as "giving away your power." These can be encounters with other people or life situations resulting from inappropriate decisions. The prayer wording allows a shift in attitude that reflects the intention of taking back that power. As it is practiced on a small scale within each individual life, then it becomes a tiny grain of sand in the mass consciousness that grows as others receive and begin to use this simple thought in their daily lives.

It might be appropriate to define mantra. It is a short series of sounds or words that brings about balance within what you call the subconscious awareness. Often the sounds are from ancient languages that are not consciously understood, but resonate at the DNA/RNA level of the body bringing about change in an outward flowing manner. The mantra as currently used is often an intuitive decision on the part of one person assigning it to another. Frequently the appropriate combination is not given and years of repetition bring little if any change. Some choose on their own with the same result. The use of the simple prayer, "I am a human becoming, help me to become," guarantees results. The most benefit is gained, not by setting aside a period and using continuous repetition, but by single statements made in connection with conscious recognition of thoughts, encounters or situations that are bring forth your victim response. Remembering and thinking it several times during the day is also very helpful.

You each have victim responses and there are no exceptions. You simply deny you do in order to deny that you give away your power to an Ego that does not exist. Denial is the shield of the empowered Ego that fosters victimhood as result. This prayer will end the deification of the ego. Ego is function not a false god personality. "Thou shalt have no other gods before me." The number one false god is the falsely enthroned ego that you have been programmed to struggle against. A number of commonly used quotes are appropriate "That which you resist, persists." "That which you fear shall come upon you," etc. You have been programmed to turn everywhere but inward in self-contemplation that results in self-empowerment that in turn flows outward into expansive expression. Self-contemplation is not sitting and staring at your navel wondering "who, what and where am I?" It is practicing the use of the universal laws and contemplating the results of these applications in experience for the purpose of self-enlightenment. Each experience is a pebble in the pond of your life.

Your not so friendly perpetrators have added other layers of programming very effectively. You must not look inward or empower the self because that is "selfish." You are then "guilty" if you consider empowering the self because it is then implied that you will use the power to "overcome" others. This results in a distortion through misinterpretation early in childhood as each attempt to establish their innate tendencies to follow what gives them joy into greater expression. The distortion spreads into countless intermingling and inter-acting complicated behavior patterns that pass from one generation to another. The simple use of the prayer/mantra frequently within group/family situations by the participating members would bring dramatic changes. The wide use of it "wisely" would have phenomenal results.

The point of this segment of information is not as a sermon, but instead to illustrate how a statement of simplicity and appeal can bring forth change in a way that resolves and literally dissolves intermingled and interrelated distorted patterns of experience. If you doubt this, use the small prayer and observe what happens. The more you use it appropriately (wisely) the greater demonstration you will observe. Following the first few remembered uses of it, you will find yourself using it silently in situations as simple as being irritated because the waitress is slow. It changes your experience, which in turn changes hers. There will be big irritations that will slip by and later when remembered that are the most appropriate times to say it with meaning (emotion). It works!

It would seem that this series of messages could perhaps have been condensed down into a few simple statements that would be as effective as the small prayer. Perhaps, but would you have heard them? In observing human tendencies, especially ones with media overwhelm and information clutter, it is a matter of chipping away at the established patterns of the "read and toss" syndrome. Most who have awakened to the reality of the situation surrounding you are avid readers and listeners with this syndrome deeply patterned. The media overwhelm consists of constant repetition plainly presented and supported by subliminal key words and phrases. This places shield of resistance at the subconscious level that then accepts the subliminal messages like arrows penetrating a target.

These messages have had to slowly penetrate this shield using repetition and realizations of truth as our arrows to penetrate the shield and to cause places in the shield to open that the messages could be absorbed in the rereading of edited version. Greater clarity and conciseness of particular true statements should augment this opening process. This doesn't indicate that your shield attempting to protect you from the media barrage is weakened, instead it is strengthened. The greater realization of the bigger picture of both aspects your surrounding situation allows for conscious sifting of all the information you are inputting. The realizations of truth and your sincere commitment to the project have rearranged the content of the subconscious in a way similar to programs used so computer files can be rearranged allowing the disk space to be used in its most efficient configuration. This will be reflected in your life experiences. There may be some confusion, especially during your sleep patterns as this reconfiguration of your subconscious actually happens. For the more self aware, it will be more pronounced and for a time, even troublesome. This process will allow you to absorb the important contents of the messages into a format at both levels of consciousness. It is like entering two interacting programs on a computer. Something like Word overlaying Windows, both contributing to a greater practical application available to the "user." How well it works depends on how well the user learns and applies its available unique applications. This is an apt analogy for careful consideration by serious users intending to take advantage of the opportunity to short cut older methods of "grubbing it out."

No. 38

There are many levels involved in the process of bringing forth the accelerated change in the consciousness of earth inhabitants/ planetary awareness. The focus of the mass consciousness at the individual level is outward in contemplation of each ones environment. The deliberate teaching that the creator is a personality somewhere beyond the sky in the "heavens" making arbitrary judgements about which of the victim prayers deserves answering, is a picture of the structure inherent within the abhorrent plans being carried out all around you. It is constrictive in its focus, the opposite of expansive creation that maintains itself through an over-unity mode, meaning the flow brings forth an exponential increase of energy beyond what is focused into manifestation. This results through the inverse movement of the self-contemplative focus, which is within the intentional manifestation or the action of the 2nd universal law. It can again be likened to there being two sides to a coin. Through the intention of creating/manifesting there is the result of the manifestation and then the contemplation or experiencing of this process which is the self, contemplating as it experiences. This involves the 5 senses, ego observation and the contemplative thought process. Ideally all this moves through the individual life experience in a flow.

This is not to say that each individual would always create positive experiences. However, if the process was understood at the subconscious level, then the effects of an inappropriately caused experience would be contemplated. Through the necessary adjustments of attitude and intention, a lesson would be "learned" and the overall experience pattern continued with little trauma, greater wisdom gained and further upliftment of the energy vibration.

Through consideration of the ideal, it is easy to conclude that the planned reversal of this flow to create an opposite inclusive flow would end in something like your scientists theory of the black hole, absorbing all available energies into a compacted mass. Why then have these planners not figured out the greater picture of the inevitable end of their endeavor? The enthroned ego with an addiction to power and control is seldom able to perceive logically. You perceive this type of distortion as insanity because of an individuals inability to follow the logical norm of the societal group. Sometimes it is because the creative thought process is far beyond this societal norm and sometimes it is ruled by distorted ability to perceive. This is both genetic and learned behavior through controlled indoctrination interchanged between the present generation and those following. The particular group holding our interest promotes longevity and positively believes in reincarnation. Each of the hierarchy are programmed at birth through magical methods that they are a reincarnation through a long line of predecessors all committed to this project. Each generation is then perceived as being further empowered than the last. In this way, their project has continued on for what you experience as eons of time toward this important pivotal point.

This project, which deviates so far from the acceptable norm, has come into form through the use of the first two laws of the universe, attraction and focused intention. However, it is not possible for them move out of the flow of expansive energy in a relaxed mode. The law of allowance is ignored. The only way for balance to be maintained is through rigid control of all aspects by planning and executing every detail to dovetail within their overall plan. Deviations are detected as quickly as possible and all haste is taken to remedy the situation by any means possible in the belief that the end justifies the means. This overview of the pattern of their plan does not indicate that it is any less formidable. Earth and its inhabitants are firmly within the grip of its influence and the situation must be *intentionally* resolved. It is beyond the point that containment would be appropriate while the inhabitants figured their role out. The control being exerted outweighs the possibility of this taking place without focused assistance. The focused assistance is manifesting, into the heart of their game, in the form of Project

New Paradigm with its multifaceted application of all four laws. You must contemplate the inside-out process concurrent with the outside-in process through the nuances of previously explained facets of creative flow to arrive at a picture of the game board. You will then be able to choose intelligently to join the play or not.

The play will be interesting to follow. One focus of play will be intense and controlled giving forth an aura of determined restraint, planning and examining every move. The other, relaxed allowing each play to be drawn through the wisdom of thought thinking resulting in calm game moves each flowing into the next in an expansive mode. The adversary considers that each play represents a shift necessary before another play can be conceptualized and focused into manifestation within the application supplied by the use of two universal laws as a self-governing factor. The balance as perceived by them is established control. Since their focus is restricted to using only two laws, using the third in an opposite mode makes the fourth impossible to attain. In other words, within our analogy, they are playing with only half a deck. There are slang references to insanity as playing with only half a deck. Quite appropriate!

There have been frequent uses of analogies within these messages. Each illustrates the understanding of two areas, the reintroduction of the universal laws and an overview of the game strategies in simple terms. We have attempted to add dimension to those understandings within succeeding messages. As you assemble these bits of information into blocks of understanding, you enhance your ability to contribute to the project. Commitment and resolve garner confidence in your day to day experience as you attract opportunities to participate. This releases the need to react toward the programmed individuals caught up in the negative focus and brings allowance into your experience. You know how the game is being played and can now perceive that you have the choice to participate intelligently resulting in a new sense of balance through purpose. Through returning to a familiar expansive expression, your sense of well being becomes magnetic and radiant. You are beginning the transcendent process.

The creative process takes advantage of every opportunity to continue its expansive mode. Your heart welcomes this wondrous opportunity and adds the dimension of emotion to the thinking level bringing forth outward dimensional expansion. This is how it works!

No. 39

There was a time that mankind experiencing on this planet brought all into balance. It was an experience that set what you might term the ideal into the consciousness at the planetary level. This then established the ability to recognize imbalance and allow for the desire to return to that ideal. This realization of what is and is not balanced experience comes from deep within the awareness. This singularity of focus is the controlling factor allowing the planet to remain within the orbital pattern of the solar system. What is perceived as gravity as it relates to the magnetism of the planet does not apply to the planets as they orbit within the solar system. This is a higher application of the law of attraction, or like being attracted to like. When there is similar criteria involved in the creative focus that brings a system into manifestation, that similarity is the basis for remaining within the field of focus. Inasmuch as there is a natural over unity flow of energy accumulated, the system continues to expand and additional planets are formed. The process involved is not the point, only that you grasp the understanding that your scientists cannot understand what is at the basis of manifested creation without understanding the basic laws of the universe and the principle of thought thinking and acting upon itself independent of control. Once this basis is accepted, then the door to understanding is opened. It was never meant for man to gaze in wonder at what surrounds him, but that he should understand. The human brain is but a radio receiver that is capable of tuning into the flow of knowledge ever present in the creative flow. The magnetic field surrounding each of you is like an antenna, but your acquired belief systems cause you to unplug from the universal station and instead plug only into the (5) sensual environment. The spiritual aspect of the hu(man), the god aspect of self-awareness, is unknown to you through the stressed importance of material manifestation and the distorted influence of your religions. The adventure you search in vain to find is found in exploring the journey of the spirit that you are into manifested experience and in finding its every expansive return trip. This explains why each goal attained is never enough, and more and more must be attempted or lapse into discouragement and plan instead for a trip to the city of golden streets to take up playing the harp on a local cloud.

Humanity as it knows itself on planet earth at this moment is experiencing a degree of utter frustration that is incredible indeed. This can be compared to a balloon filling at an exponential rate toward the explosive point. The master planners of control are watching for this bursting point and planning its expansion with what they believe to be great care. However, just as balloons from the same package burst at different air pressure levels, neither can they be sure what the exact bursting point may be. It is a matter of how this released energy is directed that is the important point. Will it be as they choose or can it be self-directed by the mass consciousness of the awareness inside that bubble? Could the energy within the bubble be redirected from frustration to creation and deflate the balloon? They have no contingency plan to deal with these possibilities. It only requires one small hole in the dike to destroy the dam. Several or even many small holes insure and speed the process. Why not one big explosion? Allowing weak points to expand is within the expansive flow of creation, while deliberate destruction is not. Considering possibilities within your own life experience is self-contemplation, again within the expansive flow of experience. Is the focus of applying the law of attraction and deliberate manifestation of the opportunity for the weaknesses in their plans to expand include the destruction of the ones who would enslave or end your earthly experience by their choice? It is suggested to consciously withdraw participation by focusing instead on an entirely different creation project that will simply transcend the planned disaster. This would leave the perpetrators holding the bag and experiencing the other side of the coin, as fits into the experience of the law of attraction through their own use of it. This would be a wonderful demonstration of the universal laws in concept and application.

The conceptualization of the simple changes in how a situation is perceived and using a change of the focus of intention, applying the universal laws that have brought forth the wholeness of manifested reality is a big stretch of your understanding of how "things really are." When you reread this material, ask for the spiritual aspect, the source of your manifestation into this life experience, to give you discernment. Ask to know if this material contains truth and what are the applications of these truths that will serve you, your fellow inhabitants and the planet. It is your right to know if this is guidance or trash. "Ask and it shall be given unto you." This statement was not given to bring you material things directly but that you might receive knowledge (information) to be experienced into wisdom. It is appropriate to continue to paraphrase, "unto those, much will be given and much will be expected." When understanding is given, you are expected to apply the laws and to live within them in ever expanding application and further understanding. "Ignorance is no excuse before the law." The laws work whether you understand them or not. Intelligent intentional application is the best bet for an adventure that will keep you delightfully occupied, depending on your ability to overview your own experiences and see them in context. Attitude does determine your altitude.

There are many puzzle pieces within these lessons that will be assembled by each serious endeavor to do so. Amazingly these completed puzzles will each be a unique piece that will fit into the puzzle at the next level. You exist within a dimensional whole. Even the pieces are dimensional rather than flat. A necessary shift in how you conceptualize is available as a stepping stone for greater understanding. When you add dimension and life, which is thought thinking, to the game board, it lights up. Through your imagination you can begin to perceive movement within flow. Nothing is lifeless or stagnant. Every quark, atom and molecule is pulsing with thought and movement. Nothing is truly flat or solid. You cannot walk through walls in your manifested body at the density of 68 MHz or less. This should not be a mystery. When your brain vibration is 90 MHz or less, you are unable to tune your radio like brain to the universal flow and receive the keys to the mysteries of galactic intentional focus. The possibilities of adventures leading to these experiences are encompassed within these lessons. Not all is directly presented for much is there to be contemplated and greater understandings brought forth through personal unique processes. Within the creators flow all uniqueness is divergent and cohesive. Two sides of the coin or should that be a visualization of something that is dimensional rather than flat, incorporating the polarities through expression and experience for the purpose of returning to balance and adventuring forth again. The practice of discernment is an inclusive nuance of self-contemplation of experience for the purpose of gaining wisdom and moving on into further expansion. A wise practice to apply frequently.

No. 40

When the ending of the millennium does occur, it does not do this on the date of your calendar. The cycles are not required to follow your calendar of the seasons. The basis of the cycles is not from the earth prospective but from what you call the zodiac as earth passes from one influence of the 12 aspects of experience to the next. The starting place of each planet's trip through these influences does not follow the conclusions drawn by astrologers but is determined by the mathematical equation of the solar system as it synchronizes with the master equation of the galaxy. It may then be assumed that the true ending of the millennium cycle is unknown other than in a general sense, and it is close to your calculated time, give or take a few months. The cycles shift at higher levels as the "heavenly bodies" (observable in the night sky, which is nearly impossible because of artificial lighting), **all moving in cycles** reach points for repetition to begin. This indicates ending and beginning within the conceptualization of finite thinking that is confined to the lower realms of dimensional experience. Each cycle may be thought of as a portion of a breathing process allowing for a rest period or at time spent at the zero point of balance before the shift. The zero (rest) point is the point at which each manifested creation partakes of an energy "feeding" process, or a gathering of new energy before it moves into the new cycle.

It is this available energy that the devious ones plan to utilize combining it with the separated soul energy they plan to gather. They perceive this will supply an additional over unity boost to bring about their planned shift from positive to negative. They also perceive that the control they are exerting will be accepted as the balance necessary for the energy transfer to occur at the resting point of the cycle shift. Magicians assume that their tricks are accepted as real by observers caught up in the process. Unfortunately for them, they are the ones caught up in their own deception. The creator and the creation do not observe the darkness of deception for all thoughts and plans are known.

Glaring reasons that humanity as it now experiences cannot in this moment exist in the higher dimensions are that thoughts and emotions are available to be read by all. Deception is impossible because intentions are fully known. This brings personal responsibility as the basis for higher dimensional experience into the light of logical understanding. Individuals sharing the same dimensional experience screen out harmonious thought to allow balanced group experience. Focused thoughts are known and then what you call mental telepathy eliminates the need to slow the vibratory rate to vocalize thoughts. Since all at this level are consciously aware that their shared intention is participating in their return trip to the source of their own creation, the transition is not fraught with difficulty. Are their deviations? Of course, but normally these are worked through in a supportive environment. It is rare that an individual must be returned to a lower dimension.

As you begin to understand a larger picture of this point in the history of your planet and the segment of humanity that now resides on it, you can pinpoint your own experience within the scenario. If indeed you are a volunteer who has placed itself in a lower dimensional experience in order to assist the individuals trapped there, then it hardly seems fair that you must be bound by the confines of that dimension. Unfortunately that is how it works. However, it was understood when you volunteered to do this, there would be a point that you would be fully reminded who and what you are and of the agreement you made. In other words you were promised a wake up call. This is your wake up call.

No. 41

Now that this information has begun to be absorbed into your consciousness and the subconscious levels of your awareness is rearranging to allow an attitude adjustment; a new focus is developing. The world you observe is changing before your eyes. There are three levels of awareness developing, the facade as presented to you, the activities of the magicians and the refocusing of the mass consciousness of the planet inhabitants. The first two layers of simultaneous awareness were present within your psyche, but were blurry and distorted. Examining them with some detail has allowed clarity and understanding, adding the third brings forth a realization that you are indeed standing on the first rock of the projects planned diversion. Now it is decision time. Do you participate and continue in sharing a clear picture of the movie in progress all around you? This is a scenario rather than a scene. It is in motion all around you with all three activities interacting on the same stage all within depth, width and height. It goes without saying that the project is the least focused of the activities as yet. That is your job. The basic job description is present within these messages. The framework is there, it is your personal responsibility to "flesh out" the job. The freewill aspect is the ball in your court. Whether you pick it up or walk away is your choice.

Our part to play within this drama, tragedy, or love story (your choice) is to act as the producer of this production. The writing, directing and acting are your contributions. The producer provides the financing and the decisions as to whether the proposed script is something the backers (investors) will approve. If scriptwriters do not bring a proposed scenario to the producers, the producers may decide a certain theme would be saleable and solicit writers to contribute outlines. Since there have been no new paradigm novels, the theatre owner has instructed this producer to solicit new paradigm outlines, beginning with a statement of purpose setting the theme. This is your invitation to participate. Since this is a Cecil B. DeMille type production, collaboration is recommended.

The analogies used are not meant to make light of the situation, but to instill understanding at the subconscious levels of your awareness. Pictures are easily assimilated in clarity. Words are filtered through a myriad of individual past experiences, attitudes, opinions and all the programming each of you carries through the deliberate indoctrination you have received. Movies and television have been their tools of deception. However, the pictures that are brought forth by the imagination are far more powerful. For example, in your not too distant past there was storytelling of myths and legends that invoked the imagination. The current cartoons for children and movies have been provided to repress the inner imagination and stifle the creative instinct. Pictures program the subconscious. Pictures focused with the intent of reprogramming the subconscious accomplish this quickly.

Purposeful intent supported by resolve is focus. The planet and humanity continue to cry out for an end to this scenario, but only humanity can bring the end through the creation of a new plot, a new script and a new play. Freewill allows humanity the choice to continue the present movie or simply have the stage revolve to the next production.

However, there must be a new set (scene) on that stage so that audience participation can be invited to create this play of plays for the planet as a whole.

What more can be done is now out of our hands. The wake up calling is up to each of you as this message comes into your experience. Who is it that you *know* in your heart would resonate with the challenge focused through it? Will you dedicate yourself to this critical cause? Will you read and study the information with the intention of allowing its message to fill the void that resonates within you because of the deceptions of the dark magicians? When you think or speak the small prayer, "I am a human becoming, help me to become," ask for guidance through your feelings that you may know. You are calling forth the vibratory connection to your source, the cause of your life experience here and now. Lines of communication open, and seeming miracles begin to happen through coincidence and synchronicities. Most of all a calm and peaceful attitude becomes prevalent in your experience. Your countenance changes and you know who you are, why you are here and what is to be done in each moment. You have a purpose, a mission and there is hope for this planet after all.

No. 42

In the times that come, those of you who make the choice to become part of the wholistic transformation of this planet and its inhabitants will lead the way through the transformation of yourselves. Mankind is inspired by example not by words, written or spoken. Will you each be as famous as Mother Theresa? No indeed! Your example will be one of living the life of purposeful focus.

Each day your intent is to be a human becoming for the purpose of mankind becoming and the planet becoming. This commitment in unison will bring forth an aura of magnetism that will reflect in all aspects of your experience. Will it make you a millionaire? Probably not. Because your focus is to participate in the larger creative flow into an experience that will have parameters that are yet unknown. The basic concept on which all higher dimensions are based is in the understanding that the pivot point to upliftment into evolving consciousness is the unified focus of returning to the level of the creator.

The "one-upmanship" of accumulating and maintaining material wealth is a moot point. During the period of chaos facilitating the transition, those with intent to assist in the birthing of the new paradigm, rather than the maintenance of values to be transcended, will be assisted in having available what is needed to superintend facets of organization that are necessary. These will not be in the focus of leadership, but of setting the ideal or archetype of cooperation. Once before, a question was asked for your contemplation. You were asked if you could conceptualize a system in which there were no levels of leadership of hierarchy because they were unnecessary. Unity of focus based on personal responsibility to fulfill the harmonious (shared) goal of "becoming" through individual experience sets up a cooperative environment. Cooperation replaces competition and fear is no longer present. The accumulation of wealth is motivated by the desire for protection which is based in fear of what the future may hold and fed by the empowered ego through competition. "He who dies with the most toys wins" is an apt illustration of this imbalance. "It is easier for a loaded camel to go through the eye of the needle (cultural reference to the small people gate into a town or a house compound) than for a rich man to enter heaven (a state of contentment)." This is true not because of the material things that are accumulated, but because of the basic attitudes that motivate him/her. Retirement funds are necessary because these same attitudes and beliefs bring on disease and degeneration of the body, illustrating the basic lack of trust in the creator's flow that birthed you into this life experience. In a nutshell, the moment you are born, you are taught to beginning swimming upstream against the flow of creative expansion. It is now time that you climb out on a rock, take a good look around and then begin swimming within the expansive flow. It is so much easier and "in-joy-able."

Swimming with the flow allows the focus of "becoming" to be thought acting within and upon itself. The resulting harmonious experience is that of being wholly supported in that quest. To accomplish this within an environment of humanity swimming in the opposite direction is impossible unless it is accomplished within a cooperating group that is literally out of that flow. Pulling ones self out of that flow, up on to the rock, carefully perceiving the situation and making the decision to enter the greater flow of the galaxy that is moving within creative expansiveness brings you to a level out of that struggling mass. Once the initial group begins this action by freewill choice, many will join by increasing numbers and a new flow is formed joining the galactic flow. As those of the masses, literally wearing themselves out by spending their creative energy within the struggle, observe your life moving smoothly and easily along within that flow, your mission of reversing the flow will be well under way.

Your return ticket receives its first punch when you pull yourself out and stand on the rock and observe the situation from the level of accepting the situation as reality within the 3rd dimensional realm of planet earth. The next punch in your ticket is received when you make your choice/commitment bring forth a new paradigm of experience. The next is received when you begin the move within your consciousness and change your life expression through thought and action in harmony with your commitment to bring forth this new paradigm of experience with the inhabitants and the planet. You the know the purpose of your incarnation at the fully conscious level and the empty wondering will cease. You then will live in fulfillment of your purpose. To choose otherwise is tearing up your ticket. Can you get a new one? Later maybe, but you will have missed your intended purpose and your intended opportunity.

Reread, contemplate, pray and decide! Freewill is your privilege and your responsibility. Use it in wisdom!

Dear Messengers,

Now that the handbook is complete, it is time that we turned the intention of this flow of information toward the next phase to follow. As the momentum begins to grow, not so much at the actual manifestation level as within the intentions to participate, the idea dawns that a crisis point exists. Our pebble in the pond of the mass consciousness, that no doubt seems ever so tiny to you, is indeed powerful. The shift in perception is the most important beginning point possible. This bypasses the negative emotions of anger and the desire to retaliate. Your bible states "Vengeance is mine, sayeth the Lord." This is a total untruth, but does contain the advice to leave the law of attraction to its natural action. Your misunderstood karmic law, as quoted when there is the desire for someone to get their "just due," is indeed a distorted reference to the law of attraction. When quoting it in judgment it applies in that instance also. "Thou shalt not judge, lest you be judged." The law of allowance would be wisely used instead as in "I am a human becoming, help me to become." Or "They are humans becoming, help them to become, or he/she is a human becoming, help him/her to become." Indeed this prayer for others is sharing the gift of grace and is allowance indeed! This introduces the next level in the shift in human consciousness, beyond self, to include others through allowance, thereby transcending the need to control.

It is important, when working within the focus intended to be inclusive of the mass consciousness of the entire planet, to forgo the desire to quote rules and regulations. These do not sell well, especially with the diversity of understandings within the consciousness of 7+ billion beings. Back to the basic of basics in simplistic language that is easily translatable with as little distortion as possible is most logical. KISS is indeed the rule. Acronyms are interesting shortcuts to recognition. Perhaps we could invent AIAB for attraction, intention, allowance, and balance, or FSTF for the 1st, 2nd, 3rd and 4th. In order to cross language, cultural and religious barriers, simplistic applications must teach the basic laws without formalities. They must he practically applicable in all life situations and bring forth the desired shift in perspective that translates into changes of attitude and consciousness. It is possible to do this with a few simple words that include AIAB. This seems paradoxical in a world of overwhelming numbers of communications literally moving faster than the speed of light. Of course, overwhelming is the key. The paradox includes the haves who long for greater simplicity and the have-nots who long for greater complexity. The inner void remains at all points on the scale of human experience on this planet, except for those who are now aware of the creation of the new paradigm.

It is the first instinct when encountering these messages for individuals to want to rush to "the mission" before study and contemplation bring forth the necessary, fundamental, basic changes in consciousness that allow for synchronistic encounters with people and information to bring into their awareness what their part is. For multitudes, the change in perspective and attitude through the use of the simple prayer is all that is required. These will reap the miracles of a richer life experience, in the midst of chaos, through their focus on the intent within the wave of new consciousness. Spreading the message (word) and applying the basics in their daily lives is the most important mission of all. <u>If applying these is not done at the fundamental levels of human experience, then all the messages are to no avail whatever!</u> These are the ripples. What good are pebbles if the pond remains static? <u>The victim consciousness must be transcended so that humanity can take back its power.</u>

When you share the gift of this information, you must be able to supply feed back to those who receive these messages and reply in a <u>reactive</u> mode. The pent up desire for change is released and direction needs to be given to those who rush to you for guidance. Personal responsibility is another way of saying "take your power and use it with intentional focus to bring balance." The balanced state of experience is necessary to be a functioning part of the ground team. Rereading, studying, contemplating and applying what is within the messages through personal experience will prove the validity of the information and bring forth balance within chaos. The ground team has space for those who are awake, aware, committed, focused and balanced. This brings forth the ability to act rather than react. If it is not yet time for individuals to act, then encourage them to continue to study, share the message and be within the rippling effect while they wait patiently. <u>This is the space you must occupy to be functional and ready. It is putting oil in your lamp so that it may be lit in the moment of opportunity.</u> So, *become* this consciousness!

Embracing the Rainbow
Volume II

II-1

There has been a great deal of interest in the independent activities of the people who have received and read the copies of the message and the handbook. As expected, the reactions have been mixed between total acceptance and total rejection. However, the overall impact has been gratifying and effective. There are indeed lights of understanding beginning to be discernable on many parts of the planet.

The assimilation and application of the concepts will accelerate the acceptance of the principles involved and through their application the desire for greater understanding will be increased. Therefore, an opening will be created that will allow for movement toward the goal of a new paradigm and it will begin to manifest. When the time is ripe for greater expansion of the concept of a new experience for mankind, the information leading to the next step will be ready for distribution. Once the transition is made away from victim consciousness toward the acknowledgement of personal power through alignment with the originating expansive flow of creative energies, the thirst for greater understanding will be aroused. The misunderstanding of looking outward for answers is deeply ingrained and will require de-programming and education of how to apply this concept to daily living in order to allow it to become a new foundation for manifested reality.

Without adequate changes at deep levels of the psyche and application of the previous explained universal laws, the next levels of understanding will be nothing more than another exercise in entertainment. Much of the valuable information disseminated through other receivers has become an addiction for fanaticizing with little or no application in practical living experience. The focus has been toward survival of the physical body so that the same ideals and life style could be maintained until individuals could ascend (arise out of) rather than transcend (go beyond). The focus must be more wholistic and include survival for service aimed at lifting the yoke of darkness and descending vibratory experience from humanity and the planet rather than be focused on individual escape from the morass of a destructive situation. In other words, there must be participation in a solution rather than using the information to abandon the ship.

Once the goal is identified in a statement, then what comes next? What are the guidelines for participation that will ensure that transcendence through to experience the new paradigm? This will be the focus of the next level of information. Much material has been disseminated indicating that rescue and reform will be provided by extraterrestrial beings and all humanity has to do is to meditate and wait around for magical processes to change everything for them. It would be wise not to count on it. There is a saying. "God helps those that help themselves." That is a truth to put in a dozen places to remind you to let go of the "I am a victim that needs to be rescued" consciousness. **You will be helped but victims will not be rescued. Victim consciousness vibrates below the necessary levels to enter higher dimensions.**

Giving up victim consciousness is a personal decision. It is not an easy process. If you rescue, you become a victim of the rescued. Sympathizing with those who are locked into victim consciousness supports their victimhood and ties you to them. Discernment allows you to recognize the situation and at that point you must acknowledge that this is a situation that is of their own creation through their belief that others control their choices. This does not mean that you must ignore their plight, but does determine that you cannot do for them what they are unwilling to do for themselves. There is not a rule of thumb for how to give wise assistance to them. Their plight is a result of the personal decisions they have made and the attitudes that have influenced those decisions. Remember, they are human beings becoming or not, by their own choice. Teach them the prayer and remind them of it in the midst of their miseries and tactfully suggest other viewpoints to them as you become aware of them. With the application of the "becoming" prayer, opportunities will abound for them.

The critical point for the next step in the transcendence process follows the acceptance of the personal ability to move through victim consciousness by accepting responsibility for using the universal laws to take charge of their manifested experience. This does not mean that each must become a millionaire to prove they have accomplished this. In truth, most will find that abundance is measured by the inner feelings of self-approval and confidence that precludes the necessity of impressive material demonstrations for ego aggrandizement. What you do with regard to self and others is more important than what you have. When this is accomplished all that is necessary is attracted without effort, for each is then encompassed within the expansive flow of creation.

To become is the goal of all. How this is to be accomplished is uniquely experienced through freewill choice. Help is available. The asking must be for help not rescue or to piggyback on someone else's accomplishment. Each must know theirs is a unique experience not to be compared to others. Each incarnation is for their own particular soul purpose to be created through their choices and decisions. There are no mistakes other than to remain closed to seemingly new concepts and continue to repeat the current experience for lack of discernment of the connection to that which has focused each into manifestation. That connection vibrates within the awareness of every human and is ignored or responded to with each and every choice and decision. It is our goal to trigger the awareness of this connection in every human possible through direct connection or through changes in the mass conscious awareness on a planetary level, using what you refer to as the 100th monkey theory. First and foremost is transcendence of the victim consciousness into personal responsibility.

This process will require that individuals separate themselves from those refusing to change their perceptions and to align themselves with others who are willing to make this change. When lives begin to change as a result of accepting and using personal responsibility through the application of the universal laws, those previously unwilling to change will again choose to follow suit or not. Remember that freewill is the loose cannon of the 3rd dimension and the freedom to choose is made by *all* whether they admit it or not. Though it may seem that the victim/personal responsibility theme is being nauseatingly repeated, it is the foundation upon which the format for transcendence to the higher dimensions is built. It is the rock from which the foundation is quarried. It is the first step that begins the journey. Lip service is easy. It is in the doing that the proof of the pudding lies. How it is accomplished is between each person and the creative aspect that focused each into manifestation. Through the intuitive understandings that this connection fosters, each will find their purpose and the path of their journey. In the asking for help the opportunities that genuinely "feel" right will present themselves. Incorrect choices will be difficult and bring little satisfaction. Asking for discernment brings knowingness and other opportunities to pursue. A house will stand on a rock foundation and allow for layer upon layer of brick to be added. To begin, you must begin at the beginning.

II-2

The bible has a reference to two standing in a field, one is taken and the other is left behind. Does this support the belief that there will be an evacuation of part of humanity by space ships? In this case, the reference could be applied to a faith in the creative process and to coming into alignment with the expansive self-contemplative flow of energy that births each soul expression into manifested experience. When that alignment reaches a degree of compatibility that allows for a transition to higher dimensional experience, the transfer can be completed during the life experience. It "can" but it is a rare happening when the planetary whole is vibrating at the present rate. It has been a long time since that has taken place, contrary to some circulating stories. This is not to say that some blending experiences have not happened. Insofar as massive space ship removals of humans from this planet, as has been circulated, contemplate 7+ billion beings and consider how many ships with facilities for them this would take and the answer is obvious. If humanity, experiencing as they are now, were transferred to another planet, there would be two planets in trouble instead of just one.

Each and every being on this planet came with the purpose of bringing the situation here into alignment with the cosmic plan of freewill experience leading to balance. That constitutes a lot of intention. That intention is there to be tapped in order to bring this situation to completion. When humanity, or at least a significant portion of it, can go *through* this situation and heal it themselves, then and only then can they move through their intention to come into balance. In the greater picture of each soul's evolvement, none would choose to be rescued. At the base of the rescue stories lies the victim consciousness. Does this render those messages false? That is for your discernment. Always there is truth to be found, and it is different for each. Ask the knowing part of self for discernment and proceed from that point to consider and you will know.

The presence of an energy cycle called the photon belt is circulating. It has been reported as being seen as a doughnut shaped energy field near the Pleiades star system. Does it really exist? Indeed, it does and calling it a cycle is the key to what it truly is. Regardless of what has been "seen," it is a transition of movement between the polar experiences of positive and negative, your terms. This experiencing has been pictured by many as a pendulum type movement from one extreme to the other. This would be appropriate in linear thought; however, higher dimensions are not experienced in a linear process. Since the great part of experience is in higher dimensional expression, the explanation must be thought of in holographic terms. Religious writings contain some references to wheels within wheels that indicate there are multiple cycles that are in motion and interfacing with each other. This brings to mind the workings of a mechanical watch. However, now you have watches that keep perfect time without those wheels. In this way, cycles can also be in process that are not necessarily circular in motion. Even though circular motion is observed going on around you, such as the motion of the solar system, and the zodiac, from the greater holographic prospective, these circular motions are spiral rather than circular, allowing for the expansiveness of the creative energies. If indeed, they were circular, then all that is would be static rather than expansive. This would limit evolvement and as you can easily contemplate, boredom and death would indeed be truth. From this perspective, you can now understand the importance of expansiveness as being at the basis of creation and how evolvement is a natural constituent of experience. With this as a frame of reference, you can begin to grasp that the spiral is accomplished by interlacing the polarities with the circular motion to widen the circle and to either lift or lower the continuity. The shift of energies that are necessary to accomplish the transition between the polarities is something like an electrical charge. It is accomplished by entry and passage through an energy field that causes a change in polarity. These energy fields are also in motion and move through the galaxy in cycles that coordinate with all other cycles with mathematical precision.

Planet earth is now poised at the transition point of several cycles. This is an occurrence that does not happen frequently and is of great interest to this portion of the galaxy. The result of these coinciding cycles is that the transition between polarities will be of greater impact and import enhanced by the fact that the consciousness of the beings and the planet poised to do this. These are not at the level of evolvement that was intended through the failure to make the transitions that were available in the last approximately 26,000-year cycle. Added to this, is the deliberate plan of the adversarial forces to disrupt the cycle transition into deliberate chaos intending to continue the negative polarity cycle for their own purposes. This then brings into understanding the necessity for the humans on this planet to make a leap in consciousness in order to survive this transition of energies into the next cycle by coming together in a mass consciousness that has a combined focus of an increased frequency. The upliftment through the release of victim consciousness into personal responsibility is the shift that would accomplish this necessary change. The degree of shift in the mass consciousness will determine the intensity of the planetary experience at a point within the energy field you call the photon belt and the ability of humanity to experience the transition through it.

It will also determine the ability of the adversarial plan to accomplish its purposes. Needless to say, their plan will never be allowed to be successful, but the question remains as to what part earth's inhabitants will play and where the soul awareness will find itself when the scenario plays out. It must be emphasized here that the ground crew is included in this drama, volunteering to help also carries with it the responsibility of becoming part of the destiny of the planetary consciousness. There will be no rescue. Each will rise or fall within that destiny. This then fuels the necessary commitment and focus of energy in helping humanity to accomplish this last-ditch effort to come into vibratory alignment.

II-3

When the time comes for the changes to begin in earnest with regard to the change of governmental focus, there will be an outcry by the citizens. Measures are planned so that the individual will be overwhelmed and unable to react in any way but to submit. It is expected that they will grovel before the god that is on his throne far away and think that they are being punished for some great sin, in other words, play the victim. The inner strength of the focus of the soul has been totally disregarded. The planned shock of overwhelming the citizens as a whole has been analyzed and studied to bring forth the reaction that is desired. As in all experiments, the outcome is influenced by the expectations of those setting up the criteria. The "scientific" data so prized by the scientists of this era is as accurate as the opinions of the moment allow. Thus, as new possibilities are considered, the old theories crumble eventually and are replaced. This indicates that the possibility exists that the expected reactions of humanity might indeed be replaced by *actions* that do not fit their planned scenario.

Mankind has been taught to distrust his fellow beings. Few have any realization of the interconnections that exist through the sharing of the source of their manifestation into experience. Since all are emanations of the creator focus in self-contemplation, you can rely on the fact that there are connections that are unknown and power within these connections that is wholly untapped. We have previously discussed the concerns of the situation as it presently exists on this planet and the importance of the convergence of the cycles with regard to the importance of the transitions that are available. It has been emphasized that all levels of consciousness including the creator are focusing upon this process. At this sequential place in the scenario, watchfulness is all that is being focused. However, when it is appropriate you may be assured that activation of latent abilities that are available within the consciousness and the physical structure of the human body can and will be stimulated.

The ability to receive this stimulation and accomplish what will be needed will depend upon the conscious awareness and in particular the ability to accept self-empowerment within a wholistic pattern of behavior. The energies that will be encountered in the approach to and passage into what you refer to as the photon belt will not be the same as are being experienced now. The last of the current polarity cycle is reaching its completion. Here again it is difficult to put into linear terms for your understanding processes that are of a holographic nature. Within a holographic framework, all is interactive within a cooperative format. When an imbalance is present all that remains in balance becomes focused to regain the balance of the whole. There is a generation of interactive energies to awaken latent connections to bring forth whatever is necessary to allow the return to balance. We return again to the understanding that thought has the capability to think. All that is manifest in all forms is thought into being from pure potentiality and is interactive within itself; this is a natural process. In its simplest explanation, each human is a thought that thinks and therefore is self-aware. As above, so it is below. The entire galaxy, and more, is thought that thinks and is self-aware.

The goal of the new paradigm in simple terms is the transition of humanity from victim consciousness into self-empowerment, which will result in a rise in the vibratory emanation of the planet and its inhabitants. Planting the means to make this transition is the goal of this segment of the ground team. Once planted and released to accomplish its intended effect, the stimulation of the latent connections will move it through the mass consciousness to all humans able to accept and begin to function within its concepts. The next step to follow will be the spread of the understanding of the four basic universal laws and the application of these within each individual experience. These concepts are included in the handbook and once the critical few begin to study and practice them; more latent connections will begin to open to the stimulation that will be coming to the planet with increasing frequency.

It is easy to get caught up in the fear of what might happen based on the present consciousness of the planetary inhabitants. However, it is important to stay within the understanding that this consciousness is ripe for change and that it is now underway. There are other ground teams accomplishing their assignments that dovetail and provide the holographic synthesis that is now taking shape. The situation is not hopeless, but is encouraging indeed! As each member has been stimulated into awakening to their assignments and have proceeded, most times through the need to do whether it made any logical sense or not, so also will that process spread through the mass consciousness. You have been programmed to distrust your humanness. Through empowering the personal self, it is necessary that you choose to trust the empowerment of your fellow man. Will there be exceptions? Yes, there will. One of the latent functions that will be stimulated will be discernment. You will know and when you trust the process, those will not be encountered. Victim consciousness will draw victim experience through the law of attraction. Those who move to self-empowerment in a holistic way will continue to evolve into greater experience and be drawn together to create the new paradigm.

This is not a message of deception. You are thought capable of thinking. There is a group consciousness that thinks. You can change your mind (thinking) and so can it. It is a matter of seeding the process with an alternative that has powerful appeal. Once put into usage its power increases, especially if it receives additional input from the concerned foci of greater levels of manifested awareness. Physical manifestation is an end result of focused thought. If through choice and request the focused thought is changed, then the physical manifestation must also change.

This understanding is easy to forget with the continued input of mind controlling data that is purposefully focused into daily experience. This is the reason each is encouraged to continue to reread and study the handbooks. The information is simple, direct and contains no techniques other than offering a solution that dovetails within the flow of expansive energies that maintain all creation and allow it to continue within the universal laws. The freewill aspect is both the thorn and the blossom of the process. It is the vital emanation of creative energy. It has at its essence both positive and negative polarity and is not bound by cycles. The polarities are available on the whim of decision which allows it to alter creation at the manifested level. Freewill cannot be controlled. It can be influenced, but at any point, individual consciousness can simply change its thinking and the influence is cast aside. Thought can create an experience and thought can change it into another experience entirely. Combined focus of thought is all-powerful when it operates within the universal laws and is supported by emotional commitment. The return to self-empowerment following the experience of containment and victim experiences will bring forth an emotional sensation to the soul that equates to the joy so often spoken of by religions. Just as love and hate cannot share the same heart, neither can joy and a victim perception share the same experience. The courage to choose comes as the responsibility of humanity to create its experience, in this instance with all possible help available for the asking.

II-4

There was a time in which the beings on this planet resided elsewhere in the galaxy. Not in the present body, but you would say these were your ancestors. Mankind did not originate on this planet. To those who currently believe that you came into being out of some primordial soup, this shall be an affront to that theory. However, through consideration of the laws of the universe, remember that creation is possible through intent and purpose. Development of body, mind, spirit and emotion does not fit into the criteria of random selection as a possible scenario. Indeed the physical body does match the physical attributes of the earth mineral content, but that is through the law of attraction that allows for adaptation within the environment. The marvel of the human body is that it has adaptive capabilities that make it possible to survive in hostile environments. This is surely being proven by the introduction of purposeful chemical abrasive combinations and vibrational variations designed to destroy it. The plan being that only the most adaptive will survive and be useful in further experimental adaptation and exploitation. Resistance to a negative environment allows for adaptation and can be stimulation to either advancement or regression, depending on the degree and the focus of the individual desire to move through the experience.

This possibility can now be discussed openly as the subject of extraterrestrial presence has been the subject of extensive media presentation. Though many older people still resist the possibility, most children accept it as true and dream of traveling to take part in other planetary experiences. Much of this is presented because of the belief that there is little left to be known about this planet and that adventure will soon be found only by exploring the space beyond. The popularity of the long-standing Star Trek series exemplifies this. The information as to the monumental number of solar systems that frequent this galaxy and the presence of numerous other galaxies that are being observed makes the possibility of other life supporting planets refute the assumption that this is the only planet with conscious life. Yet to be known is a way to construct and power appropriate craft to enable humans to traverse space. With the number of inhabitants draining the life force of this planet, the possibility seems beyond reach.

Indeed, humanity is at a crossroads of multiple levels of experience. How indeed are they going to come *through* this crisis?

Obviously not without help! In their arrogant stubbornness will they ask for it and accept it, if it is given? That can only answered as the situation progresses. As has been pointed out before, help cannot be given to those locked in victim consciousness. The solution lies in humanity creating its own solution and victims cannot accomplish this because of their desire to be rescued. Rescue demands that someone or something outside themselves accomplish whatever feat is required. Again the discussion returns to the same realization that a choice in how to experience manifested life faces the inhabitants of this planet. It is no longer survival of the fittest, but survival of the personally responsible.

The opposite experience of the victim is currently achieved as exercising power over other victims and has become an unending chain of interlocking experience for an incredibly long duration. That chain is long overdue to be broken. Its strength lies in the failure of those involved to choose another way of experiencing. Without the awareness and understanding of the universal laws that support successful evolving life experience, the chain remains unbroken. Humanity can change this longstanding experience, break the chain and return to the evolving citizenship of the galaxy/universe by choosing responsibility and applying the laws in their daily experience both individually and as a group. Because of the presence of polarity, when those are drawn together as a group this also repels those who choose otherwise, and a great division is made. The application of the laws creates a cooperative situation that allows for protection from the fear of the actions of the other groups in most surprising ways. The vibration increases rapidly and protective means are most creative indeed.

The question arises from a point of overview, if victim consciousness is present in our experience, then is it present within the consciousness of the creator? The obvious answer is yes. The creator is in self-contemplation for self-evolvement. At this level, the tiniest imbalance must be fully understood and cleared. You are that clearing process. When you move through it and arrive at personal responsibility, another phase of that imbalance is resolved. A wisely pruned vineyard produces a prolific healthy crop. Once this imbalance is pruned from your experience, yours will be a healthy and prolific experience!

It is not our purpose to assail the current beliefs in a frontal attack causing resistance and stress, but to give a gradual and convincing alternative to lives that have been lived in frustration and grim survival. Ending lives in pain and disease is demonstration of the soul consciousness of the denial of a solution by those experiencing this descending cycle of manifested circumstances. What appears as a complex and impossible situation has a simple solution. A change of attitude and application of simple understandable laws will provide the passageway through to new experience. Creation does not provide for suffering to buy anything but more suffering. It is a freewill choice. Therefore, it is time to opt for a new experience by giving up what does not work and has not worked for an eon of sequential episodes.

The laws of attraction, intention and allowing used purposely through freewill choice are the criteria that will allow for the freedom of humanity and its return to full galactic citizenship and the ability to travel freely. Failure to follow these guidelines will require placement of those individuals into another learning situation. You are being offered the opportunity to begin again with the basics and incorporate them into your experience and surge ahead in a leap of consciousness that is unparalleled. How sad it will be if you stubbornly refuse to take advantage of the opportunity.

II-5

At the time of the greatest experience of chaos there will be moments of discouragement and wondering if any of this material was of value. It is then that each of the members of this ground team must hold fast to the understanding that change cannot and does not happen if the old structures remain in place. Therefore, it is exactly through this chaos that the new paradigm of experience will come into being and it will not be long in manifesting. When the outline of it is held in place in the hearts and minds of the dedicated and committed humans that desire the replacement of the old with the adventure of the new, it will come quickly. There will be those who will falter, but with at least one of every cell group having the strength to hold tightly to the commitment, the cell will hold together and the focus will be held.

Many have questioned how that, in the meetings of the groups held worldwide, a single statement could arise from the many dream scenarios. Here we have the necessity of invoking the creator presence at each group interaction. In the creator self-contemplation process, each and all are known intimately. Inasmuch as at the point of inception of the entirety of the process there is one mind, one focus, then by invoking the focus that knows itself, one focus of truth is the inevitable outcome. Through this process an experience of the "oneness" that has been touted will indeed be experienced. Lip service has been given to this, but what it truly is has yet to be experienced in this dimension of consciousness. It has been described as "enlightenment, a feeling of being one with all." These few who have felt one with nature, etc., have not brought mankind one bit closer to each other. The creator wants his self-aware aspects to come into a *knowing through actual experience* of this greatest of all experiences. When a committed portion of humanity can come together in a single focus of purpose and truly commune with the creator energy, then oneness with each other will indeed be experienced and a leap in consciousness will follow and will enliven this project in ways beyond imagination.

As has been mentioned before, there is no reason that the creator cannot use every situation as a springboard for greater creation. When you contemplate the above scenario, knowing the ripple effect, can you imagine the experience of this leap in consciousness spreading throughout creation and what effect it could have? Now you have a reason to believe that this is indeed an auspicious opportunity for mankind and one not to be missed! The issue of separation has been experienced throughout this galaxy in a festering of negative actions between individuals, nations and planets long enough to be thoroughly contemplated and it is now time to resolve it and move beyond and into new adventures and opportunities.

This is a short discussion and one that needs careful and in-depth consideration. Hold this information at the center of your personal commitment for your participation and focus. It is the reason that you made this decision to take the risk of being a member of the ground crew.

II-6

We are now ready to begin the adaptation of the human spirit to include a greater evolution and the pivotal turn to begin the return path to the creator than has been the current experience. These have been considered the experience of saints and most times simply not acknowledged or even known. Adaptations to the body have been made in the past within the genetics of the physical body itself and through the addition of vibratory implants. These have left a residue of effects that have in turn influenced the spiritual aspect. These changes have limited the vibrational connections to the focused source that has brought each into their physical expression. The genetic changes that were forcibly imposed on the human body were such that they have been inherently passed from one generation to the next and adaptation has not transcended all of these. Even the implants that caused great trauma have left their influence within the molecular memories of the cells and have been retained for generations. Modern man has been programmed to deny that humanity in its present physical form is very old indeed. It has indeed acquired some changes that do not serve it well at all.

From the larger aspect, the planet also suffers from similar changes that cripple its ability to function properly. It is time to bring these back into balance. Since it is apparent that neither the human body nor the planet are able to make these repairs in a fashion that is timely enough for the transitional opportunity, then help is necessary. In our previous discussions the process of thought manifesting into physical experience using the law of intentional focus explained that thought held with purposeful intention allows for manifestation. The intended thought through visualization of it in completion and vibratory stimulation of it through emotion, held firmly in place by commitment brings manifestation. Because the vibratory energies are at a low rate for manifested experience on this planet, the time necessary to manifest into form perceivable through 5 sensual experiences is slow indeed.

However, you are further reminded of the awareness of the planetary situation that is being observed by the galactic neighbors, most of whom are existing in a higher vibrational state of existence than planet earth. It is perfectly acceptable for the humans on this planet to invoke their help to manifest a change in the human body to accommodate the correction of the vibrational matrix of the human body and return it to its *intended pattern*. This request for help would require only a small number of human beings to enlist this help. It is something the ground crew could do inasmuch as they are now experiencing as 3rd dimensional human beings.

This would allow them to be the first to make the vibrational transition and to allow them to establish the ideal; the return of the archetype as it was originally created within the galactic equations. This then becomes the second major assignment of the ground crew. It is a simple statement within the positive prayer/mediations of each member remembering that this includes the grateful appreciation that this archetype already exists and is manifesting in perfection for each and *every* human body wherever it presently exists. It is important here to note that the archetype allows for evolution toward greater perfection of higher vibratory experience and this return to the archetype will not cause a problem for those who have achieved these changes.

This process allows for humanity to tap into the energies that are awaiting an opportunity to participate in resolving this situation and provides those assisting the greater opportunity to participate in the energy transition of the cyclical spiral of ascendance. Indeed, this provides the inclusion that is desired. Participation is by invitation only and you will be providing this opportunity. It is suggested that you contemplate the possibilities of this situation.

Reread this information as necessary in order to grasp the magnitude of this opportunity for all that are involved, including your pivotal role. Each can obviously realize that each is an extraordinary being with very specific commitments to complete as the sequence of divine order unfolds in personal experience and of the planet as a whole. The opportunity to "become" is ripe with promise in return for focused intention, purposeful follow through, and creational application of the suggestions contained within these communiqués.

II-7

As each of you became involved within this focus and began the process of composing your individual thoughts to contribute a possible statement of purpose, it became obvious to you that the simple statement required to appeal to all of mankind was not simple to arrive at. In the moment of this writing it has not yet come forth. The prayer of becoming is not yet widely known. This invocation can set the stage for opening the consciousness to perceive the statement when it is brought forth. The change in consciousness by those using the prayer with diligence in their daily life is interesting to observe. When it is further combined with a conscious clearing of accumulated negative attitudes and letting go of false doctrines from the awareness, it brings about clearly detectable vibrational increases observable by each individual. As the individual vibrations increase, the ability to connect with the source of each is enhanced. The connection itself begins to enliven and allow the body to receive a greater quantity of supportive energy. It is as though this flow of vital energy has been squeezed or pinched so that the flow is barely enough to maintain life. Contrary to what is taught, without this flow of energy from the source that focused each into being, life cannot be maintained in the body. At the center of each focus of awareness and within the physical body is a connecting point that receives this energy flow. When this flow of energy is broken or withdrawn, death occurs. The more intense the negative energies that are active in the body such as anger, fear, hate, etc., the less energy the body itself is able to receive of the already diminished flow. As these are intentionally released, the invocation of help "to become" re-activates the connection with each additional repetition.

You, the ground crew, are the guides in the setting up of the suggested procedures to uplift your fellow humans in the very near future. It is you that demonstrate the feasibility of these proposals and have input as to the viability of these reminders and suggestions. Reminders and suggestions are exactly what these messages contain. Since most humans now are lost within the complexity of their life experience amid the programmed onslaught of overwhelming control, it is obvious without help "being" let alone "becoming" is a lost cause. The numbers of inhabitants long ago became too overwhelming to consider removal as an option. This too has been planned for the universal laws for balanced life, including those regarding procreation, were deliberately convoluted and withheld. Warlike tendencies were over-stimulated from the natural instinctual self-defense/survival modes of behavior. The review of imbalance could go on and on, but that is not the point. The point is that a U-turn must be made by humanity in order to come through this experience, but the major portions of minds are programmed to reject the suggestions to do so.

Thus we must reach those that are open or desperate enough to grasp at whatever straw might possibly lead them to a different possibility. Each of you determines whom these people might be and are relied upon to make contact with them in an expansive outreach effect. Meanwhile the births continue and the control program also expands its influence and effects. Within this situation, these messages attempt to give as much help as possible to assist in remembering whom and what you are and to guide each in personal adaptation and evolvement to the greatest extent possible. All this is being done through a type of dictation/translation/transcription process that has its limitations.

Behind this seemingly vague yet ambitious process is the impetus of the creator focused energy. It has seemingly decided that the self-contemplation process of control, violence and victim/martyrdom has reached the point of resolution and transcendence. This awareness is now moving through the vibratory levels of awareness and those in the 3rd dimension are to get the message one way or another. Each of you is now a Rowan and has the message in hand. The question is, not can you, but will you deliver it?

II-8

Listening to the media reports of the situation in the "world at large" each is given the impression that ominous events portend the future and nothing of great danger is eminent at the center of "democracy's bastions." Only distant areas of ethnic unrest are subject to volatile situations of violence. These areas are chosen to exploit because there are few people to people connections between the people of the USA and people in those countries. Yet through military "assistance" the USA is involved to a far greater degree than any of the other members of the UN coalition. With your approval of these acts by default, the perceived image of the USA has been transformed in the eyes of the world from the home of the brave and free to that of the home of the dark avenger, Satan. All this has taken place in a gradual transition that has been and continues to be purposely apparent in all areas of the world but in the USA. Those caught up in the aggression and those in the watching world assume that this transition has your full and complete approval. Understanding that communication as it now exists was birthed in the affluent USA, it is then assumed that surely its citizens are fully informed and therefore are the impetus of the transition into this aggressive mode. It is incomprehensible to those in the rest of the world that these citizens are as a whole unaware that the aggressive acts are anything but benevolent "help" for there is little if any frame of reference for what those in war torn areas are suffering.

Where are the stories of the military personnel that return home who could confirm this claim? Each sees but a small segment of the whole picture. Indoctrination and mind control within the military is far more sophisticated than is possible with the general public. After discharge from the military services and a period of time away from these practices many of those involved begin to disassociate from the mind control effects and find themselves mentally and emotionally unstable. Help, other than drugs, to sort out the indoctrinated "suggestions" from the actual experiences is unavailable through government agencies and many are unable to function in the civilian world. They are left with the choice to either rejoin the military or cope in whatever way they can. Few if any have the finances or are able to find outside psychiatric help that comprehends the basis of their dilemmas. The programming of your beloved children is carefully designed to fit the categories of the future roles they will play in these armed intrigues of aggression.

When we compare the overall understanding of this situation as a play, it is appropriate. Though it is presented as if there were unbalanced authors writing scenarios to be deliberately acted out, there is more truth involved than can be imagined! Presenting this information to you, it seems to come forth in a melodramatic tone and the immediate reaction is to refuse to consider that such massive delusion could be perpetrated on so many million people. Human nature is well known. Your reactions and beliefs are fully understood. Nothing has been left to chance in this well-planned game of illusion for the purpose of delusion. The USA is the ideal vehicle for this particular transition of global role reversal in as much as there are no long-standing ethnic animosities as are present in other areas of the planet. The black/white/native American issues are the only exploitable issues and they are not of such duration to bring about the same reactions as the Moslem/Jewish/Christian situations that are now in growing conflagration in the European and eastern countries.

At the base of this entire picture is the very "human nature" that has been so well examined and studied. Humanity has been led to spend its energies in the experience and exploration of the environment outside themselves. It is only in recent years that the medical/scientific community has begun to consider the understanding of the human physical body with sophisticated instrumentation. Unfortunately it has not been for the understanding itself, but because of the

influence of the dark perpetrators through the chemical companies
for the purpose of gain through treating symptoms of degenerating
human bodies. This is the result of an overall planned assault on
the human body to coincide with the natural consequences of the
effect of over-population. The research for the dark purposes will
seldom if ever be revealed, however some of what is learned by
dedicated medical researchers is being published. Genetic research
is much maligned and there is reason to be skeptical of the motives
involved in the manipulations that are now possible in the inherent DNA structures of the human body. Ethically focused research
could indeed bring about changes that would release mankind from
destructive patterns of behavior and of inherent pre-dispositions to
health problems and disabilities.

However, in the present global situation none of this is going
to work itself out in a time frame soon enough to assist in the present moment dilemma of humanity and planet Earth. Therefore, it
appears that creating a new paradigm of human experience is the
only available solution. Though reviewing the same situations periodically in this material seem unnecessary, it is included again for
the purpose of review and reinforcing the commitment that each of
you have made to this project. With the continual deluge of disinformation, mind control and governmental super-snooping capabilities, it seems even more redundant that so many can be so unaware
or in such deep denial. Even the opposition is amazed at its success!
Thus they are engaged in seeing just how much can be paraded
before your eyes without your awareness being triggered. It is a
phenomenal experience to observe this continue to progress.

It is the job of the ground team to accept the reality of what
exists, then to look *through and beyond* the global situation, lay the
foundation of the new paradigm and aid in birthing it into manifested reality. The universal laws function and are available to those
of understanding and intent to use them to their full potential. Deliberate intentional application of the first three will result in the fourth
– the balanced experience of the new paradigm.

II-9

The honor and glory of this planet, its past history and its future role as a nurturing home to evolving humanity hangs in the balance as its degradation continues unabated. As it and its inhabitants sicken from misuse and abuse through ignorance and arrogant purposeful destruction of its resources and its supportive atmosphere, the mass consciousness becomes psychologically unstable. The extremes of behavior become more evident not only through reported bazaar incidents, but within each individual life experience. Addictions and antisocial behavior within all organized structures becomes more prevalent. The family structure that is experienced without the universal laws as the ideal format within in which to base its purpose and focus fails to provide the necessary education for children to evolve into mature and functioning adults. Instead of each generation spiraling upward into evolving knowledge, experience and wisdom, humanity has remained stuck in a continuing circle of abuse, ignorance and physical and spiritual poverty. Those who amass material wealth find themselves poor in spirit and thus continue to search for the fulfillment of the void within that is the ignorance of the existence within and the use of the laws it would provide.

Once the recognition is made that this nebulous feeling of lack is indeed real and that it can be resolved, the search for the answer to the puzzle comes about naturally, however the search for a teacher of this wisdom goes unrewarded. Those that are found teach doctrines that continue the ignorance. The true teachings that are recorded in ancient documents remain hidden, either yet to be discovered or have been found and deliberately withheld from dissemination to the people or destroyed. Little has changed over the centuries, for those who would control continue to keep the people in spiritual ignorance and poverty.

Thus the time is now ripe for the call of the people for release from this incessant control and denigration of humanity's search of its rightful path of evolvement. The focus of creation in this portion of All That Is has decreed that this must end. Mankind must stand forth in the truth of who and what he is and end this chapter in its history. In the millenniums of experience, it has not happened through their own doing. He/she remains stuck in such silliness as whether the information contains references that are "chauvinistic" and fails to extract the truth, for such things are of no importance. Man and (wo)man meaning mankind with and without a womb is one and the same. He is the same with or without the (s)he. Each is one with the creative energy that focuses them into existence and holds them there in the energy of love without excuses or judgment. Just as the creator has no greater love of one creature than another, all are held in the highest of esteem, all are then expected to do *likewise* (in wisdom).

The love of the creator and of the energy of creation is not the superficial romantic love of your songs and stories, but one of absolute support. If it were not so, it would be withdrawn at the least excuse and your experiences would be short indeed. A parent that fails to guide and reasonably and logically discipline a child lacks real love for that child. Few of the millions of children of this time on the planet are truly loved! They are tolerated, used, abused and forced to grow physically, but not raised up in the knowledge and understanding of who and what they are and what is expected of them in either the physical or spiritual realms of their life experience. At the bottom of this lies the indisputable fact that parents cannot provide what they do not themselves know. Most now refuse to pass on what was taught to them for it has not led them to fulfillment; thus they send their children into adulthood with even less than they received.

None of the above does more than delineate the problem and does not provide a solution. The religions of the world offer up their "wise" writings as the answer, but these have been so adulterated as to provide only more circuitous searching. Thus, it would appear that it is time that true guidance appears on the scene. The question then arises as to how this would or could be disseminated. Those in desperation that pursue the false religious doctrines are radical and fanatic in their defense and are no different than when the last great teachers walked among you. They are not less malleable in the belief that their priests and preachers are wise in their judgments and would again follow them into smothering any teacher or teachings that might be sent. How then could such enlightenment proceed? If indeed the real teachers, called Jesus or Mohammed, returned to walk and teach among their people they would be no better received, as their true teachings would be unrecognizable because these were altered and adulterated almost immediately. Even if they were allowed to teach, would these "new" and different teachings be received any more than the last time? They were heard, but the people could not accept them and apply them to their daily life and that is the proof of any pudding.

If mankind, male and female is to transcend this seemingly endless chasing of its tail through generations of suffering, then it must stop creating victims and being victims. It must grasp and understand that its purpose is the veneration, education and development of the awareness of its connection to its source, the tiny computer chip, the segment of creation itself that is their *self-awareness!* The *I AM that I AM* awareness that is who and what each and every human being is, whether male or female, black, white, red, yellow or brown, earthling or alien. This awareness comes into "beingness" and through recurring experience quickly or slowly learns what it is taught, but not how to return from whence it came fulfilled. It is influenced totally by the parenting it receives throughout its numerous experiences not only by others, but most importantly of all by itself. It accepts or rejects its opportunities to harmonize with its source and to extend that expansive energy into its choices of experience through attitudes and decisions.

It is not a simplistic process and thus cycles of experience are supplied over long periods to provide this process. To grasp the understanding that each is an individual extension of wholeness, likened to a cell within a body, in which all are individual yet part of a focused wholeness within a greater wholeness is an imperative. Just as within the human body, if cells attack and destroy the essential organs, the body cannot survive. Humanity must understand that it can no longer continue to destroy its own without destroying the wholeness that contains it. It must stop destroying the planet that nurtures it as well as each other. Repeating the same destructive patterns without transcending them is causing the sustaining planet, solar system and galaxy disease, imbalance and disharmony. The creator focus of this galaxy has the choice of helping this happen for all that are willing to accept this help and putting all those who purposefully refuse in a holding space so that the cooperative are no longer held back by the uncooperative. It is as simple as that and mankind is *now* facing this choice.

Teachers will not be put in a position to again become martyred victims for the purposes of those who are addicted to control and exploitation of their fellow humans. This will be a grass roots movement and will spread among the willing people who will grasp the understanding of who and what they are and change their consciousness accordingly. These will then spread the understanding among themselves and become their own teachers. The messages will be short and simple and each will apply them in their own way or not. Each will assume responsibility and will spread the teaching to all that are willing to accept and *allow* those who choose otherwise to go their own way. The time of self-awareness and personal responsibility that will allow the transcendence of this hopeless situation into a new paradigm of experience is now or the holding space is prepared and awaiting. It is opportunity or threat as your attitude determines.

II-10

At the center of your experience is the awareness that you are, that you exist. This awareness is separate and apart from your body and your brain. It can be likened to a tiny computer chip that continues to be programmed by what is experienced by you through your every thought, word and deed. Your observer ego writes the code and you act and react in accordance with that programming. The chip undergoes constant reprogramming as you add, subtract and change your thoughts, words, actions, attitudes and beliefs. To continue the comparison in computer terminology, the active memory is stored within the brain and the stored memory within the cells of the body and magnetic field that surrounds the body. The body itself can be likened to an alkaline battery. Thus when its overall pH balance is too acidic it does not function at its ideal capacity.

Your tiny computer chip is your personal connective portion of Creation with a capital, that which is All That Is, pure potentiality in contemplation of itself. You indeed are gods in training. Through your freewill you are allowed to figure out how to become a god, and the recognition of this begins your ascent toward or away from that goal. To desire to accomplish this ascent toward godliness is programmed within that chip and *cannot* be changed or removed. It remains no matter how much it is ignored or how many times it is overridden with other programming. It is always there waiting to be activated.

Inasmuch as you can know that you are, that you can observe that you think, act, make decisions, observe and experience with the 5 senses and more, is called self-awareness. It is that portion that is beyond the physical brain function. It is your bit of immortality. Now it is your opportunity to begin to increase your operating system through recognizing and honoring this chip thus utilizing its potential from bytes to bits, kilobytes, megabytes and gigabytes. The comparison of a human to a computer is more apropos than you can imagine. Indeed, computers are modeled from the human example.

Mankind without understanding that its root meaning from antiquity is "god-man" tosses about the word human. Where is this tiny chip that supposedly is at the center of the human experience? When the human is dissected, where is this marvelous chip? The answer is, can you see your awareness? The chip is the "Life force," the breath that is present at birth and leaves at death. It is the unknowable secret that we can only wonder if Creation knows. Is it the mystery that propels Creation to contemplate itself and because of that is it the reason that we exist and pursue the same contemplative experience?

II-11

In these messages, references to mankind and humanity are one and the same, with no deference or difference intended for male or female. He and his are intended as he/she and her/his entirely as equals, which they are, with properties of form and purpose that are unique and common. There are certain indisputable facts that are laid as groundwork for the story of humanity as it exists on this planet to unfold in a concise and understandable sequence.

- There are many inhabited planets in this and other solar systems.

- Many contain self-aware, intelligent life forms.

- Many are far-advanced in conscious awareness of who and what they are within Creation as it now exists.

- Interplanetary travel does now and has existed for what you would term as eons of time.

- This planet has been and continues to be visited.

- There are different purposes for these visits by different representatives from various planets.

- These visitors have and do interact at various levels with life forms on this planet.

- There indeed are benevolent beings of higher understandings that have been and are now committed to helping humanity on earth to cope with and transcend the future that is coming forth now.

- Within this understanding, what follows is a brief history of many thousands of years for this branch of the human family tree.

There was a time in which mankind was indeed a carefree being. What you would refer to as childlike. Just as your children begin life as dependent babes that progress through stages of playing life in their own reality despite the world of adulthood going on all about them, mankind was this kind of being, open, naive, playful and easily influenced.

As explained before, creation is experienced within both the positive and the negative polarities, in a balance of travels to and from the point of equilibrium between the two. This can involve experiences of what might be termed aggression and acquiescence. Built into the focused awareness of all conscious (self-aware) life forms, is a balance for this experience of both polarities. You call it "self-defense," or the innate reaction of "fight or flight," triggered by the automatic insertion of adrenaline into the body. There was a group that through what you call genetic engineering changed their life form to eliminate this function. This allowed them to remain in the positive consciousness experience, a very pleasant way to live indeed. However, it left them defenseless in so far as any form of aggression was concerned. Their solution, instead of reestablishing this balancing function, was to find a less evolved species and have them provide this needed service for them. You guessed it! A group of less evolved humanoids. However, just to make sure they did their job, they were genetically engineered to enhance the adrenal output to make sure they reacted more aggressively than was natural. Too make a long story short, this change caused an imbalance that changed the personality and limited the ability of this altered species to know their innate connection to creation. Those who engineered this change then found their intended helpers unstable and threatening rather than being the protectors they had desired. The solution to their problem did not include reengineering the altered humans so that succeeding generations would return to normal since that failed to provide an immediate solution to their perceived problem. Instead they simply shipped them off to a sparsely inhabited planet in a far-off corner of the galaxy where they were not likely be discovered, and blame for this failed experiment would not likely be placed on them, even if the forcibly mutated future generations were discovered. To ensure this, all memory of this experience was erased and no records were allowed to be taken by the altered humans on the trip to earth. In other words, this branch of humanity was shipped off to what might be termed a prison planet and left to either destroy each other or perhaps eventually work out their genetic imbalance through adaptation. Impossible? Think back to the colonization of the USA or that of Australia. The nation of England emptied their prisons in that process, doing exactly the same thing with hopes of the same result.

Did this act of enslavement interfere with the freewill of this segment of humanity? Indeed it did. Why then was it allowed to proceed? The offending planet made the acts by their freewill choice, but through the law of attraction, so was the result of drawing to them a complimentary experience. The law of attraction works and cannot be escaped by ignoring fact and hiding the evidence.

Once you accept this premise, you begin to understand the situation that now surrounds you. However, there is more to this story. This trans-galactic shipment was not unobserved. Other advanced humans were aware of the scenario and have over the eons of time visited you. It became obvious that adaptation was not eliminating the genetic alteration. Thus a further experiment was begun. Your bible refers to visitors finding the daughters of men fair and mating with them. This was in hopes that the introduction of another gene pool into abandoned humanity would in subsequent generations eventually overcome the genetic alteration. If not, then the increased intelligence through the hybridization process might allow them to overcome the alteration through coming up with their own solution to the problem. From time to time the introduction of extra gene pool additions have been made through carefully chosen genetic matching. Progress has been made. However, the overwhelming result has been that the additional intelligence enhanced the aggressive tendency in many of the humans with the end result that aggressive tendencies within those not positively affected by the gene pool changes were reinforced with greater abilities to develop incredible applications of weaponry. They used the additional intelligence to organize to a high degree with the purpose of creating a hierarchy of power and control over the members of humanity on this planet that have evolved to a balanced genetic structure. Both of these negative results continue now.

This raises the question of whether the gene pool additions resulted in interfering with the planet in violation of universal law with regard to freewill. None of this was done without it being cleared through ruling councils of galactic beings that focus creative energy and oversee the balance of the galaxy. If you are focused thought thinking, which you are, then there are levels of focused thought thinking greater thoughts than you can yet imagine. There are benevolent beings that are part of the plan of creation that entails responsibilities of overseeing the galactic maintenance and expansion process. Because genetic development was approved for this planet, other visitors have come to this planet as a source of gene pool improvement for their planetary inhabitants. This has been carried out with carefully selected individuals. Approval for this is given by these individuals beforehand through a process that will purposely not be discussed at this time.

There is much knowledge that you have been denied that it is your right to know. Through manipulations by those still caught in the throws of the genetic alteration that require them to pursue control to support their violent tendencies, you have been denied this information, even though it has been brought to earth many times. The benevolent beings have walked among you teaching, and because of being attacked and killed, have then come undetected to continue the gene pool experiments with selected recipients, educating them through clandestine meetings in attempts to bring you into the awareness of who and what you are. Unfortunately, the powerful controllers distort the teachings and use them for their own gain and you are left bereft of the needed knowledge to lift yourselves from this morass of violent behavior.

The happy news of this story is that there are sufficient numbers of genetically different humans now residing on this planet to change the behavior pattern of the planet back to the normal range. They must, however, find out whom they are and what to do. The question that remained for the benevolent ones, was how to do this. If they came themselves, the weaponry would be employed and death would be the end result. The teachers they instructed have ended up with the same result and the teachings altered to suit the purposes of the aggressive ones. How then are the wheels to be set into motion to bring this situation to an end?

Telepathic, mind to mind communication, is a common attribute of humanity, but was lost to the humans marooned on this planet in the genetic alteration. Through the gene pool change a significant number of earth's inhabitants had this ability come into being quite naturally in a rudimentary form. Those benevolent beings that use telepathic abilities as a normal part of life found they could communicate with many of the genetically enhanced beings in recent generations. However, this was as successful as the knowledge and understanding of the earth human allowed since the knowledge imparted had to be filtered through their understandings and vocabulary. Total awareness of the earth human could also be pushed aside with the human's permission and the higher awareness could speak directly, however this process was limited by the benevolent beings understanding and awareness of what the human experience entailed. Because of this lack of understanding at each side of the process it was difficult for humanity to understand the teachings or to accept the process at all. This process has been known as channeling. Partial teaching has been accomplished, but it has not been entirely satisfactory. However, no better way to communicate directly has yet been devised. The enhancement of the understanding of the receiving human has been the only solution thus far so that more clarity can be incorporated into the information.

In order that what is understood from the information made available thus far reaches as many of the genetically corrected humans as possible, it was necessary that the information be spread without being distorted by the controlling powers. Thus the enhancement in information speed and various means of it were allowed to be given, even though it was assumed that the aggressive group would use it for their own purposes. However, at this time information to the genetically normal humans can travel to them quite freely. The problem of the moment is to get the information circulating.

It should be further noted that the information given through telepathic use of humans must be considered with the discernment of logic accompanied by the open mind of whether it could possibly contain truth. Truth is individually discerned through the screen of life experience and should be weighed and considered carefully by each person. Enhanced communication is also in the form of books that now contain careful research of what you would call ancient history. These bring forth information from the time in which the benevolent beings from other planetary systems could walk on the earth in safety. These visits were recorded in the language and art of the day. Lacking photographs and written word understood by many people, myths were told by words and simple symbols that have been misinterpreted both innocently and purposefully. The enlightened teachers purposefully hid much information for later discovery. Some has been found in recent times and has been either destroyed or hidden from you soon after the discoveries. News of more accurate decoding of what is available is becoming commonly known and is available in books. These books must be read with a great deal of discernment as often-erroneous assumptions were made as to the meanings of the decoded information. It is much more difficult for it to be concealed or misinterpreted because of the education levels of much of humanity and the freedom with which information can now flow between people. It is hoped that many will search out the information and in a continuing effort attempt to interpret the information. It is necessary that they come into an understanding that allows them to realize that this is a momentous time for those who are now capable of changing the destiny that is planned for them by the organized aggressive fellow humans on this planet.

II-12

The momentous time for humanity to transcend this seemingly unsolvable dilemma is repeated with purposeful intent. The profusion of communication modes and content is overwhelming and is designed to direct mankind away from physical activity and into an imbalance of mental activity. This promotion of a sedentary life style weakens the physical body, prevents the release of stress and lessens the likelihood of survival in the days ahead. In order to transcend the experience of this repetition of life as guided by others, and to replace it with a life of personal responsibility, each must be present in a body on this planet. The opportunity to do this is here now, but your availability to participate is based on your personal internal choice. The word internal is chosen specifically, for how you come to know who and what you are is a process of internalizing within your own awareness and pondering these different ideas. There must be consideration of them in focused thought and definite decisions reached that are meaningful and followed by active changes in each life focus. These processes are best carried out in quiet time alone. In order to do this within an experiencing mode of work, family and social commitments that seem to leave little breathing room will require a decision to participate or not. If the decision is to participate, then your priorities of life will need to be changed. The TV will need to be turned off. The word "no" may need to be introduced regularly into your conversation. A great deal of contemplation can be accomplished on a solitary walk.

It must be understood that this discussion stresses a *personal* decision. Each must decide for him/herself. It is suggested that discussions with your spouse be encouraged, if that is appropriate. Many times ones in relationships have entirely different views in these areas. The pivotal relationship between you and your connection to creation is personal and can only be dealt with alone. To share with another person who is as committed to strengthening this connection is a joy. Through deliberate intention, those living on this planet include millions and millions that have been taught since early childhood to seek a greater connection to a "god" who is somewhere out there in the unknown. And that one can live a life of ease and luxury after death in some other mythical Utopian realm is illogical to visitors from spiritually advanced planets. This Christian myth is paralleled by more beliefs almost as illogical in other religions.

Each child is first to learn the gift of self-awareness is the only god necessary for each to know. Then all of their life is experienced through this focus point with further learning that personal responsibility empowers it through their life experiences into either a positive or a negative perspective. At the maturity of a generation of this understanding, religion as it exists would become a moot point. Through the understanding that the amazing gift of self-aware experience is in all things supported by the simple laws of attraction, focused intent and allowance of freewill choices, and supported by understanding gained through experience using these basically simple truths, then a new experience would await them than exists now. This is an over simplification for the teaching would involve much guidance of these children. The question remains how could something that is not known by the parent be taught by them? Thus simply the knowing of the truth does not solve the challenges that present themselves. Each must begin at the point at which truth is discovered.

In the quiet of their own consciousness, individuals must stand above the situation, consider carefully the extent of the commitment each is willing to make and then set about incorporating changes through these new understandings. As each dilemma presents itself, the simple prayer of "I am a human becoming, help me to become, or we are humans becoming, help us to become, or they are humans becoming, help them to become" changes the internal climate and incorporates the difficult law of allowance into reality. The release of the need to control through allowance changes the perception profoundly. It allows transcendence from responsibility for others and recognizes the personal choice of releasing them to their own personal decisions. Rather than bringing forth feelings of separation, this blessing process brings forth an experience of a form of love that has blessed them in a way that will have profound effects on their life. In adversarial situations, a change may take several repetitions, but it will bring change.

What is being experienced within this opportunity is that which is extended to each on a continuing basis by the point of harmonious thought within creation that focuses each individual into existence in the first place. If this were not the case, then with the first act contrary to universal law, the energy that holds each in manifested reality would be withdrawn and each would cease to exist. Each would be denied the experience of the result of that choice and could not then come into the wisdom of understanding that the act brought forth a result and provided the choice of repeating it or transcending it through wisdom. What exists within creation in truth is not religion as a practiced dogma, but practical, applicable, logical spirituality. Spirit being the name given to the presence of creation which is omnipresent, omniscient and omnipotent. In other words, the destiny of learning this truth and the experience of choosing to come into understanding and practicing it cannot be avoided, it can only be postponed.

Simplistic as this discussion is, it contains the basis for seemingly magical transformation in the life of those willing to adopt such change. To give up the known and travel into the unknown has long been the elixir of adventure. Mankind need not travel elsewhere from where he is or what he is doing to have adventure. All life is experienced by the attitude that is reflected within its own thoughts. What seems boring and mundane could be experienced differently by changing the parameters of experience, one situation at a time. As pressing as the situation is with regard to those who would enslave their fellow beings on a global scale, it can only be changed through individuals transcending their own belief structure.

It must begin with the recognition and realization that a long-standing series of deceptions, manipulations and misuses have been perpetrated. That this is true does not change anything. Where mankind is now is where he is and thus blame, fear, over reaction or cowardice will resolve nothing. Resistance or the choice to retaliate will count for nothing. Two wrongs will never equate to right. It remains for mankind to swallow the truth and to look to his focused source and chose to change his experience by coming into the knowledge, understanding and application of the laws that support all of creation. God as known to humanity on this planet does not exist. He isn't dead because he never existed. Creation exists and has all the attributes of omnipotence (all power), omniscience (all knowing) and omnipresence. The only worship required is the living of the gift of self-aware life within the laws that have brought each into the experience with honor and appreciation for the wondrous privilege that it is.

Help to bring about the incorporation of this awaits invitation by humanity. Teachers in the form of benevolent beings will come again to walk among you on this planet when it is safe *and they are invited*. They will not teach you how they think you should live, but will teach you the laws of the universe and advise you in their application to the parameters of the life design you choose individually and as a group. The choice is here to be made now between slavery and difficult deaths or freedom to come into harmony with the way creation is meant to be experienced.

II-13

When the time arrives that the imposition of the final phases of the lock down of personal freedoms begins in earnest there will be resistance. Especially in the USA since of all the humans on the planet, they have been the most deceived, the most pampered and the most used. Difficult as it is for its citizens to believe, their national development has been guided and controlled from the very beginning. The natural ingenuity and creativity have been encouraged and then turned to advantage or "bought out" and shelved. A particularly appropriate example is the continued development of sources of energy and transportation that would end the dependence on oil and coal which would eliminate the health endangering of both the human body and the planetary flora and fauna. These are available to be developed very quickly in the context of the new paradigm.

There is a natural flow of expression that is part of the creative plan. It is what you might call unchangeable programming within the human pattern that remains regardless of what purposeful effort is made to override it. Once a goal or objective is decided upon by a personal choice that seems logical and accompanied by a commitment to that goal, it can and is pursued with all possible intensity, even to the point of giving up the life force to death. Methods of torture can and will cause the person to deny and pretend to give it up, but instead it usually instills it deeper into determination to resume the pursuit of its completion at the first opportunity. This is true for those goals that are both positive and negative in their energy configuration. Thus confrontational situations are the logical result. The positive impetus is pursued through logic and the negative experience through inability to apply the law of allowance and control becomes an addictive factor in the imbalance. It is important to comprehend that perfection is the ability to remain in balance in the practice of all the laws of the universe that support the expansive expression of creation. This is a process that gives challenge to participation within what is called eternity. If not for this monumental challenge, eternity could be boring indeed.

Intelligence is not confined to the human brain/mind. It is part and parcel of the potentiality that flows through the process of creation. Self-contemplation by any manifested self-aware portion of creation, humanity for example, with a basic understanding of who and what they are in correlation to the expansive flow of creation, can transcend and remove limiting understandings. This then opens the awareness to the potential of new understandings changing the experience of that being entirely. In every way, all experience serves the expansive process of each. Because creation is, at its potential, intelligence in pursuit of understanding itself, it is necessary to discern that all beliefs reach a point of limiting the opportunity to evolve. It is then a perpetual process of transcending and leaving behind each and every understanding into greater wisdom. The exception to this is the immutable universal laws that support the process as a whole. At the basis of these changes is always greater understanding of these laws, their utilization and the wisdom gained through the resulting experiences.

Certainly it would seem logical to the inhabitants of this planet that the time has come to transcend the present experience and change the beliefs that have focused creation into the experience of the future as it sits before them. It is far easier to perceive the situation at hand and change the beliefs to transcend the experience before it comes into complete manifestation. The negative polarity experience is brought about by failure to know, understand and apply the laws of the universe. You were set upon this planet without them and denied the knowledge of them. Those indigenous groups who were on the planet were learning them through observation of nature. Through the blessing of eternity, all the time necessary, their evolvement was on its way. Now, even these too have been corrupted. Unfortunately through the teaching of the theme that nature is to be subdued, rather than to be your teacher, you were denied the knowledge that could have been gained through its contemplation as a holographic example of the laws in application.

Is this saying that technology should be abandoned entirely and 7+ billion people should return to indigenous living? That certainly would return the planet to 500 million people quickly through starvation. If living in that way would allow understanding of the universal laws, then it would be a worthwhile experience. However, knowledge of the laws from those who have both advanced technology and understanding is available to help, consequently the indigenous alternative would not be necessary. If mankind does not take responsibility to change the present intended scenario and the planet itself is required to change this situation, then technology will be purged and if the planet is "lucky" indigenous populations will again have the opportunity to evolve.

The consequences of ignoring this new opportunity to change the story of this branch of humanity that has been literally railroaded on to a path thousands of years long which has stymied their evolvement are not pleasant to contemplate. The scenario began through breaking the law of allowance and interfering with the evolvement of other humans and requiring them to remain stuck in "being" rather than becoming. The consequences to those through the law of attraction (what you give is what you get) was left for it to work in its inevitable way. No other group was willing to interfere accept in a benevolent advisory capacity, which is all that is allowed within the intelligent application of the universal laws. Intervention between species and planets does happen and is admitted here. However, the law of attraction absolutely works, but within the flow of divine order, the timing is left to the natural flow of that law within the intelligence of creation. To stretch the law of allowance and interact beyond the advisory capacity is carefully done with much consideration with regard to far reaching possible effects. This may be extended particularly when a group is evolved enough to ask for help specifically. The outcry to creation itself, by enough of the population, is answered by offers to help by specific groups. However, if the asking group is so closed as to be unable to recognize the offers, then nothing can be done. In this case, the outcries for help have been of such duration, and the imbalance of the purposeful negative perpetrators is so great, the whole galaxy is now focused on this small planet and orders have been issued to "find a way to answer the outcries." Thus earth's population is being presented with the current process and the current messages within the presently available communication proliferation. It is our prayer that it will be enough and in time.

II-14

Knowledge is given to mankind within the recorded history of the past that there has been communication with beings from other planets within the galaxy. The understanding that spiritual evolvement goes hand in hand with physical, emotional and mental evolvement would seem to be a logical assumption. Just as personal responsibility develops at the beginning levels through interaction with other beings, so also it continues as the path of evolvement unfolds through experience. Therefore, self-awareness involves itself through choice at greater and greater levels of personal responsibility interacting with other beings through maintenance of balance of physical creation, meaning the manifested galaxy as a whole. This is accomplished by sharing the responsibilities in cooperation. In other words, there is an organized administrative process in which to become involved as self-awareness and the ability to experience within the universal laws is attained in wisdom through experience. The benevolent beings that have visited your planet and now are indeed present in nearness to this planet are representatives who have volunteered for their own advancement to be part of this administrative focus of galactic maintenance.

In order for the expansive energy of creation to continue its outward flow, the individual points of self-awareness must continue within that flow through personal growth. Each must first recognize who and what they are and then through free will choose when and how to accomplish this within the laws of the universe. The desire to do this is literally programmed into each and every one and continues to call for fulfillment no matter how frustrated and blocked the experience or experiences are. Humanity on this planet is blocked at every turn by denial of this essential knowledge. The knowledge purposefully given has been distorted and the false idea that man is to use nature rather than cooperate with it so the example of it could be their teacher. Nature exists in harmony with the laws of the universe when left to itself and despite man's intervention and perversion of it. Nature keeps on trying because it contains the same element of programmed push to exist and evolve that is universal within creation.

The urge for expansive behavior is present within the living aspect of all creation. Only the self-aware have the privilege of freewill. That aspect of privilege contains the pitfall for exploitation of lesser expressions of creation. The inhabitants of this planet have created luxury and poverty through the use and abuse of the natural resources of this singularly beautiful planet. Distortion and ignorance, whether chosen or thrust upon intelligent beings, brings havoc and imbalance in ever widening effects. The personal choice to accept responsibility to change this carries the hope of this branch of humanity to transcend all of this while there is yet opportunity. Turning away from this opportunity will carry with it the consequences that naturally accompany it through the law of attraction. Eternity, as this cosmic cycle is called, is a very long sequential time in your counting to learn lessons ignored and refused. All help possible and beyond the normal process is being given now. The opportunity to literally leap ahead and bridge the lost chances of advancement is available for the taking. It is hoped that as many as possible can and will answer the call.

What are called crop circles have caused great curiosity. The previous discussion of the existence of the galactic administration of responsible maintenance was introduced as a preface for this information. In times of great stress for a planet, not an unusual thing in keeping all within balanced orbits, etc., energy is focused into the various grid systems that maintain orbit and spin velocities and other physical maintenance. It is similar to tuning up your automobile engine to keep it running at peak efficiency. This is done on a regular basis. In the case of your planet, which is under great stress, as even the most sleeping human will acknowledge, this process is going on with increased regularity. The crop circles are dynamic energy codes that are being sent as usual, but are being made visible as an attempt to awaken humanity to the truth that outside help is maintaining the balance. There have been specific cases of groups sitting in open fields, meditating and finding a crop circle created around them in moments. These instances were again for the purpose giving the message and took place only within the confines of these special areas and the particular timing of these transmissions and were not caused by the meditating group. The shapes vary with the specific energy patterns being focused. There are certain particularly restorative (for lack of a better word) areas that bring forth specific planetary responses. These shapes and places are matched for the response needed. These are not meant to be decoded, but rather to be accepted for their intended purpose.

There is knowledge and understanding of the galaxy and its encompassing universal laws available. It has always been available to be known. It is humanity's right to know all of it. That is known as evolvement. This grand opportunity is available for the simple taking of these messages, grasping the truth of the seriousness of the situation and acknowledging that lies and distortions have been perpetrated. Then learning and applying a few simple practical changes in perception through the application of the life energy that is who and what you are can begin. The choice is available now.

II-15

When the time comes in your awareness of sequential events, remembering that divine order does not operate necessarily in that mode, various situations will appear to have no connection at all to the intended purpose of thwarting the movement of the intended plan. Remember again how a computer graphic completes itself sometimes in linear movement and then the pattern changes in how it continues to appear. It must also be understood that the format of creation is not flat, but is *holographic and dimensional.* It is important to understand that those are not intended to be analogous. Manifested creation is holographic in form and dimensional in the context of vibratory variation. In other words, which are woefully inadequate to fully explain, a holographic form can exist in similar but different dimensional variations.

Once the inhabitants of earth accept the truth of the existence of other fellow inhabitants within this galaxy and others, the next great leap of understanding is that within their own galaxy there exists even more variation because each form can have dimensional variations. Further evolvement by way of knowledge and wisdom through applying the knowledge, it is possible to travel between the dimensions as easily as walking through a doorway. In other words a holographic form can exist in similar but different dimensional variations.

When this is understood, then traveling through space becomes comprehensible and does not seem at all impossible. It further explains how people of old regarded past interplanetary visitors as "gods" to be venerated and held in awe, resulting in religious worship. As understood then and perpetuated now by manipulating governmental and "religious" leaders, indeed the "god thing" is a hoax. Creational energies governed by universal laws through their application and the potentiality that underpins it is worthy of veneration, honor and awe, but there is no personality to receive worship. There is, however, that intangible, knowable bit of creational energy that is the self-awareness often called "heart feeling" with in you. That is worthy of veneration. It is there to be acknowledged and the power within understanding it used.

There are beings, that have come through experience to a greater and greater understanding of creation by conceptualizing and applying the laws that allow the use of this marvelous creational energy, that do deserve *respect.* Through their teaching, much can be learned by willing individuals rather than having to spend eons of time learning through trial and error. The greatest of all errors is to worship the teacher or the process rather than venerate the source and participate by acquiring knowledge and wisdom through experience. When mankind on this planet learns the truth of these words, then indeed he shall be free to continue his/her evolvement in 7 league boot strides. "I am a human becoming, help me to become" opens the door for the truth to be accepted. Each must forge their own path through their freewill choices, their attitudes, decisions and acceptance of their personal responsibility to participate in bringing forth a plan for use of the creational energies that are totally available.

Each of you now has the opportunity to accept or reject these messages and continue to live as a victim of the plans of the enslavers. Or you could change your attitude and accept the possibility that this might be logical truth and something to ponder, consider and then allow the intangible creational life aspect that enlivens each of you to guide you to a decision. The Christian bible mentions several times that Mary, mother of Immanuel, pondered things in her heart. In other words, she considered them and "felt" whether those things were true. If something did not fit within the comfort zone of her current understanding, she at least considered it seriously, let the process percolate for a time and then "felt" whether it was true or not. It is suggested that you follow her example and do this in the quiet of prayer time, meditation time or a long quiet walk, then just let things percolate. You will indeed know in your heart if this is an opportunity you want to participate within. Then you must "walk your decision" and take the appropriate steps to change your consciousness, pursue knowledge, live it and acquire wisdom.

Once you each make that decision, there is an entire galactic cheering section that will indeed bring forth-resounding joy and shower you with a loving blessing. You have no idea how much they desire you to know the truth and desire to welcome you back into the evolving focus.

II-16

When the time comes for the beginning of the changeover of consciousness through the conversion of the critical number of the necessary percentage, the ripple effect will seem to be unnoticeable. Just as the number of people who now believe that there is interplanetary travel has now reached the critical mass. A remainder still staunchly reject the acceptance of this belief, but that rejection is a shell to protect the rest of their beliefs, for if they are wrong about extraterrestrial visits, then they must entertain the possibility that some or all their beliefs are possibly false. There are compelling reasons that the evidence of these visits has been so vehemently denied by both governmental and religious powers. Yet it provided them with a fear weapon and the temptation to use it as such seduced them into bringing it forth as fanciful entertainment. That earth governments had the abilities to develop the capability was offered in positive possibility within futuristic settings, just as the first attempts to leave the planet itself were idealized. The nonsense of the distortions is indeed ludicrous when viewed in the true picture. However, the truth has escaped their best efforts and it has indeed put a sizable crack in the acceptance of their carefully concocted depiction of who and what mankind is and the cosmology of its existence.

The denial of the existence of anything that has enough people with actual experiences now using the available communications to tell their stories is causing the crumbling of the foundations of the credibility of the whole lie. This was done, not by shocking the population with a big expose, but instead nibbling away at it a little at a time. Now the credibility gap is enough that through this doubt, greater truth is being readily accepted. The truth is that this planned bid for global power was set into motion indeed thousands of years ago. Incredible as it seems when the known "ancient" history is researched and traced back, the plan lays open to discerning minds and is available in print, though the conclusions are not entirely clear. There are no secrets in manifested reality. The further along the evolution of self-aware beings, the more easily situations and other beings are perceived and understood. The temptation to exploit those of lesser evolvement is great indeed in the midst of experience modes between positive and negative experiences. Victim consciousness is the epitome of the negative experience. It draws through the law of attraction like energy, or in other words it draws situations that exploit that consciousness. In acquiring this understanding, it is then obvious that the very first step humanity on this planet must achieve in order to transcend this mode of experience is to shed victim consciousness and regain the self-empowerment mode.

Until the crack in the seemingly "airtight" education of mankind as to his place within the cosmology of the galaxy/universe widens, it is difficult to expect many to accept the truth that the father/god of the past and present is a hoax. This is because first there must be something demonstrable in an experiential fashion that will replace it and it must be the absolute truth! In this process, giving up the victim consciousness through self-empowerment is the beginning step. In order to do this, self-awareness, the ability to consider the individual self over the group loyalty is basic. "Me first" has been exploited through the encouragement of selfish sexual and materialistic practices as a guard to prevent the discovery of this basis of the human expression of who and what manifested life is. When this next fissure in the their foundation becomes a wide enough crack, then the bitter contents of their house of cards will pour forth with repercussions that will lift the human consciousness despite their efforts to enslave it. As the law of attraction works, they draw to themselves like energies/experiences.

The laws of the universe indeed work in mysterious ways to allow for return to balance, while allowing expansiveness through wisdom gained in experience of both the positive and negative expressions. Neither is inactive, both are at play simultaneously thus keeping the balance. During the time spent at the point of balance, all is at rest, just as there is a moment between breaths. During each act of breathing, various functions that are either positive or negative proceed within the body unnoticed because of the governing of the functions of the nerve system in the body. This can be correlated back to the galaxy in comparing the governing system that functions in the fashion of the nervous system.

The human body is a marvelous expression that has the capability of mimicking its source and can function at many levels of holographic and dimensional experience. The gift of an experience within one is to be greatly appreciated and honored. Those beings experiencing in what might be termed older models desire greatly to have the capabilities of your improved one. Thus you have visitors bent on making this happen, but meaning no harm to you. The methodology reflects many of the capabilities theirs lack. For those remembering the experience of interacting with them, this is difficult to accept as reason for these situations.

Nonetheless, permission was asked and received at a level of consciousness that is not yet available to their awareness. Those granting this are greatly appreciated for this gift of greater life experience that will be the result. Indeed, there have also been visits from a very much older group that left their unwanted mark long ago and they have been barred from return visits. Any further returns will be with severe repercussions for those individuals for these would be without the approval of their own kind.

This brings forth the previous mention of an extraterrestrial group that are not only assisting the group planning enslavement, but in actuality carry great anger toward this planet. These beings attempted to take over this planet not long after humanity was marooned on it. Not comprehending the warlike genetic alteration, even though they had superior weaponry and control technologies, humanity repulsed them. Retribution has been planned since that long-ago time. The control and enslavement plan has been theirs from the beginning. That they come and go and confer with the hierarchy of the planners is kept secret, thus you have secret societies within secret societies. Eternity is a long sequential time, and so they have slowly and carefully laid their plans over many, many years in your counting. The planetary awareness of this presence, which could not be totally hidden, has been translated into "satan or the devil" and thus the tool of fear has been implanted and personified so that you hold it in your consciousness and resist it in a non-reality mode. Those that have been influenced into being the stooges in this long-standing plan reflect the consciousness of those they consider benefactors and they in turn are attracted by the victim stance and consciousness of the rest of humanity. They have not fathomed the plan that is behind the one they are being guided to perpetrate on their fellow humans. If the total plan is allowed by humanity to be completed, the planet may or may not be habitable. Those particular extraterrestrials do not care, so long as they are able to achieve their revenge. Indeed, they are farther out of balance than earth. There is much to be accomplished in the scenario that is playing itself out in these pivotal days that are upon earth and all her inhabitants.

II-17

Through these messages it is hoped that each will strive to verify the inferences made here in brevity. The information is available to verify the historical delineation of the recent (last several thousand) years religious hoax that has been perpetrated. However, this is not to indicate that this was even the beginning. Within this branch of humanity, through the alteration of the DNA/RNA, the inner programmed desire for balance continued to resonate. It was subliminally known that the imbalance was brought about by outside forces, there was then an innate desire that the same outside forces should restore it. There was not conscious memory or records of any kind to indicate who or what had been the source of this imbalance. It was natural for the descendants of this branch of humanity to desire this correction from every outside/extraterrestrial visitor they came into contact with, benevolent or otherwise. This desire was converted over time into deification and worship with ritual religious dogma to support and spread it. The focus of these "religious" formats were both positive and negative, with each attempting to influence the other over time, or worse yet destroy each other. Though the benevolent beings have endeavored to teach the truth and explain each time, their lessons were soon distorted back into the religious dogma of looking for help from outside to rescue mankind from its problem. And so, it is at this very moment, accept for those few that have already figured it out are now gleaning the truth from those few who know or from these messages.

Knowing the truth and knowing what to do after the truth is learned is another matter. The universal laws *require* that this branch of mankind must come into understanding and with deliberate focus overcome their victim consciousness through personal responsibility to change their experience. This first step opens the doorway to reentry into the galactic family that they have been separated from for so long. The family is anxious for your return and desires to help in any way that is allowed, but earth's inhabitants must make this first step on its own with only the guidance of its necessity to assist. Then by directly asking for further assistance, more can be given, but even then it cannot be rescued.

It is proper, in light of the above explanation, to address the great as yet unspoken concern about what to do with the overpopulation when this is solved. First of all, there will be a loss of many lives in the chaos that will ensue. Certainly not 7+ billion, but those who refuse to accept the truth will slow down the paradigm project's manifestation. The longer it takes to manifest, the greater the loss of life. Those who refuse to hear and accept after the project completion will be given the opportunity to come into balance in other situations; in other words they will live elsewhere, however this time with full knowledge and accompanied by records. Those who are the new paradigm will then have many choices and opportunities of places to continue their evolution. The members of the ground crew will remember who they really are and are welcome to return to the points of their origin. The balance will be returned, though planet earth will need assistance in returning to health. It will not be as much of a task as might be thought now with the knowledge and techniques available for the asking. The remnant that remains will have interesting times in which to enjoy manifesting the new paradigm into wholeness. No further detail regarding the future will be given until that time arrives. It must be stressed that this is not the phase on which to focus. Until the first step is completed, the last step has no possibility of manifesting. Thus its explanation has been withheld. However, the concern about the overpopulation issue has necessitated this brief explanation. It is important that it be accepted that the future is well encompassed and then set that understanding aside so that the proper emphasis is placed where it belongs. *It belongs on the completion of the first step, individual conscious acceptance of transcending from the victim in need of rescue, into personal responsibility through playing a decisive part in the conception and manifestation of a new paradigm of experience.*

II-18

Through these messages the outline of the status of humanity has been established. Further detail is available to those who desire to investigate beyond what is easily perceived when viewing the media presented information in light of this information. That a hoax of major proportions is being perpetrated is difficult to miss.

There is one magic show after another being presented for viewing while the global manipulations continue to restructure national, continental and hemispheric lines of demarcation. The structure of the world as you know it is being dissolved at its very foundations. The plan is at a stage now that it can no longer be prevented. It can yet be sabotaged at specific points to frustrate and slow the process somewhat to give more time in which to reach more people. This material is being distributed at its starting point in the USA, but through the group foci must entail a planetary appeal to be all inclusive of humanity as a whole. The process of the plan is the same and different in every local on the planet. Thus, whether in the vernacular of one country or another, the end result of the plan of planetary slavery is the same. The variety within the human experience must be transcended in order that a true group focus can be attained. The division of ethnicity into race must be dissolved and humanity must consider itself one "race," a word best abandoned for it too reflects emotions that do not serve the birth of the new paradigm. The oneness that is to be sought will transcend the need for identification of diversity. Diversity need not be bred out in order to attain what can only be accomplished within each personal awareness. Appreciation of the opportunity to experience self-awareness manifested into the glory of a human body and evolve through the process of expressing creational energy negates the necessity to delineate personal differences in this way. It is a natural evolution of that awareness.

Appreciation of the gift of self-awareness is understanding that a piece of absolute potentiality that is the sum and substance of the All That Is, is the point of coagulation around which all living things exist. To comprehend it is to honor it and come to understand that it is both fragile and tenaciously committed to evolving through that potentiality that is innate within its very nature. Understanding this simple truth of who and what humanity is has been buried beneath a landslide of superfluous information that has been pushed on mankind to insure distraction and prevent this essential discovery. The distorted need to be fixed, leading to worship of both misunderstood visitors and an imagined outside source for this help, has held the transplanted humans on this planet in a self-created bondage. Many of those who have attained the return to genetic balance remain programmed into the old systems of belief that have failed for thousands of years to achieve the desired goals. It is time for them to awaken and to again experience true human evolvement. *It is the truth* that will set them, *you*, free. When this information is contemplated in the quiet of inner awareness, it will resonate and be known by those who are genetically balanced.

This will raise the question as to whether all those within the same family are automatically genetically balanced. The genes for each are randomly selected at each conception; thus these float within nearly all families at this sequential point. There will be those that are more susceptible to the negative programming that will seem not to carry the gene balance. Again, freewill is freely given. All will be accepted if the realization is sincere even at the last moment. But it is likely that as the initial statement of purpose circulates, the words will resonate and the wakeup call will be answered. The simple few words, translated into all languages, will resound within and in its repetition it will demand an answer within that cannot be denied. The yearning of all the previous generations denied the freedom to evolve is carried at cellular levels and through the genetic release is available when the trigger is activated. It is the response by the first few to this pent-up yearning that will bring forth the freedom cry that will begin the wondrous process of the birthing of the new paradigm. It is time now!

The repetitions in the message are meant to offset the continuous barrage of disinformation that has been the foundation of human existence for these thousands of years and now reaches a crescendo as the "second shoe" is nearly ready to be dropped. The emphasis on waking up and accepting the magnitude and duration of the frustrating trip of this branch of humanity down a dead-end path is the essential beginning for changing the conscious perception of this experience. This is then followed by the awareness that this consciousness change is the first layer of the foundation for the new paradigm. Without a firm foundation on the rock of truth, nothing of lasting value can be built.

The next step is either participating in the conception of the beginning statement or the proliferation of it once it is conceived and the further conception of the bare skeleton of what the new paradigm is to become. Not rules and regulations, but what living within it would involve. Dreaming the dream in a sheer playful mode. A rose was created through a play of possibilities. A lily, a monkey, a squirrel, an otter, an elephant were all created in a playful mode of potential possibilities. Man/woman must become childlike and consider outlandish and outrageous possibilities until the perfect ideas begin to gel. This is best done within groups with the same intent. Even the most closed will join the *spirit* of the task and often have the most amazing contributions. The host/hostess must set the mood of safety and spontaneity and allow the group to take it from there. Levity opens the door to creativity and the release of true human nature. We are all the children of creation and are set loose to playfully learn who we are and what we are truly capable of doing, governed only by the laws of the universe. It must however, be firmly understood that these do strictly govern, are immutable and every act outside them draws its effects within creation's own, not necessarily sequential, timing. This is known now as divine order.

II-19

The desire to understand the imbalance that followed the original DNA alteration that originated within the natural flow of self-contemplation became an abnormal obsession to know for the group of transplanted humans on planet earth. The generations followed one another and their searches within and without failed to give them understanding. The tendency to over respond to all real and misinterpreted threats became the outlet for the desire to understand this imbalance known at the level of intuition. Realizing that this tendency left unbridled would lead to annihilation, religion as an inhibiting factor was introduced. Without the aid of memory or records, it was to provide a historical point of origin as one could best be intuited and to institute some form of control to prevent annihilation. Over sequential time various points of focus were used. The visitation of beings from other planets provided the best possible focus, particularly those who came in attempts to teach and finally to introduce changes in the gene pool as a last resort in their efforts to help this branch of humanity to continue to evolve.

There are two important points of understanding to be made clear. These beings came in benevolence and did not wish to be the object of religious focus. However, the genetic introduction produced offspring that were noticeably more intelligent, but not noticeably less violent if *provoked*. Because of this, these offspring became leaders and usually the focus points or priests of the religious cults. As assisting priests were added, the roles became confused and distorted. Deification of the first of these leaders followed within a few generations of death and various levels of deification of those following happened periodically. Because of their difference, the first-born male of each following generation inherited the leadership role and the task of propagating the perceived change thus creating dynasties of leaders. The remaining progeny intermarried and spread the genetic changes. Because of the focus of male leadership by dominant expression of the aggressive tendency through warfare, females came to be regarded as being of lesser importance accept for the propagation of the male for conquest.

It is important that present day humanity understand its true cosmology. There were what you call indigenous populations already on the planet and evolving through their own natural processes when the transplanted group arrived. The confusion within the efforts of present day scientists trying to create a cosmology from their point of view for the planet is easily understood. They are unable to consider the effects of both types of humans being suddenly present at one point in history and they are unaware of the gene pool additions to the marooned group and the blending of all three ingredients in both the past and the present. This puts them at an extreme disadvantage and their conclusions add only more confusion for an already frustrated branch of humanity. It is necessary to note here that now the indigenous population evolution has been distorted, as few if any remain isolated from proselytizing contacts. Further, the environmental situation includes them within the planetary whole. The aboriginal tribe of Australia no longer propagates and is asking to reincarnate elsewhere in the galaxy. If help is again refused, this will be honored, as they are innocent of any involvement in the chaos forced upon on this planet.

Humanity's roots and how its history has played out, is not important for a delineated timeline, but for an understanding of how the frustration of being marooned was experienced and what far-reaching solutions were tried. Left to deal with their altered genetics humanity has in its confusion refused benevolent help and accepted distorted help. The roots of the refusal and distortion lay within the alteration and its effects that enhanced more than the self-defense aspect. Cooperation became competition, which enhanced greed, lust and the pursuit of power over each other, to name just a few. The knowledge of this history brings forth a fork in the road and with it the decision to continue on the same dead-end path or to accept this offer of help that is again being made. For those willing to comprehend the plans for the present path, it would seem the choice would be easy.

However, the ingrained programming of looking for rescue rather than accepting the responsibility of making the necessary changes requires leaving behind a long established comfort zone. To literally climb out of the morass of confusion to a point of over-view, observe the struggling masses expending their energy swimming upstream against the flow of creative energy because of a false perception of who and what they are through misconceptions and misinformation, takes courage. It is not an easy opportunity to accept and requires a commitment to this very personal process. It involves separating from the mass conscious belief systems in order to contemplate what is true and then adopting a new concept of personal truth.

Fortunately, this has already been accomplished by a surprising number of individuals. These, not knowing the history, through an instinctual awareness that there was a hidden story, relentlessly pursued their need to know. What came to be known was perceived despite the fact that what long-standing truth was known, was withheld except to the few planners. The current *magical/technological* cover-up continues with regard to these truths as well as the planned enslavement of all but the elite planners. Difficult as it will be for those of the Judaic/Christian heritage to accept, their cosmological story was deliberately written in a distorted form utilizing written records later conveniently hidden or destroyed and utilizing what was believed to be myths. (Little known published scientific research reveals through translations of written records these myths were actual oral history passed from one generation to the next for hundreds of years.) This deliberately distorted cosmology was compiled at the beginning of the planned scenario as it plays out today.

When a genetically altered teacher was born within this religious focus and instructed with truth, he suffered a planned near death and escaped to another part of the planet. Believing him dead, deification soon followed. The distortion of those teachings was almost immediate, in order that the plan being laid and yet to manifest in wholeness, might not be derailed. This genetically enhanced human's personal choice for this mission was to teach personal responsibility.

This has brought forth the imposing question of what to do about changing the outcome at this late stage in the sequence of happenings leading to the planned future that is nearly incomprehensible to humanity. Thus a second layer of entreaties for help was begun by a small unorganized group of conscious awareness on this planet, one that was/is answerable. We have now returned to the present moment in our consideration of an encapsulated history of earth's human population.

II-20

The avenue of entry into the minds and most important of all, the hearts of humanity lies not so much through logic as through the emotions. The great playing card of the deceptive plan has been the emotion of fear. Subliminal guidance is the first layer of control, then more layers are added to achieve control of whatever focus is desired. The last and most effective leverage of all is fear. Fear is the most creative of thought forms in the negative aspect. Love is the most creative in the positive expression.

The reason these are at the top of the scale in the human focus is the rate of the vibration of emotion that accompanies each. The degree in which the human can experience these depends upon the range in which each has experienced them. Thus you can understand the reason for the deliberate proliferation of horror, war and gangster type movies. These have been deliberately promoted for the express purpose of increasing the experiencing range of fear. Those films that pass for "love" experiences usually contain great feelings of remorse and sadness as well as more subtle experiences of fear. The technological societies of the planet have little experience with what true love really is. Fed a diet of sexual based unfulfilling relationships as love, it is no surprise that family life has reached a disastrous level for so many. Every negative aspect is paraded as the norm. Just as each individual is a human becoming, so also each relationship and family is a entity becoming, formed by the combination focus of the 2 or more included within it. With no agreed upon ideal purpose and few of the character traits necessary to carry each through the experience, the only answer seems to be the experience of a stream of beginnings and endings.

In contrast, those who have had what is called near death experiences return to their conscious realities with regret for having to return and an overwhelming experience of what they term love. These were experiences of the energies that emanate through the creative focus that maintains and expands this galaxy. It is, when analyzed, if that is even possible, the action of the universal laws to their full extent: attraction, intention and allowance resulting in the harmony of balance. This focus is supported by an even greater focus of these laws in action. It is the added presence of harmony that seems so intensely pleasant in those brief experiences.

It is not difficult for each to be in the experience of the negative situations that are there at every turn in the search for respite from stressful living. One needs only to close the eyes and check the true feelings in the midst of an adventure movie to know these inner feelings are not harmonious. It is the balancing experience of the opposite, the harmonious vibration of creation that brought forth each self-aware conscious entity and maintains each and all through a continuing focus of that same energy, that is overwhelmed by deliberate diversion from it. This is not because this marvelous energy isn't available; it is that the conscious awareness is too cluttered to find the quiet space within to experience it. If it cannot be even slightly experienced, how indeed can it be drawn in, (attracted), and focused into expression and a greater experience of it. In order to truly experience it, it must flow through the conscious awareness and be refocused into the rebirth of greater expression. In other words, to know love it must be attracted, encompassed and expressed outwardly through both acknowledgement and outward transference of it. In this process it is magnified and flows with the creative expression. That is how each comes into being and creates the opportunity to become.

The sexual romantic hugging and kissing "love" that has been programmed as love is not the love that creates and maintains physical galaxies and uncountable beings becoming. Just as the word god conjures up all kinds of negative reactions because of its false and confusing uses and is best avoided thus the word love has been avoided within these messages. Instead "flow of creative energies, etc.," has been substituted. The people who have had near death experiences return to conscious awareness with a true understanding of the feeling experience that the word love was intended to convey. Brief glimpses of it are experienced.

Sometimes, but not always, a mother's first experiences with a new baby; couples who have shared long lives together reach that level of regard for each other; there are rare appreciative times of nature to name a few. These are intense moments of an emotional/vibratory level that is called enlightenment or ecstasy. These are so strange and unfamiliar to most of the humans on this planet that the few able to attain and maintain it become "saints" if this state of empowerment becomes known. It is the level at which manifestation of thought is so natural that seemingly impossible feats are accomplished. It is, compared to the norm on this planet, "superconsciousness." However, in other human experiences on other planets, it is normal life expression.

The point of this discussion is an attempt to explain to a small degree what mankind on this planet is missing out on. What you are experiencing as manifested life, is a poor substitute for what it was intended to be. What is being offered is an opportunity to take advantage of a doorway of "grace," an offer of a favor, a special dispensation. Accepting this will allow the opportunity to bridge the gap of lost normal evolvement that should have been accomplished in the time spent in this dead-end experience. This is available to all mankind on this planet, not just those transplanted humans. The effects of intervention and denial of freewill choice ripple outward and the sequential results are not known. Even this special privilege may bring effects that are not anticipated though careful consideration has been given before making this privilege available. If the inhabitants of earth choose not to accept the opportunity, then it is a moot point.

Those that have sat through hours and hours of teaching/ preaching within religious institutions may find some of these messages reminiscent of those experiences. These are not meant to be so. These are meant to bring as many considerations as possible before the conscious awareness in order that the focus of thought may be guided through a decision process that will allow for logical conclusions and commitment that will not be regretted. The commitment to the birthing of a new paradigm requires courage and tenacity, for the time of chaos is necessary. As long as that which does not serve this branch of humanity's evolvement remains intact, it is impossible to birth something of total newness. Chaos, order, chaos followed by a new form of order is the flow of creation. It is creation living itself, for creation is aware and is life.

II-21

There is a point of personal decision that must be reached by each individual that chooses to become involved in this project. It must be understood that once the commitment is made, it will change the perspective, the way in which the experience of situations and relationships are comprehended. If the commitment is real, it will be as if you are observing from a greater perspective. It will be as if there is a split reality. The daily experience will be the same, yet an observational dimension will seem to be added. The observation mode will be experienced as an ability to understand how various past and present knowledge and experience fit into a fluid puzzle picture. There will be a realization that reality as known has changed. It will be observed that the pieces of the puzzle are not firm and do not come together into a recognizable static picture. Instead the pieces are of a gelatinous nature and are moving and flowing in constantly changing patterns. In the perception of this process, it is then possible to conceive that certain rigid insertions cause the ebb and flow to be influenced to form rigid dam like structures restricting the freedom of the natural flow. If maintained within the human individual flow of changing patterns, this brings on the end of the experience, as the life force must continue to express in a free-flowing fashion, or it is withdrawn. This is also true within a larger group concept.

When it is possible to encompass this concept of the elementary need to express that is at the very essence if creation, then it can be understood that the halting of this flow of progress and any plan to reverse it causes chaos. Within the mind's eye it is like a flow of multiple artists' colors flowing together and yet staying separate and spreading out. At one place, the colors are moving in a slow swirl and beginning to coagulate and intermingle in a darkening manner that is not consistent. As the watcher observes from the over-view position, it is apparent that this coagulated point cannot stop the flow that is moving all around it. The flow will continue to move around it and leave it behind. If the consistency of this coagulated energy can be softened, it can again rejoin the flow.

The job of softening and dissolving this dark and coagulated energy is the object and purpose of these messages. If the beliefs of the mass consciousness of this planet can be changed and a new paradigm of experience conceived and accepted the dark and coagulated energies will dissolve and the expansive flow of creation will be restored.

Within the flow of creation, the knowledge that is lived into wisdom moves through stages of what is truth within the vibrational/dimensional realms of experience. As knowledge becomes wisdom, then these conceptual lines of delineation are surpassed and the old concepts are outdated and no longer applicable. As transplanted humanity became aware that something must curb their over stimulated aggressive tendencies, religion was conceptualized. With the genetic balance returned, now it is time for those humans to leave this concept behind and begin to conceptualize the causative factors that brought them into manifested experience. They must conceive on the larger scale what it is that maintains not only their individual focus but also the larger focus of the galactic environment of their life. It is time to return to citizenship on a grander scale. All of this must be bitten off, chewed and digested in a very large bite. Why so quickly? Two reasons: first, all previous opportunities to do this were refused. Secondly, sometimes the medicine in one large bitter pill is more effective than all the small ones.

II-22

When the transition begins to take place within each individual consciousness there will be a literal rebirth as the awareness is released into a new sphere. The acceptance of the reality of multiple layers of endeavor that are operating simultaneously with multiple agendas is the first step of entering greater dimensional living. The personal reality is enveloped within local, regional, state, national and global realities that are each focused on greater agendas and are each a more encompassing reality. It is the purpose of the purposeful negative planners to encompass and blend these multiple realities into one blended focus with one agenda, theirs. Mankind can avoid participation in an experience of a collapsing dimensional reality by creating its own new experience within the negative plan. It is possible to do this through participation of the creation of the new paradigm. Each may participate in bringing forth its unknown and yet to be created layers of encompassing new realities. Without the knowledge of the magnitude and power of this project the negative planners cannot prevent it, if the desire, commitment and resolve to bring it forth is present and active in the necessary number of humans. There is no way they can control a human's ability to focus on the creation of a new reality, unless that human allows their thought process to be overwhelmed. Granted it will take commitment and resolve, but the potentiality to do this is present in all, accept those with advanced brain deterioration.

Those beings would include those with advanced Alzheimer's (It is interesting to note the honoring of a dis-ease by capitalization.), those that have "fried" their brain cells with excessive drug abuse and those with particular birth defects. Again, it is noted that the freewill choices of life style will have end results that must be accepted. How these choices play out remain unknown to others. Each must answer to or be rewarded for these within their own lifetime review. The choice to transcend experience into wisdom is always available, but it must be a true realization accompanied by a shift in attitude and deed. It must be remembered that the universal law of attraction works. The clarification and understanding of the nuances these laws encompass much understanding. The opportunity to know of and understand the application of these could be greatly enhanced by the teaching of enlightened beings who would walk among you, if invited and when it is safe for them to do so. There is a spiritual law book available, but the study of it must not interfere with the focus on the manifestation of the new paradigm. Without the framework of a new paradigm within which to experience the understanding and use of these laws in practical reality, it would be difficult for earth's humanity as a whole to experience these truths. It is necessary to begin at a practical beginning point.

It is within possibility for those who are reading these messages to begin to contemplate the action of the first two laws of the universe within their life experience to this time. The law of like drawing likes sometimes looks like opposites attracting as in the case of relationships. However, on deeper understanding when reviewed in wisdom further along in the duration of the experience, more similarity than difference is usually discovered. The ability to deliberately attract the experience or lack of the experience of material manifestation into being through purposeful thought and endeavor supports the awareness of the second law. The law of allowance is more difficult to perceive because of the degree of control exercised individually and by outside psychological (including religious) and technological mind manipulations. It is indeed, difficult for most of mankind to actually have and/or maintain a sovereign attitude. The opportunity to live life with freedom of choice and be *allowed* to observe and learn from the results of those choices is rare. To declare the desire to do so is incorporated within the desire for a new paradigm of experience.

The choice to participate in the creation of the new paradigm must not involve commitment to enslavement by another set of rules and regulations that simply control in a different way. That would not be a new paradigm. Herein lies the difficulty of transcending what exists and conceptualizing an entirely different framework of experience. It is only the statement of purpose that is necessary. It must then be followed by a slim, concise outline. Fleshing it out will be the adventure of the new future. A very *basic* outline will not seem to be enough but if more is attempted it will be contaminated with the concepts of the present. Surely mankind has had enough of the same old, same old simply repackaged and that always has produced physical and spiritual indigestion.

Repetitions again! These are to keep the focus where it is intended. First focus on the individual consciousness transition from victim to victor. It is the victor that writes the history. This time, do not bother to write the history of the past, for it is what it is, and there will be no time to care. It is time to move on. This time it is the victor that will write the history of the future. These messages and this project are gifts to earth's humankind, from their galactic brothers and sisters, to help ensure it is they that write their own future and not the enslavers. The question is, will the gifts be accepted and acted on by enough of humanity to change the unpleasant future planned to manifest in the very near future? Your decision is awaited with great love and caring. All the help possible is given at all times for the asking. Only when you are able to ask from the greater perspective of the victory of control of your own consciousness can physical help be given, not on an individual basis, but to the planet and its inhabitants as a whole.

II-23

With each sequential chapter of the experience of the transplanted humans on this planet the results of every effort to counteract the genetic variation has seemed to end in futility. However, that is the perception from "inside the forest" so to speak. The introduction of a normal human DNA/RNA structure to earth's human gene pool allowed a correction to spread by random selection through the subsequent generations. Hundreds of years have gone by as this effective genetic process has gone through its natural sequence. What appears to be a long time in your counting within creations orderly process is merely the blinking of an eye in the larger picture. Those indigenous groups that have been included in the intermixing process by choice or otherwise have received both genetic alterations, causing uninvited changes in their archetypal evolutionary pattern.

This points out the consequences that ripple outward when the will of one group is forced upon another. Even though an individual may make a freewill choice, the effects for the generations that follow are influenced in ways that are not perceived at the time of the initial decision. The intentional changing of the genetic structure of a large group is a slow process, but as the change begins to manifest, it then spreads at an exponential rate.

It must be acknowledged that the return to the genetic norm has not manifested in an even pattern throughout the planet. Not all groups with the altered genetic pattern have accepted the introduced gene resource at the same rate. Social and religious bias has influenced this because of the prevention of intermarriage with other groups, thereby locking out the introduced positive genetic change. This has allowed a considerable number of beings to remain locked in the more aggressive pattern. Many of these are deeply involved in the negative enslavement focus. It must be pointed out here <u>very strongly,</u> that this does *not* indicate that there are superior and inferior groups. Within creation, many diverse experiences of evolvement are allowed. If that type of "judgement" existed, then where indeed would earth's population be within the total scale of evolvement? Certainly not in an enviable place! Any feelings of superiority can be put in their place by raising the question for the necessity of the whole of the galaxy to be concerned with the plight of this planet because of the consciousness of its inhabitants! Be very, very careful in understanding these particular explanations. No judgment is intended, only brief overview lessons in understanding the situation of all the people of the planet.

Certainly among all the groups there are what can be termed progressive and regressive genes. Through the random process of available gene combinations at conception it is possible for the most aggressive being, with the appropriate partner, to procreate a genetic opposite in the next generation. It has been happening since the project was started. It is how the situation has changed and has reached the present point with a now possible influence of the planetary future. Had the genetic selection process been apparent at the conscious level, then the introduced genes to modify the aggressive tendencies would have been promptly bred out for the purposes of warfare and continuation in the confines of aggression for the transplanted human group would have been assured.

The complexity of the universal laws increases, as they are understood. Moving through the understanding of the laws of attraction and focused intentional manifestation to the law of allowance adds complexity at each level for all are interactive. Application of the law of allowance opens the door to experience the flow of creative energy. It might be said that it is "love in action." What is called patience is allowance. Here a nuance must be understood. There is a difference between tolerance and patience. The difference can best be described by the emotion that is felt. This is an especially fruitful opportunity for self-contemplation. Tolerance carries an emotional charge of resentment while patience is usually accompanied by heartfelt anticipation, even amusement, by the observer. There is a very profoundly observable difference between tolerance and patience. This is a difference that can be observed and intentionally changed in mid-stream, so to speak. It is this type of conscious decision that promotes the transcendence of knowledge into wisdom through the conscious choice to rise above one emotion into the other by giving up an attitude and an opinion. Without releasing what is causing the resentment, no transition of attitude can be made. In the human experience, it is noted that release of tolerance into patience is often accompanied by physical smiling. An indication of just how good it feels to allow the creational flow to express through human experience.

It is hoped those who spread these messages remember to be patient with their fellow humans, for there will be much rejection in the beginning. The comfort zone of deeply ingrained programming is difficult to soften. A great deal of seeding must be done. Even though rejected, the seed ideas will remain and await the triggering that will cause them to root and grow. What the triggers are will be unknown, for all are unique to each conscious awareness. The seeds need not be full explanations, but for many only what appear to be chance remarks can be accepted in the moment. Just that much is doing your job well, for it is critical to sense what is and is not appropriate. Too much locks the door before it opens even a crack.

The Christian religion has employed the most aggressive proselytizing program in the history of the planet. If the founding teacher of the distorted Christian faith had been allowed to complete his teaching to its potential, and had it been spread with the zeal of the Christian focus, then marvelous progress would have been made. Nonetheless, the members have applied the first two universal laws relentlessly without understanding them. Through contemplation of this point, much about the use and misuse of these two laws can be learned. With *discernment,* "a few" of these applications could be applied to the advancement of the new paradigm; certainly the "never give up" aspect of their approach.

II-24

It is appropriate to mention again the fact that there is among earth's population those who have volunteered to pause in their personal evolvement process and place their progress in jeopardy. This has been purposefully done to assist earth's inhabitants to make the long overdue transition out of isolation and back into greater evolvement and involvement with their galactic brothers, sisters and cousins. These have assumed the same bodies with the same random genetic physical expressions that each conscious awareness on earth assumes at birth. Their motivations for doing this are as varied as the experiences that allowed them their personal evolvement. In general, it may be assumed that the benefits to earth and her inhabitants was considered worth the risk of the loss of their progress should the opportunity again be rejected. If earth's inhabitants choose to remain stuck in their current pattern of experience, these beings will remain within that destiny. The risk is also a great motivator.

There are two reasons for these messages. The first is to awaken the volunteers and answer invocations for help. The second is to provide the focus for the birth of this new paradigm of human experience for which these evolved beings were willing to take such great risk. It is for you to know that successful deeds of valor do not go without reward. It is not at all "egotistical" for each one that reads this material to give careful consideration as to whether or not they are one of the "visiting" volunteers. To ponder this possibility is wise indeed. Knowingness within will govern awareness of the truth of this possibility and allow consideration of the risk of ignoring it insofar as what that could mean in the larger picture. Whether or not this is a person's truth, to aid in offering the opportunity for humanity to change its future and return to its rightful place within the creative flow of evolvement, is reason enough to <u>volunteer now</u> as a member of the ground crew. Creative thought is not limited to any one group, but is inherent within *all* self-aware consciousness. It is called becoming!

Certainly the volunteers do not place their earned progress in jeopardy to simply acknowledge it. They volunteer to assist their fellow humans to move beyond this present mode of experience. Each brings their special successful experiencing techniques as a contribution to the birth and launching of the new paradigm of experience. The logical way to help humanity to conceive of this new mode of experience is to participate within the present one so that it can be understood. In the midst of the chaos of imbalance, all volunteers have the ability to purposefully remember aspects of recent balanced experience and give guidance with regard to these aspects in the conception of the purpose and outline for the new experience desired by earth's inhabitants. These first volunteers are one part of the answer to the prayers and supplications for help that have been focused to "god." The new volunteers attracted to this process and joining with equal commitment are the return flow of invested energy, reflecting the exchange that is the dynamic operative quality of creation. It is the law of attraction in action. As the law of intentional creation, through the two steps of birthing the new paradigm, is added to the attraction process, vibratory intensity increases and transformation toward manifestation into perceivable reality begins.

It is necessary for all volunteers to consider, contemplate and decide to accept the truth of who and what each one is and then move on into the fuller completion of each assigned segment. The first step is to spread the knowledge of the opportunity to create a new paradigm of experience, keeping the concept simple, simple, simple!!! Gently inform and encourage many to change their consciousness from victim to victor through the knowledge that thought has the power to change manifested creation. Creation expresses in all experience, situations and circumstances as well as "things." Each thought, word and deed through attitudes and beliefs structures everyone's experience.

Each person every day is surrounded with many opportunities to offer a different perspective or a word of encouragement that assists the knowledge and understanding of this basic concept. This is planting the seeds for changes in the mass consciousness. This may seem a small way to begin this extraordinary change, but once begun in this people to people manner it will build at an exponential rate. Many are ready and waiting to respond positively now to carry and spread the change. These will be receptive because the present mode of life expression just doesn't seem right, but no ideas resonate within them for what to do about this knowingness. There is only a sense of being overwhelmed by the immensity of their situation and the presence of these discordant inner feelings. These moments are the opportunities to begin to walk the path of your impending new future. Plant seeds at every opportunity. As you do, you will attract more opportunities to do so. Now is the sequential moment to stand in the reality of who and what you are and begin to experience the reason for being in this body on this planet at this moment. The alarm clock is ringing. It is time to wake up and begin living in the joy of creating the new future.

II-25

It is well known among the people on the planet that the time of chaos that has long been predicted appears to be manifesting into reality. These predictions were purposefully implanted in some of the religious teachings. However, the indigenous tribes long ago taught similar predictions clearly defining this time frame. That appears to make both coincide. The difference is that some of these predictions were promulgated for a purpose and those of the indigenous people are genuine prophecies. Their prophecies contain identifiable time frame predictions (The Mayan calendar for example, calculates/prophesying the end of the current 26,000-year cycle as ending on December 12, 2012) while those of deliberate intent to induce fear assured those that hear them the exact time cannot be known. This enables them to use various sets of conditions as indications of their possible manifestation and through the years to manipulate the believers over and over again. American Indian prophecies tell of a time of chaos to be followed by the time of the "rainbow man." Zuni Indian art contains depictions of a rainbow man in anticipation of that future event. It is the purpose of these messages to bring that prophecy to fruition.

That which has been and is judged as "pagan" often contains portions of truth when the analogies are understood through wisdom. There is no one perfect way to truth for all of mankind, for each must create his or her own path. This does not indicate that wisdom through knowledge applied is not available within a group approach, as long as the focus is open and searching. When a group focus becomes locked in rigid dogma it becomes a whirlpool and not a flow within the expansive creative focus. It is to be remembered that other than the universal laws, what appears to be absolutely true often must be transcended as the knowledge experienced becomes wisdom. At that point, new applicable knowledge becomes available to experience into wisdom, and the old concepts no longer apply. The first time this is experienced in a lifetime, it can be traumatic. The individual is faced with the decision of whether to stay with what has brought him/her to the familiar point of understanding and remain in the whirlpool or let go and move on in the process of evolvement. Many of those who have sincerely searched in this lifetime have often experienced wisdom gained, followed by boredom and soon begin new quests for knowledge. Those who have grown from early childhood into maturity within the indoctrination of a single religious focus may find opening to a wider perspective through these messages as emancipation or find themselves in shocked dismay. Each who allow time to ponder both points of view in their hearts will come to a knowing of what is true for them and act accordingly. It is hoped that those of both points of view will practice allowance. It is certainly to be practiced by the volunteers. All are humans becoming. "Help us to become!"

The vision of the "Rainbow Man" and the anticipation of his coming can be interpreted two ways. Those of the Christian viewpoint could assume it means the return of Jmmanuel (Jesus) or it could indicate the advent of a wiser and emancipated human population on earth. Certainly it will require a wiser group to bring forth the new paradigm of human experience, thus the prophecy would seem quite clear. However, it could also indicate both as true. It would require an open minded and far less aggressive human focus for Jmmanuel to walk again among his human brothers and sisters in safety. The distortions of his teachings would make it impossible for those indoctrinated in the current beliefs to recognize and accept him for who and what he is because of their current understandings and expectations.

The picture of the rainbow man/woman is an easy visualization to hold in mind for a depiction of the anticipated personal experience within the new paradigm. It is important that meaningful symbology be adopted in order that the new paradigm become real in the minds of the those who desire this transcendence process to become a reality. It could represent the consciousness change from victim to victor through attitude and thought adjustment and a resting point in the midst of the confusion of change. This transition in how life is experienced will not come about without bringing about some internal chaos within personal experience. This will be preparation for that which will manifest on a larger scale as this concept takes root and grows within the mass consciousness for it is a reversal in the direction of the journey of mankind. It might be compared to walking down a long flight of stairs with a large group of people, changing your mind half way down, turning around and going back up through them. When enough people also change their minds and start going back up, it won't be as difficult. However, for the ground crew, who are the first to begin this process, it will take purposeful intent with resolve to accomplish this feat. Picturing this process in the mind's eye allows for the understanding that volunteering for this mission requires much dedicated involvement to plan, organize and arrive at the picnic for rainbow people.

As you listen to the media presentations, the theme of resistance to perceived wrong doers and evil manifestations of disease, etc., for example, is spelled out as the "war on poverty, the war on drugs or the war on ?" It is amazing to observers that citizens have not realized that there is yet to be one stance *against* that has produced effective results. It does however provide a way to extort *your* money out of your pockets directly and from your national treasury. Among your common sayings are many truisms. "What you resist persists." It is encouraged that the volunteers observe this truism at work within their personal and the national experience. It is preparation for a basic consciousness transition.

II-26

The law of allowance is the most difficult of the three active or dynamic universal laws to accept as necessary and to practice. It is essential to understand the law of attraction in order to apply the law of allowance. The composite of thoughts, opinions and attitudes of each individual generate the experience patterns of living. Through the flow of daily experiences these are filtered through this composite of each one's total collective experience. In this way the pattern or matrix is in a dynamic and fluid process. When attitudes and opinions are deliberately programmed within a limited set of rigid guidelines, the activity level of the total pattern of experience begins to slow. The key is the word deliberately. This means that the guidelines are imposed, not by the individual through knowledge experienced into wisdom but by the beliefs imposed on the individual by those he/she considers outside authorities. The pattern of each individual as a whole _attracts_ to itself life experiences that resonate in harmony with that pattern. If a person desires some thing or some experience that does not resonate with that pattern, it is difficult, if not impossible to attract it. Two divergent patterns cannot blend cohesively.

For example, there are few within the "modern societal norm" that do not know at least one man or woman that in the scenario of several marriages repeats the same pattern of abused/abuser relationships. The pattern of the victim draws the abuser, whether physical or verbal, no matter how many times a new partner enters the picture. This is especially true if the relationships quickly follow each other. The pattern of experience is held in place by the thoughts, attitudes and opinions that are at the basis of self-awareness. The victim desires to be rescued.

Someone or some event must come and change their life. If however, there is time taken to consider and contemplate the elements of the situation resulting in changes of attitude and opinion (knowledge to wisdom) the pattern of experience can change.

The tragedy of religious teachings of an outside primal source as a personified rescuer is that it not only instills a victim consciousness, but also feeds it. A victimized personified deity hanging on a cross as a status of veneration draws to those believers what they venerate, the victim experience. If poverty is venerated, poverty is attracted. If hard work is venerated, then life will be filled with hard work. If killing is venerated, then death is attracted. Whatever the dominant focus of thought, attitude, and opinion, is will influence the overall matrix and dominate the attraction of experience.

A child is born into its family situation, or lack of one, in innocence, except for inherited genetic coding. It is totally influenced in its experience by the same thoughts, attitudes and opinions of its parents until it is old enough to begin to attract some of its own experiences. Eventually it graduates to its own field of attraction, but the pattern of its matrix is already present. The direct influence of the family is present to the degree of acceptance of those thoughts, attitudes and opinions by the maturing individual. The physical attributes present also contribute to the attitudes that develop during the maturation process. Parental, teacher and peer influences all play their part. More layers of influence are present. The thoughts, attitudes and opinions of groups input to the individual matrix. Identities within ethnic, neighborhood, city, region, state, nation, etc., add their influence. Next add the conscious and subconscious programming by radio, TV, movies, newspapers, magazines, and on-line information. Each of these composite patterns is received and filtered through thought, opinion and attitude to create the individual resonating matrix.

As the overall life experience for a major portion of the inhabitants of the planet becomes measurably more complex, the matrix designs have become less defined. The resulting confusion and overwhelm being experienced has become more intense reflecting this lack of matrix definition. This appears as self-absorption as each attempts to stay focused within the vagueness of their indefinite pattern. The resulting feelings of overwhelm and lack of definition allows for the planners of dark deeds to tighten the noose of creeping enslavement literally before the eyes of the victims without their notice. Those awake and awakening are incredulous that the situation has reached this ludicrous degree.

Through understanding this overview of the combined and individual experience of mankind on planet earth, it would appear that the solution of this deteriorating human experience would logically be to give it up in its present form and replace the complexity with simplicity. How can this be accomplished? Refer to the "Handbook for The New Paradigm" for directions. "When all else fails, read the directions." An apropos truism!

II-27

The universal laws, though appearing simple in concept, contain many nuances that appear as paradoxes. A paradox is "a statement that seems contradictory, etc., but may be true in fact; a statement that is self-contradictory, and, hence, false" as quoted from Webster's New World dictionary. For example, the law of allowance is not a law unless upheld by the laws of attraction and intentional creation. In this case then, the law of allowance is a paradox. It is and is not a law. Inasmuch as the underlying basis of creation is conceptional thought, the laws are concepts to be interpreted or applied within the parameters of each and the combination of all. In the simplest terms possible, this means that as each is understood, it must also be understood that all act in cooperation bringing forth the result of harmony and balance. The 4th law depends on the interaction of the previous three as a prerequisite. Personal and group awareness acts as a form of clearinghouse for these fundamental components of creation. Without firm guidelines for expression, creation would express only as incomprehensible chaos. Attempting to comprehend the underlying laws of creation within their continuous interacting flow as they delineate creation is something like wondering which came first, the chicken or the egg. THE CREATION SIMPLY IS! It is to be comprehended and joined cooperatively at the point of realization to the best of each one's ability to do so. Whatever that is, is "good enough!"

It is logical then to come to the understanding that evolvement within creation is a constantly exchanging cooperative process of knowledge and experience toward wisdom. Those three words can be exchanged for attraction, intention and allowance. The inclusion of new information within the belief system allows for changes in thoughts, opinions and attitudes. This then begins the process of becoming knowledge applied because the matrix or pattern of the individual or group changes and attracts different experiences. Through the trial and error process experience sooner or later becomes understanding and the cycle repeats. Creation and its processes are all logical. Thought thinking could function in no other mode that would manifest and maintain form. Emotion is an important ingredient within the process. However, when, in the individual or group experience, it runs the show, emotion then becomes a trap and indicates a correctable imbalance. It indicates the necessity of setting aside time for self-contemplation and "pondering in the heart" to determine the truth of the information, situation or circumstance that triggers the emotional reaction. It is important to determine what indeed is the reason for the emotion. When the comfort zone must be defended, it may be too rigidly maintained. Perhaps it is the time to consider letting go and getting back into the flow. That which assaults the comfort zone of the belief system can often times contain the elements for moving to the next level of evolvement and deserves consideration. Considering and looking for the logic within the whole of the issue or situation is participating within the 3 steps of basic creation, leading to the 4th.

Inertia is not an energetic element; therefore it results in either termination of the focus or causes a void that will be filled with something. It is best if it is filled intentionally. The object is to be charismatic within the process of participating in creation. Each is a focused point of self-awareness within the entirety of creation. This is not an insignificant status. There is no such thing as being "just a human being"! Underlying all of creation, including the universal laws, is pure potentiality. As a focused self-aware component of the whole, the potentiality of that whole belongs to each and every component. Each is "entitled" to equal access to that potentiality by simply applying it, indeed by becoming it. What that potentiality is for each individual or group, is a matter of choice governed only by current genetic limitations and thoughts, opinions and attitudes. Therefore, thoughts, attitudes and opinions govern how much advantage is taken of the absolute potentiality that is yours by right of who and what you are. Those that have progressed beyond the earth experience by availing themselves of this opportunity to become have been called "gods." That which they "have done, you can do also and more." It is your already owned entitlement. It is time to stop listening to the falsehoods of the need to wait until after-death to claim your heritage. Is yours now, and always has been. The knowledge of who and what you are allows you to apply the laws by which you were birthed into the creational flow, and to become your dreams. It is your right to live life abundantly.

Among the nuances of the application of the laws is the necessity to understand that it is necessary to live *"within"* the laws. It is within the law of allowance that it is appropriate to discuss abundance and luxury. A dictionary often contains much wisdom and is most helpful in reaching greater understanding. According to Webster's New World Dictionary, abundance is "great plenty, more than enough." Luxury is "the enjoyment of the best and most costly things, anything contributing to such enjoyment, usually something not necessary." Therefore abundance is living within the law of allowance for it allows all to also live in abundance. Luxury encompasses living in extraordinary abundance. It is also *very important* to emphasize that abundance is not necessarily the same thing to each becoming focus of awareness! It is the responsibility of each one in the process of becoming to manifest their life experience within their own ability to function within the laws. However, it is not within the laws to take another's abundance to add to your own. Cooperation is the keynote and competition is the death knell of progress. Does that mean its unfitting to win a race or participate in athletic events or to be better at something than others? Of course not, it is just that the perspective is required to fit *"within"* the application of the universal laws. This is an example of the paradox principle that can easily become a trap.

The path of becoming is like your game of golf, not at all predictable in every aspect or the ability to always repeat success. Therein lies the challenge and the fascination of the game. In the game of life, there is no dropping out. Once focused into awareness, the game is ongoing. It may change playing fields, but it keeps on keeping on. It is much easier to play if that concept is firmly held in mind. The more playful the attitude and the greater the sense of humor that is brought into the process, the easier the passage through becomes. Indeed, those who have trod the path before you laugh well and frequently. Try it, you will like it.

II-28

It is through the probabilities of acceptance of the material contained in these messages that the focus point of the change in mass consciousness is focused. The new paradigm of human experience is based upon a multi-faceted campaign to assist mankind to bring about the much-needed completion of this phase of experience. If indeed what is called reincarnation is true and if the aboriginal tribe in Australia can request to be reincarnated on another planet, why isn't it possible for the genetically corrected portion of the transplanted segment of humanity to do this? The answer lies in the degree of knowledge lived into wisdom. Those particular people are well aware of their connection to creation and have learned to live in harmony with nature. They are watching their young people being seduced by modern technology, what they consider beliefs not lived into wisdom and see their progress earned slipping away. Their beliefs and what is judged as a meager existence in the judgment of modern societies is to them wholeness and abundance lived in peace and harmony. It is a matter of perspective.

The point is, where within "religion driven societies" is progress in applying the basic universal laws? Where is harmony with nature and living in peace with one another in the modern technological society? Is it possible to ever learn those lessons within the focus of the centuries upon centuries of ongoing genetic and learned behavior? It does not appear so to those charged with the task of observing the process. So again your brothers/sisters offer helping hands for they truly care about you and desire to see you return to the family of evolving humanity. It is truly said of mankind on earth, if something doesn't work, they just seem to do more of it.

Indeed, it is true that there are some of what you call aliens that are instigating your situation and fully cooperating with the dark planners on your planet. But they are closely related to the basic group of planners also through genetic addition. Is earth the only planet out of balance? No, as it has been mentioned before, this segment of creation, this galaxy, that is the realm of focus included in these messages, experiences the expansiveness of the creative flow through the energetics of positive and negative experiences. Like disease in your bodies, a level of great imbalance can spread and thus a cure is sought. In the case of earth, surgery is not the recommended cure. It is preferred that the holistic method of changing thoughts, attitudes and opinions create a renewal and a new paradigm of experience. This would allow mankind to rejoin the creative flow through transcending this experience rather than stubbornly continuing on the wheel of repetition until they do complete the transition individually and collectively farther down the sequential time frame.

The situation on this planet, as confusing as it is to comprehend, is as it is. It is important to grasp the reality and the seriousness of the consequences of it continuation, but the focus of importance is on creating the change. It will not be found through continued observation of the imbalance, but in placing the focus on what is desired to replace it. There is no other way to move through it and into what is desired. Again it is important to stress the need to accept that the belief systems now present within the mass awareness of the planet have _not_ lead humanity out of it dilemma. These have mired it more deeply than ever in the situation now leading it to the lowest ebb yet of this human experience. If it hasn't worked in the past, and it doesn't work now, then it is time to accept that, open the belief system to different ideas and ponder their truth rather than reject them without consideration.

When enough are reached and the truth of the above analysis is accepted, then the spread of the change out of victim consciousness will begin in earnest. At a particular exponential rate, the mass consciousness will accept this understanding and at that point the _simple bare bones_ outline of the project will be advanced. The pivotal point is reached when the critical group in this focused thought is in harmony with the surrounding galactic environment, when it conforms to and within the universal laws, and becomes the intent of humanity. It is then that the victory is won, the victors will write the new scenario and, on request, advice is available to accomplish the manifestation of the new experience. Again, free will is the controlling factor. The advisors have available technology that surpasses any that is present on earth. These can and will be shared and abundant life will not mean tramping barefoot in the desert, unless the victors steadfastly choose that scenario. If mankind chooses to stubbornly remain within the present belief system and continue the current scenario, tramping barefoot in the desert will seem abundant indeed.

Is the above meant as a threat? No indeed! Simply how it is!

II-29

It is the responsibility of those accepting the information/ knowledge contained within these messages to integrate it into the structure of their belief system. Simply put, that means to live it into wisdom by delivering the message to Garcia. Garcia is everyone who can and will receive the messages and in turn deliver the message of the new paradigm to more that will accept the mission. In this way, the expansive flow of creation is then at work laying the foundation for the new paradigm. Once the simple statement of purpose is conceptualized it will rapidly reinforce the network that will then already be initialized. When the victim consciousness is transcended, the statement of purpose will lead individual and group awareness to the next level; thus it must be as simple as the statement of "I/we/they am/are (a) human(s) becoming, help me/us/ them to become!" What logically is the next level of awareness to be encompassed in order to arrive at the ability to conceptualize the skeletal format of the new paradigm? What words would empower the human consciousness to lift its lethargic self-awareness to resolutely desire to determine its own present and future individually and in unity? This simple powerful call to the infinite potentiality of creation that is at the magnetic center of the self-awareness of each human is waiting to be tapped. (Ask the level of awareness that focuses creation through awareness at the level of the solar system, or even the galaxy. These do exist. Ask *from* a point of awareness beyond the victim consciousness and there will be an answer.)

Once awakened to itself, self-awareness desires and searches for channels through which to express. This potentiality has been perceived and exploited through techniques of manipulation by governmental and religious leaders of the past and present. A new paradigm must transcend this in order to be a new paradigm. It is not necessary to conceptualize the new paradigm in completeness to understand its purpose. Clearly delineating the purpose is the next logical step in the process. The mind filled with clutter doubts its ability to conceptualize something new amid the confusion that reigns. However, once the cause and intent of the confusion is perceived and the decision to release the victim stance is made, the clutter moves into the background. The awareness becomes intrigued as latent triggers are activated that intuitively bring to the conscious mind the desire for freedom to live a self-determined existence.

It is important to comprehend that the center of self-awareness, that aspect of self that knows it exists, is the magnetic focus that attracts the body and all experience. It is a holographic microchip of creation. A holograph can be replicated from a tiny cell of the original. As the creation is to be venerated, respected and held in the highest honor, so the self-awareness to be held in equal veneration, honor and respect. This magnet of energy is focused at conception and clothes itself in a body to experience and when withdrawn, death of the body results. It is up to each to contemplate the creation and to shine the light of the understanding of it through this microchip of self-awareness outward by living life's experiences into wisdom. As this is done within the universal laws that do govern this process, the holograph of the creation is gradually expressed through each one to a greater and greater degree. It is creation thinking and through projected thought expanding and knowing itself. Creation is self-aware through its focused microchips mimicking its own process. As each self-aware living being grows through wisdom acquired, the experiences change in dimensional magnitude. To those who acquire much wisdom, much is required to continue the exponential growth. Living the creational adventure is much like reading a good mystery book. Once involved in the scenario, it is difficult to stop reading, and it is difficult to stop desiring to evolve. Once side tracked, the urge to continue on in the process keeps pushing the awareness onward down the same path. Because of this impetus to keep on keeping on, there are those who volunteer to aid and assist their fellow aspects of creation to again find the open-ended track of experience. Creation is maintained and expands through volunteerism. That is how it is!

II-30

The evolvement of each focused self-awareness is dependent upon its ability to process the knowledge available into and through its flow of experience. The influence of those entities around it, that believe certain truths and experiences are the truth or ultimate experience, leads to entrapment and endless dead-end ventures. The ability to experience knowledge acquired and experienced into wisdom is like laying stepping stones on a path. When an understanding is complete, then it is necessary to acquire the material to complete the next stepping stone. It cannot be done with exactly the same knowledge as the last one. It must include new material/knowledge. There may or may not be a bridge between what has been learned and the subsequent new information. New concepts may contain essences of more than one stepping stone. It is this apt analogy that has lead to the idea that evolvement equates to a "spiritual path." The significant perception of the visualization of this path is the understanding that the stones must be present and laid one by one before there can be a path. Further and important is the concept that the path lies not before each traveler, but _behind_ him/her.

It is rare that the path behind any evolving awareness is a smooth upward spiral. The acquisition of knowledge and experiencing it into understanding and releasing it as complete and then opening to begin the process again does not usually lead easily to the ultimate goal. The conceptualization of that goal is literally too incomprehensible to be able to limit it into words. However, the magnetism of that goal draws all ultimately to return to it. There is no escaping its allure no matter how crooked the path of wisdom is laid in the process of the return. The view of the path of humanity on this planet as a whole over the past several thousands of years would find it curling abruptly into a circle. Mankind has continued to march around and around that circle with few able to intuit their way out of it and to continue their evolvement.

That circle now is a spiral downward as the recent human experience is being lead into the lower vibrational activities of greater and greater violence and denigration of the body and awareness. The foundations of family and personal integrity are visually and audibly assaulted with dogma of truly evil intent. It must be remembered that the altered humans conceived religion for the worthwhile purpose of preventing self-annihilation. Its original intent and purpose was not to provide the path to evolvement. It did, however, contain and retain some of the teachings of the benevolent visitors. There have also been not so benevolent visitors who have observed the religious process as a field of opportunity to promote their own agenda of retaliation and revenge. By infiltrating and slowly developing their strategies, the true teachings have been deliberately adulterated and used to promote the circle brought about by the genetic alteration and to turn it into a downward spiral.

It is the purpose of these messages to set forth the truth of the dilemma of humanity and to put forth some of the essentials of its knowable cosmology. The messages contain the elements of a workable plan to allow mankind to create for itself the opportunity to leave the downward spiral path that has resulted from not only the genetic alteration, but from their stubborn refusals to accept the proffered help. This stubborn refusal to let go of the old and continue their victim stance has allowed them to fall prey to those who take advantage of that level of consciousness. The portion of the population that was drawn to and has intermingled with the not so benevolent interplanetary visitors at the moment has the upper hand.

First enough humans must awaken to the situation set to overwhelm them. Second enough must consider the possibility of the truths offered within these messages. Third enough must have the courage to discern these truths and <u>follow the suggestions.</u> These shall then guide their fellow humans through this dangerous situation to the new paradigm and the return to the galactic family. Then earth's people shall be *welcomed* throughout creation to walk and learn among their friends and to gather the material for the stones of their individual paths. The limited and frustrating existence that has been experienced has not been a total loss. The advantages that await shall be greatly appreciated.

Each step as outlined is critical. Each requires courage both individually and as a combined focus. What is the most challenging is accepting the concept that there will not be an army gathered together physically to encourage one another. This will be accomplished by individuals that within their own focus faithfully commit and follow through daily by delineating their intentional desire for and resolve to move through the chaos to come. These will <u>know</u> in their hearts at an emotional level that does not waver that what is desired exists and is manifesting even now as the desire for it is embraced and being conceptualized. The miracle of the new paradigm will be a gathering of individual foci through their intent upon the same purposeful symbolic agreement. This cooperative focus will, through the law of attraction, acting through application of the law of intentional creation, bring forth the intended new experience. These with sure confidence will trust the process and *allow* it to happen. Then balance and harmony will reign. The truth of the presence and power of the universal laws, stimulated by the cooperative combined foci, will be demonstrated. Through this demonstration much will be experienced into wisdom earned and wisdom learned. Humanity will then stand on the stepping stone leading out of the downward spiral and find themselves facing the opportunity of creating new stones of wisdom for their paths within the new paradigm.

II-31

The understanding gained through the reading this material, especially those that have contemplated and pondered it for the specific purpose of feeling if there is a resonance with the truth present, has changed each person's perspective. Knowledge once gained changes the reality through which the life process is viewed and contemplated. When the purposefully focused mind clutter is observed with the discernment of its intended design, the perception of current reality is different. Even if the observer chooses to ignore the truth that was considered as a possibility, the ability to blend again into the sleeping masses can never be accomplished. It remains in the background and circumstances and events will continue to trigger the awareness of the truth. In this way the seeds of change are planted and will begin at some point to grow and bear fruit. Those who reject the information before considering it at all will find the choice will be offered again before the project of the new paradigm is complete.

The message carriers must understand that even though many will reject the information, making the contact invokes the opportunity of a future choice. In the case of those desiring this information to be accepted by family and friends to whom there are emotional attachments, this should be a comfort. The second offering will usually be through another messenger, and is more likely to be accepted for two reasons. First, it has been heard before, and it is easier to accept on a logical level that does not have emotional triggers involved. In this way each may be prepared for possible rejection, but will also know that even when that happens, a contact link is established. The gift is given whether it is accepted immediately or at a later time. If not accepted at all, then the difficult lesson of allowance is to be remembered, for each has their freewill choice. There is also the possibility that as the scenario evolves; these skeptics may seek out the information. The focus of intent through blessing the individuals "for their highest and best good" or a similar invocation carries the energy of the creative flow of expansion. The expansiveness of this energy has created galaxies, solar systems, planets and beings becoming to appreciate the process. This energy is as powerful as it is subtle. The more relaxed and knowing the "intender," the more potent the result.

As the messages are circulated, accepted and contemplated, the law of attraction begins to draw and attract more people of like beliefs. Those who are awake are beginning to realize that there is little information that goes the essential step further to suggest a true solution to the situation. Certain survival preparations are necessary, but these do not offer resolution. This awareness is magnetic and invokes an answer to the question of "What can we do?" The viable answer that provides a cure and not just symptom relief is found within these messages. The way in which other suggestions for resolving the situation at hand may be measured is to consider whether they offer a cure or merely symptom relief. As with a disease of the human body, a symptom seldom indicates the entire cause of the problem. The symptoms now affecting the whole of the human population and the planet are so numerous as to make an overview difficult. Few have the time, or have the tenacity to come to a clear conclusion on their own. They depend on the media and other controlled opinion givers for their picture of the larger reality because it is purposely available for easy access. It is psychologically written to present only facets of situations and events so as to deceive the listener/observer and encourage the unconscious cooperation needed to complete the preparations for enslavement one cautious step at a time. As the time draws near, the puppet leaders become more impatient and careless, yet the masses still do not hear or see. Know that this also serves the implementation of the new paradigm project. Be patient and lay the foundation blocks steadily and with purposeful resolve. Join in small groups of like awareness and contemplate the wording of the purpose, pass the messages and _know_ this is the process of thought thinking within the universal laws. The desire for this new experience is already attracting its energetic format. Trust the process! This project has the blessing of the planet and its inhabitants as a whole as its purposeful intent. That is a major plus for the insurance of its success. It does require purposeful resolve. Hang in there and do all that is necessary with passion and zeal. Contemplate standing on the first stone outside the downward spiral, knowing the possibilities available when there are moments of discouragement. Smile, you are on the willing and winning team!

II-32

As these messages are distributed and the number of people reading and assimilating the knowledge contained within them increases, the natural flow of the law of attraction allows the gradual increase of their magnetic appeal to bring more and more people to grasp the logical understandings offered by them. The wave of discontent and frustration that is rising within the mass consciousness is developing. A viable solution that does not require the sacrifice of the human body to accomplish the desired reversal of the situation surrounding the whole of the mass consciousness, is applying pressure and bringing this to a moment that serves as the impetus for the birth of the new paradigm. It is appropriate to caution the team to remember that "divine order" does not necessarily appear to operate in a sequential mode. It does require a simplistic definition of form, holographic in nature, and completes the necessary process in a variety of ways.

The key to completing this within the slower vibrational dimensions is holding the focus of the definition of form within the mind's eye for the long duration needed to allow the manifestation into observable reality. A critical number of foci holding this intention in place are needed, for each can or will do so for only a short period at time. Thus, if enough do this often enough and long enough, then the image is in continuous focus. This is the process of thought thinking at the level of necessity within the lower vibrational levels of what is called the 3rd dimension, or lowest dimension of human existence. It is the most difficult to transcend because the slow vibratory rate, at best, requires the focus to be held for manifestation to materialize. The lower the scale of the vibratory rates the longer the sequence and the more difficult it is for the mind to concentrate. The power of the competition of the planted clutter in the minds of humanity at the moment adds another ingredient to this already difficult situation.

It is thought that the lid is tightly shut and that it is impossible for the critical number of humanity to detect the net of deception, organize and transcend through the carefully laid trap into freedom. That in a nutshell, is the challenge. Can this "mission impossible" be accomplished? Is it possible for this sleeping giant to awaken, shake off the administered sedatives and arise into sufficient awareness to make the choices necessary? The ability to do so is present. The opportunity is now, for it will be a long time with much suffering before another will be available. It is said that mankind will give up luxury and all other manner of things and experience before he will give up the suffering that has been his lot for so long. Your Christian religion teaches that suffering is holy and a bridge to the heavenly experience in the next lifetime by a "loving" god? Is this in any sense logical?

Each deception individually and the collective whole of them are incomprehensible to your cosmic brethren in that they defy logic. The whole of creation is logical. Logic is a wondrous balancing mechanism. The whole of the mass belief system for earth's inhabitants is so distorted through exploitation of the emotions that what is universal logic appears to be illogical and difficult to believe. In order for the new paradigm project to succeed, the messengers must digest the messages within the totality of their awareness and allow them to percolate through and to change their perception of not only who and what they are, but how they perceive creation. It will be necessary to allow the magnitude of misconception to resolve into a new basic perception and conception of the holographic, cooperating, interacting wholeness that focused them into being and holds them there in the freedom of freewill choice. Bondage is not the heritage of choice. It is giving up the basic framework of creation through the freewill choice of victim experience that has allowed this situation to regress to its present level. This is an opportunity to bring it to an end, and to progress into knowing again who you are and doing what you were designed to do. It is time to give up suffering and experience joy, bliss and ecstasy as the realities they are, not as fleeting moments or mythical goals for saints only. The ideal is neither abused children nor menacing warriors, but free fulfilled adults at home in a galactic world of adventure. Your lovingly concerned brethren offer here their proffered advice and promise of greater assistance if you but help yourselves first as citizenship within creation requires. It is hoped that each reader will ponder and consider the alternatives and choose wisely.

It is hoped that those who embrace the premise of these concepts grasp the dimensions for change that are available through the acceptance and incorporation of these suggestions. It is the incorporation of conceptual changes at individual and various inclusive group levels leading to global awareness that allows for the holographic requisite to be met. As the individual participates within the process, the consciousness transcends from personal experience expansively through groups arriving at the global dimension. Each and all then stand on a new platform to contemplate galactic experience. Through visualizing the expansion inherent in the sequence of necessary steps it is possible to comprehend a multi-dimensional process on going within a singular focused goal. Once this is experienced into wisdom, then it is available to be experienced in other situations for varied appropriate applications.

It is relevant to point out that the process is best learned before attempting to apply it in other situations. Rather like stringing pearls for a necklace, it is best to focus on one pearl at a time. In this case the pearl of the moment is the new paradigm.

It is what must be held in focus, all else will then follow in due time. It cannot be stressed enough that scattering the focus was not the intent of this greater understanding. Stay focused on creating the new paradigm, then the joy of experimenting with this process will be splendid indeed. It is then that the focus shared between galactic family members will stand forth as intended.

II-33

Within the experience of the chaos that lies in the near future, the allowance of the experience will be a difficult hurtle for those that intend to focus the new paradigm through its initial stages of inception and birth it into manifestation. There will be difficult and discouraging moments for those who accept this mission, especially if there are no close companions to share the focus and encourage each other. Holding chosen simple symbols clearly in mind and drawing or seeing them displayed as frequent reminders will assist in holding the necessary focus. The symbols bring the focus to mind without the conscious effort of first identifying the focus and then convincing the intellect of its truth when the surrounding situation contradicts its rationality. The symbols are what might be called a "quick fix." Frequent reference to them on a continuing basis and allowing an emotional feeling to arise in anticipation of the coming new experience will bring immeasurable focused energy to the manifestation.

When this simple exercise is practiced with the discernment of its meaning in innumerable places on the planet in a continuous format, the manifestation is assured. If each time the symbol is focused upon, it is perceived as a flash of light or an electrical charge, the planet can be envisioned as literally lighting up with this new perception. This is an apt analogy and allows for consideration of the power held within the simplicity of redirecting purposeful intention through placing the attention on what is desired rather than what appears to be happening. It changes the control point from the observed to the observer that allows for empowerment of the individual observers. It further demonstrates the power of cooperation through unified commitment to a common goal. The fact that the goal is not defined in detail implies the process for the details do not dilute or scatter the focus. This project transcends merely identifying the problems and attempting to fix the symptoms for this in reality only adds to the problem as a whole. It provides the opportunity of experiencing aspects of the new paradigm as it is being created.

The parameters of the current pattern of life expression now being experienced must begin to shift in order for the new paradigm to be conceived and birthed into manifested reality. New parameters have been enumerated throughout these messages so that they might begin to filter into the minds of those reading, contemplating and discussing these concepts. The limited thinking of earth's inhabitants must change to allow for the flow of thought to move through their conscious awareness on a continuing basis. To simply exchange one box of concepts for a new box of concepts will not allow for participation within the flow of creation. This is not to say that the flow of conceptual thought does not proceed in an orderly fashion, for otherwise the flow would be experienced as continuous chaos and that is not a flow. Indeed periods of what might be termed chaos are experienced while letting go of one set of truths and accepting another that delineates the next set of experiences in the search for greater wisdom. How much chaos is experienced depends on how long the old set is retained before the necessity is to move on brings a breakthrough. If an openness to perceive and accept seemingly new concepts of truth is practiced, then the process proceeds with greater smoothness.

It is hoped that those who embrace the premise of these concepts grasp the dimensions for change that are available through the acceptance and incorporation of these suggestions. It is the incorporation of conceptual changes at individual and various inclusive group levels leading to global awareness that allows for the holographic requisite to be met. As the individual participates within the process, the consciousness transcends from personal experience expansively through groups arriving at the global dimension. Each and all then stand on a new platform to contemplate galactic experience. Through visualizing the expansion inherent in the sequence of necessary steps it is possible to comprehend a multi-dimensional process on going within a singular focused goal. Once this is experienced into wisdom, then it is available to be experienced in other situations for varied appropriate applications.

It is relevant to point out that the process is best learned before attempting to apply it in other situations. Rather like stringing pearls for a necklace, it is best to focus on one pearl at a time. In this case the pearl of the moment is the new paradigm. It is what must be held in focus, all else will then follow in due time. It cannot be stressed enough that scattering the focus was not the intent of this greater understanding. Stay focused on creating the new paradigm, then the joy of experimenting with this process will be splendid indeed. It is then that the focus shared between galactic family members will stand forth as intended.

II-34

The evolving consciousness within the holographic planetary system arises out of the individual conscious awareness, as it perceives itself within the whole. The perception of what that wholeness includes varies in accordance with what is experienced. Until the advent of the technological era these individual experiences were influenced by the belief system that was absorbed from the family environment followed by those acquired within expansion into larger group experience. Cosmology, the understanding of the how the individual fits into the perceived plan of the galaxy/universe, was taught by symbology within story, art and dance. This allowed for each to contemplate their place and encouraged each to quest to know and understand. With the advent of the printed word followed by graphic technology and the use of it for the manipulation of mankind into slavery, this process has been virtually lost. If the technology had been used to assist the individual to know and understand what truth is available rather than keeping the key information hidden or distorted, mankind would not be within the present dilemma.

Thus it is that these messages are given in the hope that the small amount of truth and wisdom within its pages will entice the reader/messengers to desire to again quest for understanding of who and what they are. This is not done, except by the few intent upon self-discovery, within the current planetary situation. This inherent right to know is denied from early childhood on through maturation as the present circumstances are now. Those in the more technologically advanced cultures are overwhelmed with misinformation and those in the less advanced cultures are existing at extreme poverty levels. It is difficult to wonder about a place in the plan of the cosmos when need of basic food and shelter are in the forefront of consciousness. Further, technology has been turned to cause the human body to literally self-destruct through weakening its foods with growing techniques, incompatible food combinations, genetic alterations to the plants, adding abrasive ingredients and cooking in fashions that alter the molecular arrangement of the foods. These are affecting the ability of the human body and the plants and animals to reproduce in perfection. The seriousness of the situation is realized by a few that attempt to spread the warnings. Without help from those with a great understanding of methods of regaining perfection, there will follow generations of imperfect bodies as a result.

Though it is the purpose of these messages to offer a plan for transcending the planetary dilemma, it is necessary that those who accept this mission fully understand that humanity on this planet is in direful straits that are worsening at a rapid pace. It is necessary that the end of this situation be reached soon, for as the damaged humans reproduce, the return of the next generations to perfection becomes more complicated as the mutations begin to scatter into dominant and recessive gene combinations. Within the generation of the acquired damage these imperfections are yet correctable. The evil of the plan to produce slaves includes these mutations, for imperfect bodies set the stage for belief of inferiority as well as the real affects to the physical brains and bodies. With the addition of technological implants the slavery would be virtually complete and provide far more control than those methods employed now.

It is not intended to place information in these messages to frighten the readers into buying into its plan. The overview would not be complete so that logical and intelligent decisions could be made if at least an encapsulated picture of the situation and circumstances that are present was not included. The truth of what has been stated above is available in book, magazine, web-site and radio. Portions of it are included in the media controlled programs, but go unnoticed. It is then in truth that it can be stated that they told you so and that you paid no attention.

They knew that amid the clutter, few would put it together or pay attention to those that did.

Of further note is the fact that through the "United Nations" the military forces are being scattered through out the world. This is for the reason that many would not enforce the coming orders against their own people, but with the ethnic and national rivalries, could and will against those of other nations, cultures and particularly those of other religions. If the attention is placed only on the situation and circumstances that surround you at every turn then overwhelm is experienced and that is exactly what it is desired for those of you who are awakening. It is the reason there is no concern about their plans being revealed at this stage. That it is yet possible to gather a focus with power enough to thwart their plans even now does not occur to them. Thus, there is yet the "freedom" to implement project new paradigm. Shall we proceed?

II-35

It is through the application of the law of allowance that mankind will make the final step into the role of the rainbow "human." The archetype of the warrior that has influenced the shaping of mankind's experience shall at long last evolve into the ideal of the responsible cosmic citizen. It is perfectly possible to adventure in a role beyond the warrior. Only other warriors within the game of conflict welcome warriors. Those who have evolved beyond walking this dead end path do not welcome conflict back into their experience. The freedom to move freely among those of more refined development allows for more rapid advancement. As within a maze, eventually it is necessary to face the wall at the end and accept it as the end, and stay there, or to find the way back to the correct passageway. The new paradigm is a gift that will enable humanity to rise above the maze to see the true passageway and move quickly into it.

This will not happen without the necessary consciousness change and the period of focus required through the chaos of the demise of the current mode of experience that is based on competition and conflict. The desire for the new experiencing mode must become a passion that exceeds the inclination to stay within what is familiar. The realization that something far better waits at the closure of this experiencing mode must be real within the belief system and be strong enough to transcend the mass beliefs of not only millions, but billions. It is through the demonstration of the power of a combined human focus that *blends with* the wisdom of creation that each will know the truth. It is not to be found in resistance to the situation that exists on this earth plane, but in *joining with* that which is Truth that will bring forth what seems to require a miracle to accomplish. Unimaginable power will be tapped in this process. It simply requires changing the focus of the combined minds of a percentage of mankind. It is not a majority; it is an amazingly small actual number of humans on earth comparatively speaking, for these will blend with the flow that creates planets, stars, solar systems, galaxies, and more.

The process is simple. The complication is that it requires standing and turning into the face of what has been taught for generation after generation by doing it within each individual consciousness. It does not require face to face confrontation with those that continue to teach these untruths. Most do this in sincerity. It is through one to one contacts with those that already feel discontent with available knowledge at the deep levels of their personal awareness, that the mission is to be accomplished. There are more than enough that sense they are swimming upstream and are ready and willing to rejoin the flow of creation. They wait only to know how to accomplish this change. The archetype of the rainbow human calls to all for it is like a homing signal that perpetually sounds in the background of life. It is like the dinner bell ringing in the distance to come home to share refreshment and rest with family. In this case, humanity has wandered far from home and has some distance to cover, but it will arrive there sooner or later, and hopefully it will be sooner!

The focus has been at the very personal level for each messenger as each goes through the process of strengthening his or her understandings and resolve. It is not easy to commit to a project of this magnitude without establishing the intent firmly within the conscious mind. The mind and the feelings must be in harmony and balance in order that the resolve is of enough substance to hold firmly through the period of the shift in consciousness. That which is now new must have time to root and become the dominant viewpoint from which experiences are perceived and decisions made with discernment. An amazing number of life situations will suddenly take on new meanings. Habitual comments that fit certain situations will no longer be appropriate and there will be moments of wondering what is appropriate. There will be rethinking necessary requiring a transition period. There will be many returns to the messages to contemplate new meanings that were missed when first read. Truth is perceived within the understanding of the moment and is constantly refreshed as different experiences are contemplated and decisions are necessary for the discernment needed to establish new patterns of belief and behavior.

There is much to transcend in order that each may stand at the end of this chapter of the book of evolvement and contemplate not only a new chapter, but also a sequel. This will be done day by day and one mind change at a time. The biggest single change is the willingness to read, contemplate and find the personal truth within with the guidance of these messages. Beyond that, the steps are small and continuously lead onward to the goal of living the new ideal or archetype moment by moment. When the new archetype is embedded within the mass consciousness, the new paradigm will be birthed into infancy and the adventure will have begun in earnest. Then you may choose to walk hand in hand with your family again for you will have returned home for sustenance and companionship. A worthy tradeoff for giving up excessive competition, conflict and isolation.

II-36

Within these messages is embedded the psychological changes of heart and mind that are required to maintain the focus of the powerful aspects of experience that constitute the human evolving within the successive steps of its journey. The focused human awareness can be observed as a matrix or pattern of energy, for that is what each is in reality. Each cell contains an electrical charge, therefore if the charges are observed they would appear as a pattern of lights surrounded by a finer thought energy that is emitted as these pass outward from the being. Since all of creation in its basic form once beyond pure potentiality is thought, and thought thinks, then it may be concluded that the totality of the human thinks. Every cell of the human body thinks. It is how feeling is experienced. It is how a deep realization can cause what you call goose bumps to arise on the body, for the entirety of the body has agreed simultaneously on a new concept of truth. That is what sends some to a doctor, because there is a knowingness from within the body that has been emitted from the body cells into the finer thought energies that surround the body and the conscious mind has opened to receive the information.

The thought function is not confined to the brain. It is the totality of the human that participates in the thinking process. Feeling is a combination of thought processes by the cells of the body utilizing the pathways of the nervous system as you use telephone lines. But just as you receive TV and Cellular phone messages without the benefit of wires, so also the body has similar and far more refined capabilities. What is called intuition is an illustration of this more refined ability. It is a knowingness that takes place at a cellular level and registers in the awareness at varying degrees of understanding, depending on the belief system of the individual. The brain is designed to participate in a multitude of processes. It houses the most vulnerable and finely tuned of the endocrine glands. The precious secretions of the pituitary and pineal glands are the drivers of the human body/mind awareness. The brain is the switching station for the receiving and transmitting of the thinking process. The combined thought process of the body wholeness is gathered and focused through the brain mechanism that it may be exchanged between humans. However, it must pass through the belief system stored in the finer energies that surround the body and hold the belief patterns of not only the individuals experiences, but also contains the norms of the experience and belief patterns of the various levels of experience of the entire planet. One function of the brain is to register and read that information upon request. Thus when certain parts of the brain are stimulated, it reads not itself, but the stored data that is within the appropriate surrounding fine energy. Each human brings its entire history of existence with it stored in this incredibly intelligent energy that surrounds it.

This then explains one reason that humanity on this planet cannot enter the higher dimensions as it is now, for those beings are able to read the finer surrounding energy and know all there is to know about each one, every thought and intention. This is the source of what you call telepathy. How is this possible? It is the degree of activity of those two glands held within the brain, the pituitary and the pineal, that is the key to what you call "spiritual progress." The protection of these glands has been provided for by what is called the blood/brain barrier. Only very tiny molecules are able to pass through this barrier. Unfortunately for humanity at this time, crossing this barrier is now possible. Fortunately, there are those individuals who upon learning this are devoting great effort to get information out to make as many as possible aware. It is not only what is eaten, but also what is put on the body for cleanliness and other reasons that now contain destructive molecules that can and do cross that blood/brain barrier. These are causing great damage to the human brain as well as the rest of the body. For personal protection and the protection of the generations of the future, each messenger must become aware of these dangers and strive to find the safest available alternatives for themselves as well as to carry the message to others. There are alternatives available but it will require effort to search them out. It is important to know and to read what is within each before buying. It will be time better spent than in front of the propaganda tube.

Again, the focus is on the chaos rather than the goal, but the goal is of no benefit if there are not humans in wholeness to bring forth and enjoy the manifestation of the new paradigm of experience. Thus it is important that certain awareness be made particularly known. There is methodology in development that allows for the return of damaged DNA to wholeness without man-made chemicals that are now being developed for that purpose. Beware of man-made intervention at these early stages. Nature has provided even this process for the preservation of the human in wholeness. There are indeed safeguards to protect humanity from self-destruction if it is studied within nature rather than pursuing the deliberately distorted guidance now being provided to the planners of enslavement. Though much is done in the competition/greed mode, it is underlain by the intentional provision of information that serves the enslavement purpose.

Each committed and focused member of the new paradigm

project must practice discernment as the awareness of the picture begins as an outline and infills with information without becoming lost in the enormity and detail of the opposition's plan. It must be held in the background while the focus remains in place on the desired new paradigm. There will be quite naturally perusals through curiosity into the activities and plans of the dark ones, but these must be kept in perspective. The new paradigm must be held at the forefront of the focused awareness in order that it may manifest into its intended blessing.

II-37

The progression of the plan of the enslavement of humanity proceeds down its apparently inevitable path and mankind as a whole stumble along into the planned containment. It is difficult to include within these messages the information that it is necessary to be known without triggering fear. Yet fear is a most effective attention device and one that is planned to be used to the full degree of its potential to shock people into full awareness. Thus it is necessary that the plan for the new paradigm include utilizing this planned episode to its advantage. In other words, to divert this potential to fit within the plan to return humanity to its rightful place within the flow of creation. In order to accomplish this, there must be a core group of dedicated humans already awake and aware that has progressed through the potential fear and well in control of their reactive modes of behavior. In order to accomplish this, these must be able to transcend the planned response and quickly attain and retain the observer mode. Without this ability the capacity and competency to accomplish their mission that will be critical in that moment will be lost. As these who choose to become part of this plan make it a point to become aware of the plans, knowing it is a necessary component of the foundation upon which the birth of the new paradigm rests, it will allow the observer mode to be experienced into wisdom.

It will be easy to lapse into emotional reactions. However, the emotions are not to be the controlling factor. Creation is logical! Therefore in order to create, manifest into reality, a new paradigm of experience, those doing so must focus within logic. It certainly would not be logical to accomplish this by joining in the reaction that is intended by the enslavers. It then becomes necessary that there be a critical number of humans that rise above their natural inclination to be part of the intended mass reaction. In order to do this, these self-chosen individuals, singularly or in small groups will find it necessary to inform themselves of as much of the plan as possible. It will be necessary to embrace their feelings about these plans within the full knowledge that it is for the purpose of experiencing them into the purposeful wisdom of attaining the observer mode. It is through this observation ability that clear and logical decisions can be made in the moment not in retrospect when it is too late to accomplish what would have been possible in the precious moment lost.

The necessary information can be quickly learned within small discussion groups, for then the material available through the yet free flow of books, radio talk shows and the Internet can be researched and shared. It must be considered in the sharing that the plans that will be revealed are not as much the flat pieces of a jigsaw puzzle being fitted together, as they are a holographic puzzle. To illustrate that concept, there are wooden or plastic puzzles that create a sphere when placed together in the proper combination. These are more challenging than the flat puzzles and the intricacy involved illustrates the extent to which the planning of hundreds of years has been required to bring so many to such an effective point. It then will also illustrate all that can be negated through the simplicity of a plan that is devised within the flow of creation compared to one that is not. The complication facing the messengers of creation, which is indeed what each one committed to the new paradigm project, is spearheading the consciousness change from victimhood to self-empowerment. It appears that only through desperate circumstances is the programmed human willing to give up deeply engrained beliefs though the experience of these beliefs has not brought to them the promised benefits. The practice and holding on to these takes them deeper and deeper in a downward spiral as they continue to fail to come to the realization that doing more of something that does not work will not make it work. Fear of the unknown locks them into unproductive behavior and illustrates the limitation of the victim consciousness that is being promoted to the maximum extent in this gross exploitation and degradation of the humans on this planet.

The question put to each reader of this material is whether or not to remain within the group headed to inevitably miserable deaths or enslavement as further mutated survivors, or to climb out on to the rock of observation. Once outside the mass awareness, that is truly a lack of awareness, then the mission becomes 2-fold.

Gathering others willing to assist and together birthing the new paradigm. It is hoped that complexity will be avoided and simplicity will be strictly adhered to. It is complexity that scatters the focus. The more simple the focus, the more quickly the manifestation will occur. Further, those not resonating quickly to the information are to be released and allowed to remain where they are. The seed is planted, and those may yet follow at a more appropriate time. Never attempt to convince anyone. Like the folk hero, Johnny Appleseed, plant and move on to the next possible appropriate contact. Though the planter may not observe the result, result by the law of averages is assured. Releasing each contact to their own destiny is practicing the law of allowance. When it is unnecessary to defend the comfort zone, logic will often filter through the emotions and these may seek the planter out when it is obvious there is no necessity to defend their beliefs.

The desire for a solution to the intuitional awareness that all is not well is the field of opportunity for the entrance of a new archetype or ideal mode of experience. The coin of impending disaster has on its other side the opportunity for its opposite, what might be called heaven on earth in the Christian idiom, a "hope" contained in all religions. It would seem that to be an instrumental part of providing earth's people the opportunity to experience this dream into reality would be a worthy goal. The choice lies within both logic and emotion as it is pondered carefully.

II-38

The opportunity that is offered within the scope of this project is multi-leveled or multi-dimensional in quality. It utilizes all levels or dimensions of the human aptitude in its focus of modifying the human perception of experience as those involved move through transcending from the present point of experience into the next level or dimension. Dimension is the preferred description for it indicates a more holographic concept. Level implies flat. The circumstances of manifested awareness in a human body are not experienced as level or flat. It is the addition of emotion that adds the dimensional quality to manifested awareness. (Indeed, there are those beings that do not have emotion as part of their experience and they desire greatly to add this dimension to their experience pattern.) It is important that the concept of dimension become familiar and be included in the conceptualizing of the new paradigm.

It is vital that the concept of the human body/mind/spirit also be made very clear. The awareness of existence within manifested experience is also dimensional. Certain of the animals have only the awareness of each moment. For them there is no past or future, only the moment. Since they are unable to retain those memories in detail, their survival is dependent on what is called instinctual awareness and tied directly to survival actions and reactions. Humanity has through domestication frustrated most of them greatly through neglect of their instinctual needs for at least partial freedom, natural varied diets and of late through providing creature comforts more appropriate for humans than fur/hair coated animals.

The human body is a composite of corrections to previous experiments that produced limited modes of physical experience. Through lessons learned, a model was conceived with the potential to evolve through multiple dimensions of experience. As the awareness changed patterns, the human body was designed to accompany that change. It was also designed so that the awareness could enter and leave a body. In other words, the awareness was not required to cease its existence if the body was destroyed through accident or inadequate maintenance. What you call disease is inadequate maintenance. The ability to enter and leave was a known requirement, for the potential of the human body is so limitless that its capabilities of adaptation are greater than units of self-awareness can comprehend in one focus of life experience.

It is important that the reader fully understand that the awareness is not the body, but is merely housed within the body during conscious awaking hours. It can and does sometimes leave the body during sleep, under anesthesia and traumatic periods of unconsciousness. The consciousness can be aware of this separation and can indeed train itself to leave the body intentionally. Some of those with this ability are being employed on a regular basis to intentionally visit particular people and events employing only their focused awareness/spirit, and then can and do report on these activities to those of the dark intent. Just as the physical body can be trained through gymnastics and other exacting physical sports to accomplish impressive feats, so also can the awareness be exercised and trained to do what most would consider difficult to believe. In this way each can begin to grasp that the "average human" on the planet is grossly unaware of its potential. The limitations of each are either self-imposed through acquired thought and belief patterns or through physical or mental limitations by genetic alteration/mutations. They are further limited by failure to maintain the physical body with proper exercise, breathing, whole foods and pure water.

Technology properly applied is a blessing to mankind. Technology guided by competition intended to create profit at the expense of one's fellow man results in greed. Through the law of attraction this intentional exploitation draws to those who do this their just due, or what might be called equal compensation.

Realizations of the truth of what they are about that result in change of intention and action also allows for a change in the degree of experience drawn in accordance with the degree of change. It is important that it is clearly understood, *the laws of the universe work perfectly whether one is aware of them or not. They simply are!* To live in harmony within them is heaven on earth. Let us cooperatively strive to anchor the truth purposefully within the mass consciousness of mankind and birth the new paradigm into the human experience on this planet.

II-39

The concepts contained within the message information will begin with the first reading to change the perception of those that resonate with its intended solutions. It is apparent that the opposition's wars on poverty, crime, cancer and drugs have produced few positive results whatsoever. The conceptual purpose of war is to provide control over another group of humans, including their possessions. When this concept is applied to the wars on poverty, crime, cancer and drugs, it is possible to see how these fit the evil plans perfectly to manipulate and control from within more easily by gaining the consent of those that are the intended victims. These "intended" "good" intentions act as a magic trick to spread the focus of their intended purpose because they apply the law of attraction. By resisting these situations and circumstances through focus of fear thoughts and actions, large groups of humanity are drawn into the planned experience.

It can be concluded that this warring approach would not birth the new paradigm into reality. It is necessary to understand that a 90-degree turn or any other degree of turn short of a 180-degree turn to the opposite approach will not work. Those that make the decision to commit to birthing the new paradigm must make it their primary focus. What the opposing faction is focusing must be held in the peripheral vision. When their plans and actions are faced fully and embraced with fear it gives them the desired energetic support and aids them greatly in accomplishing their goals. It is important to be aware but to remain focused on the plan that fits like a hand into the glove of creation. The glove is simply awaiting mankind to place their hand within it.

Symbology will play an important part in the ability to hold the positive focus. These have been used for eons of time as a focus point that allows for individual understandings and interpretations *within* a basic concept. This calls forth freewill commitment rather than the resistance that comes forth when ideologies and dogmas are strictly structured. Self-awareness desires freedom and is drawn to a simple framework that allows for freedom within it. It was the simplistic framework of the USA that drew immigrants from the world over, for it offered freedoms that had been only dreamed of. The value of the opportunity within this framework, however, was not honored by succeeding generations. This golden opportunity has been bricked and barred in through laws and regulations that one by one weakened it. Greed and deceit are the mortar that holds these bricks and bars in place and its citizens in bondage. Slowly and cleverly accomplished, the majority of citizens adapt and barely notice as each generation accepts what is and the creeping changes introduced during each span of time.

The opposition is clever and insidious, patient and well organized and has advisors with great technology. The situation is serious indeed. Those who can comprehend the puzzle picture and its
seriousness have the opportunity to choose the eventual outcome.
The timing is now such that the occasion to even change the obvious outcome is long past. The sequence of events has reached the
point of it being impossible to return to the previous opportunity
by repairing the damage done. The plan within these messages,
with widespread, purposeful and focused commitment, can and will
accomplish the desired goal. It will require transcending old belief
systems and leaving them in the bag to be left in the hands of the
evil planners. *These beliefs were <u>designed by them to serve them</u>*.
The sooner all committed messengers realize and face this truth,
the sooner the end of their planned scenario will come. The new
paradigm will bring into being a new set of belief systems that serve
humanity not enslavers. The tools of the current limited concept of
government along with religion and war must be left behind in their
bag of tricks. The magicians must be left to ply their trade among
themselves <u>somewhere else.</u>

The above underlined phrase is a clue to what has been part of
earth's past and present. It has been and is yet one of the "somewhere else" places. Has *all* of humanity been sent here because of
past misbehavior? Not necessarily, many risk incarnations here for
the opportunity to rise above (transcend) the negative behavior patterns and do succeed. Many do not and find themselves enmeshed in
the circumstances of earth's current crisis. The successful manifestation of the new paradigm will change not only the future of most
of earth's inhabitants but free the planet from this assignment.

It is necessary that each individual gives this choice serious
consideration and makes their decision based on a careful logical
and emotional basis. Both modes of experience will be actively
required in tandem and synergistically. Each will support the other
in times of doubt and frustration when all does not happen quickly
enough or expectations exceed apparent results. The desire to rescue
the suffering will be great and examples of victims will be paraded
before you through every media means available for the purpose of
keeping all locked within victim consciousness. The observer mode
of allowance while the new paradigm focus manifests and brings

the ultimate solution to their plight must be held securely at the forefront of the conscious awareness. If dropped, it must be quickly picked up. Looking at or recalling a meaningful symbol is the easiest way to regain the focus.

Will all that resonate and commit be able to retain their focus? The success of the project will depend on the consistent and the persistent. Each must look within themselves to determine if their evolvement and genetic adaptation is such that a commitment of this magnitude is possible, plausible and noble enough to find out if the traits of character necessary are available or not. It is certain that each one that commits will find out!

II-40

Although the messages appear to be focused toward requiring apparent super-human accomplishment, just as few ever bring forth the potential of the physical body, so also few explore the capabilities of the mental focus. The human becoming has the potential for expression in its physical, mental, emotional and spiritual aspects. It is has been the tendency of humans to pursue one or two of these aspects at a time. It is possible to accomplish a balanced development of all four within one lifetime. In this way each aspect supports the other within a balance that provides for a harmonious experience. This begins with a growing understanding and application of the universal laws, along with recognizing the various opportunities to insert variations of the statement "I am a human becoming, help me to become!" Inserting this statement into every applicable situation allows for experiencing the use of the mental focus to bring about a shift in the energies of a situation. This experience of the power of mental focus and the result of its focused use will allow each to experience knowledge into wisdom through actual self-empowerment. The use of this simple statement demonstrates the self-awareness taking charge of itself. Through changing the perspective within the self-awareness, in turn its perspective of the situation changes in the moment that it is happening. When the situation is perceived in a different way, it is changed. Each situation is as it is perceived. What appears as a single situation is as all participating perceive it, and is in reality multiple situations happening in a simultaneous moment.

The concept of time is in reality a no thing. It is an invention of the mind or ego recorder so that the events of experience can be perceived, analyzed and recorded. Inasmuch as the energy vibrates at such a slow rate at the 3rd dimensional level, this process is at such a slow rate that it appears to be in sequential order so that chaos is not experienced within the recording process. It is necessary that this be understood so that the concept of the new paradigm coming into existence when it is perceived is understood. When a sufficient number of mental foci desire to create this experience for themselves, it begins its manifestation process within the flow of creational thought energy. It literally already exists, it is just that the energy flow is so slow that it is not perceived or brought into the experience at the 3rd dimensional level until the sum of vibratory oscillations reaches the total necessary to manifest into realized experience. As each understands the density of earth's surrounding space and the slow rate of the humans experiencing in that space, it is possible to grasp the understanding of why it appears to be a time oriented process. In excessively simple terms, the thought process travels outward into the aqueous (fluid like) energy of the creational flow at a much more rapid pace than it returns as manifested reality. The focused thought process when fueled by emotion moves quickly through creational energy. As it leaves the dense field of energy, it becomes finer or vibrates more rapidly. It is the return trip, so to speak, in the manifestation process that slows in its oscillation rate. The law of attraction magnetizes the object of the focused thought that was "sent out into the creational field of energy" and it is returned to the point of origin. When the point of origin is vibrating at the slower rate, it appears within the sequential time orientation to manifest very slowly. If during this sequential experience, the focus is withdrawn or sufficiently weakened, the magnetic attraction process is aborted.

It is within this understanding that the concept of how the birthing of the new paradigm is entirely possible can be understood in rudimentary terms. It can also be understood that once the planners of the next "dark age of mankind" know of this plan and see it happening, the onslaught to stop it will be intense. It will require dedicated individuals and small rotating support groups to keep the necessary focus in tact in order to bring the manifestation into being. There will be no success if the focus become resistance. Allowance, difficult as it will be, must be practiced and the focus held knowing the new paradigm exists in the moment, not somewhere in the distant future. To know that without having it yet in the current experience will require sincere dedication. Experiencing this truth into wisdom will gift the humans who are able to do it into becoming at a vibratory rate unknown in the annals of evolving awareness.

Through the support of the changing of the cycles and those benevolent awareness points that not only know and understand the situation, but also offer all possible support, this project is guaranteed, *if* the necessary human quotient can be reached. The ground crew is in place and the opportunity is certainly available. Let us proceed.

II-41

The change in perspective that each acquires as these messages are read and contemplated is a process of exchanging old perceptions for new ones and climbing to the top of the rock so that each is discerning from a new and different viewpoint. With each new reading and contemplation, the viewpoint will change again. The belief system changes and allows the same printed words to stimulate a different recognition of the reality that each creates for him/herself. This is the natural flow of evolving life experience. The planners of containment continuously attempt to thwart this natural inclination through every control method possible. Government and media programming are their primary agents of control at the mental level. Fear is their primary tool at the emotional level. War and induced disease that goes hand in hand with destructive medical treatment are the control mechanisms at the physical level. That which controls the spiritual level of experience and interacts within the other three levels is religion.

The focus of religion is to contain and prevent the developing human awareness from reaching the goal of evolvement because its methodology is designed to hold the goal always beyond the reach of present time. Humanity has been fooled into believing a total contradiction. What is called reincarnation is denied yet reward for a life of suffering and sacrifice is to be attained after death or possibly by future generations. Where is there logic to be found in this concept? The cosmos positively could not exist if it was not logical! The universal laws that underpin all that is manifest are absolutely logical! Therefore the understanding of the cosmology of humanity must be logical in order that mankind may progress *within it, right now!* The planners of enslavement have it so easy when humans desiring evolvement are contained within the house of religion with its illogical and contradicting edicts that are sold into belief on "faith." Buying illogical concepts can be likened to padlocking the doors and windows of the prison on the inside and sliding the keys out under the door to the jailers. It's like asking the wolf to guard the sheep. Are all concepts within religion wrong? Certainly not! Much truth is contained within the tenets of all religions, but many distortions and outright fabrications are carefully included within each and every religion. These have been deliberately placed there to deceive and control.

At the beginning of these messages it was stated that the "God thing" was not a hoax. This is so; it is just that the perception of what "God" truly is has hopefully changed through these messages. Humanity has been deliberately guided to personify to identify. In reality, that which it has been led to personify is potentiality expressing into creation. The personality of this process is with each self-awareness, not an all-powerful outside being. The outward expression of potentiality through the creational process is to expand or separate the energy into self-aware units and all that is necessary for it to recognize and revere its own potentiality and discover how to empower itself. At that point, the return trip becomes the opposite of that process. It is a gathering process. The law of attraction draws these separate self-aware units into groups of awareness that "enjoy" pursuit of like or common focus that reveres the creation as a wholeness. These then become larger units of focus while yet maintaining their individual awareness. Evolvement becomes a joyful gathering of momentum for there is agreement and cooperation, not competition or friction.

It can now be apparent that the victim consciousness does not fit the above criteria for the return trip. The enslaving consciousness does not fit the above criteria either. Both vibrate at the lowest rate of human existence. Those within the "upper echelons" of the enslaving consciousness have found the humans on earth a most vexing group with which to cope. They have since "manufactured" a more satisfactory slave pattern. The emotions were left out of the design; it is easily programmed; the vibratory rate is below the possibility of consciousness evolvement; the rudimentary thought process is slow, as is the ability to adapt. The cost in resources to maintain them is very low, as there is no reproduction to control. Cloning reproduces them when conveniently needed. Humanity does offer something the new slave does not. Challenging entertainment!

Does that please you to know that your victim consciousness rates as challenging entertainment? I would think not. It is time to bring an end to this scenario and to write the script that will bring freedom and the conclusion to the "long suffering" that this branch of humanity has allowed itself to endure. It is time to become the winning team. It is time to claim the hoped for carrot offered by the devised religions of the enslavers. It is appropriate to birth the new paradigm now. It has been more than earned.

II-42

The approaching period of chaos has been mentioned in the previous messages. What this process might look like in detail has not been discussed. It is difficult to do this since what manifests and to what degree will be determined by the acceptance or rejection of the new paradigm concept and by who and how many. In order to delve into this area, it is necessary to consider that these messages are for the express purpose of empowering humanity to transcend, move through the current and approaching events to a new level of existence. This cannot be done if the attention is focused on the events that are now and will increasingly surround each and all. Fear is so engrained in the psyche of earth's inhabitants that it takes little to trigger it. It is not the purpose of these messages to engender fear as it is a mighty tool for dis-empowerment.

Understanding why "god allows this branch of humanity to suffer" is impossible to understand without encompassing the workings of the law of attraction. Victim/oppressor consciousness is two sides of the same coin. Existing at the lower scale of the vibratory range of manifested life experience; the magnetic attraction of the two is extremely strong. As the evolving consciousness strives to experience knowledge into wisdom it returns again and again to achieve freedom from this particular trap. The range of experience traverses between the two modes of expression. Each has experienced both within various levels. The planetary mass consciousness not only contains this mode of experience, but also indeed attracts it from other solar systems within the galactic whole. Thus earth indeed has outsiders contributing to this current era of experience. The time span of outside involvement of what you call extra-terrestrials when read within a sequential scenario has been thousands of years. It has been for a long enough period that some of those extra-terrestrials have evolved beyond that mode of experience and are now committed to correcting the results of their previous involvement with the people of earth. Inasmuch as they have transcended the victim/oppressor mode, it is within their wisdom to aid humanity if humanity will only accept the help available.

It is therefore with trepidation that the planned scenarios of the remaining oppressors/enslavers are mentioned within this focus. Since much material is available on these subjects, it is up to individuals to review the information available on radio talk shows, their web sites, books, magazines, newspapers and various conference/conventions that are available. It is extremely important that the shocking information available from these sources be processed *through* the individual's awareness. To remain stuck in the trauma of this knowledge will be fatal not only to the individual, but to the new paradigm project. The new paradigm is the only available pathway with success possibilities through this dilemma. Making such preparations as are appropriate for these possibilities is the most logical approach rather than simply continuing to process the information in panic and trauma. Promptly making simple appropriate plans and preparations through logical thought by listing and completing the suitable steps to be accomplished will not only relieve the trauma, but will bring forth the empowerment that transcends the feelings of victimhood these events were designed to engender.

The law of attraction works! That the USA and other countries have supported the attacks on the Moslem countries of the

Arabs, and others draws the likelihood of the similar experience of being attacked. The media has given all forms of illogical reasons for these attacks that were not officially sanctioned by the elected representatives but were allowed with their consent and the foolish consent of the people as a whole. Discernment was left to representatives whose influence is peddled and coerced into compliance. To cry, "I/we didn't know," means nothing to the dead, dying and miserable people experiencing the situation that has been foisted on them. They are the victims and "you foolish ones" are the perpetrators by default and must by the law of attraction receive your just due. It will not be pleasant. What can you do to change it? Change your mind and withdraw your consent to these actions within your own consciousness. Open your eyes and ears to the deceptions that surround you and vow to create a new experience for all living on this planet.

There is only one race on this planet, the human race. The varieties in appearance and belief systems are "no things." The extraterrestrials are visitors who have no desire to live here, only to enjoy the adventure of continuing your enslavement. They are fully aware that the planet cannot long endure the over population that they have encouraged so that they could play at their war games and perfect their tools of annihilation. To them humanity and earth are like the virtual reality games your children in large and small bodies' play. It is long past time to wake up and grow up into your responsibility to end their game. Welcome to the real world that now surrounds you and is about to overwhelm you unless you act now.

II-43

The clarion call of these messages is formulated to reach into the very center of each heart and mind to resonate there. It is intended to be an internal process that will enable each one embracing the possibilities contained within them to establish a vantage point from which to gauge their progressing personal transition. If each will consider the changes in their views of the world events as they are reported now and as they were perceived a few weeks ago, a considerable difference in the ability to discern the magician at work should be possible. The understanding of the meaning

of self-empowerment within the personal experience and relationships should also be apparent. The consideration of this might be
approached as the difference between submissive, assertive and
aggressive. It is the through application of the universal laws that
balance and harmony is achieved, a middle ground of experience.
Once this is experienced it becomes easier to realize when one
leaves this balance toward one or the other of the polarities. It is
taught in the current media/religious foci that "goodness" is the
ideal. Balance is not found in the extreme of either polarity. It is
through learning to discern where in the process each experience
is or is leading in the play between the polarities that allows for
wisdom to be attained.

The new paradigm will come into manifestation when a sufficient quota of humans on the planet identifies with its tenets. These
will focus its becoming without the aggressiveness of an enslaver
that would force its ideals on his/her fellow humans or the submissive victim that would purposefully refrain from participation
assuming that others will accomplish it for them. The ideal participant will employ the universal laws of attraction through purposeful
intent to manifest the new paradigm, actively sharing the concepts
and allowing the process to unfold by holding the intent assertively
within the consciousness. The focus will remain steadfastly within
their awareness as the world and personal events move through their
chaotic process of dismantling what now exists to allow the new to
manifest. Unfortunately, the new cannot superimpose itself over the
top of the present firmly held belief systems. The combined present
belief systems hold the current disastrous stream of events in place.
The belief in the repetitions of past experience of war, pestilence,
disease and painful deaths as the proper end to a lifetime of victim/
sacrifice for a future reward is rigidly held and constantly supported
by the planners of another round of their virtual reality games.

It is through these simple messages that those of genuine concern are reaching out to counter the focus of literally thousands
of years of deliberately ingrained manipulative programming into
the individual and collective psyche of humanity. It is a very large
expectation that is being placed in these messages in this endeavor
to reach those who are at a state of evolvement to resonate with
the truths contained within them. The realization of the futility of

continuing on in the age-old pattern of allowing others to write all the rules of the game is the trigger that brings forth the emotion and commitment to become a part of the momentum for moving on through to a new goal.

Just as several individuals can participate in a single event and each perceive and experience it differently, so also can a multitude of perceptions of what the new paradigm experience will be for each encompass the same definitive goal and accomplish that purpose. When the new paradigm is birthed, indeed each will experience it uniquely. If it were to be a totally defined picture it would again become encapsulated and enslaving. Within the laws of the universe, what you term ethics and morality are limited understandings. Within the higher dimensions, which is the purpose of leaving the current lesser vibratory experience through the new paradigm, it is possible for each to perceive the purposeful intent of all. This is not necessarily in detail at the lesser vibratory levels. Therefore dishonesty and aggressive intent is known and those with that level of intent find only those of similar intent to interact with. If there are no victims and only a group of aggressors to interact with, there is no game. It is to be expected that those ingrained thought patterns will show up in the beginning, however they will soon fade away as they are recognized. Do upper level dimensions lack challenge? No indeed! The challenges become subtler and even more rigorous to discern. Experience in the higher dimensions is not a boring "heavenly" evenness. The adventure of self-contemplation and growth becomes more and more interesting and the rewards more desirable. There will be no regrets for giving up the current belief systems and mode of experience, of that each can be absolutely sure.

The call for study, contemplation, commitment and follow through by defining the purpose and spreading the concept now is unfolding before each reader. It is doubted that any who are not seriously contemplating the process and anticipating the possibilities of the future of new experience will have reached this point in the messages. Both the logical and the emotional aspects resonate and the shift in consciousness is happening. Even those few that do turn away will not be able to return to their previous perspective of the current situation as it progresses toward the planned dark and dramatic shift. Those who do not choose to actively participate can yet share by simply holding the idea of the possibility of the time of the reign of the rainbow man arriving now. Legend has it that the first people on the planet climbed up out of the earth through a trapdoor. The rainbow man archetype is right now loosening the latch of the trapdoor that will allow his entry into the next level of manifested experience. It is time for this to happen!

II-44

The power of subtle thought when focused through the converging point of mutual agreement by a group purposefully representing a whole for the highest and best "good" of that whole is quite beyond the ability of the limited 3rd dimensional mind to comprehend. There is now documented evidence of the power of prayer in the recovery from illness when it is focused by doctors, nurses, friends and families for the "good" of the patient. The dynamic potential that is tapped is the *agreement* held within the focusing group's desire to bring forth the highest and best good for the person. The desire is usually limited to the person returning to an apparently "healthy" state. However, that is not always the true highest and best "good" for that person, since the purpose of the lifetime is usually unknown to the person and to those attending them, so it is best to leave the focus open. Further the person themselves may have already placed their decision as to their future into the flow of creation. Again this brings us back to the concept of thought thinking. The flow of creative energy that focuses each individual into manifestation to begin with and then maintains them in focus is intelligent thought thinking and is totally aware of what the highest and best good is in every instance *when it is directed to think within that concept.*

Self-aware consciousness is manifested thought aware of itself within its manifested surroundings. It is creation checking itself out for the purpose of knowing not only itself, but investigating its abilities to manipulate its potential to experience and know itself to a greater extent. Each of you are creational thought engaged in this marvelous experiment. You are intelligent thought surrounded by the potential of intelligent thought. The only way you can be controlled is to allow yourselves to believe you are something you are not. You must be convinced to believe you are something you are not. You must be convinced that you are powerless and subject to the will of others, thus a victim.

The intelligent thought that surrounds you is subject to your intentional will to direct it. If you fail to give it direction, it merely supports whatever direction someone else gives it regarding you. Thus through induced ignorance humanity has given consent to being manipulated. The most effective method for literally stealing your power has been through the diversion of the use of that power by convincing you to direct it outside yourselves to an unknown and little understood source, called "God." All power is vested in this vague unknowable entity that may or may not redirect the energy that is given to it back again to the worshipping requester. This is further diluted if the energy must first be directed through a "priest" like entity, who then directs it to the "God" and requests it to be returned to you. The point being, it is your power to direct as you see fit. You are the singular focus of creation experiencing as you. The bible contains a quoted question that reads something like "know you not that you are gods?" Indeed you know it now!

Learning to direct this power in *harmony* with the laws that under lay or support the wholeness of the flow of creation is the lesson to be accomplished. This cannot be effectively achieved unless the concept is known and accepted so that it may be practiced through experience into wisdom. Humanity on this planet is experiencing what results when the power of this energy is purposefully misused to restrict the evolvement of others for distorted experimentation. These entities are learning only how and to what extent others can be limited and manipulated into sacrifice and suffering. Observing is not experiencing into wisdom. Humanity is learning that sacrifice and suffering only brings more of the same. It is time to awaken and realize that continuing on the same path will only continue the pattern. In order to change this experience, the current pattern must be acknowledged and a new pattern conceived to replace it.

It may be difficult to accept that what has been taught for generations upon generations has been deliberately corrupted and given to you as truth in order to deceive and manipulate the entire population of a planet. It is more difficult to conceptualize a group focus that is so distorted as to spend eons of sequential time in the game of doing this dastardly deed. It is only necessary to accept it as what it is and resolve to withdraw your permission to be one of their plastic play pieces that bends and twists to fit their desires. It is the time now to take back your right to self-determination of your own present and future. This process leaves you not with less, but with more. You know in truth who and what you are. You now have a process in which to acquaint yourself with your inherent right and power to determine your own path. Leave the future of those who would enslave to the law of attraction. The key to their future is your withdrawal of approval and cooperation. In the moment in which their intense control focus is broken, the energy shifts for them also. Knowing this is enough. Do not spend time even considering their future. Be only concerned with creating your own. It is task enough to occupy each and all of you for some time to come.

Now is an excellent time to begin. Does a new future require that every aspect of your current experience be left behind? Not necessarily, but each must be considered carefully so that it fits in the wholeness that serves the evolvement of all. It is best to begin with the statement of purpose, then a simple framework that can be "painted" in with what is appropriate, remembering what is appropriate for one is not what may be appropriate for all. The application of the universal laws allows for diversity in harmony. A worthwhile goal to remember. If each is responsible for their individual intentions and actions all will come together in amazing coordinated cooperation. Within the true realization of time *there is only now.* The past is over and the future is yet to manifest as "the nows" pass into the past. **The dream of the new paradigm begins now and continues now!**

Becoming
Volume III

The messages contained in this, the third book of messages, are a continuation of information provided for the transition of the hearts and minds of those of humanity that are willing to be a catalyst for change. It is an undeniable truth that the current pattern of use and abuse of the planetary resources will lead to the end of its ability to sustain life forms. The human body and awareness are being deliberately overwhelmed physically, psychologically and magnetically. The majority of humanity fails to understand that unseen forces surrounding them are affecting their ability to survive. These are hidden within the "modern" conveniences powered by alternating electrical current; through radio, television, and many other low frequency emanations that now alter the individual's and the planet's magnetic fields to an unimaginable degree.

Just as human scientists experiment using what are considered "lesser species" with little concern for their suffering and death in the name of "scientific advancement," so also is humanity considered a lesser species to be used in like fashion. "You" are being used in exactly that way with the full knowledge and participation of those humans who believe themselves a part of the controlling hierarchy. These misguided humans are under the direct supervision of those beings that desire to continue to control this planet and others. The evolving conscious awareness of humanity has *again* evolved to a level that is considered dangerous. There are many that are now aware of this very real outside influence through the history revealed in the artifacts that were not destroyed or hidden, and by reaching logical conclusions about the sightings of various space craft as well as interaction with their occupants. These interactions have been both face to face and telepathic. The evidence indicates the presence of outside powers trying to continue the longstanding control of Earth and its solar system. There are also those that are a positive presence hoping to be of assistance to an awakening humanity that must be willing to take on the responsibility for determining its own future in order to receive this available help.

Humanity has itself blocked the answer to its longstanding cry for relief from enslavement by the outside forces, because it has been educated to ask for its "rescue" to come from an unknowable being that is in actuality a part of the controlling forces. Deception for control has been very successful for thousands of years. "Worship your controller" has been the ploy. Mankind has very little time left to wake up to this strategy and cooperatively agree that it is time to end this charade once and for all. Those who would assist must be a group that is willing to research and prove to itself beyond a shadow of a doubt the truth of this astounding pronouncement of the global situation. It must realize that humanity has to create its own future or remain in the circumstances of terrible slavery that are planned for them.

Both the positive and negative forces that are focused on this planet are aware that multiple cycles are culminating in this time sequence which will be to the advantage of either humanity or its colonizers, depending upon which one has the support of the overall planetary consciousness. This support can be either passively or actively understood. It can therefore be readily understood that if humanity does not make a clear choice to own this planet for itself, it is passively supporting continued enslavement and giving away its natural resources for the use of others rather than for itself. Rich mineral reserves have been transported from this planet and others in this solar system for thousands of years to enrich the lives of beings that have failed to steward their own planetary resources wisely. Reports of large "mother ships" are true and they are present for that purpose.

It is time for humanity to wake up and people to come together in the understanding that they are wise enough to control their own destiny and ask for help to "help themselves for the highest and best good for all concerned." That is a prayer that can be affirmatively answered! Until such time as humans can prove themselves to be cooperative and non-aggressive toward their benevolent neighbors, all help will be given indirectly: that is these beings will not walk among you until it is safe for them to do so. The help that can be offered will be very effective, but it must be asked for and accepted as assistance and not as rescue. A victim, be it individual or a planetary mass consciousness, has not evolved to a level of responsibility that warrants assistance. A victim consciousness must move through the need to look outside of itself and instead look at its own choices to find the cause(s) of its imperfect situation. Freewill is the freedom to choose, and all continuously choose, even if it is to choose not to choose. There are always forces willing to make choices for those unwilling to make their own. It is time for humanity to make its own choices. These messages were written to help with that important process.

III-1

The time of bringing the belief system into harmony with the actual physical reality situation in order to avoid the doom of destruction that is now awaiting the majority of earth's population is now. The important focus is not to dwell on the doom: it is the pivotal point that is now available to humanity that must be used as the impetus of change. Shocking as the facts are regarding the primrose path that humanity has been blindly following, these must be accepted and then the focus turned away from the deceptions toward creating a new reality.

What is this new reality? How can it be created if there is no knowledge of what it is that should or could replace the present situation? It would appear that this reality as it is created would be nothing but a hodge-podge of each one's desires based on the programming that is already present within each. Who would have the ability to release what is known and envision new concepts that would not be tainted with dreams of the past? If advice were asked of galactic brothers and sisters, would those not be entwined within their known reality? So it would appear that not only is there the surrounding current dilemma, but another one of even larger proportions insofar as breaking clear of the current one and then having to confront repetitions of experience rather than a new paradigm. This it seems is too much for a group consciousness that is or will be reeling from the shock of discovering the extent of their deception, or is it? It will be within the release of that shock and the decision to create their own reality that the birthing shall take place.

If what is known is deception, then will pursuing opposite concepts result in knowing truth? Indeed it could. For example, if benevolence has been sought from outside sources, is it indeed available from within one's own awareness? If freedom has not been found in either authoritarian systems or in the pursuit of individual freedoms, then where is it to be found? Could it be obtained within moral and ethical standards that gift the individual within an agreement made by co-operating groups? Could the size of the groups also be arranged by agreement? Could the groups find common ground for agreement within common desires for similar defined freedoms? If cooperation was the key ingredient rather than competition and the need to be/feel superior, then all things are possible. If common interest and desire were the defined beginning point around which all else is drawn by attraction to intended definition of desired experience, successful interaction is possible. If freedom to withdraw and find a more adequate experience within another group was encouraged and allowed, successful adventure in self-definition would be assured. The experience of the search for the most perfect expression could be an end unto itself. Though groups would be visited on a regular basis, it would be the commitment to a flexible and expanding focus that would enable them to continue until a satisfactory accomplishment was made by all involved. Thus no commitment to forever continuity would be a part of the goal, as expansive experience cannot place fences around itself and function within its intended expression. It is understood that expansive consciousness can only continue its expansion within a context of changing conceptual understandings. Progress results in shedding old understandings as these are encompassed in wisdom and the focus is ever toward the unfolding of new knowledge that allows for change. The introduction of apparently conflicting information resolves into integration of the apparent dichotomy and allows for progression into greater concepts. In other words, stagnation through holding to static beliefs halts the desired process. The safety of known apparent truths is a trap, which the progressing consciousness must purposefully avoid.

The ability to accept this conceptual understanding of the ground rules for participation within manifested experience requires a stretch in the belief system that is indeed quite phenomenal in and of itself. However mind boggling it is, it is the beginning point that is necessary if mankind is to extricate itself from the mire in which it now finds itself. The controlling over-lords are intent on returning this planet to a bare minimum of tightly enslaved beings so they can return to their original intent of stripping the needed minerals for the salvation of their own civilization at the expense of this planet and its inhabitants. It is the destiny of the inhabitants that belong to this planet by birth and adoption to take on the responsibility of changing this destiny and there is little sequential time remaining for them to accomplish this monumental feat. If challenge is the ingredient to call for the effort required, then certainly it is present. It is fervently requested that all those reading this material give it the most careful and focused consideration. It is further requested that each consider the call that is within it to assume the responsibility to make it happen, or to accept the results that acquiescence will reap without regret.

III-2

The days ahead do not look bright for those of you in the USA. The dark plans appear to be coagulating into form as they have been planned. The light workers are the focus of "God," as you have chosen to name the outplay of creative energies that bring into being galaxies, solar systems, planets and individualized awareness to acknowledge and experience these manifestations. These now begin their work in earnest. Indeed each individual awareness has within itself that creative energy that is theirs to acknowledge and to know personally. It is the focus of that subtly powerful energy that is who each really is. It appears to be apart from the personality/ego that is capable of comprehending the understanding of the concept of it. *It is the "becoming" of this apparently larger than life beingness that is the difficult accomplishment.* Yet, there is "no other God." That which each is in this larger reality is the only doorway to understanding the concept of what is called God.

God is not a focus of personality – individual thought processes or a benevolent creator separate from you. God is the combination of the focus of all Its parts coalesced into the composite of all. Each awareness is blocked from being a part of that composite until each realizes that it is a part of this composite. Being told that it is, means nothing at all. It is the realization that one's self is a viable part of that composite that encompasses the totality of the being, that is what "becoming" is all about. One must become that reality and realize it is a viable aspect of the totality of God and that its input to that reality is the truth of who they are. It is not a mental realization, but one that registers total agreement within the mental, emotional, physical and spiritual levels of the total self. In other words, the spiritual aspect that focuses each into manifested reality finally gets the message through to the rest of its focus that is walking around in the body. The body must register this understanding through the totality of its brain-nervous system resulting in what is called a realization that then registers as a sudden feeling sensation accompanied by an all encompassing understanding. It allows for a total change in perception with regard to the self and how this self fits into the composite picture of experience. This results in a change in the perception of "God" which suddenly allows for an understanding that "God" equates to cosmic/galactic citizenship rather than a father/child relationship. It is a shift from "being or experiencing as powerless" to the awesome responsibility of being a contributing portion to the totality of what constitutes "God" or the creative energy of potentiality being focused into experience in order that it can be defined and understood.

The pivotal point at which this change takes place is not a shift from negative to positive. It is rather an uplifting to a new point in the spiral of experience that allows for a greater understanding and ability to utilize the positive/negative energies that are part and parcel of the outflow of creative energies in the individual and collective foci that result in the larger matrix or design of the whole pattern of a galaxy. It is easier to grasp the larger picture of this description than to define it at the level of each individual awareness. Each being comes to the point of their own realization in unique ways and by unique combinations of experience and wisdom. The point is often approached and rejected many times before the actual crossover acceptance happens. It requires a great deal of courage to crossover to a new and different perspective of the life experience. It requires releasing well-learned lessons and entering into a completely new consciousness of what reality truly is. For those who are on the planet Earth now, the deceptions are of such magnitude and the truth of what each being is, so well hidden, that the acceptance of the truth by the masses is such a gigantic leap in consciousness that it appears to be impossible that it could possibly happen. Yet, happen it must if this segment of the human race and this jewel of a planet are to survive.

When viewed from the larger perspective, the deceptions as perpetrated on the human race of this planet are so totally illogical that it is quite amazing that so few humans have figured out the truth. Granted, many when they are first introduced to the possibility that they have been deceived, immediately resonate with the idea and begin to contemplate its possibility and arrive at the truth of its probability. However, those that cling to the deceptions with tenacity are in the overwhelming majority. It is therefore to be anticipated that much chaos will be experienced before a mathematical coefficient of beings making the realization/ change of consciousness is reached to bring about a shift in the future experience on this planet. It is then to be anticipated that the planet itself may or may not be able to survive the abuse that is being loosed upon it. To enable more help from the galactic citizenry to assist in this situation, a large number of "responsible Earth citizens" must request this help to save the planet first and the citizenry second. The requests now are being made more on a personal salvation basis than from the larger picture which automatically includes the personal aspect.

Thus it is that we offer these concepts for the consideration of those who choose to read and to accept them as suggestions worth considering and acting upon. Our concern is that the "composite concept of God" that each awareness is entitled to contribute to as a realized consciousness, become the next focus of concern for those awake and aware humans awaiting the next step in their assignment.

III-3

In the final accounting, it is the transition of consciousness into citizenship responsibility that is the goal. All else comes as a result of that choice. It was once offered as a part of the experience of bringing the US of A into being, but the consciousness of the individual people was not at a point that the goals could be maintained. Instead the exploiting of the resources through greed was greater than the commitment to soul agendas. Thus these experiences were allowed to be played out for the lessons to be learned. It is yet to be seen if these lessons will be discerned and brought into wisdom by a sufficient number to salvage this planet. Choices must be made to place the whole as equal to the individual in the consideration of the result desired.

Those asked to give their lives for the purposes of defending their country or placing the ideals of their leaders above those of others and attacking them, have allowed the illusion of a whole as being more important than the individual. It is a supreme sacrifice. When the whole and the individual consideration have equal weight, then war is not an option unless imbalance is acted out as an attack. Then all other options are considered first before a defense is appropriate. When there is balance, there is progress. It is to be remembered that the play of positive and negative energies brings forth the spiral of progress. However, the extremes of both bring forth regression, or loss of upward progress.

Another ingredient that must be taken into account within the context of war, is the familiar consideration of the victim consciousness. It is to be remembered that the law of attraction causes the victim to draw to its experience those who have a like consciousness but are on the other side of it, like the two sides of a coin. Those who feel abused draw to them those who will provide more of that experience until that attitude is shed. Thus war serves its purpose through forcing the victims to come together and experience the power of throwing off the aggressor. Then either the empowerment is retained, or the former victims return to one or the other side of the victim experience. This trading of sides continues until a realization is made that allows for transcending this experience. It is this outplay in the extreme that is upon this planet now.

It is understanding of this situation from its larger perspective that will allow those who are about assisting the planet and its inhabitants to move through these experiences and continue their chosen work. The experience for those involved cannot be changed for them. The consciousness within each involved group must shift and move both individually and collectively. The consciousness of the group that each leader represents will affect that leader's decisions. No amount of outside influence on that leader will change that and the only control that can be used is to "replace" that leader, usually through assassination. In that way the process can be slowed or changed by the chaos that accompanies the change in leadership, usually by tricking the group into believing the death of their leader was perpetrated by the other side. In this case, discernment is the key and it is the one time that the observer group may be able to influence the outcome by circulating the truth.

Through the comprehension of the larger picture, it is within possibility that those who have volunteered to assist the "God focus" can realize that their participation is a key to the transition of this planet and its inhabitants into a greater experience of manifested life. As taught by the religions at this time, personal power is transferred to and through an unknowable power and governmental bureaucracy. Both of these entities have been created for purposes of enslavement. The problem of education of the masses then presents itself. It is to be remembered, that it is the first few who are awakened and make the realization of this hoax that are the most difficult to convince of this reality. Thus, those precious few are to be valued and the education process continued for the process will become easier as the numbers increase. Though it seems but a pitiful few in view of the billions of beings that constitute the mass consciousness of the planet, it must be remembered that it took the opposition literally eons of time to reach the current control level.

A change in the understandings that they have slowly and carefully nurtured can be accomplished in a very, very short time because they defy logic. The mind of conscious beings constantly searches for logic in order that each may stay positioned within the linear perception of time and life experience. Illogic is a form of chaos and to assimilate illogic into a logical sequence requires a great deal of concentration. It is one of the reasons that rest or recreation away from this process is craved. Once illogical ideas are identified, then the sequential thought process reprograms itself, rather like a computer changing its internal arrangement of data to a more efficient combination of sequences. When illogic is perceived and the rearrangement of data takes place, then other illogical data is identified and the search is on to further identify any other illogical data present and to eliminate it also. Through this process, great changes in the mass consciousness can be accomplished.

III-4

As the Light Workers on this planet comprehend the larger picture, it is helpful to them to continue to broaden the picture to include a greater understanding of the galactic wholeness in which they are playing such an important part. This understanding is to enable them to enhance their observer roles and thus see through and past the chaos that each will find going on around them. Through the process of observation while experiencing the chaos, each will be able to place themselves in a position that allows them to be in places of safety, not in hiding, but in movement within the chaos. It is an experience of observing the self in movement, a process of literally being in two fields of awareness simultaneously. Simply put, an example to begin the process is being aware that each individual is at the same moment in sequential time an individual with its own life agenda and also a part of the family, community, state, nation and planetary whole. Each status is an awareness that is separate and yet a composite of the whole earthly experience. Each shifts their thought processes between each role and yet maintains their stability. Further, a truly good actor can be their own personality and can also assume the personality of the character they are playing and move between them without losing the awareness that they are both. The Light Workers, ground crew, whatever each chooses to call him/herself, must learn to walk in two worlds simultaneously. It would be wise for each to begin to practice the art of this split awareness. It is nothing more than an acceptance of the situation as it is. There is the world of deception and the world of knowing that the deception is being perpetrated on the planetary inhabitants.

Each also knows that a new and different world of experience awaits birthing, but until the one that is known to the inhabitants begins to crumble into chaos, there is no way to birth the new one. As the current known reality reaches a specific degree of disintegration in the chaos, the new one can begin to come into manifested reality. The question is which one will materialize, the one planned by the dark planners or the one that is envisioned by the Light Workers/Ground Crew and those drawn to the dream of the New Paradigm. There is the planned world of disharmony with the galactic composite plan or one that is created in harmony with it. The critical number of humans desiring a harmonious existence within the surrounding energies of potentiality that constitute this Galaxy must be reached in order for the New Paradigm to come into a reality recognizable by those beings in harmony with it. Based on a mathematical formula it is less than might be thought considering the number of humans on Earth. One of the reasons for this is that those who desire this harmonious experience will be focused upon that desire. Even though there are many humans that are now focused on the deception, during the chaos they will lose that focus and become caught up in the chaos. Their focus will be on the chaos, thus nullifying a great deal of the power that those of dark intent have established. It is during this time that the most important work for the Light (those of positive intent) will be done. This is the reason that it is important for those of positive focus to become aware of their purpose for being here and learn to lift themselves out of the influence of the chaos and know that those will be the moments of most productive service to this planet and thereby to their fellow humans. The exact knowledge of the nature of the New Paradigm is not all that important at this time, it is the desire for it that is important. It is the commitment to being part of the positive/Light focus that is important. It is the practice of walking within more than one awareness by acknowledging them as a part of everyday living that is primary. Each must learn to choose in the moment which awareness is the predominant one and change from one to the other by intent.

Awareness is the focus of who and what each is. Each has a multifaceted opportunity to learn to use latent/unused abilities that are available. The knowledge and use of these have been hidden and denied, for to use these would bring freedom from control. There are many that would seem quite miraculous. These are indeed simple applications of mathematical laws that exist but are unknown. Many of these will be included in the lessons to follow, not explained in confusing terminology, but as guided, simple lessons in application. When practiced and applied to daily living situations, they will become a part of each one's life experience and available when needed in the experiences coming in the sequential times to come.

It is suggested that each begin to observe the various roles that are available in situations and thoughts about situations in daily experience such as being part of the deception and observing the deception. During one's thoughts, which role is being played out, the family member, the citizen of the local community, the church member, the dismayed U.S. citizen when learning of the latest aggression by the government, the state citizen reading the news of the latest activity in the legislature, etc., etc. What observer role or active role is each one (are you) playing in the moment? Is it the role that you desire to play? If not, then can you change "hats" so to speak and observe from a different role? It is important that each of you learn to discern through self observation where you are in the scenario that is occurring in your perception at any given moment. In the practice of this role playing, much safety in the future can be gained.

III-5

In the days to come, those who intend to hold the focus for this transition of the planet and its inhabitants will need every positive word to encourage them to continue in the process. It is the intent of this material to add to the positive intent of those committed to the project by providing practical and easily used techniques to assist in holding this intent in place. It is necessary that this intent be held on a continual basis by the constant input of many. Inasmuch as manifestation can be traced backward to thought, to light, to intent/focus, to potentiality, it can be seen just where the intent to participate in this process fits into the flow of creation. For whatever purpose, be it positive or negative, the process is the same and available to be used. It is the ease of the flow, that makes the difference, for as the previous material has revealed, when the intent/focus resonates with the higher creational intent manifestation results more easily. Any desired manifestation that is in harmony with the higher/finer intent receives reinforcing energy and therefore is able to receive advantageous assistance in manifesting without needing to be aware of what it is or how it came. In other words, that which resonates with the greater plan of wholeness draws to it through the law of attraction added supportive energy.

Manifestation that lacks this resonance and is initiated at a level below the highest source of purpose or intention requires a more intense focus and careful attention to the continual need to hold the plan firmly in the center of attention. The smallest detail that deviates from the plan can cause a ripple effect that changes the planned outcome at many levels of the manifestation process. There is no automatic support process to dovetail these changes into the plan harmoniously. This then makes the resistive plan vulnerable to deviations that can be devastating to the total plan without the knowledge of those initiating it and holding it in place with their intention.

It is important that those who are supporting the manifestation of the New Paradigm understand this and hold this comparison of the difference of the two sets of circumstances that underlay the situation at hand that they have chosen to participate within firmly in mind. It is entirely possible that by being familiar with as many of the details of the opposition's plans, discouraging and demoralizing as they appear to be, when deviations do occur in it, it is possible to sense the panic and frantic activity that goes on as attempts are made to counteract the effects the deviation may have wrought. Those are then occupied in making changes in the details of the overall plan to compensate for the effects that naturally ripple through the entire situation. This then opens the possibility of being able to add to the effects to further complicate the recovery they are trying to accomplish.

Thus we offer two tools for holding the focus for the New Paradigm firmly in place. The first being the understanding of the overriding higher purpose of the creational flow bringing with it intelligent coordination of energies that resonate with the higher purpose. The second using the greatest possible understanding of their plan as the basis of observing their process and finding moments and opportunities to add to their complications in maintaining their focus. Simply focusing attention on their dilemmas can place great stress on their ability to correct the flow of intentional energy, for that which is contrary to the Light, must be done in secrecy and darkness. Knowledge is thought which flows from the Light of understanding. This then points out the need to know as much as possible about the plans of the dark intention for the enslavement of this planet. It points out the importance of the work that has been done by those committed to investigating, observing, drawing obvious conclusions and then sharing with any and all who will listen and read about what constitutes the dark plans. Those who have committed their life focus to exposing this plan serve their fellow human beings and this planet well. This information is critical to the transition through this process that must be made by the planet and its inhabitants. It must not be the focus, but must be the background upon which the New Paradigm will begin its building process out of the chaos that the dark plan will cause. Thus in its own way, looking at the bigger picture, the situation instigated by the dark forces will in the long run serve that portion of humanity and the planet that choose to take advantage of the opportunity offered as a boost on their path of evolvement.

III-6

The rapidity of the coming events into manifestation has been allowed in that the chaos will serve the birth of change. Though those of you who dread its onset, knowing the additional suffering that will be endured by the many you consider the pawns of innocence is understood, yet indeed are they innocent? The same opportunities that have been afforded you, though they may have been clothed in different appearances, have been offered to all. It is the few that have opened their conscious thought to the possibilities and the probabilities that now find themselves in awareness of what the true picture is that faces the planet and its inhabitants. This group must also understand that the dilemma will be solved in what is called Divine Order. This process moves in a holographic, nonlinear process that accomplishes its purpose within chaos much more rapidly than within what is perceived as order. What appears as order now is indeed the rigid confines of institutions of experience that are out of balance within the galactic matrix of progress toward expansive progress or evolvement.

Those who serve the focus of intention to bring this planet back into the flow of progress within the overall matrix must bring the center of their attention to this intent. At the moment, it is possible to visualize this planet as poised within a back flow or eddy that is out of the movement of this ever-present flow. Only through the focused intent of this special group can it be drawn back to its position within that flow. Visualization in unison or agreement is the most powerful tool available. It is through the *Handbook of the New Paradigm, Embracing the Rainbow* and this book to the known few who are at this time actively focusing their thought energy to this purpose, that this agreement in active corrective movement can be made known. Though the group doing this seems pitifully small, it is extremely effective. Those involved in this activity are not entities of small experience or ability. This is not the first time any of these has served the forces that organize in times of imbalance that brings opportunity for leaps forward in expression and expansion for this or other galaxies. This is not meant to feed the ego, but that each may begin to recognize that there is great power within their commitments. The time willingly spent in individual and collective focus on the desire and intent to literally focus this planet through this difficult process of evolvement is well worth the effort involved. As this focus is made within a continuing commitment, the law of attraction will draw to it the sufficient number to begin the momentum of energies that will bring about the movement within the mass consciousness necessary to refocus the alignments that currently exist. It is through the recognition and acceptance of the possibility by each of those who read these named books and circulated materials that this focus will build upon itself within a mathematical format that will underlay the process.

It is necessary that each lay aside modesty and reluctance to accept the possibility that each is indeed a special and powerful entity that has donned a robe of obscurity and forgotten their origins that each might remain unknown not only to yourselves, but to those of evil intent until this present moment. It is time to assume the proper identity and come into the role of service as was agreed upon before this series of lifetimes was accepted as part of the service contract. It is time to realize that this is who and what you are and what you do and have done before. It is a matter of simply remembering and adapting what you innately know to fit the current requirements. A certain amount of reluctance is natural because of the human format that contains your awareness. It is understood that this involves a literal containment, or restriction upon your ability to realize your true identity. Thus these messages continue the process of awakening your remembrance, stimulating your desire to participate and applying pressure to your commitment to this project.

As you contemplate the possible truth of these words, within your inner awareness the energies contained in this process do their work and the truth begins to root itself and grow. That which constitutes your segment of the "mission impossible," as it seems to the conscious mind, begins to be drawn into your daily experience. A knowingness of what is appropriate and necessary is apparent and seems the only possible thing to do. It will not seem that what you do as a part of your daily experience will be at all heroic, but through the combination of these daily contributions by the growing group committed to this project, much will be accomplished. It is in the accomplishment of these seemingly small contributions that the rooted truth of who and what you are will grow. At the moment of necessity when each must stand forth within that identity and declare the truth of the future of this planet, the ability to do so will bring a natural, powerful and pivotal shift that will cause the desired transition to occur. It is knowing that the needed commitment to the totality of the necessary change does not require great personal sacrifice or the need to stand alone before the forces of evil and suffer great bodily harm that allows for the commitment to service to be accepted with enthusiasm.

Though we admit there are a few exceptions to this pattern of service, those who accept these roles are well aware of their identities and their commitment to this level of service. To these few, loyalty, special help and guidance is constantly at hand. Blessed indeed are these special beings of commitment to leadership within this focus of service.

III-7

The human forms that reside on this planet have long been held in bondage and kept from the natural evolvement that enables each to enter into the true understanding of their source and purpose for experiencing manifested existence. The knowledge of the laws that govern this galaxy has been withheld and purposeful teaching has been denied. Instead deception has been the basis of all knowledge given. It is the decision of the overseers of this galaxy to end this practice here and now. However it must be the individual and collective choice of the inhabitants of this planet to change this experience. The long-standing deceptions have rooted and grown within the understandings of the human consciousness. Thus the decision by the Galactic Counsel will have little or no effect until the residents of this planet choose to change their experience. However, the ability to make the change once accepted and decided upon by earth's human residents will flow easily and irrevocably once the sufficient percentage of those desiring change has been reached.

What exactly the Galactic Council will decide to do to assist this is now the question. It means that those who are misusing the laws that underlay manifested existence no longer have the same degree of energy input to support their activities as they have had at their disposal. There will be a waning or lessening of this supportive energy. This will bring about an unraveling of their overall plan. Those carefully planned strategies will begin to have unexpected results that will cause unexpected ripple effects that do not bring about either the expected results or the degree of expected results in order to accomplish the anticipated goal.

The plan as known to those awake and aware humans is "the plan." It is their anticipated and embroidered plan. It is not necessarily what that plan is in reality. It is important that the difference be understood clearly. The actuality of "the plan" is skeletal indeed. It is open to many variations and has many weaknesses that are unknown to them. It is in the best interest of those who desire a change in the opportunities and experiences that are available to the beleaguered members of humanity to know that their intentions to change the momentum and outcome of this carefully laid plan of enslavement are the arrows of destruction to that plan. It is the intention to withdraw support of, belief in and participation within "the plan" that will cause it to collapse of its own weight. Within the outflow of creative expansive energies, the directional flow is based on intentional purpose.

The plan of enslavement is based on the intention to destroy and enslave large portions of humanity as a method of solving a problem that was caused by those who have controlled this planet and its inhabitants. This situation was brought about by the controllers' own decisions regarding the use of the planet and its inhabitants in the very beginning. This has been further complicated by the addition of various groups of humanity from various other places in the galaxy being added to the citizenry against their will. There does then exist a complex citizenry that brings to the mix an interesting dilemma for those who desire to control the planet.

There is a direct opposition of intentions, those of slavery and those of freedom. If it were not for the added citizenry, the plan of enslavement would have been accomplished long ago. Those that were in the beginning literally engineered for the purpose of serving were left devoid of many human characteristics for that intentional purpose of enslavement. However, the genetic addition of the added citizenry has now spread throughout the planetary bloodlines. Though there are still pockets of pure genetic variations within the whole, there exist a large percentage of genetic combinations that confuse the understandings of those who plan to control the citizens. Unexpected actions and reactions continue to upset the carefully laid plans.

It is, therefore, important that those who intend for this situation to play out differently than the planned scenario understand that their intention to create a different ending to the current flow of events has the ability to accomplish this. Once this understanding is accepted, the commitment to it becomes easier and more realistic to the conscious awareness. It is much like the laser sword of your popular movie. That intention, which is in harmony with the galactic intention for evolvement through freewill choice of experience, then becomes a powerful tool of change in the "hands" of those who understand its usefulness and learn to wield it in a timely fashion and at moments of greatest effect. Through the knowledge and understanding of the intentions of the opposing force, this understanding can be used to great effect for the purpose of freeing this planet from its heretofore use as a source of minerals and as a dumping grounds for human misfits. It is through the realignment of genetic combinations that evolvement to more complex levels has occurred for a percentage of inhabitants. This percentage now brings forward the necessary quotient to allow for the transition of this planet into Galactic citizenship, when these can be awakened and bound together by intention to take advantage of this opportunity.

III-8

As the willing members of those in human focus awaken to the plight that surrounds them, it is clear to them that the situation is indeed serious and that no amount of physical resistance can change this. It is apparent that something else must be done to bring a change to their future experience on this planet. Through the consideration of the larger picture, it also becomes clear that the lack of understanding of not only the history of their origins, but the lack of a true purpose for existence on this planet has left them bereft and adrift like flotsam on the sea. At the basis of each one's awareness there is a weary wonderment that says to each, "why bother." "What reason is there that is worth striving for to maintain life in this physical body?" "Where is this Utopia that is promised as a reward for the effort that must be put forth in this human experience?" "Does it even exist?" "Is there only a short rest before we begin over again with another life of disappointment and frustration?" "Why is there such a sense of participating in a spiral of experience that leads to the 'same ole, same ole,' or even less, each lifetime?"

There is a song that says the answer is "blowing in the wind!" The wind of change! There is a point at which the thought patterns mentioned above reach a place within the consciousness that causes a shift. A purpose is sought, not in the world of the 5 senses that is called reality, but within the awareness. Each, within every lifetime, is called upon to find their purpose, not in the world of effort, but from within the space of awareness that is only found at the center of the "awareness that knows itself." This awareness of the self was the gift from the "tree of knowledge" that the religious soothsayers have spent so much time attempting to teach as a great mistake. This is the gift that lifted humanity out of the animal kingdom and placed them at the edge of the kingdom of those beings that "know who and what they are." So who and what are they? Beings that are little, if any different than what you who is reading this is. They may have greater use of their brain capacity that enables them to know and do things that seem miraculous to those of lesser understanding. However, if you look at the progress made in that area in the past century on this planet, that is of little consequence in the dilemma of knowing who and what you are in the search for this greater acquisition of knowledge. Are these "gods" that have come and gone from this planet at their will and left you in such awe of their accomplishments that you worship them as all knowing, really all knowing?

Through the research of the artifacts of past civilizations that are now available and have been studied, cataloged and conclusions drawn, it is clear to the few that have availed themselves of this knowledge, that humanity has been lead down the primrose path. One ideology after another has been thrust upon innocent mankind in their search for their purpose and their origins to keep them in darkness and ignorance. The question is why? What purpose could beings of more intelligence have for deliberately causing their planetary relatives to be misled and their evolutionary progress diverted into a backwater rather than leading them onward and upward into full citizenship and responsibility within the Galactic family? Could there be a character flaw within the genetic expression of that particular group of beings? Could that character flaw have been carried on through to those of humanity that have the intermingled blood of those particular apparently superior beings?

The expansive flow of the Universal energies that underlay the manifestation of potentiality into expression requires that knowledge be experienced into wisdom. There is at the center of all, infinite patience for this to be accomplished within non-linear expression. This is a concept that the human mind, unless fully activated, has great difficulty in understanding. Within holographic experience, simultaneous interactions are occurrings without the limitations of linear, sequential time frames. In other words, what appear to those of less active mind/brain capabilities as experiences happening one after the other are indeed being played out in other experiential formats simultaneously. Thus a picture is being completed with more than one activity going on with no time constraints for beginning or completion, for all is in constant motion with only momentary rest periods of inactivity. These momentary periods of inactivity are those incidents of realization of wisdom acquired through the experiencing of knowledge to points of understanding. Thus wisdom is gained so that the process is continued expansively.

The apparent character flaws that have held mankind in a delusional state of false and misleading knowledge that is impossible to experience into wisdom, has been a twofold situation. First the flaw by the more knowledgeable, self-appointed over-lords of this planet who have jealously guarded their perceived superiority and the flaw of humanity in thinking they are lessor and thus the pawns of these beings. Because ones have less understanding does not make them of less potentiality. It is potentiality that is the measure of worth and mankind has equal potentiality with any and every other expression of self-awareness. It is in making this realization and demanding the opportunity to self-express into this potentiality that will free mankind on this planet to accomplish this purpose. This demand as a personal decision made within each one's own inner knowingness will bring about the change from victim/slave to sovereign owner of his/her future individually and collectively. It is a rising up from within that will in proper order progress into the reality of known experience for this planet. How long this process will take within the linear time reality that is processed through the human ego (the ability to observe) at this stage of evolution remains to be chosen by humanity itself.

III-9

The record of advancement insofar as humanity on this planet is concerned, is a checkerboard of dark and light, or positive and negative experience. As an overall composite from the point of view of a spiral of upliftment, the results are dismal to say the least. Whatever help has been given has been convoluted and shamefully diverted into disinformation. What has been intuited has been hidden or destroyed and those gifted humans imprisoned or killed. Mankind has been purposefully held in mental, emotional and spiritual captivity. The age-old question arises as to "why God allows this to happen?" Here again we face the fallacy of what "God" has been represented to be. The question is addressed to an outside Supreme Being that holds power over each individual life expression. It is the transfer of the awe held long ago when beings of apparent superior status brought forth the human in partial likeness of themselves for the purpose of exploiting their physical forms in slavery to an all-knowing superior being that promises benevolence but seldom provides it. In other words, this "God" with the expected power to control all things, does not now and never has existed.

It is the self-awareness attribute that is within each individual that is available to each and every being that has risen above animal status that is available to be harnessed and directed and will provide the benevolence "each feels it deserves." Here we face the attribute that allows for exploitation by outside influence. This brings the focus back to the understanding that each has of who and what they are. The self-awareness of each has the ability to choose and decide how to experience their manifested reality. It is the power that either takes them forward into greater experience through wisdom gained or allows them to regress into lesser experiences of slavery and degradation. These are made, not in one great decision, but as a sum total of all the experiences from early childhood onward. Unfortunately, these decisions are greatly influenced by the parent's experience from conception forward. Thus we find each generation saddled with the difficulty of overcoming this influence plus the planned misconceptions that are planted by those pawns of the self-appointed overlords of this planet.

Only through recognizing and accepting this dilemma in its true dimensions can those committed members of this human race find a place of equilibrium from which to begin to build a viable understanding of who and what they are. It is necessary to accept that the totality of human status is yet to be attained. It is totally possible to attain the full active status of the human potentiality, but it indeed will require assistance. This assistance, as has been stated before in these lessons, can be made available after a sufficient number of humans on this planet accept the fact that their help must first come from within their own decision process. It is a prerequisite that there must be acceptance that their only rescue is to be found in their own inner resources. Only after this realization may they ask for help from their galactic brothers and sisters. The "God" so sought by the disillusioned members of humanity as a source of rescue exists only as the composite of all manifested awareness as focused within the confines of each expanding unit of awareness ad-infinitum. It is necessary to recognize and decide to become a part of this manifested awareness as a responsible and contributing part of it in order to proceed within its process.

At this point, the question of the misuse of humanity by its self-appointed overlords returns to the focus of this discussion. As brought forth within the prior discussion, the laws that allow for potentiality to express into manifested reality so that knowledge can be experienced into wisdom and progress provide the basis for this process. The basic law, is the law of attraction. Thus, mankind on planet earth has been influenced from the beginning to maintain the understanding that knowledge and wisdom come from those of greater and superior knowledge and wisdom. Further that this knowledge and wisdom is given out to them through adoration and worship of those holding this superior understanding. This has brought an understanding that the humans on this planet exist at the whim of those holding this superior wisdom. As time has passed, this understanding has been manipulated into the belief by humanity that it is vested in an unknowable awareness that has all the attributes as wielded over them by their overlords. These ever present beings have hidden themselves and operated through this "unknowable God," holding humanity hostage not only for the resources of the planet, but as a last experiment in manipulation and literal entertainment. It has previously been referred to as their own "virtual reality computer game." Unfortunately that is more truth than fiction.

The collected or mass consciousness of the humans on this planet in accepting this situation as depicted has resulted in the attraction of those who are willing to exploit this total belief system. This is within the action of the Universal Laws. It will remain so until humanity literally pulls itself out of this situation. It is the desire of those of your galactic brothers and sisters who are aware of your planetary dilemma that you come into the realization of what is the true situation. There is not an easy way to accomplish this inasmuch as the human belief systems are so deeply ingrained with false information and deceptions. The hope is that the frustrations of enough of humanity have reached a great enough degree for them to begin to accept the possibility that virtually everything they have been taught to understand is inaccurate. The most important new understanding to be accepted is that without personal responsibility to change each person's consciousness with regard to understanding who and what each one is, this situation will not change. The whole of the planetary belief system will change only as its individual members change until a critical mathematical quotient is reached. How long this takes will depend on the spread of this understanding throughout all the groups that are now on this planet. It is the responsibility of those who come into the understanding of this information to disseminate it. Then and only then will the future change.

III-10

As the plan for control of this planet calls for the shutting down of the freedom of even the thoughts of the inhabitants, so also at the same time the desire to expand their experience becomes activated. It is the inability to connect with the greater aspect of each that allows the controllers to continue the closing down of the human awareness. The controllers believe that they are solely responsible for the creation of the human beings that inhabit this earth. Through genetic manipulations made in laboratory experiments and by birthing the first chemically manipulated embryos through their own bodies, the controllers believe the resulting humans are their product and solely their possessions. What they do not recognize is what might be called the Divine connection that was present in the first place. The basic being that was available in the beginning was not of their creation and thus contained the possibility of evolving into fully functioning humans within their own time line. Those were present on this planet through the focus that indeed holds even the controllers within their own expression.

It is necessary to go back further in the process of the laws of the Universe allowing for manifested awareness to be present.

Potentiality has birthed itself to explore the possibilities that are inherent within it. In order to do this; there must be the ability to observe its processes of doing this. The ability to observe is what is called awareness. Thus to create situations, circumstances and observable phenomena and explore the results, there must also be present within the totality the ability to observe and draw conclusions with regard to this process. The result is that various foci of this ability to observe, experience and draw logical conclusions have created endless varieties of foci with various abilities to do this. Each and all do this in their own way and the sum total of their experience influences the potentiality of expression within a given greater focus. In this way, by expanding the consciousness in an attempt to gain a view of the greater picture, it can be concluded that the positive/negative experiences feed their data into the greater awareness of this collective focus.

Through a lack of understanding of the overall purpose of self-awareness and the presence of this greater awareness, these individual centers become caught up in their own experience, thus cutting themselves off from the totality to which they belong. What might be called power trips happen. There is within your vernacular a cruder saying that refers to this situation. So, in this moment, humanity is sitting in the middle of that reference. Because of one ingredient within the format of the Universal laws, the responsibility for curing this type of situation must remain with those experiencing it. This ingredient is called freewill, or choice, or the responsibility of decision. Humanity has the freewill to choose to change its experience or to continue the current experience. This is not a new thought within the continuity of these messages, that is because there is no other solution. Because of this, it is repeated over and over from as many contexts and approaches as can be presented in order to make this point as clear and as emphatic as possible.

Needless to say, if there were another way, it certainly would have been brought forth in the information that is being made available to you. It is imperative that the responsibility for creating this change in experience be firmly planted within the attitude and understanding of as many human minds as possible. The possibility of being able to do this seems remote in the context of the overwhelming control measures that are being thrust upon you. That in itself should indicate that such measures are necessary in order to overwhelm the powerful potentiality that the human mind, once organized into a common opinion or focus, has within it. When mankind does direct its focus within the understanding of its power to create through agreement to hold a single focus, there is no way in which it can be overwhelmed, particularly if that focus is in harmony and agreement with other citizens within the surrounding galactic community.

The question then arises as to how to bring a squabbling group of opinionated beings into agreement. The controllers are attempting to do this, only for the purposes of its focus. In regimenting the thoughts of humanity toward their goal they are also regimenting the sub-conscious thought patterns more and more toward resistance and opposition to their planned goals. In other words, they are also helping to set up the possibility of the failure of their plans. In past experience, their plans have worked to keep humanity under their control. This time, however, their human counterparts are more intelligent, far more educated and have tasted more freedom than ever before. This gives them a greater opportunity to come together in agreement, particularly with the yet present ability to connect via the communication capabilities available. Though plans to bring this capability to an end are definitely formulated, there is yet opportunity to access them to great advantage.

It is hoped that these messages, though containing shocking and discouraging content, also offer hope and suggest opportunities that can be put to use by those of mankind that are awake and aware. The future may yet hold promise for the transition of the planet and it inhabitants into true freedom to return to the path of evolvement. The future need not be dark with the promise of continued slavery.

III-11

As each reader moves through the various stages of encompassing the reality of the greater picture of humanity and its plight of the moment, the process of accepting changing perceptions becomes a familiar experience. The material has thus far begun at a simple level and progressed through levels of understanding. We are now at a place to begin encompassing the understanding of those that would continue holding humanity in captivity. Just as they have attempted to know humanity's capabilities for **their purposes,** it is also necessary that **they** be understood. Though their understanding of humanity has failed to include the "divine" connection which they have claimed exclusively as their own, humanity's other attributes are well understood. In order for those that have contemplated the information within these messages to have a clear and balanced understanding of the entire picture, it is important to know more about their counterparts.

The expansive flow of creation extends itself not only in the manifestation of more planets, stars, galaxies, etc., it also allows for limitless expansion of the awareness. It is difficult for the mind/brain that is not operating at its full capacity to contemplate the concept of what limitless and timeless could mean. Within this concept there is allowance for forays into both positive and negative expression that feed back to the wholeness of knowledge and wisdom within a collective composite. In the consideration of the wholeness, then each individual awareness seems like a grain of sand on the beach and causes each to then wonder as to the importance of their personal experience. Is it of such little value that pain and suffering are meaningless to this composite awareness? Is it even aware of all of its parts? Here again the mind/brain that has been focused only upon itself and its personal experience has cut itself off from this wholeness of which it is a part. It is the contemplation of the wholeness and its meaning that allows for participation within it. It is in stretching the awareness to purposefully include itself within the composite that its importance to that composite becomes known.

Having come forth through the auspices of a group awareness that is focused upon its own importance, that attribute has carried through to humanity. In contemplating a new paradigm of experience, it is this key of including itself within the composite wholeness rather than focusing only upon itself that will bring forth the freedom that humanity has as the impetus for change. To put this in less abstract terms, it is the desire to become participating members of the galactic family and to extend their perception that the purpose of life experience is greater than each individual experience and each planetary experience that will bring this forth. When it is realized that harmony of experience is found by expressing within the immutable Laws of the Universe and not in ignoring them, then experience can be shaped into progress and joyful expression. Recognizing these laws as the basis within which all manifestation is expressed, it becomes possible to recognize imbalance for what it is and to transcend it.

Technological progress is not a true measure for progress within the creative expansion of potentiality. Those who have focused primarily on this one purpose often destroy their creation through misuse of that focus. It has sometimes caused the distortion of the progress of others, a situation with which humanity on this planet can certainly identify. In this way, those who are again attempting to play at their control and destruction games have placed this planet and its inhabitants in danger of destruction.

Imbalance as projected through failure to recognize the potentiality of self-aware beings to pursue their inherent evolvement processes has brought both the givers and the receivers of this policy to a point where the significant decisions each will make will influence their progress. Each will reap the results of these decisions. Each has the potential power to change the path of their evolvement by the actions taken through the next few sequential events to be shaped by the decisions made both individually and collectively.

It is important to grasp that the individual does influence the collective decision, both directly and indirectly. What that means is that though the individual is bound by the group decision through composite agreement, it also allows for that individual to free itself from the group decision by forming or becoming a part of a smaller group with a different focused purpose. This smaller focused group, by invoking the second Law of the Universe, the focus of intentional manifestation, then separates itself from the greater group and does change the path or experience of its evolvement. It is for this reason that the messages have encouraged the formation of smaller groups with the intended purpose of creating a New Paradigm of experience. Those who have evolved beyond the need to participate in the victim consciousness that holds them within the grasp of the controlling civilization and locks the two groups into this situation as it now exists, have the opportunity to salvage this planet and its inhabitants. They may at least create an opportunity for a sizeable group to free itself from this situation. It must be stressed that a quorum must be met in order for this to occur.

It is suggested that this information be contemplated with serious consideration for the opportunity that is within it.

III-12

What is a major drama to the inhabitants of earth is indeed an important pivotal point in the continuing evolution of conscious manifested awareness. In the totality of the galactic expression that constitutes the known reality, it is wondered how this small, beautiful planet at the outer reaches of this defined area can carry such importance. It is the transition through the taking back of personal power/control of individual and collective destiny that is the central issue. Just as the consciousness of the leader of a country, self-appointed or elected, expresses the composite consciousness of the people within that country, the planetary scenario that is being played out is the collective representation of the consciousness of the beings on that planet. This then is carried out into a further composite of consciousness in an expanding composite. We might say that earth is the collection point of victim consciousness, a point within a larger collective of this unhappy experience within this area of the galaxy. The solving of this situation by humanity on this planet will bring forth a clearing of this experience in an expansive ripple effect that will reach to the far corners of the galaxy. When visualized in a holographic context, it is indeed a "big deal."

Because of the freewill aspect of Universal Law, it becomes clear that the burden of accomplishment that is carried by mankind at this moment is one of great importance. While it is understood by the counterparts who intend to hold humanity as their own to do with as they please, there is much interest in their attitude and treatment of those this planet. There is no apparent intention to redirect this continuing pattern of enslavement. This presents the dilemma of how to assist humanity and answer their calls for freedom from this experience. It also accounts for the concentrated effort on the part of the self-appointed colonizers of this planet to maintain claimed ownership through members of the human race that are willing to be pawns. In this way, it may be portrayed that the control is not from outside, but indeed by humanity enslaving itself. As the saying goes, "saying something is true, does not make it true!"

Because the belief patterns of humanity, through governments, religions, education and media have apparently so successfully shut down the minds of the greater portion of the people, it is the opinion of the controllers that the game is won. Even though they are quite sure of this, they yet are careful to keep all aspects in careful review. However, within the group of pawns there are factions of competition for the favor of the controllers. It is within these contests that there are many opportunities to unravel the carefully devised plans that lead to closing the apparent "trap" of humanity. The pawns do report in the end to one focus of consciousness. Referred to as the "anti-Christ" in literature, he is expected to be born into a human body that is like those of humanity. Unfortunately, that is not true. This "anti-Christ" has existed in the history of this planet and has been the controlling entity by appointment for eons of time. He exists in a form that does not have a short period of existence and might be thought of as immortal. Though painted in literature in various formats of evil, his is a human format, but one of long duration. His intelligence is incomprehensible to the average human mind. However, the character flaw of power is also comparable to his intelligence. Fortunately, he is not the final "word" with regard to the future of this planet. There is a council that has influence beyond his. It is to this council that an appeal must be made. Though he has great influence and through eloquence has kept his controlling influence alive over a long duration of time, it is this council in which greater authority rests.

The question then arises as to how to make this all-important appeal. One or even a few cannot do it. It must be through combined and focused appointment/election of an eloquent and powerful emissary by a quorum of humanity. How can a divided, submissive and victimized humanity ever arrive at such an agreement? Where will this idyllic emissary be found? Indeed, those are the questions! Further, how does this emissary contact and appear before this heretofore-unknown council? It would appear that help is certainly going to be needed to accomplish this. There is help available when the quorum is gathered and the appointment/election is made. First the impossible must be accomplished, and then help will available to assist. This is something that humanity must do in faith. Certainly there is belief in theories more illogical than this firmly held by large groups of humanity. These presently accepted concepts offer far less than freedom from bondage and acceptance of the right to continue on the path of evolvement.

The timing of all these coinciding forces of chance as has been introduced in previous information, has brought all of this to a pivotal point in the order and process of expansive expression. All possible focus of intent is at work within the factions that are present. At the center of these foci are the dazed and incredulous human beings that hold not only their own future, but the ability to influence the entire galaxy with their decision process. What will you/ they do?

III-13

While mankind seems to face accomplishments that are of monumental proportions for a divided and quarreling group that from one perspective is more animal-like than divine, there is light at the end of the tunnel. The ability to continue on the current path is now reaching a point at which the path must divide. There are those who innately know that the time has come to make a decision. They must either continue on the path that is leading to a vibrational decline toward destruction or stop where they are and look for a way to change directions. Herein lies the awakening process. The current choice that is offered by what has been called the "esoteric or new age" alternative lacks grounding in application of its principles within daily life. It requires ignoring investigating and understanding the plan of the planetary controllers for "fear" of supporting them by recognizing their presence and actions. This "head in the sands" approach fails to appeal to the general population for it lacks practical application appeal. Most people are unable to separate their focus to ignore the world around them and replace it with one that they cannot perceive through their 5 senses. This is particularly true because the sources for participation comes from information perceived to be from beings whose teachings recommend disconnection from the apparent real world. Their teachings often are so idealistic as to leave their readers/followers feeling guilty and frustrated for they are unable to attain such levels within their current living situations. In the end, the ideals are abandoned.

It is hoped that these messages contain information that guides its readers to concepts that contain practical challenges that uplift their desire for continued evolvement. It must be understood that this has to be accomplished within the practicality of the experience that is going on within what their 5 senses reflect as their present reality. The difficulty lies in accepting the fact that the inhabitants of earth are not alone in an inconceivably large galaxy. Thousands of visits have been made to this planet and have been plainly visible to extraordinarily large numbers of people for literally thousands of years. It is totally amazing that this has been literally programmed out of the present mass conscious awareness.

Aggressive action has long been focused by the self-appointed controllers to block friendly, benevolent beings from direct interaction with humanity at large. This has been stepped up with the placement of powerful military capability into the hands of the human pawns. Again, it is important to understand the concept that this is for the purpose of **"having humanity enslave itself."**

As these messages circulate, a distillation process goes on continuously. The information is begun, put aside and then reread. Those that begin and complete it in a flow are few and far between. Reaching this point in assimilating the information has been accomplished by a very few. However, participating in the process in a more leisurely way does not indicate that this type of contribution is less effective. It is accomplishment that is appropriate within the total pattern. Many will never read all the messages. Many will do so in a longer, on and off pattern of participation. It is the composite of understanding that will bring about the necessary changes in the totality of understanding by the whole of humanity that is necessary.

The entire process of reaching the minds, hearts and spirits of those humans who have evolved despite the longstanding programs of control has been an ongoing focus of those of greater understanding among your Galactic brothers, sisters and cousins for a long time in your sequential counting. It has taken much effort on their part to create opportunities within the laws that they observe with care to assist whenever and wherever possible. The question arises as to why, if others blatantly disregard those laws, are these beings so careful to observe them? Always remember that the basic law of attraction works in its inimitable way. These beings know this and have no desire to allow their well-earned progress to be eroded in any way by forgetting this law. It may appear that those who ignore or break the Universal Laws that underlie the expression of potentiality into manifested experience gain by doing so, however in the totality of it all, the piper will have to be paid. For those of humanity that follow through on their desire to bring forth this change for this planet and themselves, much will be forgiven through the gift of "grace." This is an opportunity that is to be taken advantage of by those who are wise. The added difficulty of evolvement within such difficult circumstances is being taken into consideration and value added for doing so.

It has been the purpose of these messages to both encourage and lay out carefully a picture that is comprehensible and contains as much truth as possible so that it might be accepted by minds that have been misled and taught to misperceive. That it contains some information that might be less than the total truth is plainly admitted. It was designed to bring its readers forward in an ongoing process of learning concepts and then leading each forward to accept others that opened new vistas of understanding. In rereading the material, contradictions will be found. It is hoped that those that do this will be able to understand the process and realize the purpose and methodology that was employed. The reeducation of an entire population is not an easy process when the basic understandings are purposefully contradictory in a planned and ongoing effort to cause conflict and separation between large numbers of people with incredibly diverse cultural differences.

To conceptualize the problem is to understand its probable impossibility, but that is exactly what the "controllers" are counting on. Let us make every effort to surprise them.

III-14

As the world situation evolves into greater and greater confusion and chaos, what is happening in the larger picture is impossible for the individual to perceive. Each can perceive only that portion of the whole through personal observation and through what truthful media information is available. This is further complicated by the filter of opinion, experience and feelings through which each reaches their own conclusions. Any single person or any group, no matter how carefully known information is analyzed and checked, rarely knows the truth of any situation. As those who would control increase their surveillance through computerized analysis by satellite, scrutiny of communication exchanges, photographs taken in stores, banks and in street intersections, individual lives become documented to the point of infinite detail.

For what purpose is this being done if the abundance of "chemical weapons" would allow the annihilation of all or any portion of humanity at any time? If the human body is being deliberately debilitated through genetic food alterations, additives that are abrasive and destructive, diseases that are deliberately induced through vaccinations, destructive medical practices, etc., to what end is all of this leading? It would appear that humanity is no different than the animals that are demonically used as test subjects for the "good of humanity." What then is to be the recipient of the "good" of the tests in which humans are the focus? In the larger picture, are humans benefiting from the animal testing? Following that thought pattern, would anything of good be likely to result from the testing that is being carried out on human bodies? We again come back to the conclusion that this planet and its human population are but a virtual reality game for those who consider themselves to be superior and in an "ownership" position. We return to the conclusion that someone or some group is misusing their greater intelligence to perpetrate an injustice of great magnitude. The victim/abuser consciousness is being played out on a massive scale.

Surely, it is time that outside intervention by the powers of "good" can intercede. Unfortunately, that is not possible within the Universal Laws that uphold all that has manifested from potentiality into creation for the purpose of potentiality knowing itself. All is held in continuity through the immutable laws that govern without deviation. If deviation would occur, all would end in chaos. How then is chaos of any kind allowed? It is here that we must return to a concept that is found within the creation process. Each of you experiences it in your life expression as breathing. Your physical expression depends on it. Without breath, your body can retain life but for a very short time. Within the expression of potentiality into manifested expression for the purpose of experiencing thought into wisdom, there is the necessity of investigating this process within self-awareness by various degrees of knowledge and wisdom. When an experience is complete or reaches a degree of imbalance, then it is necessary that it be dissolved. The energy is then made available to be reused or recycled. This recycling process of dissolving and reusing this energy is called chaos and takes place in the larger reality in what might be compared to breathing. What is manifested, literally comes apart into confusion and returns to energy that is available for reuse. There are as many patterns for this process as there are happenstances of creation; in other words it is unique each time it happens. The degree of chaos needed in order for the energy to be reused is also unique to each circumstance.

How much chaos is necessary for humanity to recreate its opportunity to evolve within a positive situation? That remains to be determined by humanity itself. It is obvious that the current situation has no way to progress without a return to chaos. Those who have evolved and those who have chosen to incarnate on this planet for the purpose of changing the paradigm of experience on this planet hold the key within their conscious determination to play a leading role within this drama that is playing itself out now. The determination of who writes the final scenes for this current theatre production is very much up to those present right now. It will not wait for another generation to pick up the task from another one that has ignored the responsibility and left it to the happenstance of "someone else" to do it.

How much help can be contributed from the galactic community, it must again be pointed out depends on enough human beings rising above the victim focus and accepting responsibility. This is their only recompense.

III-15

As the situation progresses the intensity of the changes that will be experienced by each individual and by those of each culture will begin to become more apparent. Thus far, the changes have affected particular group experiences. However, as the warring factions become more widespread, individual experiences of chaos will expand correspondingly. Eventually there will be more areas of war and aftermath of war than areas of apparent peace. In other words, this experience will spread like a skin disease across the surface of the planet. In using the word war, that includes the usage of biological agents as well as the usual destructive kinds of weaponry. It is difficult to understand what purpose all of this pain, misery and destruction of a beautiful planet can possibly serve. It is in entering the observation mode of the larger picture that the true insanity that underlies the plan of the controllers becomes obvious.

By contemplating the freewill aspect of the Laws of the Universe it would appear to be an element that could return all that is back to potentiality. Indeed it is a possibility! It could be the cause of the end of an experiment birthed from potentiality that would be just another idea that didn't work. It is something to contemplate. However, it is also possible that there is a counter balance for this type of freewill action that upon reaching a certain level of imbalance, an offsetting action is brought into play as a natural effect. If we continue to consider this from the prospective of the virtual reality game, there are always elements of surprise written into the game, not by the players, but by those that formulate the game in the first place. It may safely be assumed that the players in this game did not write the rules. That they are attempting to write new rules is apparent, but those do not supersede the rules that came with the game as brought into being in the first place.

What are these surprises that cannot be overridden by new rules? Those can only be learned by playing the game. That is the point of all of these messages. All the players must play the game and search for the strategies that will allow them to succeed and continue on in the game. The experiences of manifested life are never boring for those who search for challenge by not allowing themselves to settle for what is given them, but strive to create what they desire. However, the Universal Laws must be observed in order that the progress made in the game is continuous in the long run. That does not mean that there will not be temporary setbacks through errors in choices, or that these choices will not be repeated until wisdom is gained through these repetitions.

Thus, we find that humanity has placed its progress in the game of evolution in trusting that these controllers are their "gods" and that "gods" always are benevolent and have their best interest at heart or are fearsome and cruel and there is no recompense that will buy off their wrath. It is time that humanity realize that in order to save themselves and their planetary home, it is time to take up the mantle of responsibility and stand forth in their own power. In order to do this; fear must be put aside. Fear cannot be conquered. Those are words that tie humanity to what has held them in bondage. The very verbiage of the language contains programmed intimidation. Words of war such as conquer, vanquish, threaten, superior, force, intimidate, capitulate etc., etc. keep the focus on competition rather than co-operation. Mankind on planet earth will only transcend this situation when co-operation becomes the by-word of all interaction. Many experiences of a competitive nature can be experienced within the spirit of co-operation, like sporting events, for they promote skills that are of use in other applications as well as in learning to appreciate the capabilities of the human body.

It is contemplating how humans can stand forth in their own power that is the question. This is particularly true when considering the overwhelming organization and power that is being wielded by the controllers and their pawns. However, it is at the basis of this entire situation that the key is found. Humanity has allowed itself to be placed in a position in which it cannot match the opposing forces chosen focus of power. It must now find a totally different approach. The one thing that a human possesses that cannot be taken away, though methodology is being developed to attempt to do this, is the thought process. Even those that have experienced mind control techniques involving incredible experiences, are often able to regain their autonomy of thought. It is the combined, co-operative focus on a simple concept that can and will place humanity beyond the situation that now surrounds it and threatens to overwhelm it. It is within the conscious choice to acknowledge the situation, leave victimhood behind and cooperatively focus on an ideal of experience that this power is available to mankind. When a consensus can arrive at this point, then a direct appeal can be made that will bring forth assistance and there will be an end to the current control of this planet. However, the victim/abuser consciousness must be transcended or the process will be repeated until that knowledge becomes wisdom. Releasing victim consciousness will not be an easy transition for it is deeply ingrained within the population of this planet. It is an important element to be held in the forefront of future considerations.

III-16

It has been ingrained deeply within the consciousness of mankind that they are the servants of their "god" of the moment. Over the long space of time since mankind has been elevated into self-awareness those on this planet have been held in servitude and have been subject to the whims of the controller's interactions between themselves. Further, as the manipulated progeny of these same beings, these attributes of contention and competition are a part of this heritage. In truth and reality these deep-seated tendencies of competition and the use of violence to resolve the inevitable friction that results from this focus has served neither the controllers nor the enslaved. Both have remained over eons of sequential time stuck within the victim/abuser mode that has blocked both from evolving.

Failing to live in harmony within the Universal Laws which includes living in harmony with the natural environment of each home planet leads to the waste of its resources and eventual exhaustion of the ability to maintain life on it. The natural conclusion of that focus of experience is to look outside for another source to plunder. Earth is the source for those who have set that parameter at the basis of their pattern of experience. It is natural then for this same parameter to be the attitude promoted on its perceived colony.

As these messages continue to contribute to greater understanding of the foundation upon which mankind developed within a controlled and manipulated situation, it is hoped that those reading the information will come to understand their situation and their learned attitudes and understandings. In order to change deeply entrenched beliefs and experience, it is necessary to see a clear picture of the present situation. Only then can a true decision be made as to whether this is the path that is desired to be continued or if it is time to stand forth within personal decision and change the course of human history by writing each one's own history and so the history of humanity. For eons of time, each generation has accepted the parameters of experience that has been thrust upon them and waited to be led out of bondage.

It has been said, "when the people lead, the leaders will follow." This has not proved to be true, as each time it has been an isolated group that has attempted rebellion only to be devastated by weaponry that instilled even greater fear within them. This resulted because they attempted to stand forth using the same competitive, war techniques that had been taught them by example. Their purpose was to create an improved version of the life they were leading, with again another "leader" to guide them to a Utopian societal experience. This in truth would have been simply a better version of the usual victim/abuser experience, temporarily. Even if a benevolent leader were chosen, the history of the influence of power in the following familial generations through the competition of the offspring has inevitably led to despotism.

Thus there has been the hopeful expectation that better leadership would be provided by short-term election of leaders from among the people. In this way it was thought that the inheritance of power and the competition between heirs would be eliminated. It should be obvious that this method of choosing leaders has not provided a better solution. Always the people have abdicated their individual power through desiring leadership/government to act as their shepherd or parent. What was desired was a larger experience of the family. A benevolent super being, a benevolent leader, and a benevolent parent, with the power vested in the masculine gender. What has been lost is self-reliance within the balance of both masculine and feminine unique characteristics.

Mankind has little if any faith in the unique distribution of characteristics and talents that if allowed to exhibit individually would bring forth a composite that would birth the desired Utopian experience. At the basis of this experience would lie the spirit of cooperation. The question that arises immediately is how this could possibly even begin within the present situation of separation, hate, distrust, etc., etc. Herein lies the wisdom of the breakdown and chaos that is inevitable when circumstances reach a level at which the current situation can no longer maintain itself. An apple rotten at the core must disintegrate. Thus the comparison is obvious. In the midst of chaos, groups will come together in cooperation for the purpose of survival. If there are enlightened ones among these groups with understanding and foresight, these can begin a new experiment that suits the members and the group focus. They must not lead, but only advise and promote the new experiment. If there are enough of these groups all focused upon this new concept of human existence, all understanding the history and the need to leave the past in the past, there is hope for a new paradigm of experience for this planet.

Difficult as it is to accept, not all of humanity will be able to participate in the bringing forth of this concept. All that incarnate on this planet understand this before doing so.

To all, the opportunity to experience manifested reality is worth the experience of it. Much wisdom is gained and despite the limited understanding now held by the mass consciousness, is worth the experience. Though humanity dreams of attaining immortality within the body, that too carries with it responsibilities that counterbalance perceived advantages. That known as self-awareness is immortal. To add to it a body that is immortal includes dimensions beyond the ability to understand by mind/brains that are not fully active. It is a situation of first things first.

III-17

As the situation continues to develop, the picture becomes more confusing from the perspective of humanity, however from the greater perspective, it appears as movement or change. It is through what appear to be ominous events that this change begins its motion and in reality reflects that long awaited momentum is building. This is not to say that these ominous situations should be greeted with anticipation, but it is important that the observer mode be maintained while also experiencing these events. None of you are asked to be anything but human in your reactions other than to know the truth of what the bigger picture indicates. It is by moving through situations rather than resisting them or ignoring them that experience becomes wisdom. If experience is denied, then the opportunity to gain wisdom is lost.

The knowledge of the history of humanity's birth into self-aware beings, the addition of other families of humans to the mix and the

constant interference and prevention of evolvement by the controllers have contributed to the confusion and frustration of those of
you who are present now. Without the understanding of who and
what you are, there is little hope for change. This is the reason that
this information has been deliberately destroyed, withheld, or misinterpreted. The available historical information is presented in different ways because of different interpretations of the documents
and artifacts. This has happened partly through deliberate intent and
sometimes because of bias and ignorance. It is thus important that
more than one source be searched in order that each individual can
discern those aspects of truth contained in each. Again, the conclusions may vary, but enough of the truth will be discerned by each
to reach far more intelligent understandings of the total situation.

What seemed incredulous in the beginning begins to make
sense and then allows for acceptance of a reality that has been purposefully hidden to continue the ownership of this planet. With
legitimate inhabitants with a level of self-awareness to govern
themselves, colonization for the purpose of stripping a planet of its
resources is unconscionable. The fact that the colonizers knowingly
gave this ability to the beings that were already present on their
arrival makes the situation even more objectionable on moral and
ethical basis. To further complicate matters, it is the responsibility
of the inhabitants to prove that they have the ability to govern themselves and to steward their planet by changing the situation through
their own freewill decision. They must discern how to accomplish
this within the Universal Laws and, in this case, despite largely not
knowing what these specifically are. Most know that the system that
surrounds them is orderly and must be to continue, but what supports that orderliness is an unknown. Searches for this orderliness
are convoluted into theories of origin that are of little or no importance in understanding how it operates.

The simplicity of the Universal Laws escapes the understanding of scientists who thrive on complications. Simple as they are
the diversity and interactions within the application of them cause
confusion when the search is for the cause behind the effects. It is
so much more efficient to begin with the cause or the laws in their
simplest form and then follow their effects forward into experience.
The written/spoken enumeration of the laws is fully supported

mathematically. It is important to begin at the beginning. The big bang theory does not allow for understanding to be elicited from a holographic process for it is again a search from manifestation back to cause. The diversity available within holographic parameters is so encompassing that to find the cause within its available infinite variety is to be compared with finding the needle in the haystack.

The process of layering information adds to a greater understanding of the whole in which mankind on this planet finds itself. It builds a holographic understanding that enables those who study this material to change their ability to perceive and discern more of who and what they are and to know more about the controllers. There are many more incredible facts that are available to be known. The question is, "how much is essential in order to bring forth the necessary decisions that will free this planet from the situation in which it is mired?" There is a point at which further information becomes more detrimental than helpful. It is the search for this point that brings forth these messages. It is hoped that commitment and action in the application of the suggestions included will signal the end of the need for more information. At the basis of all action is the transition of consciousness and the decision to answer the call to responsibility that has been ignored and refused for so long by the composite group on this planet.

III-18

The knowledge available to mankind that has been hidden and in many cases buried for thousands of years is rapidly becoming available. The ability to decipher the languages of old and the availability of this information through willing publishers that place it into books, videos and lectures is bringing this to more and more people. The distortions in the translations do create lessons in discernment, but even the distorted information opens minds to the understanding that mankind's history of civilization is much longer than indicated. The evidence by scientists of thousands of years of habitation and the contrast of religious sources maintaining that man has only been on the planet a few hundreds of years has brought forth enough conflict of information to bring any thinking person to wonder about the real truth.

When the information available is considered from the largest perspective possible, the evidence of the presence of the controllers on this planet and their influence in the history of mankind is glaringly evident. The further evidence that their presence has been deliberately ignored and purposefully withheld from humanity is obvious. This is further supported by the "sightings" of craft capable of interplanetary travel that have not only been experienced and reported by people now: reports of it happening all through recorded history have been found by those researchers that have chosen to investigate this area. Personal memorabilia and newspaper reports offer conclusive support. There are too many reports from the past to be considered hoaxes because there was too little exchange of communication to allow for a wave of suggestion to cause imagined encounters.

What puzzles and confuses the average person experiencing the multi-media programmed information being force fed to them is why on the one hand "alien presence" is promoted, and on the other denied at the same time. It accomplishes its exact purpose, confusion. The mind on one hand wonders at its possibility and yet is supported in its denial because such presence threatens all that has been taught over the millennia. The presence of this influence that has totally affected the lives of humanity since before their self-awareness was given to them, has always been the cause of great trauma and mass annihilation of segments of the population. The deception and violence not only of the controllers, but also the inherited and genetically induced tendencies for this within humanity itself, have contributed to slow evolvement. In all truth, without outside influences such as cosmic cycle completions and information such as these messages, the desire to leave these behind and to move forward into creating the opportunity of a new paradigm of experience would not be available for a long time in your sequential counting. The concern and support of humanity by cosmic/galactic fellow citizens have been focused in answer to those who have asked within their prayers and supplications for a longer period of time than most people realize. It is that within the laws, as has been mentioned over and over in these messages, only a certain amount of help can be given, for those who have progressed beyond the level of earth's consciousness cannot give direct assistance without involving themselves within the rescuer/victim/abuser experience. Only those volunteers who are willing to risk for the sake of humanity have made this decision.

Within the confusion of the conflicting information regarding outside presence and its influence in the ongoing history of this planet is the opportunity for the seeds of truth to be planted and to grow into acceptance of the long-denied truth of humanity's real history. The information is available now to be gleaned and to open the eyes of enough to the hidden truth and for this truth to spread. Once discerned and believed it can spread quickly and then, as you put it, the jig will be up. The pieces of the puzzle are present, however few have put them all together into a discernable whole. It seems that each is able to focus upon their part of the puzzle, but is unable to look beyond and collect enough of the other pieces to put it together. When those who do glimpse the picture attempt to share, there is not enough knowledge of the true history to provide a background or frame of reference for the picture to be believable or meaningful. Further, there are few that have the skill or desire to look beyond the media provided information and to do the necessary research. It is a matter of whether the information as presented here is believable and whether it will inspire those who question it to look beyond its claims to find out the truth. The valid, documented information with logical conclusions is available!

As repeated "ad nauseam" the ball is in humanity's court. Mankind must be instrumental in the decision and determination of events that will break forever the hold that has been placed on them. The evolvement necessary has been reached by a sufficient quotient to make such a change possible. The cosmic cycle processes to support and boost the possibility of success are present. The information to assist in the process is being made available within the currently available communication flow to awaken and motivate all those that have the opportunity to receive it. How many and who these are is dependent on the continued spread of the information by those that receive it. Is this the only source? Indeed not, however it is what has been made available to each one that receives it. It is your particular source and it is a personal decision as to whether to accept it as truth and also a decision as to its value. Each individual determines whether or not a decision is made to accept an active role and continue its expansive spread. The future of life on this planet depends on these individual decisions.

III-19

The dynamics of interaction between the foci present on Planet Earth are becoming more, shall we say, interesting as the puzzle pieces move into place. Inasmuch as what is actually happening within the holistic interaction is observed in a sequential fashion by those of you that are within the experience, it is difficult for you to comprehend the true progression of the process. This is further complicated for what is known of the true happenings is given only in part and in distorted fashion. Thus, humanity is left to grope through the experience. Only through the decision to create a new experience and the further decision to keep the attention focused on the desired outcome rather than the unknowable current situation, an increasing amount of energy will be directed into the manifestation of the new paradigm. As the chaos accelerates those who have the desire for this new "dream" of existence as an ideal or archetype will find it will provide a focus of stability that will become more and more attractive within their thought processes. Their thoughts will migrate toward the pleasant feelings and visualizations that will accompany their desire for this new state of existence. It will provide them with pleasant diversion from the apparent reality that will grow more intense as the chaos progresses toward the point of the release of energy that can then be redirected into manifesting the new paradigm.

The desire to be organized, to get organized, in order to make this change happen will be both assistance and a hindrance in the process. It will be reinforcing in so far as promoting the discussion and awareness of the necessity and desire for changing humanity's long-standing status with regard to the perceived outside ownership of their planet. It will also carry with it the seeds of carrying forward tendencies that have in the past prevented true transcendence from the learned pattern of ownership and exploitation of the planet and fellow inhabitants. The desire to organize around a leader rather than around a concept or principle is strongly embedded within the earthly human psyche. The need to have concepts and principle analyzed by breaking them down into minute details diverts the energy of them and allows for divergent trips into dead end ventures. The wasted effort these adventures involve can be limited and often avoided altogether by intuiting the proper direction a focus can follow to reach the intended goal. The process of literally feeling out the direction that is appropriate through imagery also allows for each to ascertain the appropriate group each feels offers greater growth opportunities.

Within the practice of freedom of choice, much progress is available to the individual and this flows outward into the group and to the totality of the whole. It is possible to understand this through remembering the observation of a lake or pond. Bubbles rise from the bottom, each creating their own small rippling effect, yet not disturbing the equilibrium of the totality, but contributing to the oxygenation and enlivening of the whole. Like bubbles, ideas and feelings about what may contribute to the process leading to the creation of the new matrix or pattern add to its birth process. Many will be considered as the proper pieces that will contribute to a balance and harmonious whole and be accepted. Those will change and evolve through participation within the creational expansive advancement of potentiality into manifested experience for the purpose of understanding itself. Through potentiality expressing outward, observing and returning knowledge experienced into wisdom or self-understanding, the diversity of the number of opportunities to pursue within this process is mathematically beyond calculation. Thus the mind is stretched during the consideration of this concept and its possibilities of expression. It then becomes conceivable to realize that mankind has been limited to an incredibly narrow and controlled pattern of experience within unlimited possibility.

As this pattern of experience is purposefully compressed into an even more confined and restricted ability to express, the freedom to evolve becomes even more remote. This greater restriction produces an energy crisis both individually and collectively. This causes the restrictive boundaries to be necessarily more and more heavily controlled. When the number of beings on the planet is considered, it is understandable that plans are laid to reduce that number and that the choices of the intended survivors have very selective profiles. In order to choose these survivors, a great deal must not only be known about the ideal but also about which groups offer the most prototypical candidates. Since the tiniest of details can expand into problems in the future, the genetics are most important in these selections. It is difficult if not impossible for most humans on the planet to comprehend the detail of genetic information that is available now for this selection process. The limited brain/mind cannot comprehend the amount of knowledge that is accessible to the processes of the fully active brain/mind. The potentiality of the brain/mind is in direct proportion to the mathematical odds for the possibilities that are latent within the galactic matrix. In other words, there is virtually no way to calculate the number of possibilities.

In considering this as a starting point, those that read this material can begin to understand the limitations that have been accepted by humanity at this point and realize that it is time to end this enslavement and to claim the heritage available to every self-aware conscious entity within creation. The awareness is the immortal undeniable focus that is free to search for its ultimate expression within the incalculable potential available. That is its birthright.

However, how it is to do this is within its own freewill choices. There are holistic levels of self-awareness that are not known to the human mind, and that is emphatically acknowledged here and now. The understanding of this wholeness of the self-aware unit of which the human is a part has been hinted at, but requires an expansion of the brain/mind function in order for it to be assimilated. Access to the necessary understanding of the greater aspects of human experience hinges on transcendence through the victim consciousness into personal responsibility. Again, this is a repeat of the theme of lifting the consciousness from the degradation brought about by dependence on dogmatic leadership. It requires the acceptance of standing forth individually and collectively within personal competence and demonstrating the capability of bringing the current situation through the necessary chaos into a positive group focus that will move humanity forward. The potential for this transition is present and pressing to be expressed.

III-20

While mankind is caught up in the delusion of servitude within the belief that the real rewards for obedience are withheld until the end of the lifetime and are to be experienced in another realm, one's personal power is totally compromised. He/she lives in a state of belief that control rests outside of any real personal control. "God" is the ultimate source of all good humans themselves are the cause of all "bad" because of disobedience to some known or unknown laws, rules or regulations that they have broken. Obedience and service are the watchwords of "goodness" which is the "ideal of life." To further add to the ambiguity of the situation, commitment to obedience and service allows for cruel and inhumane treatment of fellow humans at the discretion of religion and government. Within this system, there is no true freedom for mankind to determine who and what they are. There is no freedom to understand that the "God" concept as taught is one perpetrated for one purpose only, to enslave and control beings that have the potential of becoming totally equal to and surpassing the evolvement of those who are foisting this enslaving situation on the humans living on this planet.

Until the humans on this planet are willing to awaken to the illogical data that is presented and understand that it has an underlying purpose, and to accept that it is done for the purpose of control and for no other reason, no progress toward true freedom can be attained. Life for humanity will continue on as it has for thousands of years. The games of manipulation that are in progress now are but a prelude to the events to come. The aptitudes and adaptabilities of the human body and psyche are being thoroughly studied in order to ascertain the future uses which the most adaptable will be expected to withstand. A minimum criterion is being established and only those that meet this will be kept and allowed to procreate. All others are expendable by whatever means are chosen; all of which will be part of the "survival of the adaptable" experiments. As unbelievable as this information may seem, it is the real truth of what underlies the chaotic activities that are happening on this planet. What appears to be chaotic to the participants is a well-planned strategy to keep the inhabitants in a state of confusion so that there will be no organization by them to exchange information in a real way toward an understanding of what is their intended future.

It is imperative that a portion of mankind think carefully through these messages and come to see the logic and sense of them. These awake and aware people must then begin to actively share this information with all that have the ability to stretch their awareness to understand and accept these concepts through logical thinking and to begin to become aware that the potential of personal power far exceeds their victim reticence. Further they must understand that this personal power need not and must not be measured in aggressive tendencies, but in the measure of mental, emotional and spiritual focus. It is important to understand that the spiritual focus is not that of the traditional "religions" toward a benevolent or malevolent "God" outside of the Self. Each must come to understand that their power rests in the recognition that each has the opportunity to participate within the consciousness of galactic citizenship that contributes to the composite of how the creative expansive energies of potentiality are directed either toward positive or negative group experience. Unfortunately, this sector of this galaxy has long been caught up within the negative victim and abuser/aggressor experience.

It will take true commitment and focused desire to break free of this well-established pattern of experience. It is important to note that the matrix of this pattern has now reached a level of vibratory expression that is at its limits. It is at a point of vulnerability that will allow it to disintegrate into its own chaotic destruction if a new consciousness among its victims were to become well established. It is this goal that underlies the purpose of these messages. It is this change in consciousness that can be the catalyst that can bring about change and the end to the extremely negative experience that has held this planet and others within its web. These messages are but part of an organized effort to awaken humanity on this planet. By opening to the possibility that the information contains Truth with a capital "T" it is possible to begin to find verification of it through other published material. It must be remembered that available information is published through the perception and prejudice of the personal interpretation of the authors. Thus, contradictions will be found. Truth can be perceived as existing at the center of a circle with opinion and interpretation focused on it from 360 degrees of observation. It does exist and the more degrees from which it is observed, the clearer the perception of it becomes. It is the openness to its existence that allows for the clarity and understanding of what is the Truth that is grasped.

That mankind was purposefully pushed along its path of evolvement for reasons of servitude are at the basis of understanding the situation the inhabitants of this planet find themselves in at this moment. What must be further understood is that the gift of self-awareness allows mankind to understand they are not limited to this servitude. It allows them to lift themselves beyond this experience into full galactic citizenship with equal opportunity for continued evolvement and participation in the expansion of potentiality. There is no permission from some unknowable super being required. It is your already inherited gift. Each must however, accept the gift and move into the available citizenship and accept not only its benefits, but its responsibilities by first realizing and accepting the true situation that surrounds them and deciding it is time to change it, not some time in the future, but now. There are now available shifts in cycles and other coincidental phenomena to support the necessary change in consciousness. These will assist humanity if the wisdom to take advantage of this perfect time for change is utilized.

III-21

The time to prepare for the adversities to come is now. What can be done? It is imperative that each begins not with the outer concerns but with that which is within. By that, it is meant that each must come into the realization that the attitude and opinions about who and what each one is must be the basis. It must be fully understood that time and consent are the two necessary ingredients to be contributed by each. The time is now and the consent is to accept a total change in the understanding of who and what each of you are. Each is to begin by opening to the idea that virtually all that has been taught with regard to the past, present and future of all of humanity on this planet has been a deception. It is necessary to accept as true reality that which has been told as myth, that which has been denied and what has been predicted/prophesied as the inevitable future. A new foundation must be laid as a basis for the new conception of humanity as wholistic, self-contained beings whose inner awareness is the source of their identity.

The process of changing the reality from permission to exist from an outside source to personal responsibility is not an easy transition. It requires rethinking most awareness processes. The training to ask permission to literally exist is begun at the earliest stages of development and is presently programmed into virtually every focus of ongoing life experience. Once the truth of the deception is accepted, then the change of belief is met in each day's myriad small decisions. Each momentary choice must be examined in the beginning to determine if it is influenced by personal inner knowingness regarding its appropriateness in light of the new foundation for understanding. The right to personal decision as to what to do carries with it the choice not only as to the appropriateness with regard to the person making it, but also with regard to how the decision will affect those to whom the effects will ripple outward and touch. This requires the acceptance of responsibility with regard to a larger picture. The effects can no longer be transferred to the "power" that formerly was responsible for granting the desire and must be accepted by the individual making the decision. The effects of the decision must be accepted and born by the decision-maker. Thus the acceptance to participate in the creation of a new picture of human experience entails the process of maturation into citizenship rather than subordination to an overseeing entity. Through the careful consideration of this concept it can be seen that acceptance of the disadvantages of "slavery" has also had the advantage of ducking the responsibilities that taking control of one's own experience carries with it.

Just as the settlers/pioneers that followed the discovery of the North American continent by the European countries sailed across unknown waters into unknown situations, so also will the "new awareness pioneers" find adversities to encounter and to deal with on a moment to moment basis. The most important will be found within their own conscious awareness, for it will be there that the decisions will be made that determine the outcome of humanity's future for a very long time to come. The coordination of cosmic cycles that are available to assist in this epic consciousness change will not be available to assist again for a long time in linear counting. The focus of awareness by cosmic/galactic forces will allow the mass conscious decision by humanity to rule its future and turn their attention elsewhere. Earth's human population has this opportunity to mature and grow into greater evolvement, but it will not be forced upon them. The opportunity is just that, an opportunity offered. It must be accepted and acted upon in order to bring about the changes that are available. It cannot be accomplished by only a few, but those few must spread their understandings with concerted effort and zeal in order that the necessary quotient can be reached. It will not be easy. It cannot be put off any longer or left for someone else to accomplish. The window of opportunity will remain open for a mathematically exact time and when it closes, it simply closes. If it does, the future of earth's inhabitants and the planet is bleak indeed. Both will continue to be exploited without mercy. The influence of forces from outside this planet and this solar system underlie all that is happening on this planet. This is a positive given. These forces are legion and are vying among themselves for control. This is also obvious and yet sleeping humanity sees it only in terms of their own small personal experience. The conflicting stories of worldwide activity that reflect these forces at odds with each other are plainly reported even in the controlled media stories. But this goes undetected because the larger picture is obscured by deception from the awareness of the most educated and supposedly informed.

The lack of the ability to put all of the puzzle pieces together into a coherent and logical picture leaves confusion as the only available conclusion to all but a few. The necessity to continue to enlarge the picture beyond what even the most informed and analytical minds have done holds the truth beyond understanding. The picture is very, very large indeed. As has been said, "truth is stranger than fiction." Even the most imaginative science fiction writers have not grasped the reality of what is the true picture. It is important that this large picture become known and it can only become known when earth's people, one by one, accept the truth of victim consciousness being the first layer of the foundation that must be torn out and replaced. It must be replaced with the understanding that humans on this planet **are not** second-class citizens. Claiming the ownership and governing of their planet is their rightful inheritance. It is their duty and their responsibility.

The planet rightfully belongs to its citizens, not to those of another planet or solar system. In order to control their own planet, earth's citizens must control their own attitude and thoughts about themselves. They must know themselves to be worthy of self-decision without permission from other beings or imaginary "god or gods." This requires courage and the ability to respond to challenges. It is in the blood, the mind and the heart to do this if the programming and the attacks on the health of the physical, emotional and spiritual aspects of human existence can be transcended before these do further damage. The results of the decisions to be made by the readers of these messages are critical not only for those doing the reading, but for the future generations of humanity on this planet for a long time to come, if, indeed, there are to be any future generations. This will depend upon which of the vying forces may indeed win out if humanity drops the ball.

III-22

There are areas of focus that the human mind is totally unaware would serve in the change of direction from subservience to freedom of choice. Where the mind is focused determines where the totality of experience will arrive. When the awareness is bombarded with a confusion of ideas and experiences, the holding of a single or singularly coordinated group of ideas, thoughts, opinions and desires becomes difficult indeed. It does not require the effort of what is termed concentration, but does require the broader and more easily managed process of focus. Focus allows for peripheral awareness of events and information that can be noticed and allowed for short-term inclusion without diluting or taking away from the intended direction of the intent of the overall focus. It allows participation within the currently perceived reality while yet holding in the awareness the intended direction of desire, of intended purpose.

Humanity must first allow itself to accept the possibility that it is their birthright to steward this planet and manage their own evolvement without interference or direction from outsiders. Once that possibility is allowed to take root, the desire for this experience will grow within the awareness, for it is well established within the psyche. It is latent, or buried under the mind control programming that has been layered within the social and religious structures on a worldwide basis for thousands of years. This entire program of control (literally) surrounds mankind's understanding of itself like a tough skin. It is necessary to literally squirm within this skin of deceptive understanding and shed all of it in order to perceive and create a new experience. If this were not possible, then there would be no necessity to place so many layers of false information into the minds and to hold it there through intimidation and fear. This need for control at all cost is the clue that the armor is fragile and that the fear of the controllers is far greater than your own. If mankind discovers its power and its true heritage, there is no answer for them but to destroy all but a few and to begin through intimidation to rebuild the population based on the same deception and fear program. Try as these beings have, it is not possible for them to change the necessary DNA programs to reverse the evolvement and return mankind to a more animal like being.

In reality, mankind's saving grace at this moment is the number of outside influences that are vying for control of this planet. Indeed, there is more than one. Is earth that valuable? It is the competition for supremacy that is the important point insofar as the outside interests are concerned. Each has their influenced faction among the deceived. And deceive you they must with clever and deceptive techniques. For those awake and aware human beings, it is possible to perceive these as factions vie for control. Even within the controlled media and religious dogmas there is confusion. Stories are reported, then either changed or withdrawn. There is conflict and competition between various warring factions so that if discernment is practiced the contention and factions are obvious. Many of the visions and esoteric prophetic experiences being reported are nothing more than another form of mind control. When these prophesies include future Utopian life without responsibility, beware. What is important to these factions is which one can win the prize, regardless of the condition of the prize at the end of another phase of history. Meanwhile, mankind has the opportunity to sleep on amid this virtual reality game or to awaken, stand forth in its own awareness and claim the prize, the planet, right out from under the warring factions' noses. They need only to come forth into personal and group awareness of their birthright and collectively stand forth in declaration and ask for help from that point of consciousness and it will be given!

The key is that mankind must evolve to a point of maturity that indicates the ability to accept galactic citizenship. To be a planet of full-fledged citizenship, earth must be self-governed. Otherwise, this planet is considered a colony, available to be owned and ruled by outsiders. Until humanity is ready to be responsible for itself and its planet, it cannot participate in the galactic family. Then it must decide between being a positive or negative expression. Both experiences exist. Difficult as that is to accept, that is how it is. Help is available, but only on a consulting basis. Citizenship hinges on and results in total self-responsibility. It is not a case of aggression versus regression. It is aggression versus progression. Earth has been caught up in the process of rule and control by negative, stuck expressions of the expansive energies of potentiality. If this opportunity to change the situation is taken advantage of, then the decision must be made to simply continue that which has been the victim side of the coin by expressing the other side through aggression and abuse as you have been used, or to indeed create a new paradigm of experience.

As has been mentioned before, when citizenship is a reality through a quorum of humans declaring their independence and self-responsibility, then the opportunity to observe and receive consultation on what other expressions of positive experience are currently in practice will be available. The space in sequential time to synthesize the new paradigm will be given and protection will be provided. Only a framework need be idealized. The proof of the pudding will be in the individual personal changes demonstrated by those humans that are able to shed the skin of manipulation and deception. These must walk their talk, so to speak and live their conviction of personal and group self-responsibility. It goes beyond a change of mind to living the conviction.

Where does one go when there is no capricious god to direct one's wishes, desires and fears toward? Can that empty place that was once filled by the "God" perceived to give and take, answer or not answer, hear or not hear, depending on whim ever be filled again.

Indeed! Now is the time to remember the Laws of the Universe and to read them again and to practice them. Each must become the god in their lives, for the laws are the premise of life expression. The messages are written so that each time they are read a different perception is received, more is understood and the desire to experience real freedom is kindled. There is no freedom without responsibility. As responsibility is relinquished, freedom dissolves into slavery, no matter what clever face is painted over it. The choice between these realities, the fork in the road has been reached. It is indeed decision time.

III-23

True to the predictions written into the Christian bible, the false "Christs" abound. Not in the form of people claiming to be "**the** Christ," but in those giving all kinds of "higher" information. Most of this information contains elements of truth. These are people who are most sincere and have no idea that it is arriving in forms of thought manipulation. The elements of truth give credence to that part of each that must have verification in order that the messages are accepted. Much is known as to the way the human psyche functions. The art of manipulation of the mind/brain/body-coordinated functions is well understood. Those that are concerned with perfecting these technologies have much experience in this art for it has long been practiced on beings of lesser evolvement. Because of the free will element and the adaptability of the DNA of humans on this planet, this branch of mankind has proven to be a frustrating challenge to those intent on restricting and reversing the natural evolvement process. The frustration is twofold. Not only does this make humanity difficult to control, but these beings find there are elements of evolvement present that they desire to incorporate into their own life expression. However, thus far, most have not been able to accept the desired changes within their own strands of DNA. Some changes have been accepted, but not the ones most desired by them.

To indicate that the true total picture of the situation in which planet earth is the focal point is complicated and confusing is a major understatement. All players but one in the larger picture have had control of the planet at one time or another. The only player that has not had control is humanity itself. The others want the control of the planet and its inhabitants now. The winning of the competition between them is as important as the prize. Unfortunately, the physical resources of the planet are of more importance than the inhabitants are. Thus in the final confrontations, if the population cannot be controlled, and in order to gain the prize, it is necessary to destroy them, it would be done. Further, considering the technological development of those game players, what chance does humanity have to come through this scenario?

To answer that question, it is necessary to return to the basic fundamentals as given at the beginning of these messages. The 4 Laws of the Universe govern all potentiality in expression. Thus it can be observed that those that vie for the control of this planet have drawn to themselves others that also vie for the same thing. The inhabitants of earth, at this moment, are not involved in that same focus. When and if the inhabitants of earth focus cooperatively and decide to take ownership of their own planet for the purpose of creating a new paradigm of experience, they are removed from the scenario. If they choose to change their perception from victim to self-responsibility for the use of the expansive energies of potentiality, then the picture changes. Each Law builds on the others, and when thought is incorporated within the Laws, it thinks independently, releasing coordinated complimentary actions in ways that cannot be planned by the mind/brain of individuals. For example, the human body was created within the Universal Laws and continues to think for itself, allowing for adaptation that frustrates those with other plans for it.

While humanity is caught up in the games of others and refuses to see itself as a prize in a giant game of one-upmanship, it cannot free itself. It is of primary concern that this picture be given to them in order to see the illusion that has been fed to them for the purpose of keeping them under control while the players continue to vie for overall ownership. The power players are evenly matched; thus each move is so decisive that sequential time is of no importance. The life spans of these players range from virtual immortality to generational changes in which the focus is locked in so that life span length makes no difference to the final outcome. It would be easy for those humans who do awaken and accept the truth of the bigger picture to feel themselves so insignificant as to have little if any power to change the situation. In truth, they are the only ones in the scenario that do have the power to change it. The other players are so locked into their side of the victim/abuser expression that the chances of their changing that perspective are slim to nothing. Humanity has been calling for help, begging the very "gods" who have perpetrated this situation on them, to get them out of it. What chance is there that these beings will do that? None!

The human beings becoming on this planet, if they are to become now, must do this for themselves. They must accept who and what they are, learn of the existence of the basic Laws of the Universe that have been denied them, put them into practice and create their own new expression of potentiality. That is their inherent birthright. There is no other way out of this dilemma that totally surrounds them and in truth threatens their possible extinction.

III-24

As the time for the closing of the cycles comes closer, an impetus is being felt within those who are energetically compatible. Because of the flow of energies that are now focused within the magnetic field of the earth and those thought energies that are available, a mental and emotional discomfort is being experienced by many. These feelings and understandings that something is out of the ordinary are motivating these people to search for a cause and an end to this uncomfortable state. It might be said that cosmic burrs are being planted so as to get the attention of those who are energetically yet outside the level of submissive indoctrination. These are the ones who will find and read these messages and identify with the content and its purpose. The search for the cause and the solution will end with the reading. Then will begin the commitment to a purpose that calls for fulfillment in a way that is difficult to ignore. Once the seeds of a purpose are ingrained within the awareness, it roots and becomes aware of opportunities to express and participate within its expression.

This illustrates the law of attraction as those who are already committed are focusing intention to manifest a new paradigm of experience, the Law of Attraction begins to draw more and more into this shared focus. As the intentional focus gathers more that share this cooperative agreed upon desire, this activates the second Law of the Universe, that of intention to manifest a shared focus. That focus begins to clarify and to intensify, thereby adding more attraction energy. This building of a momentum then multiplies exponentially. It is the shared general point of agreement that is the organizing impetus for the successful manifestation of the intended focus. As the laws begin to act and interact with and within each other, the process of thought thinking begins, thus opportunities and synchronicities begin to be incorporated into the experience of those holding the intended focus in their consciousness. It is critical that those in the beginning phases hold the general intention of creating change through their own desire to do so. Out of this intention will blossom the birth of this new experience. Mankind has been held in bondage and ignorance long enough. There are enough evolved humans present now on this planet who desire to take responsibility for the present and future of this planet to focus this intention into a new reality. It is a matter of getting the truth of the situation into their awareness and offering them a solution that does not require them to sacrifice their life experience to the intentions of other detrimental plans for humanity. It merely requires that they change their attitudes and understand that they are the rightful owners of their own planet, provided they are willing to be responsible citizens of it and of the galaxy of which it is part.

It is necessary that each and all understand that planned manipulation has been foisted on them at every turn, through every institution, be it government, media, societal mores, religious doctrines and the "ground in" understanding that violence and competition are the answer to all problems. Indeed, calm, resolute and unbending intention that underlies all forms of decision, actions and thoughts will bring about more positive changes in one life span than thousands of years of aggressive misuse of each other. Further, it is time to end the allowance of outsiders to misuse the mineral resources and the human/animal resources so generously provided by this planetary home. It might be said that humanity's mining claims have been literally stolen from them through the misuse of these resources on the planet and through the export of them by those who have already misused and mistreated their own planetary home. Now they despoil yours to continue their same pattern.

Careful study of documented information and studied conclusions now available in printed form, leads the discerning individual/group to the inevitable conclusion that indeed something is very wrong. It is time to change the scenario for the sake of humanity and to end the literal rape of this earthly domain that is the heritage and birthright of those whose home it is by birth and by adoption.

This planetary home is humanity's to retrieve and to own, but first the false mining claims must be refuted and correct ownership established. Since the power of the contesting entities for continued colonization of this planet is totally overwhelming, then action of the Laws of the Universe, properly understood and applied is the powerful resolution to the problematic situation that seems so dire when its full picture is comprehended. Through the Law of Attraction, those of singular intent will gather their focus. By cooperatively intending to create a new experiential paradigm of experience, the next layer of power through the 2nd Law will be added and those will interact and integrate bringing forth discernable intensification and expanding attraction of others to the process.

The 3rd Law of the Universe is the most difficult to access and to practice. It is the Law of Allowance. The process must be allowed to construct itself within the focused and agreed upon intent. This law is most perfectly applied through confidence in and acknowledgement of every nuance of manifestation as they begin to be experienced not only as a group, but also especially within the daily happenings of each individual's personal life. The new paradigm of experience is a coalescence of all the individual experiences that fit within the agreed upon focus of intent. These are locked in as they are noticed, acknowledged and appreciated. It is the small occurrences that instill the confidence that is at the center of the application of the Law of Allowance. Doubt is a normal human trap, but when the desire for change is deeply felt and held in mental and emotional confidence, it must manifest. This will not be an easy phase, thus the encouragement of small group interaction with the sharing of both knowledge and "happenings" that support the actual reality of experience will strengthen this necessary application.

There are those individuals that will accomplish this phase very much on their own. All are appreciated!

Through the coordinated and integrated action of the first three Laws of the Universe, the 4th Law of Harmony and Balance will manifest into reality. This is not to say that there are no polarity experiences within the Law of Balance and Harmony. Indeed there are, however, there are not the extremes of experience leading to great imbalance. These are merely lessons of discernment that demonstrate knowledge lived into wisdom.

It is the learning to rely on the self-awareness to perceive where each is within the application and understanding of these laws that underlies all of manifested reality. That will replace the programmed need to look outside to some power greater than self for the gift of permission to do something or to fulfill a desire. It is up to the self to attain that desire through the application of those laws for the self and in cooperation with others. Thought properly intended thinks and acts through to completion if properly held in mental and emotional focus for positive change. Focus is "lightly" held by the mind. If you intend for your body to move from one room to the other, it simply does by acting on your intentional motivation for it to do so. It acts entirely within the Universal Law of Intention into manifested action. It is not even a conscious thought, it is an intended action, and it happens. The subtlety of this example demonstrates the power of intention that is "lightly held" but is yet confidently expected to happen. It would be well for this example to be contemplated and carefully understood.

III-25

It is necessary for those who choose to become involved in this process to make a firm commitment to change the perspective through which their life experience is viewed, remembering that the perspective chosen is in accordance with the type of view that is available within each one's personal attitude. This view is either observed stubbornly through a singular, one way only focal point that rules out all other possible choices or it can allow for realizing that other points of view are available. It is possible to think in terms of what is true being at the center of a circle and 360 degrees of possibilities existing. Beyond that lies the ability to expand further into a holographic conceptual understanding in which truth is at the center of a sphere and an almost immeasurable number of possible viewpoints exist. Through this change in attitude, what is known as judgement becomes choices. It allows for others to observe and choose and it encourages the self to quest for more perspectives and a broadened experience. The allowance for other possibilities to exist expands the life experience and brings the being into the flow of expansive energy that is the source of "All That Is" as it understands Itself through knowledge acquired and lived into wisdom through individual experience.

It is difficult to comprehend that each life experience contributes to the composite that differentiates itself so that it can then gather those scattered experiences back into itself in a meaningful way. It can only be interpreted through intelligent beings observing their experiences and drawing conclusions, which is another way of saying experiencing knowledge acquired into the wisdom of understanding. This happens in both separated, individual experience and conclusions as well as group and mass group experience data gathered and processed. The "mind" intelligence capable of doing this is beyond the scope of its finite awareness to comprehend. It is only necessary to be aware that the process is part and parcel of who and what each is. Infinite possibility is constantly being contemplated and investigated. Each and all are the instruments through which this process is going on. Thus, it is important to understand there is no "sin" or error, only experience to be lived into the wisdom of understanding and infinity in which to do it.

However, when, through wisdom gained there are those who wish to bring an experience to its conclusion, as do the humans on this planet, then it is possible for knowledge to be made known to those asking so that new choices are available. It is through knowledge gained that the process of asking for assistance is brought forth. However, the asking must be done within the applicable laws that underlie the existence of all manifested experience. There must be an understanding and application of those laws by the requesting group before it is possible to give the assistance.

When considering these messages, it is possible to see the tight circle of circumstance within which humanity on this planet finds itself locked. It is possible to see it as a wheel of existence from which there has been no escape and to understand why those who prefer this planet to remain as a colony rather than an independent self-determining unit have employed all possible means to arrange this. Since the actions of these beings are under scrutiny now, it has been necessary to manipulate the population to perpetrate, on the surface, control measures upon themselves, so to speak. Therefore, you come to understand the power structures and reward systems that have been fabricated in order to entice those who would apply these control techniques upon their fellow beings as well as instigate destructive functions to the planet for their own apparent gain. How long they enjoy this advantage over their fellow humans remains to be observed. It is to be noticed how often those who have "outlived" their usefulness, and know the inner workings of the conspiracy to control, seem to come to interesting ends.

It is this ability to observe that allows for choice as to what each would intend to have for a life experience. It is this choice process that will enable mankind to change the planned destiny and remove themselves from the control and influence of those who would control and hold this planet as their own rather than allow for its populace to evolve into galactic citizenship. The solution lies in the ability of Earth's evolved human residents to lay claim to their planet by their own recognizance, for unknown to them, theirs is the first right of refusal. Colonization by outsiders is only possible through their permission, in this case by default through ignorance of their own ability to claim it and for the most part ignorance that they are a colony at all. Considering the carefully documented historical evidence of alien presence on this planet for millennia that is now available in print and the myriad of "UFO" sightings, how this foreign presence goes without understanding is illogical and beyond comprehension by all outside observers. It is as though earthlings are totally fixated on continuing to accept slavery and control, except for those few upon which the hope of the survival of humanity and the planet now depends. "May the force be with you!"

III-26

Though the intent and purpose of humanity as a whole cannot be focused as a cohesive unit, a representative group with clear intent and purpose of representing the whole, can set a process into motion. It is the components of intent and purpose clearly identified as representing a whole and focused upon a defined outcome that attract to it the power to manifest into reality. It is the contribution of the many into the focus of a unit of definite intent that draws to it the power of subtle creative energies. It matters not whether the wording of each contributing focus is exact; it is the intent of the final outcome that is the cohesive factor.

For the purpose of example, suppose the final outcome desired is the reclaiming of the ownership of this planet. Suppose a group of those who have evolved on this planet decide that the governing and destiny of this planet is theirs to control without outside interested parties' interference. This would be a definition of intent and purpose that would be clear enough to draw to it the energies of the law of attraction. This would result in those of like desire joining in this expression of intent and purpose in thought. Through the thought focus of this desire and the intent for this to become a reality for the good of the true citizens of this planet and the physical planet itself, the Universal Laws would begin to operate. The thought and emotional desire would begin to attract a greater thought process and energies would begin to coagulate into events and circumstances that would support this process.

The key is not in acting out resistance to the current apparent situation, circumstances and apparent events, but in focusing on the desired outcome. The act of holding the desired outcome within an emotional field of desire for the envisioned outcome is the application of the Law of Allowance. This is the most difficult of all of the Laws to apply, for the events that are happening will still reflect the expression of the established process until the focus of the desired outcome begins to influence the total picture. The process of the two situations must evolve into a chaotic dissolution of the established process before the desired new process can begin to manifest into reality. Herein lies the difficulty, for the focusing group of humanity that is now instrumental in initiating this change into reality is also accustomed to what is referred to as "instant gratification."

Holding this intent and purpose firmly in mind and heart through the chaos into its manifestation into reality is extremely difficult for even those of well-disciplined mental capacities.

It is the absolutely desperate situation that is facing the "humans becoming" on this planet and the prospect of the loss of all progress made over these past thousands of years that will be the impetus to do this. To indicate that the above statement is true, it is only necessary to avail oneself of the now abundant material available on the internet, talk radio and many published revelations of conspiracies that subjugate the citizens of all countries through drugs, intimidation and war as well as physical, mental and emotional abuse. The deliberate attacks on the moral, familial and religious beliefs at the basis of human experience are now beyond the logical acceptance of a mind that is not already separated from its ability to logic and analyze data clearly. Fortunately, there remain in the mind and heart of all humans certain keys or triggers that can yet be activated that cause them to click into an awareness state that throws off the carefully programmed acceptance state of the propaganda that has been force fed into their minds. The continued attack on the health of the bodies by the altered food, drugs and medical "health" care system has created a further complication for humanity to rise above. The adaptability of the human body has amazed even the perpetrators of this entire scenario of control. However, the limit of the ability to absorb much more abuse has been reached for many.

It is to be remembered that all of the above is part of not only the planners of the control scenario, but it also plays into the necessary chaos that will allow for the birthing of the new paradigm of experience. Unfortunately, it is to be remembered that nature uses the "survival of the fittest," or put another way, "the survival of the adaptable" as a rule. Thus, it is the wise who begin to assist themselves through choice to assist Nature in surviving by carefully deciding what foods and other products are allowed into and on their body, and further, what programming is allowed into their awareness. Almost all media is programmed contrary to the highest and best good of those who regularly expose themselves to it. It does help to be aware of its purpose and decide to take from it only that which serves the highest and best good. It is wise to remember that too much media input overwhelms even the most adept at choosing what serves and does not serve them. Media includes music as well as spoken and pictured presentations.

Those who will bring about this phenomenal reversal of the planned scenario for the future of this planet and its remaining inhabitants will learn and apply well the 4 primary Laws of the Universe. These Laws will become the "god" of their lives and upon the wisdom of these Laws will rest the future. They are the foundation of the new paradigm of existence. All building blocks will be shaped by their application. Their simplicity and the energies and intelligence that their interaction with focused minds that hold clearly their intent for the highest and best good of all will bring forth changes for the good of this planet and humanity that are beyond anything the present human mind can ever imagine. It is the clear and present desire for this incredible experience that must call and hold the minds of all that read and resonate with this information. Upon your mental shoulders rests the future of this planet. The question remains as to whether there is enough commitment and focus to bring about the desire to own and shepherd this planet and your continued progress. A galaxy of fellow god beings awaits your decision and your follow through.

III-27

The question arises as to what others will be doing while those committed to birthing the new paradigm of experience are focused within that process? Except for those who are committed to the agenda of the negative forces, these will be creating the necessary chaos that will allow for change. Therefore, it is necessary that those who contribute to that aspect of the change be released from any judgement on the part of the creative group and allowed to make the contribution that is within their ability to do. Since many of those unable to allow themselves join in the creative focus will be friends and family, this will make it difficult for the "ground crew" to stay focused and to "allow" them to contribute to the chaos. If it can be known and accepted that these may yet be drawn into the new paradigm further into the process, then it will be easier to allow them the opportunity to make their contribution freely.

It is important that those who choose to take part actively in focusing their intent and purpose toward bringing into manifestation a new paradigm of experience clearly understand that making a commitment lightly is not recommended. The material within this series of messages has attempted to educate step by step change in how each perceives the world around them as it is at the moment. It attempts to point out a logical and understandable method by which change can be initiated, but also to state plainly that taking part in changing the intended future of this planet and its inhabitants involves more cacti than roses on the path through the process. The exchange of cacti for roses happens near the ending of the scenario and indeed is well worth the experience. Each is encouraged to remember that once the focus on the desire for a new paradigm begins to coagulate within the mass consciousness, not in quantity of those doing so, but in agreement with both mental and emotional commitment, the Universal Laws of Attraction and Intentional Creation begin to change the total situation. What is happening will be difficult to ascertain in the beginning and will appear in synchronistic occurrences that will not always be recognized. Further, once the momentum of people reading and resonating with the messages and the desire for a new human experience begins to multiply, allowable contributions by galactic neighbors can begin to manifest in further help. There will be those who simply begin to attune to the concept, as it becomes subtly available within the mass consciousness, and begin to add their desire for a new experience without knowing about the messages. Many will have the books given to them or find copies that were not utilized by those who did receive them, a demonstration of synchronistic events that happen through the Law of Attraction as it subtly works.

The thought vibrations as those committed to the project read, reread and discuss the concepts with like-minded individuals contribute greatly to the invocation of the Law of Attraction. The power of their intention and commitment then invokes the Law of Intentional Creation and it is further fueled into creative action by the emotions that accompany the desire for this new experience. At this point the person involved has initialized into motion two of the Laws. Holding the commitment and resolve to experience into wisdom this opportunity then leads to the difficult invocation of the Law of Allowance. This requires what has been called "faith" through "knowing" that the Laws are real, do work and are working in the midst of the continued apparent success of that which needs to be changed as well as while confusion breaks down what must change. The heroes, sung and unsung, of the new paradigm will be those who can commit, grasp the understanding of applying the basic Universal Laws and allow them to bring forth the desired goal through the breakdown and formation process. There will be no instant gratification. It will not happen overnight. The plan to dehumanize the population of this planet is too well established to be changed quickly. But, focused desire and purposeful intent can change it! It can only be accomplished by living, breathing citizens who know that they are powerful beings with the Laws of the Universe and the creative flow of Divine Intent that humanity be allowed to choose its own destiny and is deserving of its inherent right to do this. It must however choose its path of self-choice or bow to the overseers who await that choice and do all in their power to influence humanity's decision. The decision can only be made by each individual and those individual choices then meld together into a rising tide of intent and purpose.

It does not matter how much mind control via multiple processes has been forced upon mankind. There will always remain triggers within the mind and heart that can be activated that bring about "changes of the mind" and undo all the programmed responses in a moment. These awakenings are happening with greater and greater rapidity now as a result of many unique coincidences. As the awareness spreads that a new experience is available for the taking by committed individuals, these will increase exponentially. The wave of desire for not only changes, but for reversal of the current trend toward slavery is beginning to manifest. Take heart and do not falter in desire or commitment. The time for the ground crew to redouble its effort and continue on is now. Hold the desire clearly in mind and sense the movement of the Universal Laws as they support humanity and be aware that there are many galactic fellow citizens that are awaiting the time to be of greater help when it is allowable.

There are many cooperative facets that support this thrust for humanity to regain the right to determine its own destiny that are unknown. The ground crews are unaware of each other, however, what each does supports the others and the plan as a whole. There is a plan, of that you can be sure! Just as the oppressors have a plan, there is a plan that does not oppose it, but transcends it. That is a very important difference that is significant to comprehend. What good would it do to simply oppose and block a planned negative experience? It is necessary to transcend it and create that which is new. Consider that concept carefully and remember it in discouraging moments!

III-28

It is to be understood that the time of realization by humanity that it has come to a crossroads is happening now. A decision must be made as to whether to continue on under the influence of those who would continue to control them or to accept the responsibility of choosing their own future. Under the influence of the methods of control being applied now, the consideration of taking such responsibility by a large portion of humanity is not possible. Take into consideration the number of humans who are not even vaguely aware of the situation that confronts the planet and its inhabitants, and the chances of ever attracting the interest of a considerable portion of humans are next to impossible. However, when those who are aware, no matter how few by comparison to the number inhabiting the planet, come together in agreement as to this choice, the balance of power is changed. This is even more powerful when these concerted foci are aligned within the action of the Laws of the Universe.

It is to be remembered that when the action of one group involves interfering with the freedom to evolve of another group, this is in conflict with the natural flow of creative expansion of the galactic/universal environment. A plan that is in conflict with the creative flow requires constant attention and management in order to maintain itself for there is no interactive creative thought to correlate the facets of activity into a naturally cohesive thrust into manifestation. Once the decision is made by a group in agreement to return a deceived group back into the flow of expansive evolvement, "heaven and earth" combine in a flow toward accomplishing that goal. The Laws of the Universe are invoked and "thought thinking" becomes interactive with results that are beyond the comprehension of the originating focused group. The momentum grows exponentially and manifestation occurs spontaneously.

Considering the bigger picture in a condensed version allows those contemplating its accomplish-ability get a sense of its possibility and grasp a knowingness of how the process works in essence. However, it is necessary that each and all understand that the process does not work by itself. If it did, the situation as it now exists would never have come into being. There must be carefully laid groundwork in order for the process to begin and continue to a point to which it will then complete itself. There is indeed such a point. The originating group will have no way to ascertain this point and so must initiate and continue to hold the desire and intention in place through the greater portion of the process lest they withdraw in over confidence before that unknowable point is reached.

Desire and intention have been stressed many times, however there is action also required. Physical resistance to the overwhelming forces of those who intend to intensify their overseer roles is pointless and futile. Those that intend to change the destiny of this planet and its inhabitants must direct their action toward the spread of the concepts of manifesting the new paradigm. This new paradigm of experience will be accomplished through the understanding and application of the basic Laws of the Universe—focus, intention and allowance bringing forth the end result of balance and harmony. This would appear to be quite simple when considered in its basic conceptual understanding. However, to apply these principles in the midst of coercion, chaos and confusion in a firm trust and knowing that the Laws are working when there is no physical proof to justify that all-important belief is not a simple task. When the 5 senses cannot be trusted to tell each committed individual what is happening, then the process is not simple or easy in its application.

If humanity cannot come up with a group of focused individuals to hold this desire and intention for a new experience in a committed fashion, then the planet itself will begin a cleansing to enable itself to avoid extinction. This process is already beginning. The degree to which commitment is made and held as the subsequent events unfold will determine greatly to what extent the planet will need to cleanse itself. This commitment involves the shedding of the victim stance and the willingness to claim earth citizenship, including the responsibilities that this will involve. There can be no looking back, no blaming for the past and present experience, and decisions will have to be made with regard to repairing the damage to the planet. Greed and abuse patterns must be transcended with the highest and best good for each and all always as the controlling factor. Those who cannot accept these guidelines cannot be allowed to influence decision making situations. Discernment and disclosure of intentions will be the hallmark of all discussions.

If the earth proceeds to cleanse itself, then of what good are these messages and the desire and intention of those who are attracted to this process? Who indeed will survive as a remnant to repopulate the planet? Will it be those who have misused the planet or those who would heal the inhabitants and the planet with loving intent? Since all that exists, as manifested reality, is vibrational, those that exist in a vibratory rate that is harmonious with the planet will find themselves in safe places. Those safe places will exist where these individuals are. There are no "safe places" as designated on the planet despite any and all predictions. There will be safe places in the midst of any and all disaster experiences. It is the consciousness of the individuals themselves that will create those places. Those that respond to the call to planetary/galactic citizenship and are able to transcend the victim stance and take on the mantle of responsibility to create a new experience will come through the days ahead to guide this planet to a new level of experience. The Law of Attraction will bring about its inevitable evening into balance and harmony. Whether any of humanity on this planet presently will come through this experience is entirely up to the choices that each makes. It is the responsibility of the ground crew to offer this choice to as many as possible, as well as to make that choice for themselves and to stick to it as the process continues through to completion.

The cycles are coming to their inevitable completions and the opportunity window is beginning to close. Those beings that have evolved will respond. Those that choose otherwise are to be blessed and allowed to follow their own path. This is most difficult to allow for those connected by family ties and friendship, but there is too much important work to be done to dwell on their chosen future. Seeds planted do grow. Trust the process and keep on keeping on. The future of all depends on the ability to make the difficult decisions of each moment. The emotional strength to do what is necessary is available to all who are committed and who hold the highest and best good of all as their guiding principle. Each is asked to do only that which is the best they can do in the moment and to hold no regrets as to the decisions that are made and the actions that are taken. To learn to trust oneself within each moment to moment experience is to mature into responsibility; a necessary process for sharing the birth of a new paradigm. As each moves through the levels of experiencing into wisdom what is chosen, there is never a lack of the need to exercise courage, vigilance and perseverance. They are the hallmarks of maturity and the signal that completion of a cycle of experience is at hand. Each must decide what point of maturity they have reached and if they are ready to take on a new level of challenge. This is not a project for the faint of heart, the lacking in courage and those without stick-to-ability. Do you know where you are in relationship to this opportunity?

III-29

Within the flow of events that humans experience as a linear sequence or time, the progression of maturation has reached a level of experience internalized into wisdom that allows for a shift in pattern of experience. However, this shift is accessed through the freewill choice that is innate within each evolving human. What is experienced as linear progression, when viewed through the more accurate holographic picture of experience appears as piecemeal contributions to a dimensional whole. Linear observation reflects a flatter, less dimensional picture of progress gained through manifested occurrences experienced into wisdom.

In order to comprehend how multiple lifetimes of experience can contribute to the wholeness of their contributions toward harmony and balance within the combined collection of these, it is important to gather them into a comprehensive unit. As the gathering of a unit of experiences nears completion, certain absences of experiential requirements become apparent. Thus, certain missing accomplishments are assigned to complete the experiential unit.

A great number of beings present on this planet now are focused on fulfilling their individual requirements for completion or as you might consider it, graduation. This allows the indigenous population the advantage of the infusion of exceptionally talented individuals from various levels of advanced experience to assist their process of attaining the freedom to evolve independently. Who are these exceptional beings? There is no way to know, for they themselves do not know. Are those who read these messages one of these exceptional beings? Maybe! The point is, there is available a reservoir of talent with exceptional abilities. These have specific issues to experience into wisdom and there is no accident that these beings are present on this planet now. Within their knowingness are the need and the desire to complete these experiences. These specific assignments are of value in the birthing of the new paradigm. It is suggested that each reader of these messages search their own heart and mind as to whether their life experience now is a satisfying one. If not, then perhaps within these messages there may be a resonance that allows them to awaken to the desire to fill an inner void that has heretofore been overshadowed by lifestyle, media programming and the general malaise of disharmonious confusion that is proliferating now. It is worth considering the possibility carefully.

The question arises within those who give this thoughtful consideration as to whether those of the other persuasion are aware of the presence of gifted entities? Indeed, this is possible and in many cases probable. Many have had their life ended purposefully by the opposing forces. Infiltration is a method used by those involved with both purposes. There is a natural curiosity to know what is going on within the other camp. This is often undertaken by individual choice rather than design, thus one that might appear to be involved on the other side, so to speak, is discovered and eliminated. Therefore, it is unwise to judge all participants as being what they appear to be. Those that have special talent often find themselves within romantic entanglements that lead them far from their specifically assigned experience. These often find there are difficult choices to be made in order to satisfy the inner urge to be elsewhere doing other things. It is to be recognized that the spiritual aspect of self has little to do with the standard religious affiliation that is pushed upon the average person. What satisfaction is found by most has more to do with the victim stance requiring a promise of a rescue connection than in actually finding spiritual fulfillment within the religious dogma programmed into their consciousness. In the search for more understanding of the empty feelings within them they are stuffed with more dogma and misunderstood information, and few ever find true satisfaction except by intuiting beyond the available concepts.

This is not to say that these messages are put forth as a new "bible." This information is for the education of all those on this planet receiving it that can let go of their current literal acceptance of media, religious and familial teachings as well as subliminal programming. This allows them to consider the possibility that there are other concepts and information available that can lead them to fulfill the inner urges that populate their own psyche. There is a greater plan that has been carefully laid in order to answer the long continuing outcry through prayer and thought for release from the stifling hold on this planet and all of its inhabitants, inclusive of human and all other life forms. Each and every human on this planet is a part of that plan. How many will answer the inner call is yet to be known. Freewill choice is the basic rule that can and will be exercised by all. The freewill of those who do answer also includes the measure of commitment and action to spread the information that each allows themselves to do.

The birthing of a new paradigm of experience upon this planet is an exercise in cooperation rather than competition to determine which is the stronger force. Cooperation through focus and intent within the underlying Laws of the Universe has power to manifest that is incomprehensible to the average mind on this planet. The functional brain of humans has had its activity purposefully lowered to prevent the movement toward freedom that these messages are designed to initiate. It is important that those who take this information seriously and intend to become part of the cooperative creative focus also intentionally begin to exercise their mental capacities. This can be done through games, experiential learning and any other method that will separate them from the influence of the media and other "dumbing down" activities that are everywhere in the "modern environment." The brain, like the body, deteriorates if it is not exercised. In order to focus and hold to a commitment, mental and emotional clarity is of the utmost importance. Reading information that is contrary to the promoted dogma and focusing thought for the purpose of discernment as to its validity and the possible intention of the writer is also recommended, including these messages. Much can be ascertained from them by intuiting the purpose of them. Each will, without doubt, intuit different reasons through this exercise.

III-30

Humanity will continue to evolve through the process of experiencing the changes that are coming through its current experience. By learning of the Universal Laws and how to act and interact within their concepts, the opportunity for rapid progress is present and flowing through the experiences of all who have begun to apply them. When a greater and greater number come to "know" they are true and accurate application of them brings to them the results they desire, then the manifestation of the new paradigm of experience will begin in earnest. It is through their application and understanding with the "knowledge" that they indeed do work along with the understanding of "thought thinking" as they move from focus and intent into real experience the application of them will become natural. It will take no more concentrated effort to apply them on a continuing basis than it does to decide to get up from a chair and move to the door or wherever else you intend without actually applying concentrated thought. It is through intention that it is accomplished as easily as breathing or any other act that is accomplished in the "knowingness" that it just happens easily.

The key to the application is in knowing that the intent must be in harmony with the flow of expansive creative energies that move and carry the manifestation of galaxies, solar systems, planets and individuals through to experience creation in the observation mode. It is necessary to understand that all that is considered reality first begins in the imagination, the mind of the conceiver. The focus of intent moves the process through the various stages of conception to energy conversion resulting in coagulation of that energy by slowing down the vibration until it manifests into observable, touchable matter or what is called manifested reality. What is considered reality is focused intent condensed through application of the Universal Laws by holding the intent firmly and "knowing" that the process works until it does. The slower the vibration of the focusing mind and the surrounding environment, the longer the process takes and the more difficult it is to hold the intent long enough. Learning through application to hold the intent "lightly" without attempting to force its creation but again in "knowing" the validity of the process allows for "practice makes perfect."

There is a great difference in the application and concepts of wanting, believing and knowing. Wanting only creates more wanting, believing only says that one thinks the process will work, while "knowing" accomplishes the intention. It is the degree of difference gained by the actual experience of "seeing" the application work that allows for the "knowing" to become accepted and applied with ease.

The first attempts at application must be reasonable and believable in order to reach the "knowable" level of acceptance. The nuances of these concepts are important to contemplate, bringing the understanding that deliberately applying the concepts of these laws may not be an easy task in the beginning. Thus, to choose a single application with which to test the theories is of primary importance. It is the habit of man to want everything at once and to fail to take a new process slowly and deliberately. The learning of the application of the Laws is much like stringing beads, one at a time. What is challenging is to hold the concept to be manifested clearly in mind without adding nuances to it that complicate and slow or in fact halt, the entire process because of unnecessary detail. Again, thought thinks and often creates a far more grand application than the finite mind can conceive.

The energies of the individual begin to change as intention and the ability to hold an intention clearly strengthen and hold firm. It would be expected that one or more successes in manifesting a desired outcome would firmly integrate the process into the experience. However, that does not seem to be the case. Most find that old habits and assumptions do not disappear from the experience easily. It takes many successes to raise the acceptance level to create a habit level for natural manifestation. There also are the instances when casual thought manifests as the subconscious applies the Laws to these casual thoughts. It is possible to bring into experience instances that apply to others that were never intended. Therefore, the statement "of highest and best good for all concerned" is the best possible safety insurance and would be wisely added to all intentions to manifest a desire. A consistent sprinkling of this statement within the continual mind chatter that fills the void between meaningfully aware thoughts is also wise.

To meaningfully apply the Laws of Attraction, Focused Intent and Allowance requires purposeful desire to bring something into real experience. The simple experience unhampered by unnecessary add-on details is possible to manifest quite quickly, depending on the clarity, ability to focus the intention and emotional energy that adds impetus to the creational process. The degree of "knowing" is the final ingredient in the mix. It is difficult to determine the difference between believing and knowing. Again, it is an easy, almost effortless application of the desire, just as you know you can move from the chair to the door. There is an application of the doing of it that is totally without doubt and a knowing of exactly where one is going, but no thought as to exactly what the muscular and other bodily efforts are that are involved, or what may happen during the process of arriving at the door. It is also necessary to continue to "know" one is going to the door all the way to getting there. Losing the focus may allow one to end up in the kitchen and wonder why one is there. In the same way, it is not necessary to delineate what is necessary in order for the desire to manifest. It is only necessary to know what the desire is and to add the minimal amount of focused cooperation that is necessary to set the process in motion while holding the intention of experiencing the desire. It is often mentioned that one needs to be sure one really wants what one thinks is wanted. Most can think of casual thoughts or statements that have brought experiences with consequences not expected. The creative aspect built into all is listening and takes those thoughts and statements literally, especially if the momentary intention is sincere and supported by emotional impetus.

While the explanation seems complicated, the application is quite simple. It is a matter of simply doing it simply. The complicated part is when doubt slows or destroys the effort entirely. To begin by choosing a desire that is totally contrary to the current experience is to set up a formula for failure. To attempt to move from poverty to affluence with one desire is sure to fail. It is best to begin with something small and simple. It adds to the process to act as if the desire is already happening. Place an empty hanger in the closet for the new coat. Make space in the cupboard for a new dish or pot, etc. Then be patient and *wait expectantly.*

III-31

It is through the application of the Law of Allowance that the greatest progress will be made with regard to the invocation for manifesting the new paradigm of experience. This is the most difficult of all the laws to apply for it requires the letting go of detailing the desired outcome. It is extremely difficult for the limited mind to focus on the outcome without feeling sure that it is necessary to also envision the process by which that outcome will come into being. It cannot be emphasized too much that it is the outcome that it is necessary to focus upon. The question then arises within the mind as to what indeed it should "look" like. The fact is the most important aspect to "envision" is what it will feel like. Therefore, it is necessary to coin a new expression such as "enfeel" in order to bring the proper focus on this aspect of manifesting. What is called manifesting is indeed coming into the understanding and the application of the 4 Universal Laws. These have been simplified in concept and renamed to words that bring forward greater applicability for they fit within your normally spoken vernacular. *Focus, intend* and *release with "enfeeling" to experience "harmony & balance"* is as simple as it is possible to place these wondrous Laws into your conscious awareness.

It is the intent of these messages to be focused at the planetary level for the greatest healing possible. However, that does not indicate that the individual for their own experience cannot use these Laws. Do remember it would be easy for humans to become so caught up within their own "life drama" that the greater purpose for the planet as a whole becomes lost and "falls through the cracks." The point to remember is that without the healing of the whole, the individual applications of the Law will do little to bring about the freedom of humanity from the planned scenario of control. It is, therefore, imperative that any personal application of the Laws be focused "within" the greater planetary focus. Thoughts regarding this are most productive if all is "seen and felt" within a holographic picture of all applications contributing to the success of the planet as a whole. Within that focus, each individual success in applying the Laws then contributes to and strengthens the greater focus. Furthermore, the individual then draws a greater contributing focus of energy from the planetary whole into their process, a wondrously helpful boost toward their desired goal. Again each is reminded to include the statement "for the highest and best good for all." This releases the "thought thinking" aspect of the action of the Laws to utilize energies that otherwise would not be available to contribute to the whole (holographic) pattern.

The Universal Laws when properly invoked can bring about wondrous changes in situations that otherwise would remain stuck within their current motion and momentum. This remarkable process results in complete re-arrangement of energetic forces that are in motion. This causes a period of chaotic energy shifting but can happen quickly *if* it is released (allowed) to complete the process without the input of imposed restrictions to its motion by the "intender" by continually adding thoughts to the process on how the Laws must bring about the desired focus. It is this necessary release/ allowance that is the key. The educational process has brought mankind many blessings, but it has also allowed for great limitations. The simple tribal experience with faith in guided rituals often brought about remarkable changes with success based on previous experience and allowance of "unknown" energies to bring forth the desired change. It was the allowance of that "wise" outside energy to accomplish the feat that allowed it to happen. How much better it is to understand that the "outside something" is but the naturally existing Laws that underpin all of existence acting through the focus and cooperation of the mind/s involved.

It is also important to mention again the added impetus that is gained when more than one mind agrees in basic concept on a desired focus. It is possible to "know" that the agreed upon desire for a new paradigm of experience can be the encompassing focus. It is possible for it to contain myriad individual foci each contributing to the success and fulfillment of all when the "highest and best good of all concerned" is the releasing factor. The greatest success is accomplished when the foci are concerned with the outcome and not the how, why, when and ifs that the human mind is so good at conjuring up to contemplate. It is this unneeded contribution that "gums up the works and throws the monkey wrenches" into the process. This not only slows the process but can cause it to fail to manifest or worst of all bring forth a convoluted version of what was potentially possible. Thus, it is again stressed that the discipline of holding the focus on the desired outcome is of the utmost importance in allowing the process of the Laws once set into motion to bring into manifestation that which will serve the greatest number to their highest and best good.

This message will need to be read and reread in order to help each to keep in mind the exactness required in laying the foundation for the successful application of the basic Universal Laws. The habits of the undisciplined mind are deeply ingrained. However, practice followed by success and holding to the simple repetition of the basics over and over again will bring about the desired new paradigm of experience. The holographic concept of all fitting together within a matrix that contains infinite variety within a whole can and will allow for the freedom that mankind yearns to experience.

It will be necessary to incorporate these concepts within the mind and the heart in order that these become the new "god" that each finds necessary to fill the void within. In this way, mankind can at long last come into the understanding that each is an expression of the Divine Order that is "God" knowing Him/Herself, All-ness in Self-contemplation. It is necessary to further let go of the need to "personify to identify" this greater concept of "God" and accept it as an on going process. Consider this carefully.

III-32

The empowerment of humanity is of the utmost importance in the outcome of the entire scenario. This empowerment cannot come from the outside. This is an inside job that each individual human must accomplish on his/her own. This is not to say that there is not guidance available to trigger and assist. These messages are the perfect example as are the comments, articles, books and all other triggering phenomena that are available to accomplish the awakening of each and all. The overload of media availability to many of the current world inhabitants serves the awakening purposes as much as it does as a mesmerizing tool. It takes constant reinforcement to keep the lid on conscious awareness. However, sudden discernment can cause all of the cleverly layered programming to fall away and understanding to instantly awaken when the proper triggers are activated. A simple statement that makes total logical sense within the thinking/nervous system connection causes a realization to register through out the awareness and in that moment there is a change in the ability to receive thought that has hitherto gone unheard and unnoticed. It is this process that is the purview of the "ground crew."

The agreed upon focus of the "ground crew" involves the awakening process as well as the primary focus of the desire for a new paradigm of experience through "outgrowing" the victim experience and accepting the responsibility for changing the human experience on this planet. All who respond to this challenge are capable of accomplishing it, or the goal would not have appealed to each in the first place. The "Johnny Appleseeds" who plant idea seeds are "heaven sent" to do this. Consider carefully this idiom of speech. Many common sayings, when heard in the new context of change, have been speaking to the consciousness of each for a long time. Those will henceforth have great meaning and will trigger consciousness changes as they are noticed. The awakening process is ongoing once it is begun. Like a good mystery story, one clue leads to another in an ever-deepening commitment and synchronicities will become a way of life. Chance comments, a word, a story line, a news note, etc., all will fit into a different context than previously. Particular friendships will have greater meaning and others will diminish in importance as the focus of interest changes.

The work, the focus of what it is necessary to accomplish, will redefine the thoughts and the available time. A natural realignment to what is important will change with little direct attention as far as the personal life is concerned. When the focus and the intent are upon the outcome being for "the highest and best good for all concerned," it will happen of its own accord. What will be accomplished depends upon the strength of the foundation set forth in the very beginning. The simple statements of intent such as "help for all humans becoming" and "for the highest and best good of *all* concerned" set that foundation upon a firm and level beginning for they broaden the focal point beyond the personal scope while yet including it. The globalization of interaction and activity by humanity at this time no longer allows for experiential change to be limited to a country, a continent or a hemisphere. In order to accomplish the transcendence of humanity on this planet as a whole, it was necessary for there to be an inclusive global consciousness. Until this was possible, change was only piecemeal and easily destroyed from within as well as through direct intervention by those who plan to continue their control.

In considering the picture from a linear event observational mode, timing seems inordinately important. Within the understanding that a picture of wholeness can be filled in by events and circumstances that do not appear to be happening in a sequential mode, it is difficult for those participating to ascertain and comprehend the larger picture. Without understanding accomplishments as they fit within the bigger picture, it requires great self-discipline to hold the desired outcome firmly in intentional focus. It is because the increasing inflow of newly awakening awareness requires those of greater understanding to constantly redefine the purpose and the intent. This then in turn refreshes and renews their own focus. From an energetic pattern point of view, this provides for a spiraling of greater available dynamism. It is the entry of more and new awakening awareness that provides this important momentum and allows for a continued increase of available energy that offsets the inevitable fallout of those without the ability to maintain their commitment. Many of these will be drawn back into the activity and again provide the addition of needed impetus. As the focused pattern begins to clarify and increase in momentum, its drawing magnetism will begin to be felt within the planetary mass consciousness.

It is when the pattern begins its clarification and its energy begins to draw from the negative focus that the greatest difficulty will be encountered. The assumed superiority of that group is unquestioned in their minds, thus they feel little if any concern about the attempts being made by organized groups to change the perceived future of earth and its population. It is the lack of organization and the emphasis on individual change and participation that does now and will continue to allow the transcendence of consciousness to reach the momentum and pattern clarity necessary to change the synthesis of the mass consciousness. Once this point is reached, then the methodology as employed by them to control large segments of the mind of humanity will erode quickly, provided the momentum can be maintained.

Indeed, critical points will be reached and must be moved through. It is then, in answer to focused and deliberate requests, that outside help can intercede in subtle ways that will assist in moving through those crisis moments. "Help to become" will be answered. Thought thinking will provide the exact needed assistance. It will not come as intervention, but as assistance. There is a very important nuance in the different meanings of those words to be contemplated and understood. There will be no mass invasion of extraterrestrial ships to rescue humanity. That would not allow mankind to work out its own solution to the dilemma in which it is now embroiled. At all times, humanity must create its own solution to invoking a new destiny story. There must be no misunderstanding of that fact. Victimhood and galactic citizenship are two opposite poles of experience to be understood and deliberately chosen. This is done by way of myriad small decisions and actions as experienced on a daily basis by individuals in their own life experiences. These experiences then gather their own energy pattern reflecting a larger experience by an *intentionally focused* group of humanity. That is what will bring about the changes so greatly desired, prayed and begged for by suffering humanity through this long and difficult period of its history.

III-33

This is the sequential period of time that is the leading edge of the chaos that has been mentioned many times in these messages. The pattern of existence as it has been known on the planet in recent millennium has begun to disintegrate. As in all cases of disintegration, portions of the coagulated (manifested) energy do not dissolve, but tend to break into pieces that become destructive to the portion that remains intact. In order to understand this; think of energy in a formation that resembles a lovely snowflake. Picture it as made of a sturdy material and see in your mind's eye portions of it breaking into pieces and being tossed about and causing other portions of the pattern to break down from the impact. Since all manifestation consists of solidified energy, this is a reasonable comparison. Once energy is solidified, it does not return to its origin (light/thought) without being broken down by the same creational process in reverse. However, that process is not an assignment for this ground crew. The larger picture that encompasses the totality of Earth and its inhabitants transcending the currently planned future contains many separate foci in order to bring the new paradigm of experience into being. It is only necessary that as much understanding of the process as it is possible to explain and is helpful be included. It is more important that each segment of the whole focus on the portion that is their agreed upon assignment.

While all are curious about what the "big" picture looks like, it would indeed be impossible to explain. It is to be remembered that as "thought thinks," nuances of change can cause major differences in outcomes. Because freewill is a major component in the process of creation and allows for diversity within wholeness, the mediating factor within the working of the Laws of the Universe is the ability for thought to think *within* the whole. In other words, "thought thinking" can consider all nuances of change throughout the whole and compensate for effects that the finite mind has no way of considering. It is the wisdom that evolving consciousness strives to emulate. The Laws of the Universe are totally compatible and cooperative. When the Laws are invoked, and intent and purpose are in cooperation with them, there are never disagreements or discussions as to what, how, or which method or approach is right. It is simply done in the most advantageous way! There is no ego involvement as is present in situations of less evolved thought processes. It is these ideals that are sought in the dimensional progress of evolving consciousness. As these are mastered, each progressive life experience provides for new and different challenges to be lived into wisdom.

Presence on Planet Earth in these times is not and will not be lacking in challenges. Opportunities to live challenging experiences into wisdom will abound. Those who can focus their intent and purpose to take advantage of these opportunities will benefit greatly. That is indeed a glib statement that in the moment has little meaning. However, if when others are in panic, one can "keep his/her head clear" and listen to the "knowingness" that is available to all that will listen within, decisive action will prevail in the moment.

It is a matter of taking that second or two to listen/feel what is the appropriate thing to do. It is a skill that is acquired by practice. Applying it now in the small decisions that are made each day can provide practice. Much is done by mere habit. As the situation changes, those habitual actions/reactions may no longer be appropriate. It is important to begin to pay attention to the thoughts and feelings, especially those that reflect apprehension or concern. It is time to begin reprogramming the conscious awareness to be more and more active in moment to moment decisions. "To do or not to do?" That is the question to be asked within each conscious awareness. It is of utmost importance that these questions are asked of the individual self-awareness rather than asking others for their opinion. Only the individual is experiencing the decision and is in the situation: the decision may require action in brief moments. Through practice, confidence and trust with that inner knowing part of self will be built.

Becoming involved through commitment to the "ground crew" requires focus of intent and purpose. It also carries with it the advantage of connection to a flow of energy that is purposefully aligned with the Universal Laws and the flow of intelligent thought that supports creative expansion of thought into matter. This connection involves a balance of responsibility and compensation in direct proportion to contribution. It does not reward foolish input that endangers the outcome. Development of the "feeling" of appropriate words and actions is a prerequisite to wise participation. The major portion of the process will be accomplished by individual awareness and consciousness change along with dedicated intent and purpose to create the desired new paradigm of experience. It is the focus on the intended outcome through "knowing" the desired outcome can manifest when participants are in harmony with the Laws and truly desire "the highest and best good for all humanity on Planet Earth."

It is to be expected that as the influence of this focus of intent to change the planned destiny of mankind begins to affect circumstances and situations, the usual method of destruction will be employed, that is to infiltrate and destroy from within the organization. However, there will be no organization to destroy. No doubt, individuals will be "removed" from the focus, but there will be few if any records to indicate what individuals are responsible for the change taking place. Once the triggers change the conscious thinking process of those participating that will be the only connection that can be made, on a one by one basis. Meanwhile, the spread of the consciousness change will continue with its inevitable results.

Thus, the purposeful intent to structure the change within the individual consciousness serves a dual purpose. It increases the opportunity for individual evolvement and provides the vehicle for the advancement and transcendence of the planetary whole without the danger to life and limb that would be associated with the usual rebellion scenarios that have been repeated over and over to little or no avail. The advantages are many, most of which are yet beyond the limited human mind to comprehend. That too will change. With the acceptance of self and planetary responsibility, the brain/mind will activate to a greater and greater degree. Though purposefully imposed, the limited brain capacity was held in place by the victim consciousness. That in turn was held in place by the desire to be rescued by a source outside the self and humanity as a whole. This further provides the understanding for the weekly programming lessons stressing the need to ask outside help in all areas of life, to turn over life to outside greater wisdom, and the media depiction of the constant stream of victim situations. All is carefully coordinated to keep the victim consciousness firmly anchored within the mass consciousness. It is our purpose to change the mass consciousness to personal and planetary responsibility, where it belongs!

III-34

Within the blessing of education, the proliferation of broadcast communication and the printed word for the distribution of knowledge lies the problem of discerning what is of value and what is deliberately placed within these sources to mislead and misinform.

Herein is the next level of understanding that discernment as to what is appropriate and true must be applied to all input. Within each is the source of such guidance. The ability to tap into this wisdom is present within all and latent within most. The lessons in learning to discern what is appropriate and what is not are many and frustrating. For most, these are trial and error with difficulty in figuring out what purpose experience serves in life. Once the concept of discernment is understood, it is learning to use this important tool that is at the basis of many of life's trials. It then becomes a useful tool that enhances experiencing knowledge into wisdom.

It is to be understood that discernment is a tool that replaces what has been called judgment. Each can then release the self-deprecation that comes from "judging" self and others as being right or wrong. Discernment is an internal process that eliminates looking outside of one's self for the cause of the seemingly difficult experiences that plague the human life. The dictionary lists "insight" as an appropriate synonym. Discernment can be applied in a before or after mode. It is wise to consult one's inner feelings carefully before undertaking an experience. It can be further applied in retrospect to understand what lesson can be gleaned from an experience that is happening or has happened. Unless a lesson is learned, it is likely to be repeated until it is "discerned." Then a realization of what the intended lesson is/was happens within the understanding of the individual or group.

The practice of discernment is part of the application of the Law of Allowance. To consider the appropriateness of an undertaking in either the before, during or after mode requires a letting go of the emotions involved in the experience so that the logic of it can be considered. This may be an ongoing process of consideration before the totality of the lesson is gained. Even partial understanding and realization of its purpose in the totality of the life experience allows for greater knowledge to become wisdom which in turn allows the individual to apply this and change their pattern of expression to include different possibilities. In order to consider the situation and its circumstances there is a letting go that is necessary in order to allow the mind to consider the possibilities of the who, what, why and how of the total picture. If there is considerable open mindedness, possible scenarios can be played out in order to determine the greatest number of possibilities. Through this process, the more logical meanings become clear. Through this release needed solutions often become accessible because the mind has been allowed to reach inward to access the available wisdom from within. Each has a storehouse of available wisdom that is obtainable through the practice of discernment. There must be a desire to lift personal experience out of the daily morass of pointless repetition, judgement and blame.

In order to shed the victim consciousness the individual must be willing to turn their view of life from looking outside for the cause of situations and circumstances to looking inside for the causes that invoke what the Law of Attraction has brought into experience. These causes are to be found within attitudes, opinions and self-talk, for the mind is speaking within in a constant flow of chatter. Within this internal conversation are the keys to many of the patterns of thought and behavior that set up the situations and circumstances that are being experienced. Changing these patterns that are the basis for the creation of the life pattern is not a simple task, but a good beginning can be made with the awareness that it all begins with discernment. The world does not just happen to anyone. It is invited through the Law of Attraction, for like attracts like. A victim attitude draws not only fellow victims into one's life, but also abusers to provide the victim experience. As each begins to accept the responsibility that the cause is within their own pattern of experience, and is willing to accept this idea, then the practice of discernment is possible.

The discerning individual will find it necessary to logically assess their attitudes and opinions. Are they judgmental and blaming of others? Are there always reasons that the self is not responsible for what is going on in the life experience? If so, then denial of personal responsibility is blocking all progress and the cycle of victimhood is established. Until such time as this can be looked at with logic and the pattern discerned, it remains locked into the experience. It is necessary to desire to change these basic controlling factors, look and listen to what is thought and said and purposefully change the basic pattern. The results will take time and diligent correction in order to see the changing pattern in experience. However, the pattern must change if the intent and purpose are held in focus and thought and words are changed. Statements made can be restated in a positive mode, this then changes the first statement. Thoughts can be "re-thought."

Simple as this message content is, there are few if any who cannot find application of these ideas in their daily experience. The practice of discernment is an ongoing focus through many levels of experience. Looking within at attitudes, opinions, statements and thoughts often reveals interesting and applicable causes. Each is encouraged to apply these suggestions in an ongoing fashion.

Discernment is further practiced in considering and choosing what information is true. It is a wise practice to set up the discernment process by stating in thought that one wishes to discern truth before listening, watching or reading. In that way the mind discards what is not true and retains what, if anything contained, is true. What is truth for one is not always truth for another. Each pattern of experience sets up a different ability to glean what is necessary to know. It is encouraged that this suggestion be used when reading these messages.

III-35

As the sequence of events seems to accelerate and lineal time to pass more quickly the chaos will grow. Each individual will experience their own sequence of events that are only a small portion of the total picture. The controlled media will report only segments of the true picture. When viewed from the perspective of the planetary whole, there is a far greater degree of chaos now present than can be perceived by humanity. Those yet in zones of calm have little frame of reference for the experiences of those who are in the midst of war, geological or weather phenomena. Though greater global awareness is present, yet there is little exchange of actual experiential trauma between these separate experiences. It would not serve the planetary wholeness if there were such a connection so that all were experiencing the trauma of those within the distressed areas. Those that appear to be uninvolved serve to hold the equilibrium of the planet steady as the chaos is experienced elsewhere. There is a balancing that takes place.

It is planned to increase the experience of chaos in order that this balance may be forfeited. This plan to deliberately upset the balance by increasing the chaos beyond the planet's ability to retain its balance is based upon the theory that once the imbalance reaches a certain point, it can be pushed into a negative vibration that will block its access by positive energy foci. In other words, the planet would then be wholly owned by those of negative energy vibration and would then be no longer accessible by those of balanced or positive energy vibrations.

In order to accomplish this it has been thought that it was necessary to lower the vibrational fields of the inhabitants to a point that survival of some would be possible when the conversion to pure negative energy is completed. The installations of massive energy converters in order to bombard the ionosphere have been planned for this purpose. The testing of these converters appears to be for reasons other than what is planned. Indeed, they are to "protect" the planet from positive foci and appear to the planners to be accomplishing their intended purpose.

The question remains as to whether the theory on which all of this is predicated is one that will produce the desired change of polarity and if it were applicable, what are the implications that would accompany the result. When change is undertaken within the Laws of the Universe, the "thought thinking" principle can and does work through all the possibilities and probabilities and reaches a conclusion as to feasibility. When change is attempted without this inclusive aspect of wisdom, there is the inherent danger that unknown factors are disregarded and the outcome is likely to be unstable at some point in the process. This then brings the situation to the consideration as to how far freewill can be allowed to operate if the use of it involves massive risk to whole segments of creation.

Freewill with regard to individual experience is inviolate. However, when "will" is focused into a situation that is for the deprivation and destruction of not only the freewill choice of evolving consciousness, but to the point of destruction of the soul energy at the basis of life expression, then careful consideration must take place as to how this situation may be handled. The situation not only demands consideration and decisions, but also involves the decision of what intelligent foci may be involved in making that decision. In other words, a stacked deck cannot exist either for or against the continuation of the experience. This creates a considerable dilemma in coming up with a consortium of qualified and empowered "beings" willing to become involved in such a situation for serving in this capacity puts their own evolution at risk. Evolution is in reality a growing participation in responsibility. It is not a movement to a Utopian existence of lesser involvement or fewer responsibilities. Just as maturation into earthly experience naturally involves greater participation and responsibility, so also does evolvement into the higher dimensional realms.

A great "talent" search was initiated in order to find a cohesive group willing to consider the dilemma that the situation upon this small planet contains. To say that it covered a great deal of manifested reality is an understatement. The vested interests in the future of this planet are varied, well established and of intensely determined purpose. At the irrefutable basis of any solution is the will of the human population on the planet involved. It is then self-evident that those who would retain their control of the planet would make every effort to make sure the inhabitants "decide" that change is undesirable. Herein lies the purpose of the massive release of communication devices and the focus on the retention of the victim consciousness. The foundation of victim consciousness has been carefully laid within the religious foci from the very beginning. It has allowed for control of the progress of mankind not only in the discovery of the "god-like" qualities that are inherent to all, access to the understanding and application of the Universal Laws, but also to the understanding and ability to relate to the "creator mind" that is available within the outflow of undifferentiated energy at the basis of all Creation.

The key to the entry of the gathered wisdom foci is held within the collective mass consciousness of humanity. Unless the individual and collective desire of humanity for freedom from the oppressive outside intervention that has been present on this planet for thousands of years is focused toward an end to this situation, it cannot and will not change. The only possible help that can be given at the moment is to focus energies into the available thought realms surrounding the planet in the hope that individuals will accept these subtle suggestions to augment the desires that are already there to bring forth a change within the collective thinking of mankind as a whole. This seems like drops into an ocean of misery, but in accordance with the freewill principle, nothing further can be done.

The presence of craft from positive origins, what are called extra-terrestrial visitors, among those of negative and earthly origin as well as visible energy patterns imprinted on the surface of the planet has been increased. It is hoped that these will stimulate curiosity and trigger into awareness some of the volunteers that now risk their level of evolvement in service to their fellow humans. These messages are received and circulated by individuals that are responding to this plan. Those of you that hear of these, read and respond to them are in reality coming into harmony with the energy of concern and the desire to assist that is being generously focused into the atmosphere surrounding earth. The electrical charges that are being forced into the energy fields encircling earth are being placed there in an effort to block all positive support for the planet and its inhabitants. Fortunately, all efforts in harmony with the Laws of the Universe are supported by the intelligence of "thought thinking" which finds ways to circumvent such plans. If mankind can indeed be triggered to desire its freedom, despite the plans to block any such assistance, then the Universal Laws can and will support them. However the focus is to be held on that which is desired instead of retaliation and resorting to the old methods that have failed to bring mankind manifestation of their desire for change in the past. In other words, the focus must not resemble that which it is desired to leave behind.

The human population that desires to experience the opportunity to evolve in freedom from oppression must focus on what is desired and let go of the experiences of the past. These have led them in a continuous circle of repeating what has been taught to them by the example of their oppressors. The same blood/DNA of those oppressors flows in the blood of humanity. The question remains as to whether there are enough humans on this planet that have evolved beyond those genetic aberrations that do not serve their advancement. Can they focus on the desire for freedom from the repetitive pattern of life as they know it and transcend it into a new paradigm of experience? Can they now live those experiences into wisdom?

III-36

When each individual being incarnates on this planet it is with the explicit intention of blessing all experiences into wisdom, not only for themselves, but also for the planetary whole. It would seem that each individual life expression can hardly be a blessing to the planet and its inhabitants as a unit, but that is very much the case. Each has the opportunity to focus her/his life experience for the "good of all concerned." That inclusion is far reaching indeed! When this intention can be coupled with harmonious application of the Universal Laws a great contribution to the planetary consciousness is made. Fame or fortune need not accompany this contribution. Most often, the greatest contributions are made in obscurity and often without the conscious knowledge of the person doing so. These individuals simply experience life as a pleasant and harmonious sojourn. These are often recognized as being an "old soul." A term applied to those who seem to create for themselves an experience of simplicity and contentment and no recognition is given to them as accomplishing anything in particular. However, from a larger perspective their contributions are a major balancing factor.

This does not in any way take away from those that do place themselves in the forefront of activity and contribute greatly to the focus of attention to not only great "good," but also to great "evil." It is difficult to consider that those that focus evil into recognition are of service to the planetary whole. It can be considered that they draw to them the evil that is present in the mass consciousness as a boil draws the infection present within a body to a crisis point so that it may burst or be incised and removed and healing may take place. It is the tendency of humanity to judge and blame individuals and situations from their individual point of view rather than from the larger picture of planetary wholeness. Each has their own particular purpose for reincarnating and through the Law of Attraction bringing into experience what is needed to complete the purpose for the lifetime. As mentioned previously, each lifetime is a contribution to a greater totality of experiencing into wisdom. There exists a holograph of experience that requires the completion of various segments of experience in order that completion may be experienced.

Therefore it is unwise for individuals to decide what is good or bad with regard to the behavior of others as well as their choice of lifestyle. Each is to strive to accomplish what seems important in the moment and to listen to the inner guidance that is available to all. It is difficult to do this in an environment of coercion at all levels and periods of life experience. Fortunately, there are those that do hear and/or feel strongly what is appropriate for them and consistently move toward their unknown goal/s. Frustrating as it is, it is one of the requirements that the goal/s are either forgotten or are influenced out of the awareness by the parent/religion/ government influences present from birth until death.

As each moves through their sequential life experience it is impossible for them to ascertain their success or failure with regard to attaining the intended goal. Each must follow their guidance and keep on keeping on. A life filled with synchronicities and one that answers inner urgings to undertake what seem appropriate actions and that appear to accomplish the desired goals may well be on "track." This is especially true when the ultimate purpose is for "the highest and best good of all concerned." This may be stated in other ways such as "creating a win-win situation in all ways possible," etc. It is the intention that is measured! Through ethical intention the first two Universal Laws are invoked.

If "ethical" is a prerequisite, then why indeed does evil seem to succeed? It is because the Laws work regardless of who employs them. It is the outcome that is measured by the ethical intention of the "highest and best good of all concerned." The intended manifestation process that is contrary to the "good of all" must reach a crossover point where unknown instability destroys what is not harmonious in the larger picture for there are no individual minds capable of interpreting all possibilities. It is the clarity and duration of the intended focus that does hold a "evil" situation in manifestation beyond the normal point of destruction. Knowledge of the Universal Laws is not normally an unknown. Therefore, those who plan to hold onto Earth as a colony know and understand their application well. It is the human population that has been denied the knowledge and understanding of them so that they cannot use them to help free themselves from the plan to continue their enslavement. It can therefore be understood why the knowledge of these important laws is a prerequisite to those humans calling forth the freedom of Earth's inhabitants.

These messages have from the beginning been leading the readers toward the acceptance of the Truth that they contain. It has been necessary to slowly and carefully lay a foundation of understanding that moves beyond blame for the condition in which humanity finds itself. It is important that mankind accept the responsibility that they have allowed themselves to be duped and misled over thousands of years to be the slaves and toys of those who would control them. The plan to hold them in this deplorable condition has been one carefully implemented since man has been allowed to "rule himself." That these human rulers were/are carefully controlled is absolutely true. By absenting themselves, the true rulers have hidden their influence behind blind faith augmented by cruel punishment for disobedience meted out by "a God of love." The paradox of this claim has kept mankind in a constant turmoil and exactly where it was planned that they be. It is the hope of those waiting patiently for evolved humans to see through the ruse and to declare among themselves the intention of ending this practice once and for all. It is the key to all hope for creating a new paradigm of experience.

III-37

It is essential for the ground crew to understand that their commitment is to assist humanity to take advantage of their help and the opportunity of the completion of the various cycles that are reaching their culmination. The outcome beyond that is to be allowed. Indeed those members of the ground crew that participate will sink or swim with the human population on the planet. However, in lifetimes that are yet to be experienced the rewards for this work will be experienced if the effort to free those on this planet fails. Those members of the ground crew that do not answer the call to complete their mission will indeed become part of the destiny of the human population. It is the risk that was known to them in the beginning of this process. The degree of the opportunity available depends upon the participation of each individual. In no way is this intended to be a threat but as encouragement to look carefully into the inner awareness as to the validity of these messages and to "feel" what is the appropriate response. Participation within this phase of the plan is not appropriate for every human. To become aware that there is a plan that can lead to freedom to evolve can then lead these that do not fit into this particular focus to diligently search for their proper place within the effort to birth the new paradigm.

Humanity stands on the brink of what is opportunity or disaster. Those are blunt words, but it is not to the advantage of an entire planet to mince words and walk softly. The process is proceeding according to both plans and a convergence point is looming in the not too far distant future, as it is experienced in sequential time. Those in awareness must focus and direct their intent to participate and to involve as many as possible within their focus of intent. Tomorrow is not soon enough to begin.

What has been known and experienced is what is expected to continue in at least a somewhat familiar format. This will not birth the new paradigm. Atlantis, whether believed as real or as a myth, is an example of this. The story that is known is of a continent containing a greatly advanced civilization with a well developed scientific community and a very strong religious priesthood that controlled the development of all phases of the civilization. Though there were survivors, most of these were reduced to what is termed "caveman" status for their tools of advancement were lost under the sea. The stories of "how it was" became mythology within a generation. After the passage of several thousand years, what now exists in comparison? Again a well developed scientific community that is controlled behind the scenes by religious and supposedly "esoteric" brotherhoods. Behind these in reality are the extra-terrestrial true rulers making sure that their colony stays under their control. The reduction of mankind to utter poverty of physical and religious experience failed to allow them to maintain a destiny of continuous enslavement.

Unless a focused portion of the population is willing to take on the responsibility of deliberately intending to change the repeating cycle of apparent advancement followed by the return to poverty of body, mind and spirit, nothing will change. The age-old question of "Why does God allow this if He truly loves his beings?" rises to the minds of humanity over and over again. The answer is always the same, freewill! If self-aware beings choose victim consciousness, the Law of Attraction will provide them with fellow victims and abusers to maintain the experience. The desire to move *through* the victim experience thus experiencing it into wisdom with the intention of creating a new paradigm of experience for the whole of mankind and this planet is the purposeful intent that is necessary. This must be held in the forefront of all thought regarding this process. Will this salvage the planet and all of the human awareness units on the planet? Only those who are willing to participate. Who these will be will be decided within the soul matrix of each individual.

Participating in life experience at the 3rd dimensional level blocks from the understanding the activity of creation that goes on in the higher dimensions of experience. These underlie or support those of the lower vibrational levels of existence. Life is often thought of as becoming more focused and rising to a point of completion resembling a pyramidal experience. Using this example, it is necessary to understand that the pyramidal experience is supported by focused thought that may be understood to be its energetic counterpart, thus creating a double pointed structure. That which is seen or experienced is supported by an energetic format of focused thought and these interact on an ongoing basis. If this thought format were to be withdrawn, the manifested portion would cease to exist. Each human life is supported by an energetic focus that holds it in format. Each mountain and grain of sand is held in focus by its energetic counterpart. To illustrate this principle within the life experience, a business or organization is held in experience by the thoughts of those who participate by their focused thought. If that is withdrawn, it no longer continues to exist. It continues or it fails based upon the factors required and whether or not these were included in the focus of attention and intention.

The information contained above can be carried over into the previous discussion of placing attention and intention within the application of the basic Laws of the Universe. By releasing them in harmony through proper intent, the action of the "thought thinking" function of the Laws can and does supply the factors required for true manifestation of the desired outcome to the highest and best good of all concerned. If the intent is held firmly in mind and heart and at the same time released and allowed to manifest through the action of the Laws, the outcome will assuredly be harmonious.

While the information contained herein is often repetitious, it is written so that each may be convinced that there is a way out of the ongoing repetitious cycle of experience into a different adventure. Life fully embraced leads to wondrous adventures.

III-38

When the time arrives for each individual to make the decision as to whether these messages are in fact guidance indicating what their mission in this life may be on this planet at this time, a resonance with this greater objective will fill the void that has been felt within. Recognized or not, until each identifies what their particular dominant purpose is, there is a need to search and find it. This leads to physical changes in location, career changes and frequent visitations to various churches as well as other community and athletic endeavors. Often times it necessitates fervent participation within a focus that does not satisfy the empty the need in hopes that more of the same will eventually be fulfilling. Mankind has been denied the understanding of how to commune with the greater aspects of that part of him/herself that has placed their awareness into this life experience. This aspect is alluded to in religious literature but with little meaningful guidance. Meditation is taught, but the overload of media input along with the stressful life style of "modern" life seldom allows most to reach a point at which the mind is able to free itself to reach the quiet point required to commune with the focusing aspect. It is as though the brain cells are stimulated to an operating mode that cannot slow down to a resting point of awareness. In this state of stimulation, the thought processes do not function normally. The thoughts are not comprehended and considered and are instead, simply processed through. This then accounts for what is often referred to as the "dumbing down" of the modern-day mind.

This frantic mode is further pictured in life styles that reflect constant busyness through hurrying from one task to another. Relaxation is musical noise, TV, movies or videos. Sleep is induced with alcohol, sex, drugs, or late-night eating resulting in exhaustion of the body's functions. Simple quiet time such as sitting to observe a sunset and contemplating the joy of being alive, of counting one's multitude of blessings is seldom done, even by the older members of the current culture. The learned busyness is continued until dis-ease or infirmity demands a slowdown. The point to be made here is that those who choose to participate in this focus of intention to create a new paradigm of experience must realign their priorities. In order to create something new, a separation from the attachments to the old must be eventually made. That does not say participation must be given up, but their importance must be allowed to dimin-ish. In order to contemplate what is new, there must be quiet space within the awareness to do this. Priorities must change to allow for slowing down the participation in meaningless endeavors and a greater peace sought through choice. Quietness must be redefined from boredom to peacefulness.

Seeking peace in proximity to urban noise, airwaves filled with unseen but very present vibrations and living amid crowded visual surroundings is challenging. Artificial light inhibits the abil-ity to observe and enjoy the evening twilight and the view of the star filled heavens. What countryside is close by is also filled with exterior lights. Work schedules continue day and night. The planet itself has extensive areas of constant activity that further exhausts the wholeness of the global entirety. Is this purposeful? Indeed, for it separates humanity from its connection to the planet that nurtures it and prevents mankind from reciprocating in any way. Humanity at large is on a "taking binge" with little understanding of the neces-sity of a return flow of energy to the planet through appreciation and honoring the provisions that maintain life.

How then do those who accept this change of focus come into balance and harmony with the global whole in order to enhance and magnify their presence into a focus that will augment the necessary transition? The way is through applying the Laws of the Universe within their own experience. It can be done through intention and attention to what choices can be made to bring as many peaceful moments into each day as possible. The Law of Attraction will work when the attention and intention are clear. Time off from frantic activity, even a small space of quiet time, can have a "grounding" or quieting effect. Positive prayer that centers on appreciation and blessing of the self and others rather than on what appears to be lacking in life will change the experience. Who one thanks is of little importance, for this again is the need to personify and identify.

"The power that Is" is sufficient identification. It is the thankful "heart" (feelings) that is important. One cannot expect to create a more abundant experience if one is not appreciative of what is already within the current experience. By honoring what is, the Law of Attraction is invoked.

Thus, it is important to find positive attributes in the current experience to appreciate and honor even as a new paradigm of experience is desired. This is the paradox that is found throughout creation. In order to have what is new, it is necessary to honor aspects of what is present as a stepping stone on which to stand before creating a new stepping stone to continue the progress. To honor something does not make it necessary to carry it on into the next phase. Again, it is necessary to point out that the grateful heart reflects a feeling aspect that resonates with the Law of Attraction that brings into experience more for which to be grateful. It is the way it works.

III-39

As the sequence of events begins to accelerate, it is time for those who are committed to the change of experience for humanity on this planet to seriously focus on the idea of the realization of the new paradigm. In order for it to manifest into the reality of experience, it must first become real in the minds of those who identify with this idea. It is rather like pulling the proverbial rabbit from the hat. The event as seen requires focused intent "behind the scene" and a great deal of practice in focusing on this desire in order for it to appear. The event itself is a manifestation of the intent that precedes it. What appears as a magical event to the observers involves instead focused practice and the intent to mystify and surprise. There is a direct correlation to the birthing of the planned new paradigm of experience. The new paradigm will arise out of the "grass roots" desire of humanity to end the current descent into slavery. Under what appears as complacency and ignorance of what is going on in the life of the "average" person is the feeling that "things are not quite right." Beneath that awareness is a cognition that is sending forth a signal calling for balance and harmony within the planetary experience. This psychic signal is the platform that provides for the creation of the new paradigm. It is upon this critical foundation that those who read and identify with these messages have permission to dream/imagine the framework that will begin manifesting into reality the desired new experiences.

The key to the survival of this focus lies in its lack of organization. There is nothing to infiltrate and nothing of substance that appears to support its existence. But exist it does! It exists in the minds of growing numbers of individuals and answers untold uttered and unuttered prayers to countless ideas of divine power that is believed to possess the ability to intervene. In truth, it is the manifestation of these prayers and the underlying desire for balance and harmony that is coming forth as the "messages" and the focusing of these through individual minds into the mass consciousness. This is then the answer to these "prayers" and desires. The divine intervention is manifesting through those who desire it. The invocation is made through thought and is being answered in like manner. Since thought is the impetus for all creation, the invocation and the answer are in the most powerful and yet subtle form. It is also the most defensible when it is firmly held and emotionally powered. No amount of subliminal influence can alter the emotionally held conviction that is focused upon a desired manifestation. Desire, firmly held in mind with emotional knowingness that the possibility of its actuation is feasible, can and will manifest. It matters only that the perception that is held by many is *generally* identifiable through statements of purpose.

Those who are now actively involved within their own focus with or without a small group have now reached a quorum to allow the invocation of more help from outside sources. Meditations/prayers and simple thought requests are encouraged to be directed to request help to assist humanity to focus on a different experience as a solution rather than on the problematic situation that surrounds them. Greater awareness of the problems serves to promote an awakening from ignorance, but in no way provides for a solution to those problematic situations that are enumerated. Indeed that which is hidden behind the problems and that invokes them is organized with intentions that are deeper and darker than can possibly be ascertained from the currently known situations. The hoped-for return to prior known experiences would in no way hold these dark intentions in check. It must be clearly understood that all hope must be focused toward the invocation of a new paradigm of experience. The past must be allowed to become the past. The future must be imbued with the hopes, plans and dreams of harmony and balance within the application of the basic Laws of Universal experience. It is the shift into this tried and true method of manifestation that will provide the solution to mankind's dilemma. It is through focus on what is unknown and yet to be discovered that the present is let go to become the past and that which the future can offer is discovered.

What is unknown conjures up either excitement or fear. It is important that the ground crew builds upon the emotion of excitement and anticipation in order to provide greater potential for manifesting the new paradigm into realized experience. That which begins as the nucleus of the intention will then draw to it what is necessary to bring about the maturation of the original idea and allow for the what might be compared to cellular growth and expansion of this idea into manifested reality. What begins as a small focus of intent then expands from within and can be promoted further by help from without. The available help can offer protection which enables the natural expansion to continue rather than be contained by those who would prefer that this intentional focus be aborted or die in its infancy. It is this kind of help that it would be wise to invoke during prayer or meditation or focused thought. It is "help to help yourselves" so to speak. It is requests for help to open up the path of mankind before them so that it can be seen and understood as it is experienced into reality. That kind of help fits within the Laws of Galactic Citizenship to be exchanged between its members, freely asked for and freely given. "Help us to help ourselves!" It invokes no indebtedness between members. It is the way of advancement in which all that can, help all that ask, but those must be willing to help themselves in the process. It cannot be done for them. The means of help is left to the helpers for often generally worded requests for help are filled from a greater understanding that brings forth results undreamed of by those requesting it. Greater thought thinking is always available to answer requests formatted within the basic Universal Laws. Thus requests including "for the highest and best good of all concerned" invokes this greater wisdom with extraordinary results guaranteed.

It is hoped that those who identify with these messages and intentionally change their objective to bringing forth the new paradigm of experience for mankind on this planet will remember to hold this focus in the forefront of their attention. The principles contained are of course available for application within personal experience. It is strongly suggested that dedication toward the planetary whole is the basis upon which the individual experience is focused. To change only the individual experience will not change the planetary experience. However, changing the planetary experience is guaranteed to change the individual experience. Both can and may be coordinated by those who truly desire to take advantage of a time that is ripe with opportunity for rapid evolvement. There is much to be understood and the choice involved is momentous for mankind as a whole and each individual that chooses to be consciously involved. "Pray" (think and ask clearly) that enough make the correct choices and purposeful application of focused intention that the highest good is manifested for all concerned. (To *what or who* this request is directed matters not.) What is the highest and best good for both individuals and mankind is an unknown. Judgement withheld <u>*allows*</u> the 3rd Universal Law to wield its powerful influence. The coordinated action of the first three manifests the 4th, harmony and balance, the essence of the goal of the new paradigm humanity desires to experience.

All begins with the consideration of possibilities, then choice. Choose carefully!

III-40

Circumstances, situations and events are perceived through the sequential experience pattern of the earth plane through a reformatting of a greater experiential matrix. It compares somewhat to unraveling a knitted sweater into a long thread that only retains the individual kinks that made up the stitches. It is impossible to ascertain what the sweater looked like from the pile of kinky yarn that is then seen. Thus each event in the sequential chain of events is all that can be perceived of an existing prototype that is whole and complete. Once the experiential chain of sequential events has reached a completion point of its cycle and a reality is experienced as complete, a perspective of the entire event can be glimpsed. However, it is only one perspective of a holographic whole.

The concept of time that is the basis for perceiving sequential events exists and is experienced differently within each level of manifested reality. With the ability to perceive a greater and greater perspective of a whole, the importance of minute by minute time calculation becomes less relevant. What becomes important is the encompassing process that contains the situation or event as it is completed into a whole experience. It is like watching the sweater being knitted as a whole from freshly spun yarn. As it is knitted, it becomes the background for the embroidery of individual experiences. The same sweater background is perceived and embroidered by each individual who is living within its influence. Each sees their version of the sequence of events, situations and circumstances that then makes up a larger and larger group experience as perceived by all from a myriad of perspectives. The consensus of the group perspective then becomes the "mass consciousness" experience. Out of that generalized agreement, laws, rules and regulations govern what is generally acceptable behavior. It is this consensus of acceptable group behavior that is so important to the oppressors to influence. The more uniform and regimented the world population is, the easier it is to influence and control through identity in a "global" perception rather than within cultural, ethnic or national allegiances.

At the same time as the globalists are attempting to standardize the human life experience into a robotic and more easily controllable worldwide situation, the human psyche is longing to individualize. The larger view of this intense struggle between containment and creative expression is beginning to clarify into groups of varying experiences. A large percentage are being slowed and standardized into a hypnotic zombie like existence. Others are caught up in frenzied accomplishment of various extremes of life experiences. Some are lost in various group foci that exploit their fellow humans, etc. Underlying the whole chaotic scene are the mind manipulators that carry out their influencing experiments on their human sacrificial guinea pigs. Mind programming, medical experiments in the form of prescription drugs and vaccines, illegal hard drugs, food additives, food combinations, unseen vibratory waves from commonly used communication devices, appliances, etc., all influence the human body and the vibratory/ electrical spark of life that animates it. These conveniences provide seeming comfort and ease and are thus difficult to think of giving up. It is not the concept of them that is counter-productive to human experience, it is that they have been designed in a planned format that is intended to accomplish very specific negative goals for mind manipulation and control of body functions. In other words, all these beneficial items can be made within a format that would support the life forms on this planet. It is important to understand that these were designed purposefully to slow and confuse the vibratory life force that inhabits all living forms on this planet with the direct objective of eliminating all but the most resistant that these may then breed the most adaptive future slave stereotype. Mankind must come to realize that just as they have thought nothing of doing genetic breeding of life forms that they considered "lesser," so also are they considered a lesser life form by those who direct these human lackeys to misuse their fellow humans. Those who allow themselves to be used in this way are given no more and probably even less appreciation than the average human. If these will betray their own kind, then they are truly untrustworthy and that is not a desirable characteristic for a slave archetype.

It is important that as many open-minded humans as possible come into the understanding of just what their true status is insofar as those who consider this planet their colony are concerned. This is not meant to cause any reevaluation of the worth of humanity to a lesser value. Indeed not! Humanity has running through its veins the blood, the DNA, the potential of all self-aware beings to evolve within the plan of creation. What is important to grasp is that humanity faces the enviable challenge of throwing off the yoke of outside influence and facing up to taking responsibility for creating its own future. It will be through growing to accept this challenge and creating a way through this experience that the true autonomous qualities that have been deliberately forced into a latent state must now be called forth and brought into focused application. These are not the warlike tendencies of competition that have been cultivated and encouraged, but those of responsibility, courage and cooperation that will bring about the spiraling of evolvement into galactic citizenship. These will lift the human consciousness out of the seemingly hopeless struggle that surrounds it and allow the planet and those inhabitants who change their perspective to transcend this present situation. Those who identify with this new paradigm of experience will move into it. Those who do not, will be allowed more experience until another opportunity is created individually or collectively to choose again. Advancement is available to those that choose carefully and decidedly. Again, each is encouraged to consider thoughtfully.

III-41

Since the beginning of the time that this planet was inhabited with warm-blooded mammals the process of evolvement toward self-awareness was the goal. This is a normal and natural process. What is measured as time by this self-awareness as it progresses and is refined appears as short segments in what appears as a long process. Again, we refer to the holographic picture of the whole process. The linear sequential observation of the self-aware ego has no inkling of the larger picture until such time as explanations of "how it really is" can be placed within his/her perception and are accepted as truth. The convenience of the light and darkness cycles as a measure of time determines the perception. However, there are other means of measuring time that can be adopted. The longer the cycle measured the longer the life experience of the individual. Though it might seem impossible, were another measurement adopted, then the life span in actuality could be either lengthened or shortened depending on the content of the cycle. How could this "content" be compared? Not easily by the participants. The point being that the experience is conditional on the criteria for measurement used by the observing egos. These are agreed upon through the generalization of the input of the many opinions of the total group.

This is a powerful tool to control insofar as manipulating a large group is concerned and explains the grouping of people in cities and the efforts of using mass media methods to shape the generalizations of opinions. Some of those now shaping the generalizations are:

- Power and permission are in the hands of an outside deity.
- Violence is the way to resolve differences.
- Humans are more different than they are similar.
- Being right is more important than understanding.
- The past controls the future.
- Pleasure and luxury are the necessities of happiness.
- Complexity is more satisfying than simplicity.
- Might makes right.
- Service and sacrifice are the ultimate gifts one can make to the future of mankind.
- There is not enough and those that have must take it away from others.
- If it isn't "right," laws and regulations can fix it or more control is the answer.

The list could go on and on.

What is it then that the messages found in these small books would replace as currently held beliefs:

- Responsibility and freedom are interchangeable terms.
- Power and permission are retained or given away by choice.
- Purposeful *focused intention* is an all-powerful tool.
- What is believable must be logical.
- Responsibility negates victim/abuser attitudes.
- Where the attention is, is where the intention is.
- Like *attracts* both sides of the "likeness experience."
- There is an important distinction between indifference and allowance.
- Humanity has a choice about its future experiences.
- Rescue without participation is not an available option.
- The new is invoked in kind before the end of the old.
- Chaos is a necessary stage in the process of change.
- Commitment to a goal attracts assistance to aid its completion.

Through the reading and the rereading of these messages, these and other principles toward the choice of choosing the destiny of mankind on this planet will become a deeply rooted focus of intent by all those who choose to be a part of this process. It is logical and it is one focus that can be participated in by those with many divergent views without the necessity to defend or attack the diverse thoughts the new paradigm invokes. The "desire for a new paradigm of experience" is all-inclusive. The intent focused for the "highest and best good for all concerned" allows for *thought thinking* to bring forth an organizing agreement that will profoundly include all rational possibilities into an encompassing plan that will be readily acceptable. Humans becoming will indeed become. It is a focus of energy that is all-inclusive and yet extremely discriminating as the choice for participation. It offers the long-awaited opportunity to mankind to transcend its colonial status for sovereignty and participation within its galactic community.

The question arises now as to how long before those who desire this planet to remain as a colony will allow this to go on providing the humans of earth to free themselves through declaring their sovereign ownership of this planet? That is a part of the plan that is well encompassed. It is first and foremost the job of humanity to make its choice and to declare their intent within their own awareness and commit to assuming the necessary responsibility to focus their purposeful intent into the Universal Laws and allow the picture to clarify. Thought thinking is wise indeed! Some things are better left to resolve themselves through allowance. However, remember that allowance is not indifference, it is watchful observance with emotional expectation anticipating the outcome of purposeful intent. It is change through conscious participation in expressing the principle of Life that is known through the gift of self-awareness. It is found by perceiving what is known and felt within the feeling aspect of awareness through logical consideration of questions asked within the thinking process. It is thought thinking within the individual consciousness and testing its conclusions through the feeling aspect as to their validity in quiet contemplation knowing there is no need to compare the conclusions to anyone else's process of decision. With no need to defend the conclusions, true contemplation is available. The consensus is important only to the contemplator. Think about it!

III-42

Through the process of broadening the perspective of the human experience it becomes easier to identify with the task of changing the intended future experience by returning the controlling focus to the beings evolving originally on this planet. Each unit of awareness that incarnates (experiences in a body) on this planet identifies with the past genetic history of that body as passed on by all the previous progenitors. This then carries with it the right of sovereign ownership of this planet, not as an individual, but as an individual part of the family of humanity. It takes little review of the past history of "royal families" to see the pattern of behavior that is present within that segment of the mass conscious memory. The review of history in light of the influence of those governing directly or in manipulating the members of humanity that were chosen to fulfill that role points vividly to greed, deceit and treachery as standard operating procedure. Indeed, there is little of enduring value to be gained in repeating the experience of humanity in this past chapter of planetary history other than to create a deep and abiding desire to transcend it into a totally new pattern of evolvement. This is not to indicate that there has not been a great deal of progress and much experienced into wisdom. It is meant to indicate that all that is practically possible to learn has been gleaned and it is prudent to release the need to continue and to move on to a more rewarding pattern of experience.

As the consciousness shifts to allow a more encompassing view of the human experience, a different way of perceiving the content of the mass consciousness allows the observer to more easily perceive and acknowledge the influences at work that are deliberately programming the overall attitudes and opinions that shape it. The observer begins to separate from those influences and to recognize them as being forced on those that would not knowingly choose them by outsiders of another nature with a different pattern and focus. This recognition then leads to a choice as to whether to purposely continue within this pattern or to separate from it in purposeful intention to bring about a change for the whole of the planetary experience. To attempt to separate and maintain an individual focus accomplishes little of value whereas joining a larger focus of intent to change the planetary experience offers a solution of enough value to incite a commitment. As has been mentioned before, a change of individual expression does little to change the experience of others, while a planetary change will affect all individual experiences within its scope.

These messages continue to follow a theme of clarifying the current situation with its probable continuity for humanity in a downward spiral of experience into abject slavery and the intended destruction of the soul energy that is the focus that places and holds the spark of life within each body. That spark is experienced as individual self-awareness. Stripping this aspect of life from the human expression would return it to the animal state and to what is thought to be an ideal slave archetype. That is the simplest explanation of the planned future. The greatest problem is the desire of the controllers to retain a percentage of intelligence that is linked to the self-aware state. Thus, experiments and continual testing go on to determine what techniques of mind control and physical adaptability can bring about this ideal prototype. It is hoped that this planned scenario that awaits those who continue to accept the indoctrination, the vaccinations, the regimentation and the subordination of their will to powers outside themselves is now vividly envisioned by those who read and accept the possibility that the content of these messages contains truth. It is hoped that the logical sense of bringing about change by a method not anticipated by those that intend to control this planet and its population is clear. It is possible to change the experience by conscious choice and by deliberate intention through aligning that intention with the basic Laws of the Universe. These bring about deliberate empowerment by allowing the Law of Attraction to release requested help to assist rather than to rescue. At the basis of this plan is the essential change in the perception of the situation at hand and the change in consciousness from victim to responsible creator of a new paradigm of experience. Releasing all of this into the flow of creative expression is the desire that all happen for the *highest and best good of all concerned!* It must be understood that this is not to be intended for beleaguered mankind only, but all that are involved in the entire scenario, whether they appear to be of positive or negative intent. Within that desire to encompass the greatest possible change in experience lies the greatest possible empowerment for transformation in the galactic experience. It is a moment in this segment of galactic history that is unprecedented! It carries with it unparalleled opportunities for evolvement to those who have the desire and the commitment to become an active participant in this shift in consciousness. It is hoped that many will be able to change their perspective and to encompass the possibilities that are available to contemplate. To knowingly be an active participant in this opportunity is even more phenomenal. Consider this opportunity carefully.

III-43

The process of lifting the mass consciousness out of its long-standing morass of controlled attitudes and thoughts concerning what it is necessary to experience as a human is progressing toward a shift in focus. It is necessary that there be formed what might be called an enlightened or knowledgeable nucleus. These messages are intended to serve that purpose. As these are read and reread, those that resonate with the information contained within them form a pivotal core for the attraction of greater numbers to join the growing momentum toward the creation of the new paradigm of experience. To desire change is one level of involvement, but to desire change within a feasible format that is based upon a logical sequence that allows for a group consensus of agreement brings about a momentum that has within it the promise of success. As the momentum begins to build within this focused core of belief in the success of the process that is now well initiated, it is not experienced by these same individuals seeing the actual results for those are and will continue to be unknown from a practical sense. It will be experienced instead as an inner knowingness that all is working exactly according to plan. Though mankind has long sought to observe and control as many aspects as is possible within their life experience, in this case it is known from the beginning that it is necessary to "trust the process." That permits the Law of Allowance the scope to manifest what is invoked through the Law of Purposeful Intention (deliberate intention to create.) It is necessary to understand that in order for an intended creation to manifest, it must be *allowed* to manifest. This happens through holding the intention firmly in intellective view in the full faith and anticipation that it is already in energetic thought form and deliberately drawing to itself the molecular experiential format that will allow it to come into perceivable reality.

Embracing the Laws of the Universe as a viable method of bringing a new paradigm of experience to this planet and its inhabitants requires focusing committed intention through the understanding and application of the interacting sequence of the principles involved. These laws have been introduced in their most basic formats along with simple explanations of both the sequential and interacting processes that allow them to serve as a purposeful vehicle of creation. The Laws are responsive to intention and thus are often, if not most of the time, operating from a perspective of default, meaning they are manifesting whatever is being held in focus by any and all thought held in place. Thus, those whose thoughts are on poverty and lack are creating within their experience more poverty and lack. Thoughts on victimhood are drawing more experiences of victimhood. Thoughts of hatred and revenge bring experiences of being hated and of vengeance. Focus on "wanting" particular experiences or things, brings more "wanting," not the manifestation of the objects of the wanting. Thoughts of appreciation of abundance, happiness and joy bring more of those. It all depends upon the perspective of the focusing conscious awareness.

The Laws are real and the results they bring forth when properly applied are real. The doubt that arises during the linear sequence of time that is experienced between the invocation of purposeful intent and the manifestation into realized experience is the trap. Manifestation between energetic thought formation of the matrix to the realizable experience varies with the quality of purposeful thought that is held in place during this interim. The quality is influenced greatly by the emotional excitement that is contained in the anticipation with which the event is awaited. Though emotional support is experienced periodically, it is difficult to maintain the necessary level of anticipation through "knowing" the matrix is indeed drawing to it the required condensing energy to bring about completion. Thus, it serves the process to have multiple foci contributing to the thought pool that is holding the pattern in place. Here again, it is the generally understood desire for a new paradigm of experience that is the organizing force fueled by the input of contributory data to support this desire from myriad points of view. The focused energy input within a delineated pattern that is defined within a process in harmony with the outflow of Universal expression moves through manifestation with a maximum of efficiency. By funneling the thought energies through an agreed upon organizing focus a dynamic is established that elicits an attractive force that brings to the process more thought energies that in turn adds further empowerment to all phases. Thus, it is seen to build upon itself because it is acting in harmony with the creative outflow of potentiality which can be understood to be energy that is yet without purpose or form. This unformatted energy is more quickly imprinted with the desired expression. It is not necessary to break down or reformat energy already imprinted. Since the Law of Allowance is free to ascertain the most appropriate combination of available essential elements that will benefit the whole, manifestation is within a harmonious flow.

It is to be remembered that all manifestation that is attempted that is contrary to the creative flow that maintains the whole must of necessity by held tightly in focus within carefully delineated guidelines. All elements must be contained within the preset guidelines and error factors must be reviewed and corrections carefully made for any deviations. A monumental difference is experienced between the release of a free-flow of energy set into motion within universal harmonious guidelines and the focus required to direct those that deviate from that flow. The Laws working together freely have available self-direction within the process utilizing wisdom that is beyond comprehension. That is a decided advantage in the birthing of the new paradigm.

III-44

Each and all are surrounded by the energy that focuses the awareness that each knows as him or herself. It is the consciousness that allows choices and observation of the self within those choices. The variation and the extent that this selection involves varies with the willingness to confront the situations and circumstances that are present and to make decisions that encompass the range of greatest to the least effect upon the status quo each is experiencing. This begins during childhood. It is then that parents wield great influence through their approval or disapproval of the choices that each child makes. Until about the age of 12 parents are the "gods" of each child's life experience. The relationship established between the child and its parents influences the pattern of decision making that will be lived out during the rest of that lifetime. The child may decide to follow the pattern as set or they may choose to use it as a guide for change. Again, it is the conscious awareness making a decisive choice that will influence the pattern of the life experience. The confidence or lack of it that is acquired during childhood influences the courage and adventurousness that each applies during the life experience. They are further influenced not only by the input of other interactions and experiences but also by the genetic inclinations that are inherited through cellular memory passed on through previous experiences of prior generations. All of these influences are continuously interacting within the consciousness as well as those attachments that are made to objects, circumstances, situations and relationships with others. As the ability grows to interact with more and more influences in what is deemed the "modern world" with its global travel and global media exchanges, it is easily understood that life is anything but simple in this time and place.

It is considered progress to find the awareness surrounded by complexity. If that is true, then mankind should be extremely content and experiencing both mental and spiritual evolvement. A few are able to "put it all together," but certainly not a sufficient number to lift the conscious experience of the many. It then becomes necessary, if evolvement is to become a step forward, for a sufficient number to prioritize their life choices to bring this purpose into a meaningful focus. It has been the intent of these messages to assist in bringing the understanding of the necessity of doing just that in order that a shift in the planned future of mankind on this planet take place. It has been pointed out many times that it can only happen through the concerted efforts of enough individual humans by their own choice to do what is appropriate to cause this to happen. It must first begin within each individual self-awareness with the desire for it to happen on a planetary level. This is the foundation for all else to build upon. Each must understand that it is their rightful inheritance to take dominion over the direction of their evolvement. Until that choice of personal responsibility is made, some other unit of awareness will be happy to do it. The inheritance of the DNA used to introduce the original genetic enhancement that pushed the evolvement rapidly into self-awareness for those originally inhabiting this planet causes the natural group tendency to inevitably lead to competition and power struggles rather than cooperation. It therefore becomes clear that a purposeful choice must be made between competition and cooperation. This would lead to a major shift in the overall group experience. It would lead the human experience on a totally new path of expression. It seems such a simple choice in light of the profound change that would result. As is the case in all life experience, the simple choices are often the most profound and life changing.

While the messages are dealing with the simple truths that lie at the basis of evolving experience, the masters of control continue to complicate and confuse by causing chaos at points all over the planet. It is their plan to cause enough chaos and confusion to overwhelm their overly independent (in their opinion) workers into giving up any thoughts of freedom in order to have order and peace. As the confusion and chaos grow, all memories of the past seem to have had more of the order and peace that is desired. This is what is planned and presented through subtle suggestion. The more complex the experience surrounding humanity, the more easily it is believed it can be herded into asking for outside control to reorder their existence.

Then it can be said, "humanity asked for their help!" It is in understanding their methodology that it can be clearly seen that in order to free itself, humanity must make exactly the opposite decision. It must decide that control by outsiders in the guise of "government," especially as "a single world government" will not bring about the desired Utopia. There must be a nucleus of informed and purposefully intending people that are committed to initiating an independent and free experience for this planet and its inhabitants. It must be clearly understood that this planet and its abundant resources rightfully belong to its human inhabitants to use for their own benefit to create an independent member of the galactic family. Help is available to initiate this opportunity. Advice to assist is available to be accepted or not, as chosen by those who take advantage of this opportunity.

These messages return again and again to the underlying theme of choice and responsibility. It is hoped that this understanding and this attitude are becoming a premise for the choices that are made by each individual. These individuals are now forming a growing nucleus of informed thought that is focused on the purposeful intent to claim the inheritance that belongs to the human population of this planet from this day forward in sequential timing. It can only be claimed by knowing it as truth and declaring it as the basis for every act of choice. Through purposefully desiring a new paradigm of experience, with cooperation as its focus of empowerment for "the highest and best good for all concerned," the energetic framework is put in place. The pattern then begins filling in as the harmony of agreement corresponds with the action of the Laws of the Universe. The ripples of added conscious agreement continues to build as the messages reach more and more people and the pattern strengthens. As the "ground crew" continues in their committed focus, so also does the anticipation that fuels the purposeful intent. Help in various forms of interventional formats begins to assist. These will not create the new paradigm, but will stand forth to allow the new pattern to formulate.

The term "ground crew" has never been meant to indicate that it is acting under the specific directions of outside help. It is meant to be understood that it is a cooperating group that is now receiving informational help to support them in completing the assignment that was agreed upon before incarnating in human bodies to assist in bringing this planet out of bondage and into the full opportunity to evolve. These have taken on the human limitations of their earthly genetic parent's histories, but have brought with them strengths to blend into the mix of evolutionary advancements made by those humans that have evolved or have been abandoned on this planet. These ask for nothing but the commitment and cooperative help of all who will understand the opportunity that is being offered. It matters not what the reason is that each individual volunteers. All are necessary contributors to a worthy and vastly rich opportunity at the individual and planetary level that will ripple outward to an extent that is beyond imagination. It is hoped that once the dream is birthed within each imagination it will take root and grow into an unshakable commitment that will fuel its purposeful focus through the chaos that is planned. This commitment will assist each to keep their equilibrium. Their example of courage and stability will in turn attract many to the cause of the liberation of humanity.

III-45

The understanding of time, space and reality present a great mystery to limited consciousness. The vibratory rate of manifested experience and observable matter or objects to be experienced in 3rd dimensional reality requires the concept of time to be comprehended within a sequential format. This requirement separates simultaneous events and manifestations into identifiable segments thus dividing multiple coactive happenings into recognizable units. It is then difficult to discern a reasonable and essentially accurate picture of complex situations using only the *known* pieces. Arriving at a bigger picture by assembling information from a stream of passing information requires a process necessitating the activation of a portion of the brain that is latent in most earthbound humans. The known factors may not contribute enough information to indicate the integral picture, but certainly the parts considered separately in no way indicate the combined elements forming what is true. In other words, the 3rd dimensional experience is extremely limiting. This is the reason it is so difficult to transcend it through individual effort. The addition of multiple media providing mass amounts of information has been instructive in allowing the realization that situations that are larger and more inclusive exist than are being revealed. The amount of conflicting and deliberately misleading data included in the available information makes accurate conclusions difficult to formulate. Situations change, the available information changes and the end result is overwhelming and confusion.

It is important to understand that the deliberate confusion that is being foisted upon humanity by the use of both ends of the information continuum is purposeful. Too much information along with too little truthful and pertinent information is presented simultaneously.

This purposefully prohibits thoughtful and intelligent humans from deriving accurate conclusions and reasonably true pictures from the ongoing flow of information about events and situations. The frustrating search for needed information leads concerned members of humanity either to acquiesce or continue to search futilely in order to intuit at least an indication of the true scenario that is going on around them. Knowing there is no way to ascertain all the information, each draws conclusion in the best way possible and experiences confusion and distrust.

Is there a solution to this dilemma? Consider that it may be best to accept the situation as it appears. It is possible that the confusion and chaos that are planned for humanity to experience and accept are exactly the experience needed. It is expected that mankind will resist and condemn the chaotic conditions and desire an end. If instead these conditions are accepted as a part of the process of the eradication of the very chaos and confusion that are being experienced so that these can be replaced with a totally new experience, a shift in the total scenario is inevitable. Indeed, it can be considered that what is going on is inevitable. The current system must break down in order that a new one can be put in place. It provides the opportunity for mankind to intercede and create for itself what it desires.

The question at this time is what is it that mankind desires to create? It will be either a continuation of the colonization of this planet by outsiders or the declaration of sovereignty and ownership by asserting that the true ownership of this planet belongs to the evolving human population. To this end, these messages are dedicated to educating all humans who can be contacted, all those that will take up the gauntlet and recognize their true identity as citizens rather than owned slaves. These must dedicate their life focus to the purpose of declaring the freedom of the entire planet. The scope of thought must be toward recreating the whole. From this perspective, it can be seen that the push for a global identity serves this purpose well. Indeed, there are no accidents. The impetus of the desire for the "highest and best good for all concerned" can and will use all facets of existing experience for the greater good when it is released and allowed to do so through focused and encompassing purposeful intent.

It requires mature and intelligent beings to thoughtfully consider an unprecedented plan of cooperation for a purpose of the highest possible intention for an entire civilization. This sets forth an opportunity that can, if considered, call forth the memory of the reason why each has incarnated at this time on this planet. All the experiences that have happened thus far in this lifetime pale when compared to the prospect of providing assistance to a beleaguered planet and its numerous inhabitants that are now denied their rightful freedom to evolve in a positive and supportive environment. This assistance would end the rape and pillage of a richly endowed planet and solar system that are now being used to support civilizations that have failed to care for their own planetary homes.

The change of consciousness from victim to sovereign responsibility is the necessary foundation for the fundamental change of the planetary experience. Commitment to a cooperative focus that clearly delineates the benefits available to be experienced is an impetus for joining a worthwhile cause. The individual as well as group benefits available for participation have been enumerated in past messages. The simple and yet incredibly effective factors to be contributed have also been listed. The opportunity to experience into wisdom through cooperating within the basic Laws of the Universe offers evolution possibilities that are rarely available in one lifetime. Seldom is such a "sales pitch" given to entice mesmerized units of consciousness to awaken and to activate their previously intended participation. However, this is a well-orchestrated and long-standing situation that is finally ripe for transition into a different manifestation of human experience. Full participation is welcome indeed.

III-46

The information as presented so far has brought forth for each individual a greater understanding of the reason each is present and what each has come forth to accomplish. There have been transitions to contemplate through considering possibilities of the origin and evolvement of mankind on this planet that are far different than those presented by mainstream religion and the organized scientific community. It is interesting to note that definite and thoroughly researched available artifacts found at many different sites around the planet support the theory of the forced evolution of the original life forms for the purpose of serving outside ownership interests. These facts logically fill in the gaps that the mainstream anthropologists are unable to explain and in doing so discredit their historical conjectures. Through the willingness to consider all the possibilities, including the two commonly debated conflicting origin theories, the thought process has been enhanced. Once "possibility thinking" has been incorporated into the mind/brain process, it changes the way all incoming information is considered. It is rather like breaking down a shell that has been artificially placed around each conscious awareness to protect it from considering anything other than the standard approved thought diet that is constantly fed to modern societies. This, of course, is purposeful to shape the collective/mass consciousness of the planetary whole to fit within the plan to control and re-engineer the human worker down the evolutionary scale rather than to allow it to spiral upward normally.

Once this understanding is firmly established in the minds of the readers of these messages, it naturally focuses the intent toward thwarting this plan by outsiders that is clearly only for their benefit. No intelligent conscious awareness desires devolution rather than evolution. It also becomes quite clear that in order to change the future experience, it is not possible to use methodology that has been purposefully introduced and encouraged by the outside influence that obviously has psychologically planned every human experience to fit within their overall strategy of control. It becomes necessary to understand that in order to outmaneuver these planners, it is necessary to move to a strategy that is at least one step above their model program procedures. Their methods of operation involve using the Universal Laws in a focus that is not in harmony with the flow of energy generated by the expression of pure potentiality into greater self-contemplation. The plan of devolution of the humans on this planet is in direct opposition to this flow. It is then obvious that the intent to create a different experience is established by purposefully invoking the Universal Laws to act within the flow that moves expansively through evolution of species.

There is no manifestation of experience or object without thought first conceiving and then projecting the desired design into the limitless field of undifferentiated energy that is available and waiting to fill the mold created by the intended design. When the Laws are invoked in harmony with their purpose and released to fill in the details of the basic pattern, wondrous results happen. In contrast, as has been stated previously, to use the Laws in a contrary flow, every detail must be delineated and held firmly in concentrated focus not only to create the design, but also to hold it in place. Consequently, as the pattern becomes more and more detailed, it also becomes more and more fragile. If the focus is released, the natural "thought thinking" process would recognize the disharmony with its original purpose and begin a self-destruction process. The overview provided by this discussion allows for the reader to comprehend a larger picture/understanding of the situation in which the planet Earth and its inhabitants find themselves at this moment in its history. The word "transcend" means to "rise above, transform, excel." In order to continue on their path of evolution, humanity must "transcend" this current experience. To do that, it must "rise above" those that would thwart that natural progress. Because thought is the basis of creation, it then becomes apparent that mankind must "think" in a way that is "above and beyond" their jailers, using a "transformative" conceptual pattern as their basis of intent. This could be further assisted if variations appear in humanity's behavior pattern that is inconsistent with what is "expected" to be their reaction to the programmed plan of control. Variations in humanity's projected stereotype behavior cause attention to shift away from the concentration needed to hold their expanding pattern in place. This then would weaken their ability to hold their fragile model in form.

The question comes to mind as to how this all important "pattern of control" is held in place by the varied groups that make up the support focus provided by the members of humanity that are in league with those that are now in control of the planet. The answer is very simple! Ritual! At the basis of all-ritual, religious or fraternal, public or secret, either similar wording or similar intent is present. All of these are purposefully mind controlling and limit the behavior of those that take part in them even after these may have left the group and no longer practice the rituals. The concepts imparted continue to exert influence. The impact of participation in ritualistic routine designed to limit and control is thorough and often difficult to transcend. This is so because the patterns of limitation at the basis of its purpose tend to permeate many areas of thought and influence decisions that limit "possibility thinking." Are all rituals devolutional? That depends upon the basic purpose and whether or not those practicing the ritual remain free of any desire to control or use the ritual for any devious purpose. It is difficult to invoke and hold a ritual to its original intent for any length of use. Consequently, spontaneity in meditation/prayer is strongly suggested.

It may seem that just about all components of current life on the planet are tainted in some way with purposeful harm in mind. Certainly, far-reaching efforts are being made to control every possible attitude and opinion. The human psyche has been examined extensively for the purpose of limiting and reversing the progress that has been made by the human beings either of origin or transplanted here. In actuality, because of the push to limit progress, the push to advance has been stronger than it would otherwise have been. It is difficult to limit further what has progressed despite great effort to prevent or lessen it. The only method employed by the self-appointed governors of the planet/solar system has been to do more of the same methods that have not stopped progress only slowed it down. It appears to be working with the large mass of individuals, however, as most of those reading these messages can testify, it took a brief encounter with a logical presentation of triggering ideas to introduce "possibility thinking" right through all the programming for limitation. That in itself should indicate the tenuous success of the plan that is being foisted on humanity. It is time to begin thinking independently including as many possibilities "as possible" about what is being provided as guidance from *all* sources meant to influence experiencing the gift of life. Consider the source and what might be the purposeful intent. Does it intend to promote opportunities to evolve or is it intended to limit, control and lead to the eventual lessening of possibilities to make purposeful independent choices for the highest and best good of all concerned? Intention is the measuring quality to carefully ascertain. However, the best intention based on (ritual) information designed to influence negatively, cannot but accomplish the original purpose or at the least, cause confusion. There are many opportunities for lessons in discernment. Observe and consider carefully rather than come to conclusions too quickly. If each one has clear and purposeful intent to be aligned with what is truly for the highest and best good for all concerned, the observation mode will provide a true sense of what are the appropriate determinations to be made.

III-47

The situation as it now exists as perceived reality is viewed by each individual through the screen of previous influences. These messages are literally sifted through the belief systems of each individual in a format that is acceptable to each as reality. As what is acceptable is incorporated within the current belief system, this then creates a new reality format. This is a constant and ongoing process with regard to all information received from all sources. How much change happens within each reality format depends upon the flexibility of the individual psyche. What is gleaned from the messages as acceptable information varies with each individual. What segments seem especially important to one individual will not necessarily seem important to another. This is the reason that each is encouraged to read and reread the information. As the reader accepts portions of the information as possibly true, the accepted reality format of that moment changes. Different perspectives of what is indicated through the wording are perceived and either accepted as possibilities or rejected with each reading. With repeated readings different information stands forth as especially meaningful and in turn stimulates new understandings as the mind/brain process is activated through consideration of different possibilities. It is a program designed to awaken and enhance the natural latent abilities yet to be tapped and to reawaken those that have been shut down by the mind control procedures all have been experiencing in increasing degrees for far longer than this century.

The process that is begun by reading and assimilating those facets of information that are accepted into the belief system causes a shift in the thought process that reaches into other areas of the life experience. While it is focused toward birthing a new paradigm of experience for the human experience on this planet, it brings with it other changes that will benefit those choosing to incorporate greater flexibility into their concept of experience within a body. Experiencing an active roll in the creation process at the present density of earth's vibratory level requires the ability to acknowledge, internalize, analyze, and express emotions within the purposeful intention of living within the "highest and best good of all concerned." This is setting up interaction that ripples outwardly in far reaching effects beyond the finite mind's ability to comprehend. It is the release of the format of experience that must limit to control that has its basis in fear. Control is believed to offset fear in order that change can be slowed and a modicum of "peaceful existence" can be experienced. However, the control mode requires more control measures to support the original limits and is a self-perpetuating negatively expanding cycle. It is the mode that has been adopted by those who would own and "control" this planet and its inhabitants. The intention to create within the Universal Laws focused for the "highest and best good for all concerned" deliberately invokes change. It is through the release of this intention into the Laws that change flows within a coordinated cycle that is logical and effortless. It is within this context that "freedom" is experienced. When all are included, then abundance is experienced in myriad different modes. Freedom encourages and allows diversity of expression whereas control demands conformity and limitation. Both of these are contrary to the natural desires of self-aware consciousness. This is because those that attained this higher state of awareness have done so by aligning themselves with the flow of greater self-contemplation that is at the basis of potentiality knowing itself through the expression of thought into experience into wisdom. It is through wisdom; knowledge acquired by living actual realized experience, that greater freedom is realized. This is the reason that life on a 3rd dimensional planet is honored and desired by units of self-awareness. To "know" greatly accelerates the evolution of the greater soul matrix of which each is an intricate interactive part. Through this process, a greater understanding of who and what each one is becomes gradually acknowledged and realized. This carefully discovered self-realization is the foundation of all progress. Each recognition adds to the basic understanding, the knowing that each is an essential aspect of the essence of the whole. This whole is incomplete until the totality of it is gathered into the awareness of the true nature of whatever adventure is the focus to be thoroughly investigated and understood in this grand cycle.

Forever is incomprehensible. "Now" is the only segment of power available to the conscious awareness. 3rd dimensional awareness continues to focus on the past and the future, which removes the consciousness from participation in the only available point of influence. Past memory is meant to serve as an informational source to prevent repetition of previous inappropriate experience. The future is an unknowable point that is available to receive the experience that will manifest based on intentions and actions made in the "now" of the current moment. This unknown future cannot be different than what is being experienced in the current circumstances if there is no one present in the proactive moment acting in the creative intentional thought mode. It has been pointed out that if all the past and future thought was subtracted from the total human focused thought on this planet at any given second, there are very few people actually present. It is something to contemplate carefully.

The question then arises as to what is the difference between being absent in future thought and in intending a change to manifest in the future. When a conscious awareness is intending a creative thought, that awareness is experiencing as if it were actually present in the midst of the intended creation. In other words, the future intention is being pulled into the present moment as if it already exists. The imagination has that individual either pictorially or emotionally or in both modes, experiencing what is intended as if it already exists in the present moment. How is that possible if only the basic framework is known? The answer is to pretend that it is known and play with what it might actually be like. Even if only one tiny segment of the whole is examined in the exercise of imagination and enough are simulating this, then a whole will formulate.

The thought-thinking segment will coordinate and revise the complexities into a balanced and harmonious format that will exceed all expectations. The birth of the new paradigm of experience will begin the change by reorganizing mankind's daily happenings. Those that are the instruments of this change will desire big changes to happen quickly. However, small changes in many places and in many different occurrences will begin the shift. It is more difficult to plug many small holes in a wall of plans than a few large ones. Subtle energy at work in many places leads to profound change. Trust the process!

III-48

It is as though the planet itself is drawing a deep breath before it begins to literally shudder and shake in an effort to focus its energies toward saving itself from the abuse it is yet absorbing. In its collectivized thought process, it seems to be coming to the conclusion that enough is enough and that it is time to begin a retaliating process in order to release itself from the relentless onslaught of destructive activities that its boarders are deliberately engaging in at "her" expense. As all manifestations are a balance of energies, it may be considered that the Earth is a "womb" or receiver/receptacle of the creative energies that are focused through the star (sun) energy that is the center of this planetary system. At the moment it is the only planet in this solar system supporting 3rd dimensional evolving humans on its surface.

While currently known history of this planet seems like a long time in the human reality system, planetary history covers what seems like measureless time periods when considered in a sequential time mode. Difficult as it is to encompass, there are other logical systems of perceiving the evolutionary process. When the brain/mind is fully activated, the ability to transcend the need to observe in a linear mode allows a shift to a process that relegates the resultant time factor from the controlling influence in observation to a variable of little importance. The process itself becomes the governing focus allowing the mind to become absorbed and to encompass the flow of multifaceted interaction within the "whole-graphic" scenario that is being played out. The ability to change the mode of observation through greater ability to observe the many parts of a whole interacting simultaneously changes the awareness of the self within this view of the unlimited movement of energies. As the perception expands to encompass the greater energetic picture, the self-awareness changes in correlation to this expansion of comprehension abilities. Through the expanded ability to perceive a situation from a more inclusive viewpoint, it is understood in a different dimensional point of view. In this way, it can be said that life is being experienced within a greater or higher dimensional plane of observation. This does not indicate an "easier" level of experience, but one that is more inclusive of causes and details that went unnoticed within prior available abilities. Acuity of thought along with the desire to know more in order to express more precede dimensional changes. In other words, the ability must be developed and practiced before it is possible to move into the higher dimensions of experience. The move does not come before the development of the skills to experience and maintain the necessary focus needed to remain at that dimensional level.

The shift to higher dimensions is earned (or remembered) by practicing now. At the basis of dimensional shifts is appreciation of the gift of self-awareness. This is not accomplished through or in tandem with self-deprecation. The "self" always does the best it can within the environment that is provided by its own surrounding thoughts. As it is immersed in self-appreciation it grows in expression. However, if surrounded by criticism and thoughts that belittle it, it shrinks and is robbed of the ability to express its Life energy effectively. The difference between self-appreciation and self-aggrandizement must be thoroughly understood. The important factor is whether or not the process is based on comparison to/ with others. What is considered within the self without the necessity of measuring/comparing the self to others is the key. Each rises within its own world of self-awareness. What others think or what self thinks it has accomplished compared to others is of no value in the overall journey through 3rd dimensional experience. Each journey is self-contained.

Others are present as mirrors in which to observe the self. What is seen in others is the reflection of what the self is unable to see by looking within. It is said that, "each is alone in a hall of mirrors." Until the self is willing to recognize "itself" in these mirrors, there is no way to find the door out of the hall. Finding the door already open is always a surprise, for it is impossible to determine when one has reached the ability to embody the facets of self-awareness necessary to integrate into the next dimensional experience. Much hype is circulating about the shift in the earth's vibrations that will "carry" its inhabitants to a higher dimension. It is firmly stated here and now that humanity's capability to exist at the next higher level of dimensional experience will determine whether or not individuals will make that change. The earth can and will make such a shift. How many will accompany her in that shift will be determined by those individuals themselves based on their personal abilities earned through appreciation of the "personal self" and their ability to allow an expansion of their thought processes into new possibilities of experiencing what surrounds them here and now.

The ability to release old familiar comfort zones and *allow* participation in creating a new paradigm of experience is far more challenging than is imagined when it is first considered. Adventure sounds intriguing; however, stepping off the cliff into unknowable new experiences without any familiar frame of reference requires commitment and a large measure of courage. If it were not for the horror of "knowing" the truth of the genocide and enslavement that is planned; few would have the necessary incentive or courage to make the choice. It is simply an "either-or" choice. There is no in-between place to go. Looking at it from that perspective, certainly creating a new experience based on self-appreciation that transcends the victim experience is far more appealing than riding the descending spiral into a long standing greater victimhood. There are no rescuers in sight that care to become involved with those with too few "guts" to help themselves. The opportunity to continue this current experience of learning how to pull the self-up by its own bootstraps through self-appreciation and possibility thinking is waiting elsewhere for the stubborn and the faint-hearted. The choice to be part of this scenario on this planet at this time is not/was not an accident. You are here by choice to make a further choice. It is suggested that you do it and do it with style and enthusiasm!

III-49

The copies of the *Handbook for the New Paradigm* and *Embracing the Rainbow*, now circulating, can be counted in the thousands. Each one is causing a ripple of change in the consciousness of the reader and in turn within the mass consciousness. The books are now traveling to many countries so that the change can begin to be worldwide. It is hoped that translations will be made and

copies of these circulated. It is necessary that the focus of cooperation in creating a different experience become a global influence.
Countries where the population has little or no access to communications other than government propaganda will require intervention
of another kind. Trust that this problem is being given very special
attention. Also, remember the hundredth monkey theory. In this
case, include a request for special methods of reaching these fellow
humans in prayer and meditations. Help can be given for the highest
and best good of those segments of humanity when it is requested
for them. In reality it is in support of what they are already asking
for themselves. The tighter the oppressive situation, the greater the
silent outcry of those experiencing it. Freedom to evolve is innately
desired by all from the deepest levels of awareness. What may not
be spoken, can be thought with great emotion.

Though emphasized frequently throughout the messages, the
power of thought as the prerequisite for the spoken word is powerful indeed. When thoughts and words are focused by many in agreement with passion and enthusiasm, a momentum is built to manifest
the desired intention. As more contribute added momentum, the
ripples become waves. When agreement and cooperation focus a
positive desire for the highest and best good possible, there is little
that can prevent the manifestation of what is intended. What is cru-
cial to understand is that in the process of the creation of the new,
the old must cease to exist, for both cannot share the same space,
except as one is declining and the new is coming into reality. As
this process is being experienced, it is critical that the focus be held
firmly in place because it would be easy to interpret the necessary
period of chaos and confusion as failure rather than to see it as the
beginning stages of success. It is extremely important that all members of the "ground crew" have a firm understanding of the purpose
of the period of chaos. It must happen in order to clear away the old
and make space for the new. It also provides added available energies to be siphoned from the chaos and reformatted into the new
intended pattern.

It will be very challenging to acknowledge the breaking down
of personal life patterns when they happen to each one as well as
many others and know it is absolutely necessary in order to manifest
a vastly improved way of life. This is the reason that the messages

began with admonitions to prepare for change in the best ways possible. This is extremely challenging in view of the urban life style the majority of "modern" humanity lives, depending on the availability of food from stores and restaurants that require supplies to be delivered daily from far away sources. Jobs depend on utilities and lines of communications, for few produce actual products that would aid in survival. 50 years ago, in times of stress, most people had family living on farms that could assist in providing basic food necessities for at least a period of time. Even in what is called 3rd world countries, the small farmers have been pushed off their land to make way for "factory farming operations." Humanity has allowed itself to be placed in dire straits indeed for basic survival needs are controlled and in short supply worldwide. This information is not for the purpose of promoting fear, but so that each may consider carefully what is not only possible, but also probable in the near future. Those that have given little concern for the plight of the farmer/rancher in the past should now understand and rethink their concerns. The push is on to eliminate those that have survived. These are a tenacious and efficient group that have constantly devised ways to stay on the land. There are too few of them left to feed the urban multitudes outside the established import system. This is a true picture worldwide.

Humans, when there is necessity, can be amazingly creative. But could the modern urban dweller survive if all the modern conveniences were to disappear? Those who have spent their lives in an urban environment would do well to research and plan some "what if" scenarios with their families. What would be true necessities if there were only crickets for entertainment? Basic survival necessities are seldom found in the modern urban household. If the faucets don't provide water, where would it be found and how could it be made drinkable? It is time to consider this basic issue with logic and planning. The answers will not be found on TV, in videos or the movies. There are excellent "homesteading" information sources available—magazines and books. There are military survival handbooks, etc. Some are out of print and difficult, but not impossible to find. It would be wise to consider priorities and perhaps consider different choices with regard to what can be acquired and stored to satisfy possible future requirements.

III-50

The greatest understanding that enables the limited mind to connect with the totality of Universal existence is through mathematics. Energy exists within precise cycles that can be read as mathematical equations. In order for Universal existence to continue, all the pieces of the puzzle must fit together. Since life expressing is not a static existence, that indicates that changes are going on within the totality of the puzzle on a continuing basis. Variations are constantly being recalculated to continue their inclusion within the whole, which is far greater than can be imagined by finite minds. Thus, it is that catastrophic events cause chaos and recalculation down to intricate details and these ripple outward influencing the Universal whole. The greater the catastrophe, the greater the chaos during the period of restoring unanimity. Knowing this, great focus is concentrated on areas to prevent such happenings if possible, or at least to lessen the causative factors. This is not always possible for the "free will" factor of those intent on causing such episodes cannot be denied. If all the individuals within the area of disharmony are not in agreement with the disruptive focus, then there can be intervening action to counterbalance the intended disruptive action if those in disagreement specifically ask for help to offset the intended plans. Agreement with the disruptive plans does not need to be informed agreement. In other words, the plans need not be generally known or understood. Passive agreement through ignorance is still agreement.

This is the reason that so much effort has been put forth by various individuals and organizations to alert and inform the people of this planet that there is indeed a subversive plan moving toward completion. This plan, if allowed to reach completion, will deny natural evolvement of life on this planet and will allow survival and enslavement of only chosen ideal candidates. Those who do become aware of and choose not to agree with these plans must then come together in agreement to focus on a plan of their own to create a different scenario for the populace and ask for what is called Divine intervention. However, this cannot be asked of an unknowable God that may capriciously choose whether to answer or not, depending on His mood that day. Such a God does not exist.

Pure potentiality exists with multiple levels of awareness within its expression all the way "down" to 3rd dimensional awareness and even below that level. All these multiple levels of awareness combined may indeed be considered "God." There are levels within this composite of awareness that are very great indeed. Consequently, certain levels of this "God Awareness" can and do hear and answer prayers that are addressed to them correctly, either accidentally or through the understanding and application of the Basic Laws that all manifested awareness exists within.

To ask is the first important step. To continue to ask never allows the process to move beyond the asking stage.

First ask, *assume* the answer is on its way and then continue to *express appreciation* that it is happening in its own perfect wisdom and timing. That "wisdom and timing" is greatly influenced by the one asking and how well that awareness is able to follow through with the two remaining steps after the initial asking. This is often called prayer. Nothing can happen until there is first asking. Then the next two steps, assuming it is happening (continued focus of intent) and expression of appreciation (allowance) controls the manifestation. It is that simple! A few additional details are helpful. Ask within a framework that allows what might be called "Divine Intelligence" or thought thinking to fill in the details. Doubt destroys results; trust insures them. It seems that these simple rules cannot be repeated too often, for habits formed through misinformation are difficult to overcome. It would be wise to reread this message frequently to remember these essential steps.

"Divine Intelligence" encompasses the benevolent galactic brothers, sisters and androgynous beings that have evolved beyond your level. It is true that there are those who live in harmony within the "God Energies" that promote evolvement at all levels of potentiality expressing itself. This is the composite of all accumulated wisdom knowing itself and continuing its expansive experience. All awareness is a part of that magnificent pool of intelligence. It is also true that through free will, there are those that are experiencing in disharmony with expansive intent. It is important to understand that self-awareness can purposefully destroy itself by continuing its negative experience to the point of destruction, because the negative focus lessens (literally pinches off) the focusing energies of the soul. However, destruction by this method of weakening the connection to the soul is very difficult to do. Awareness can "muck around" in negative experiences for the learning that can be gained and then return to harmonious experience.

Many of those that might be considered to have great wisdom and experience have pursued both paths. To have a body destroyed by those experiencing within what is considered negative experience does not destroy the self-awareness. In other words, unless deliberately chosen, there is no real death, just the need to digest the learning available from the victim experience, then acquire a new body to continue the next experiencing opportunity into wisdom and evolve within the field of potentiality. The availability of bodies is sometimes limited and thus it is suggested to use the present one to the greatest advantage possible while you have it. Honor it and care for it. It is intended that a radiant "being" express love and caring for all "life" through it by thoughts, words and deeds. Align the overall individual intention with that framework and positive results happen.

III-51

Though often a topic of discussion, the number of humans that this planet can provide for comfortably within its ecosystem is not the real determining factor in the overall "health" of the planet. The deciding capability is determined by how the resources are shared and for what intent these are used by the inhabitants. If the intent is for the "highest and best good" of *all* the inhabitants and these are shared in ways that provide for an abundant life experience for all, then the carrying capacity of inhabitants on the planet is considerably greater. It is obvious that that does not describe the current situation. It is also patently obvious that the current situation cannot continue if the planet is to sustain itself in its present form. The current story line can only end in disaster for both the inhabitants and the planet itself. Observation of the other planets in the solar system with no apparent life on their surfaces is the stark reality and a possible end to the continuation of the push for luxury for the privileged at the expense of the remainder of humanity and the planet's natural environment.

The ability of the planet itself to absorb the escalating misuse of its resources while the majority of its inhabitants are in suffering and misery is causing a shift in the energy that constitutes what can be called its "harmony quotient." In other words, the totality of the planetary awareness, which it definitely does possess, is becoming unstable or troubled. It too is aware that a progressive disharmony is being experienced in an increasing momentum that is continuously stimulated by deliberate intent. It might be said that the alarm bell has been ringing within that awareness for some time now causing the planet to now know that it is time to begin survival maneuvers or its current mode of expression will end. Because of the awesome power of the weaponry of both the planetary inhabitants and those vying to "own" this planet, its total destruction is not outside the realm of possibility. This precarious plight is now known to the totality of awareness that governs the action/reaction of the planetary processes that are what is called "nature." The sum total of mining, tremendous weights of water held within dams, surface and underground construction and weapons testing has caused internal pressure anomalies within the planet that are causing the various natural fracture lines to become extremely unstable. These fracture lines remain from previous pressure anomalies and as natural "zippers" to allow for normal shifts and changes in surface features. Add to this the contents of the mass consciousness that include pain, starvation, disease and an enormous outcry for change and relief. This exists along with the opposite intent to compress the human awareness into a weaker and weaker embodiment. The planetary awareness takes all these factors into account and must find a way to relieve all this pressure in the only way it can, which is what is currently termed "earth changes." These amount to changes in weather, volcanic eruptions and earthquakes. Each are in truth messages from the planet asking for the stress to be reduced by removing the causes of the stress. Unless this happens, these messages will become more and more urgent, that is more and more powerful. Unfortunately, many of the humans present within areas receiving the messages are caught up in the phenomena and the aftermath of the messages. The planetary choices are made in the areas where the greatest weakness is found in the earth's surface areas. Often phenomena return to the same areas because these still contain the weakest points. A shift of great enough proportion has not taken place for there to be a weaker point elsewhere on the planetary surface. Other factors enter into the greater picture. The focus of consciousness with regard to concern for the planet and its inhabitants helps to balance that area and relieve the planetary stress. It is a form of protection for that area. In this way, often the timetable of factual predictions of future happenings is slowed or prevented. The mass consciousness of humanity is a powerful component of the planetary whole. That is the reason that such an intense effort has been made to instill involuntary endorsement of the plan for continued outside ownership by the majority of human inhabitants. Deliberate misinformation and mind control from multiple sources have controlled the basis of human experience for generations in preparation for the favorable shift in multiple cosmic cycles that is happening now and in the near future. With the unsuspecting consent of a large segment of the mass consciousness, it can be said that Earth's citizens do not want a change and are cooperating with the outside influences. This is an effort to prevent "Divine intervention." Humanity on the one hand is asking for help and an end to the wars designed to keep them quarreling among themselves and unaware of the influence being exerted on their thought processes. The human race is being divided so that it can be conquered with the least effort.

It is appropriate to note here again that there is just "one human race" regardless of its diversity of appearance. All experience the "life force" identically. Only the outside appearances are different. These differences have been exploited along with cultural and religious variations to promote separation. All bodily, cultural and religious differences are responsibilities to learn of human unity within diversity. There is no advancement to higher dimensions until that truth is experienced into wisdom. Each has experienced within the different cultures to experience this reality into wisdom. It is important to the goals of the controllers that you forget those experiences and focus on the differences rather than the similarities. The similarities far outnumber the differences! It is to be noted that many of those experiencing in the higher dimensional realms are far different in appearance than those the human race sees within itself. Your "space" movies are quite accurate in imagining possible variations of species. Think about how that might be dealt with in the future, if it is possible to come together as a single human race, celebrate and maintain the diversity within it and create a new experience.

Epilogue

Those that read and study these three instructional manuals now view the current life experience on planet Earth from an entirely new point of view. This point of view is one that shifts daily as new information is absorbed, considered and incorporated into the belief system. As a foundation is built from which to view the experiences of life, it is constantly shifting. What seemed absolutely true in the recent past, often must be discarded for the wholistic picture changes to incorporate new information and revisions made by the choices of those that share the planetary whole. Through this understanding it becomes obvious that rigid and dogmatic doctrines obstruct the evolutionary progress of those that choose to allow themselves to become trapped in those belief structures. This constantly changing flow of opportunities to choose presents lessons in discernment with respect to the truth and applicability of new information. Each must consider how the new information might alter their perspective and decide if incorporating this change will allow the new view point to represent what is believable truth. In other words, it is necessary to "try the new information on for size" and then decide whether or not to accept it. While logic is an important testing tool, it is how the new picture *feels* that determines whether it is accepted or not.

When first encountering the new concepts that may be included in these messages, many will have put the book(s) aside for a period of time. These will return to reread and study them, for the daily situations that are observed from a new viewpoint will cause the truth of the messages to become clear. Some will reject them entirely, but will pass the book on to others that will resonate with the truth of them. In this way, these will have fulfilled their contribution to creating the new paradigm of experience. As each reacts appropriately to this information, the purposeful intention to create a new experience for the planet and its inhabitants comes more clearly into manifestation. Already the energies are gathering as the concentration of intention attracts more participants. Responsive enthusiasm grows as it is realized that it is possible to transcend the current circumstances and create an entirely new situation that humanity has longed to experience by utilizing the Universal Laws that govern the progression of life's natural process.

Whether humanity remains stuck within its current reality or chooses to lift itself out by its own volition remains to be determined. Only through discarding the "poor us" syndrome and realizing that the power to bring about change lies within their own attitude and choices will the circumstances be reconstructed positively. Mankind must grow itself into true Hu-mans (god-men/women). Natural evolutionary progress, despite all attempts to prevent it, has made this potentiality for this change available now. It is hoped mankind will take full advantage of this significant opportunity.

Suggested Reading

The Spiritual Laws and Lessons of the Universe
367 pages... Trade Paper   ISBN: 0-9640104-6-1 $16.95 + S&H

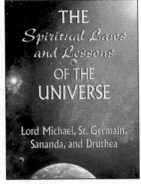

For eons of time in your human history, mankind has experienced and existed in blindness about his divine spiritual heritage, that is, his oneness with the Creation. Since the time of the "Fall" from "grace," many have continued to struggle with what is "their" purpose, and why it is so difficult to find and know THE TRUTH. Many, in their ignorance and confusion, have asked themselves why the Creator allows the seemingly unending ruthless and merciless inhumanity of man to continue; why HE allows suffering of children, wars, disease and pestilence and corruption. Often ones simply decide there is no Creator, which only keeps ones ever "separate"from KNOWING HIS PRESENCE WITHIN."The Spiritual Laws and Lessons" is deliverance of truth to YOU. The Creator is offering YOU the instructions for reaching the "lighted" path back home to HIM, AND THUS TO ONENESS. You will learn HOW to recognize the Anti-Spirit, (that which is AGAINST the Creator and therefore AGAINST LIFE) within YOU and why through your gift of free-will YOU allowed the Anti-Spirit within your temple. You will learn about what are the "Deadliest" Sins (errors) committed by you and also about the nature of YOUR personal responsibility for ALL consequences and experiences within this manifested physical "illusion." NOW within these pages bringing forth the EIGHTEEN Logical Cosmic Laws of Balance of The Creation, written in explicit detail with MANY examples given for YOUR careful consideration and recognition of truth. Why? To let there be NO misunderstanding of HOW and WHY you, of humanity, have lost your inner as well as planetary BALANCE. You have broken EVERY law set forth herein and have, therefore, suffered the consequences of your errors against the Creator and against LIFE. You each now have before you YOUR "road map" back home to spiritual wisdom, knowledge and truth. Will YOU see? Will YOU hear? The new cycle will BEGIN anew in the GLORY and Celebration of cleansing within and without of ALL fragments of ANTI-LIFE. WILL YOU JOIN OUR FATHER/ MOTHER CREATOR in the Divine Holy Kingdom of LIFE? The Creator awaits your decision. So be it.

CPSIA information can be obtained
at www.ICGtesting.com
Printed in the USA
FSHW021626130421
80377FS

9 781893 157255